NEWCOMER'S
HANDBOOK
for
Minneapolis-
St. Paul

2nd Edition

FIRST BOOKS

3000 Market Street N.E., Suite 527
Salem, OR 97301
503-588-2224
www.firstbooks.com

Authors: Elizabeth Caperton-Halvorson, Maris Strautmanis
Series Editor: Bernadette Duperron
Publisher: Jeremy Solomon
Contributor: Nancy Olseth
Cover/Interior Design, Production: Erin Johnson
Maps: Dennis McClendon, Chicago Cartographics
Chapter Icons: Matt Brownson

Transit maps courtesy of the Metropolitan Council Transit Operations.

ISBN 0-912301-45-7
ISSN 1087-8467

Printed in the USA on recycled paper.

Published by First Books, 3000 Market Street, N.E., Suite 527, Salem, OR 97301.

CONTENTS

CONTENTS *(continued)*

CONTENTS *(continued)*

House and apartment hunting in the Twin Cities, real estate agencies, tips on what to look for in an apartment, details about leases, security deposits

CONTENTS *(continued)*

IF ALL YOU'VE EVER HEARD ABOUT MINNESOTA IS THE HARSH climate and its colorful governor, the prospect of living here might be daunting. But be assured that national surveys consistently pick Minnesota as one of the best places in the nation to raise a family, and 97% of those residents surveyed believe the Twin Cities region is better than any other in the whole country. So what's so great about Minnesota? Many believe it's the quality of life!

Living here you'll enjoy one of the nation's most economically robust regions, not to mention forests, rivers, lakes, parks, ski slopes, golf courses and more shopping than you could ever need. There are Fortune 500 businesses and nearly as many theater seats as in New York City; vital downtowns where people like to live and want to play; a small enough population for breathing room, but more than enough to support two internationally acclaimed orchestras and several major league sports teams; and safe neighborhoods with clean streets and well-maintained houses. Most important, you'll be living in a place where art, culture, sports and recreation are easily accessible and affordable.

And what about the weather you ask? Well, it's what pulls Minnesotans all together, creating something to talk about, and prompting plenty of good Samaritans who will stop to help if you spin out on the freeway.

More than half of Minnesota's residents live in the thirteen-county Twin Cities metropolitan area, for a total of about 2.6 million people— 368,383 in Minneapolis, 272,235 in St. Paul, and the remaining two million in the suburbs—a pattern which contributes to the region's biggest problem, urban sprawl. Third-ring suburbs Woodbury, Eagan and Eden Prairie all doubled their populations during the 1980s and '90s, and current growth is occurring even farther out—in Maple Grove, west of Minneapolis; West Lakeland Township, east of St. Paul; and Farmington and Savage, south of the Minnesota River, an area recently made more accessible by the new Bloomington Ferry Bridge.

Upon arriving, the first thing you need to know is that while called the Twin Cities, Minneapolis and St. Paul aren't twins. Sitting on the Mississippi's west bank, Minneapolis is the power suit; it has demolished layer upon layer of its architectural history in order to create a skyline profile of sleek office towers and hefty industrial sites. In contrast, on the east bank, St. Paul is warm and inviting. Even though it's the state capital it has a slower, more settled and provincial feel, with attention being paid to architectural preservation. If Minneapolis is gray pin stripes, St. Paul is a flannel shirt, plaid.

The suburbs, too, have their own look and feel, ranging from post-war practical inner-ring municipalities like Richfield and Roseville to upscale Lake Minnetonka, North Oaks and Sunfish Lake. Newer suburbs range from new-house-and-strip-mall subdivisions like Eden Prairie and Eagan to the new urban development of Maple Grove and Woodbury, which emulate the small town live-where-you-work neighborhoods of the past.

Like much of the US, the Twin Cities' economy is strong and unemployment is low. Local corporations Pillsbury, 3M, and General Mills, are household names. With over 200 medical research centers and a large employment concentration in surgical and medical instrument manufacturing, the Twin Cities have been dubbed "Medical Alley" by *Business Week* magazine.

One contributing factor to the area's job stability is the state's well-educated population. Public and private elementary and secondary schools rank among the nation's best, and Minnesota's Post-Secondary Education option gives high school students an opportunity to take free college credits. The University of Minnesota, one of the largest universities in the country, is a major research institution. The U of M main campus along with a dozen private four-year colleges, six community colleges, nine technical institutes and several trade schools are located within the metro area.

Civic pride is a strong sentiment in Minnesota. Honeywell Corporation has been a major force in reclaiming the Phillips neighborhood, and citizens throughout the region are actively engaged in their own communities, from solving neighborhood problems to volunteering in their children's schools and sports programs. "Quality of life" issues are addressed by civic and government organizations and include primary prevention of violence, clean drinking water, environmental protection, and affordable housing.

Speaking of which, affordable housing is increasingly hard to come by here. Minneapolis alone is an estimated 15,000 units short of affordable places to live and the "affordable" range has crept up toward the $150,000 mark. On the plus side, this is forcing residents to rediscover "old gems," structurally sound, often beautifully crafted early 20th century houses that are being updated to meet the needs of modern families. In another step back to the "good old days," new development often embraces "urban village" goals of integrating low-income with high-income housing and creating public spaces to encourage community interaction.

Living costs in the Twin Cities continue to mirror the average of US urban areas. According to the 1998 American Chamber of Commerce Researchers Index, the Twin Cities ranked more affordable than New York, Boston, Philadelphia, San Diego, or Washington, D.C. Compared to the other large metropolitan areas, costs for health care and transportation were higher than average, while housing, groceries and utilities were on the lower side. Housing costs, however, have been going up, though experts say that prices are unlikely to catch up with the East and West coasts due to the cold climate and the area's seemingly never-ending supply of room to expand.

This is an outdoor kind of place, despite the famous weather which ranges from minus 30° to plus 90°. Sports and recreation are year-round pleasures here, and indoor facilities have been built for everything from horseback riding to ice hockey. Walking trails and bike paths snake the metro area's 136,900 acres of parks and 19 wildlife management areas. Minneapolis and St. Paul each enjoys its own chain of lakes and operate parks that cover thousands of acres and provide public access to the lakes and rivers. The park lands along lakes and rivers are connected by parkways—one-way streets following the shoreline that include bicycle and walking paths. In winter, half a dozen downhill ski operations are in and near the Twin Cities, with mountain skiing available at Lutsen on the North Shore of Lake Superior.

Even though the region is home to the largest urban Native American population in the US, it remains the least racially and ethnically diverse of any of the nation's 25 largest metropolitan areas. Its population diversity is increasing, however, as active church groups have reached out a helping hand to a flood of Southeast Asian, Hispanic, African and Eastern-European refugees. As a result, certain parts of the Twin Cities are undergoing dramatic changes. The principal effect is felt in the schools, where racial/ethnic groups account for approximately one-fourth of the public school enrollment.

HISTORY

A recent play about Minnesota history opened with the untamed rhythms of a Native American chant in raw counterpoint to the genteel strains of a Victorian waltz; a clear metaphor for the cultural conflict that has accompanied the settling of Minnesota.

Native American tribes hunted and migrated over these rolling hills for centuries before the Europeans arrived in the mid-17th century. One of the area's earliest known place names was Im-in-i-ja Ska, given to the tall white sandstone bluff that creates a sharp curve in the Mississippi River at the center of St. Paul. The first extensive European description of the region was written in 1683 by Father Louis Hennepin, a Franciscan adventurer who traveled with a party of Dakota guides up the river to a wide falls which he named St. Anthony. Where Hennepin was standing is now the center of downtown Minneapolis.

Minnesota was acquired through the Louisiana Purchase in 1803, and Congress sent the US Cavalry to explore the new territory and find out what treasures the country had gained. Lieutenant Zebulon Pike found two different groups of Native American tribes living here, the Ojibwe and the Dakota. Pike signed an agreement with Little Crow, a Dakota, in 1803 that ceded to the US nine square miles of land at the confluence of the Mississippi and Minnesota Rivers where he built Fort Snelling. Settlement began during the 1820s, and soon fur traders and farmers were comfortably established down river from the fort. In 1841, an earnest missionary named Lucien Galtier built a log church on the east bank of the Mississippi and named it after St. Paul, the Apostle of Nations. The name stuck for the settlement, which soon became the capital of the new state of Minnesota.

Entrepreneurs also moved up river to St. Anthony Falls where they used the hydraulic power of the Mississippi to mill flour and saw lumber, giving Minneapolis the nickname "Mill City." This east bank settlement was originally known as St. Anthony, but Charles Hoag, a teacher, proposed a different name for it, combining Minne, the Dakota word for "water," and polis, the Greek word for "city" into Minneapolis. Today the cobblestone street of old St. Anthony has been preserved as Saint Anthony Main, a shopping and entertainment district across from downtown on the east bank of the river, in what is known as the Mississippi Mile.

Relations between white settlers and Native Americans in the area were not always harmonious. There was an agreement by the US to send food and supplies to displaced Indians, but during a recession in 1862, federal food rations were not sent, and a group of hungry and desperate

Indians raided a homestead and killed the people living there. More violence followed, leading to the Dakota War of 1862. When the fighting ended, thirty-eight Dakotas were executed by hanging, and the Indians were pushed west into what are now called the "Dakotas."

It was the Mississippi River that opened Minnesota to the world, and the newborn cities on its banks experienced booms in the late 19th century as waves of immigrants, particularly Scandinavians, Germans and Poles, moved to the frontier. In 1867 Minneapolis was incorporated as a city; though, at first, the transportation hub of St. Paul was the larger of the two competing hamlets. During the 1880s, however, Minneapolis began to overtake its neighbor both in population and commerce. Rivalry between the cities was fierce, and led to the Great Census War of 1890. The first census results showed that Minneapolis was population champ, but St. Paul officials charged fraud, and a scandal ensued. A deputy US marshal arrested census workers in downtown Minneapolis and results were recounted. Investigators found that counters in both cities had inflated numbers with "residents" who lived in cemeteries and office buildings. The recount confirmed that Minneapolis had more residents, and it has remained the larger city ever since.

Although St. Paul has gradually garnered the reputation as the sleepier town, it hasn't always been that way. During the Prohibition years from 1920 to 1933, mobsters running liquor from Canada brought their ill-gotten gains and their wild ways to the city of St. Paul. Ma Barker and her sons hid out at here and the infamous John Dillinger was involved in shoot-outs around town. Arrests and indictments in the late 1930s led to the end of St. Paul's "gangster city" era.

With a large rural population, Minnesota was fertile ground for labor and agricultural reform movements. When the state's Farmer-Labor Party merged with the Democratic Party in 1944 (forming the Minnesota DFL), it began producing national leaders with a strong liberal bent. Hubert H. Humphrey served first as mayor of Minneapolis, then as Minnesota's US senator. A strong advocate for civil rights, he gave up his congressional seat to serve as vice president under Lyndon B. Johnson, and was the Democratic presidential candidate in 1968, losing to Richard Nixon. Humphrey's protege, Walter Mondale, succeeded him as US senator and also served as vice president under Jimmy Carter.

While the state's political reputation was growing on the national front, the Twin Cities were becoming the industrial, commercial and cultural center of the vast fertile Upper Midwest region. Unchecked by geography, area growth erupted outward into the surrounding farmlands after

World War II, and the rings of suburbs that were created lured population away from both Minneapolis and St. Paul. Extensive redevelopment, begun in the 1960s, continues to this day, bringing people back to the metropolitan core. The early 1970s construction in Minneapolis of the Investors Diversified Services (IDS) building, the area's first skyscraper, signaled the emergence of Minneapolis as a financial center for the upper Midwest. Soon many downtown offices, apartments, stores and theaters in Minneapolis and St. Paul were connected with indoor, above-ground skyways, making it possible to live and work in the city centers during the bitter months of winter without ever having to step outside.

Also, it was during the 1970s that investors and government officials finally became concerned with building preservation. Numerous revitalization projects were undertaken, including restoring the Landmark Center in St. Paul and renovating the Warehouse District in Minneapolis. These initiatives have kept alive some of the early history of the two boomtowns, and now the presence of these historic buildings is helping to attract affluent professionals, young families and senior citizens back from the suburbs to live in the cities' central cores.

WHAT TO BRING

A car and a coat—both in good shape to take on winter. The Twin Cities' bus system, MetroTransit, offers express connections to several suburbs, but getting around totally by bus is difficult and time-consuming. After years of legislative reluctance, light rail transit is becoming a reality, with the first segment connecting the Minneapolis downtown to the airport and the Mall of America expected to be operational by 2003, but light rail for the rest of the area is still a dream. Still, many Twin Cities residents get back and forth to work either by bus, bike, carpool, foot or cross-country skis, and Metro Transit works hard to support their efforts (see **Transportation**).

A map—there are places where Twin Cities' streets and highways follow a perfect grid, and places where streets are laid out at crazy angles to the grid. This guide will help you to get to know the neighborhoods, but for the full picture, you'll need to accompany it with a map. *Hudson's Street Atlas,* which is published locally and sold at bookstores, is a comprehensive spiral-bound book that shows every street in St. Paul and Minneapolis and the surrounding communities.

THE LAST DECADE HAS BEEN GOOD TO MINNEAPOLIS AND ST. PAUL. The Twin Cities, along with the rest of the nation, have prospered—crime rates declined a little and the tax base increased a lot. Many area communities used their newfound revenue for projects, such as renovating housing, historic preservation and rediscovering/making accessible the Mississippi River. The state approved funding for Light Rail Transit (LRT), the first section of which is being built along Hiawatha Avenue through the east side of Minneapolis. This development, coupled with an influx of new-comers desiring an urban rather than suburban living experience, is rapidly metamorphosing the Twin Cities cores from gritty to trendy.

The downside to the recent urban migration—a problem which is shared by many major metropolitan areas across the US—is that housing here is harder to find and more expensive than it was just a few years ago. According to the Minneapolis Assessor's office, some neighborhoods have seen a 40% increase in property values in as little as two to three years, and the North Loop in downtown Minneapolis has skyrocketed over 100% since 1997. In such a market, renovation becomes economically feasible. Consequently, some of the neighborhoods that were undesirable five or ten years ago are being stabilized and gentrified.

That said, there are still sections of both cities that old-timers usually tell newcomers to avoid: North Minneapolis, north of Highway 55, between Wirth Parkway on the west and the Mississippi River, extending into Robbinsdale and Brooklyn Center; South Minneapolis, south of I-94 and east of Lyndale to the Mississippi River, as far down as 46th Street; St. Paul, along University Avenue east of Snelling and north of I-94 as well as the northeastern quadrant of St. Paul, north of I-94 and east of I-35E. While these regions do, in fact, include active neighborhoods with strong associations, particularly Seward and Powderhorn in south Minneapolis, there may be safer Twin Cities locales.

A few suggestions to get you started with your hunt: while this is an over-simplification, most people will say that you won't go wrong if you stay west of Hennepin in Minneapolis. Many young single professionals choose to go straight to Uptown or the southwest districts of St. Paul. Bryn Mawr has been voted one of the most livable neighborhoods by the *Twin Cities Reader*; Nicollet Island is a treasure trove of Victorians worthy of restoration; and Northeast is generally considered a stable place to look for affordable housing.

As you explore the Twin Cities, you may notice certain types of housing cropping up again and again. In fact, it's nearly impossible to differentiate among neighborhoods by their housing styles. The Midwestern square is an example you will find throughout the Twin Cities and some older suburbs. These simple houses, consisting of a two-story wood structure with a front porch, dormer windows, and high ceilings, date to the turn of the century, and many have been split into duplexes. Arts-and-Crafts bungalows, often with stucco siding, were mostly built between 1910 and 1930, and are common on the quieter streets close to the edges of both cities. Typically, the bungalows have handsome built-in buffets and window seats. Near Lake Harriet and Lake of the Isles, you will find Prairie-style houses. These low-lying, natural wood and stone houses with narrow windows, pioneered by Frank Lloyd Wright early in the 20th century, are distinctly Midwestern. Colonials, two-story box-like houses with symmetrically arranged windows and a central door, line many older streets of the inner city such as Pillsbury Avenue in Minneapolis. Also in the older neighborhoods you will see many Tudors—the houses with steep roofs and sides decorated with dark wood timbers and stone arches. Some Tudor-style houses were built as recently as the 1940s. Finally, grandiose Victorian wood-frame houses, dating to the late 19th century and adorned with gables, towers, and outside bric-a-brac, stand out in older neighborhoods. Victorian-era houses can also look quite plain, with only a small wooden decoration under the eaves and a tall front porch. And bad news for our car-dependent society: older city houses usually have one-car garages.

When asked where they live, residents in Minneapolis and St. Paul are more likely to give the names of their neighborhoods than their street addresses. This can be confusing, but don't worry, it's actually quite orderly. Minneapolis, which has six geographic areas: Central, South, Southwest, North, Northeast and Southeast, is further divided into 11 communities and 81 neighborhoods, which are organized around parks and schools. The Central community, for example, includes the following neighborhoods: Downtown East, Downtown West, Elliot Park, Loring Park, North Loop and Stevens Square/Loring Heights. St. Paul, on the other hand, is sub-divided into a much more manageable 17 districts, many of which coincide with historic designations or earlier independent villages.

Virtually every neighborhood is represented by a neighborhood organization. Call the Neighborhood Revitalization Program in Minneapolis, 612-673-5140, and they will put you in touch with the current president of the association of the neighborhood you are considering. These groups are an important source of information and advice, and they can also help you feel at home in your new community once you've moved in. The Minneapolis neighborhoods which have web pages can be accessed through the city of Minneapolis' web site, www.ci.minneapolis.mn.us. In St. Paul check www.ci.stpaul.mn.us or www.stpaul.gov. Another site for both cities is www.tcfreenet.org.

NEIGHBORHOOD SAFETY

While 911 is the emergency number throughout the metro area, for safety information in Minneapolis, check with Community Crime Prevention/SAFE, 612-673-3015, a unit of police officers and crime prevention specialists who work in partnership with communities to make Minneapolis a safer and better place to live. A recent innovation in Minneapolis, called CODEFOR, uses computers to identify crime patterns. Check www.ci.minneapolis.mn.us/citywork/police/stats for crime statistics. The Minneapolis Police Department also publishes an "Official Uniform Crime Report." Copies are available at the City Municipal Library located on the third floor of city hall and at the downtown Minneapolis Public Library sociology reference desk on the second floor. You can also join the SafetyNet discussions online at www.tcfreenet.org. To investigate neighborhood safety in St. Paul, call Community Resources (FORCE Unit) at 651-292-3712, or check the STATMap which details the different levels of crime throughout the city. You can get this information and a copy of the annual police report by calling 651-292-3501, 9 to 4:30, weekdays.

Just as in any other metropolitan area, pay attention to your gut feelings when looking around town for a place to live. Drive or walk around the neighborhood to see what's going on, and try to experience a prospective neighborhood at different times of the day, particularly at night. Ask yourself if you feel comfortable there.

Note: You can get zip codes for particular addresses from the US Postal Service through one central number, 800-275-8777, or www.usps.com. Using the zip code number, your insurance agent can provide you with additional statistical information concerning your prospective neighborhood, including the crime rate and how much insurance coverage will cost you if you decide to move into that area.

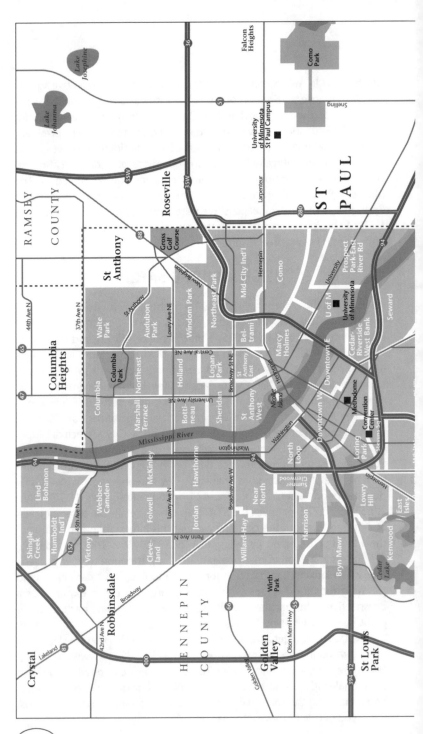

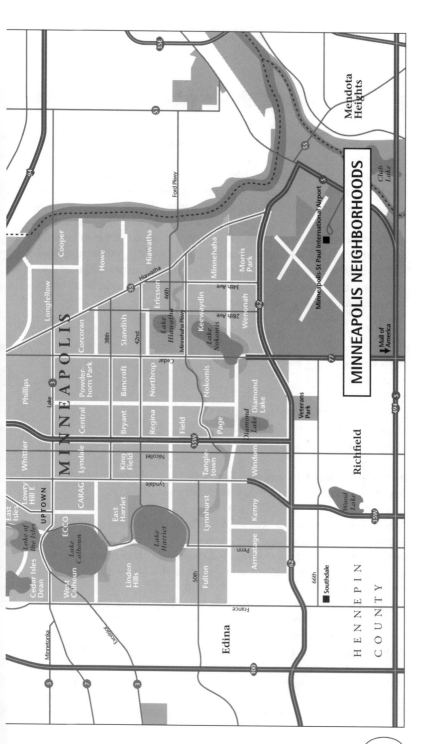

MINNEAPOLIS NEIGHBORHOODS

MINNEAPOLIS

Though Minneapolis has shrunk from its peak population of 550,000 residents in the 1950s, mostly because of suburban flight, you shouldn't take this as a sign of urban decay. Minneapolis is making a comeback. It is meeting the needs of its burgeoning population—both individuals and families relocating to the area, as well businesses that go from local mom & pops to international mega corporations—with rehabilitated and newly-constructed housing and office spaces. The river is being cleaned up and biking and walking trails added. Community gardens overflow with flowers and vegetables in even the poorest of neighborhoods, and some have city-commissioned gateways, sculptures that welcome visitors and symbolize neighborhood pride.

CENTRAL COMMUNITY

DOWNTOWN WEST
NORTH LOOP
DOWNTOWN EAST
STEVENS SQUARE-LORING HEIGHTS
ELLIOT PARK
LORING PARK

Boundaries: North: Plymouth Avenue, Mississippi River; **West**: I-94; **South**: Franklin Avenue, Highway 12; **East**: Interstate-35W

People enjoy living in the heart of downtown Minneapolis. It offers easy access—to a job, city offices, the Central Library, shopping and entertainment, dining out, and relaxing river walks. However, though downtown is getting a Target, a major grocery store is still on every downtown dweller's wish list.

    Downtown West (Park Avenue to Hennepin/2nd Avenue North, along the riverfront and west to 12th Street) centers around Nicollet Mall, an eight-block commercial strip closed to cars, and the restored Warehouse District, an area of nightclubs, restaurants and galleries along First Avenue, north of the Target Center. This area's corporate tone is matched by plenty of high-rise apartment buildings with luxury suites, and condominiums. Downtown West is also home to empty-nesters who left their single-family homes in the suburbs and moved into the high-rises and townhouses to be close to the symphony, the theater district, and the shopping. You'll find loft apartments created out of 19th century flour and blanket mills in the warehouse districts of the **North Loop** (2nd Avenue North to Duluth Avenue, west to I-94 and east to the river), **Downtown East** (Park Avenue to 35W) and Downtown West. These warehouse districts are turning the riverfront into the trendiest places to live in the city, and are home to professional artists, entertainers, corporate suits, retirees and young people.

Only a short hop away, **Stevens Square-Loring Heights** is bracketed between the busy streets of Lyndale Avenue, I-35, I-94 and Franklin Avenue. The original buildings here were constructed roughly between 1890 and 1930. Loring Heights, west of Nicollet, is a neighborhood of grand houses, developed in one of the upper classes' first moves toward the south and west of the central city. Its layout of curved streets on a ridge is the classic mark of the Victorian romantic suburb. The small apartments of Stevens Square, on the other hand, were built as a mill-town for small families and single tradesmen. Recent decades brought freeway construction to this little neighborhood, and along with it, urban decline, including the conversion of many of the large houses of Loring Heights into multi-unit housing, group homes, and businesses. The 1990s, however, began a period of restoration, and now modern townhomes stand beside reclaimed mansions and updated apartments to overlook the city. Nearby **Elliot Park**, surrounding the Hennepin County Medical Center, has fared less well and, according to the Minneapolis Assessor's Office, is one of the few downtown areas where property values have actually declined.

LORING PARK

If you live in Loring Park (Lyndale to 12th and Hawthorne Avenue to I-94) you'll never have to wonder where to go for food, entertainment or people watching. Lovely turn-of-the-century, brick walk-up apartments and large stone houses surround Loring Park, with its pond, shuffleboard courts, and summer movies sponsored by the nearby Walker Art Center. The air of grandeur in this community is enhanced by the Basilica of St. Mary, the Women's Club, and Hennepin Avenue United Methodist Church. Loring Park residents are made up of a mix of professionals, artists, and students, and the area is a popular residential choice among the gay community. Visiting film crews and out-of-town celebrities are often spotted in the Loring Cafe, 1624 Hammond Place, a cosmopolitan bistro. A slew of interesting coffee shops and cafes line the north side of the park. On the south, the 510 Groveland Building is one of the best addresses in town. Independent theaters such as the Red Eye Collaboration, Loring Playhouse, Walker Art Center and Guthrie Theater are all nearby. There's a lot of action here, and residents' major complaint is sleepless nights from traffic noise.

Web Sites: www.ci.minneapolis.mn.us, www.tcfreenet.org

Area Code: 612

Zip Codes: 55402, 55403, 55404, 55405, 55411, 55415

Post Offices: Main Office, 110 South 1st Street; Loop Station, 110 South 8th Street; Loring Station, 18 North 12th Street; Butler Quarter Station, 100 North 6th Street; Commerce Station, 307 4th Avenue South (all post office branches can be reached at 800-275-8777).

Police Precinct: 4th, 1925 Plymouth Avenue North, 612-673-5704

Emergency Hospital: Hennepin County Medical Center, 701 Park Avenue South, 612-347-2121

Library: Central Library, 300 Nicollet Mall, 612-630-6000

Public School: Minneapolis, District Office: 612-668-0000, http://mpls.k12.mn.us

Community Resources: Neighborhood Revitalization Program, 612-673-5140

Community Publications: *The Alley*, 2600 East Franklin, Minneapolis 55406, 612-692-8562; covers Elliot Park and Phillips Neighborhoods; *Stevens Square Community Organization Herald*, 110 East 18th Street, Suite 112, Minneapolis, MN 55403, 612-871-7307

Transportation: Bus Lines: Most city bus routes pass through downtown Minneapolis. You can get around downtown by bus on any major street, and downtown fares are reduced. Check a transit map (719 Marquette Avenue transit store) or call 612-373-3333, 612-349-7000 to have one mailed. These are also the numbers to call with questions about specific routes. Minneapolis/St. Paul Intercity Express buses 94B, C and D provide connecting service between downtown Minneapolis, I-94, Snelling Avenue, the Capitol Complex, and downtown St. Paul.

CALHOUN–ISLES COMMUNITY

UPTOWN—EAST CALHOUN (ECCO), CARAG (CALHOUN RESIDENTS ACTION GROUP), LOWRY HILL EAST (THE WEDGE)
BRYN MAWR, CEDAR-ISLES-DEAN, WEST CALHOUN
KENWOOD, EAST ISLES, LOWRY HILL

Boundaries: North: Bassett Creek; **West:** France Avenue; **South:** 38th Street; **East:** Lyndale Avenue

Visitors and residents alike fall in love with Minneapolis because of the Calhoun-Isles community with its linked "Chain of Lakes" and the myriad activities possible here: running, roller-blading, biking, swimming, sailing, people-watching, etc. Calhoun is one of the top lakes for windsurfing in the Twin Cities, and the running/biking paths around all these lakes are part of the Grand Round Parkways (see **Lakes and Parkways**).

The Calhoun-Isles community was the first Minneapolis suburb, and it's still one of the most popular places for newcomers to settle. For those working in the northwest or western suburbs, this is a particularly convenient place to live as you'll be able to travel on Highway 7 and Cedar Lake Road and avoid the gridlock on I-394. For those who work in downtown Minneapolis, the office is only a short walk, bike ride, or brief bus ride away.

Calhoun-Isles can be divided into three distinct districts: the trendy, populous rental neighborhoods commonly known as Uptown; the meandering streets along the southwest border of the city that make up Bryn Mawr, Cedar-Isles-Dean and West Calhoun; and the city's most expensive neighborhoods, Kenwood, Lowry Hill, and East Isles, which wrap around Lake of the Isles.

UPTOWN

EAST CALHOUN (ECCO)
CARAG
LOWRY HILL EAST (THE WEDGE)

Uptown spreads outward from the Calhoun Square Shopping Mall, which is at the corner of Lake Street and Hennepin Avenue in East Calhoun. It includes **East Calhoun (ECCO)** and **CARAG** which, together, extend south from Lake Street to 36th Street, and east from Lake Calhoun to

Lyndale Avenue. The northernmost section of Uptown is called **Lowry Hill East** or **the Wedge**. It is a large, roughly triangular shaped, rental area that stretches between Hennepin and Lyndale avenues, north of Lake Street, to the point where they meet above the I-94 tunnel. The up-and-coming Lyn-Lake business district, at the corner of Lyndale and Lake streets, is also an entertainment center. Bistros, art-house cinemas, ethnic eateries and beer-and-burger bars all thrive in this area, along with small performance spaces and galleries. Uptown landmark Sebastian Joe's on Franklin, west of Hennepin, is one of the best ice cream stores in the Twin Cities. On the first weekend in August, Uptown hosts the country's largest outdoor art fair along Hennepin Avenue.

As a general rule, the houses and apartments closest to the lakes are the most expensive. Sturdy Midwestern-squares, many of which have been divided into duplexes, predominate, and stately brick apartment buildings built as far back as the 1890s still survive. The major building period, however, occurred during the 1920s as part of a plan to convert East Calhoun into an "apartment district." Mediterranean-style structures from this period can be identified by their ornate decorations and clay tile roofs. Low-rise one- and two-bedroom apartment complexes built in the 1960s and '70s can be found here too.

With living quarters in abundance, the downside is traffic. The intersection at Hennepin and Lake is said to be the busiest in the Twin Cities, and the future LRT train crossing Lake Street every few minutes is expected to make Lake Street gridlock even worse. In an effort to make commuting by bike easier, area residents have been among the most active promoters of the Midtown Greenway, the below-grade bike path parallel to 29th Street, that will eventually run from France Avenue all the way across town to the Mississippi River.

BRYN MAWR, CEDAR–ISLES–DEAN, WEST CALHOUN

Close to the parks, but out of the traffic, the hilly wooded neighborhoods on the west side of the lakes contain moderately priced, single-family homes that are slightly newer than the houses to the east. This park-like setting of architecturally-varied, well-kept bungalows, ramblers, and colonials offers comfortable living amid the more imposing Tudors and grand Mediterraneans built along the scenic parkways. High-rise apartment buildings in **Cedar-Isles-Dean** and **West Calhoun**, along Highway 7 and Excelsior Boulevard, have picture-perfect views of sailing boats beating through the deep green waters of Lake Calhoun. **Bryn Mawr**, which is sliced in two by east-west running I-394, does not experience as much of the recreation traffic, even though it is adjacent to Cedar Lake and the Wirth Park Woods. Residents in these neighborhoods tend to be professionals or executives, many of whom work out of their homes, so there are people about throughout the day.

KENWOOD, EAST ISLES, LOWRY HILL

While Calhoun seems like a summer kind of place, **Kenwood**, on Lake of the Isles, is at its best in winter when the crowds have gone home. Winter evenings bring groups of skaters and scents of hot chocolate and cinnamon wafting through the frost-bitten air, and the most important building on the block becomes the east shore warming house. In late November, this affluent neighborhood seems twice as impressive, with its large Mediterranean, Colonial, and Arts and Crafts homes dressed up for the holidays. So muffle-up and take the three-mile walk around the lake, and don't miss the "Mary Tyler Moore house" on the corner of Kenwood and 21st where Ms. Moore hung her hat after she sailed it in the air in the opening clip of the TV show.

Not all residents live lakeside, many of the skaters, bikers and joggers you'll pass live between Kenwood and Hennepin Avenue, where the hills of **East Isles** sport several architecturally significant houses and many well-maintained apartments. The Purcell-Cutts house at 2328 Lake Place is considered one of the best examples of Prairie School architecture in the state. Young professional families live in these large houses where the neighborhood personality is both active and sophisticated. To find an apartment here, look for discrete signs posted in yards or windows—rarely do the best ones make the classifieds.

At the north end of the lake, the steep streets of **Lowry Hill**, from I-394 to 22nd Street, west of Hennepin, span the arts and the ages, from turn-of-the century mill-owners' mansions to the Walker Art Center's collection of contemporary art. Some of the houses here have been pulled down or turned into offices, but many of them still exist as private homes with craftsman details intact creating a wonderful air of elegance and grace. Despite the heavy traffic, residents of Lowry Hill enjoy their neighborhood, happy to be so close to the Guthrie Theatre, the Walker Art Center and downtown.

Web Sites: www.ci.minneapolis.mn.us, www.tcfreenet.org, www.carag.org

Area Code: 612

Zip Codes: 55403, 55405, 55408, 55409, 55416

Post Offices: Loring Station, 18 North 12th Street; Lake Street Station, 10 East 31st Street; Elmwood Branch, 3532 Beltline Boulevard, St. Louis Park (all post office branches can be reached at 800-275-8777).

Police Precinct: 5th, 2429 Nicollet Avenue, 612-673-5705

Emergency Hospitals: Hennepin County Medical Center, 701 Park Avenue, 612-347-2121; Methodist Hospital, 6500 Excelsior Boulevard, St. Louis Park, 952-932-5000

Library: Walker, 2880 Hennepin Avenue, 612-630-6650

Community Resources: Neighborhood Revitalization Program, 612-673-5140; East Calhoun Community Organization (ECCO), http://freenet.msp.mn.us/org/ecco, includes a crime-site map, environmental, recreation and school information, and a welcome packet for new residents. Packets can also be obtained from any ECCO board member or Block Club Leader.

Community Publications: *East Calhoun News*, P.O. Box 80535, 612-823-6005; *Southwest Journal*, 3225 Lyndale Avenue South, Minneapolis, MN 55408, 612-825-9205; *Hill & Lake Press*, Kenwood Recreation Center, 2101 West Franklin, Minneapolis, MN 55405, 612-377-0892; *The Wedge*, P.O. Box 80510, Minneapolis, MN 55408, 612-377-5181

Transportation: **Bus Lines**: 1: Apache Plaza/Kenwood/Downtown; 4: Southtown/Lyndale Avenue/Downtown; 6: Downtown Minneapolis/Hennepin Avenue/Lake Calhoun/France Avenue/U of M/Rosedale; 8: St. Louis Park/Bryn Mawr/Downtown; 12: Glen Lake/Methodist Hospital/Downtown Minneapolis; 17: Knollwood Shopping Center/Hennepin Avenue/Nicollet Mall; 21: Lake Street/Marshall Avenue (St. Paul); 23: 38th Street/Lake Street/Becketwood/Highland Park

SOUTHWEST COMMUNITY

ARMATAGE, KENNY, WINDOM
LYNNHURST, FULLER
LINDEN HILLS, FULTON
EAST HARRIET, KINGFIELD

Boundaries: **North**: 38th Street; **West**: France Avenue, Xerxes Avenue; **South**: Crosstown Highway 62; **East**: I-35W

While young singles head straight for Uptown, hip young families usually prefer the post-depression bungalows and mini-Tudors of the other south-west communities. Life here, while still close to the city lakes and park-ways, is far enough away to make quiet, tree-lined streets and well-kept yards feel like small town living. No more than ten minutes' drive from the high-rises of downtown, this is the most heavily residential area of down-town Minneapolis.

Single-family homes and duplexes predominate, although apart-ments are available, especially in the Windom neighborhood. Most homes date to the early 1900s through the 1940s. Colonials and Midwestern squares line central streets such as Lyndale Avenue, while stucco bunga-lows are common toward the outer edges of the community. Homes sur-rounding Lake Harriet and the Lake Harriet Rock Garden are expensive, and some of the most beautiful in Minneapolis. Moderately-priced ideal starter homes abound away from the lakeside.

Numerous parks add to the tranquillity of the community. Lake Harriet, encircled by a parkway, has a bandshell on its north shore. Martin Luther King Park to the northeast has indoor tennis courts. Lyndale Farmstead was the original home of Theodore Wirth, the turn-of-the-cen-tury "father" of Minneapolis parks. It features after-school programs, films, and an ice skating rink. The Minnehaha Creek Parkway runs through the community to the south.

ARMATAGE, KENNY, WINDOM

Located between the 62 Crosstown Highway and Diamond Lake Road, Armatage, Kenny and Windom neighborhoods boast well-built two- and three-bedroom starter houses, most of which pre-date the 1940s. Houses in **Kenny** tend to be newer, and sometimes larger. There is a stable mix of old and new families and, according to the Kenny Neighborhood Association, the homes are about 95% owner-occupied. Apartments can be found in **Windom**, along 35W, where housing runs the gamut, dating from pre-WW II through the 1970s. Neighborhood concerns here include airport noise, freeway issues and preventing pollution of Grass Lake. Kenny School (K-5) in the middle of the neighborhood is a gifted-catalyst school (it's an enhanced program for gifted students) with an active Parent-Teacher Association.

LYNNHURST, FULLER

The community milk-cow (you read it right) once grazed in a pasture on 46th Street, and the neighborhood of **Lynnhust** somehow retains that idyllic sense. With fine period homes and the parks along Minnehaha Creek and the shores of Lake Harriet, many believe this neighborhood to be one of the most pleasant in the Twin Cities. Extending from I-35W, and then west to Penn Avenue, between 46th and 54th streets, there has been steady upward movement in assessed values of these properties, and quick market turnover. Many residents cite the attractiveness of the houses as the main reason for choosing to live here. "Tangletown," inside the Fuller neighborhood, is a hilly tangle of curved, wooded streets that are unusual in the mostly grid-like South Minneapolis layout. **Fuller** can be described (though perhaps not for long) as a neighborhood in which you can get a lot of house for the money when compared to neighborhoods closer to the city lakes. Major issues in this vicinity are increasing airport noise and the volume and speed of traffic, as well as traffic spillover onto the residential streets. Shopping is conveniently located in five commercial districts along Penn Avenue, 50th, Bryant and Lyndale, with many new shops and small restaurants being added.

LINDEN HILLS, FULTON

Linden Hills was built as a "cottage city" in the 1880s to entice homebuyers away from downtown and out to the waters of Calhoun and Harriet. Only a few cottages remain. Most have been torn down and replaced by large bungalows, prairie styles and Tudors with three and four bedrooms and two-car garages. Property values are moderate to high, even for houses in deteriorated condition. The remaining ivy covered cottages with details like oval windows are considered desirable remodeling gems.

Many families choose Linden Hills to be in Southwest High School's attendance district, and the sense of community—wine and cheese welcomes and summertime block parties where everyone's invited, is another draw. Best of all, it's quiet—a tranquil haven in the middle of the city. **Fulton** is a bit less placid. Located between 54th and 47th streets, and Penn and France avenues, it is bisected by the main artery of 50th Street with its extended commercial district which offers boutique shopping at 50th and Penn and 50th and France. Linden Hills' shopping area, at 43rd and Upton, includes country antiques and stylish accessories for the home.

EAST HARRIET, KINGFIELD

Talk about quiet neighborhoods—most of **East Harriet** is occupied by Lakewood Cemetery. That's supposed to be a joke, you'll hear it a lot if you move into this neighborhood. You'll also be treated to a list of all your celebrity "neighbors," including Hubert Horatio Humphrey, Minnesota's senator for many years and vice-president of the United States. Joking aside, this neighborhood does include some of the city's finest amenities: Lake Harriet and the Lake Harriet Rose Garden, and the T. S. Roberts Bird Sanctuary off Roseway Road, that features a boardwalk through the marsh and an osprey nesting platform. Houses in Lake Harriet tend to be large two-story Tudors, Colonials and Mediterraneans with sun-porches. The homes are set back from the streets under leafy, old growth canopies. **Kingfield's** houses are similar to those closer to Lake Harriet, but are usually a little less expensive. Many of them have been updated with additional bathrooms and new kitchens. While this is largely a middle-income neighborhood with single-family homes, it does have some apartment buildings, multi-family residences and commercial areas.

Web Sites: www.kenny-mpls.com, www.ci.minneapolis.mn.us, www.tcfreenet.org

Area Code: 612

Zip Codes: 55409, 55410, 55419

Post Offices: Lake Street Station, 110 East 31st Street; Edina Branch, 3948 West 49 1/2 Street, Edina; Diamond Lake Station, 5500 Nicollet Avenue (all post office branches can be reached at 800-275-8777).

Police Precinct: 5th, 2429 Nicollet Avenue, 612-673-5705

Emergency Hospitals: Fairview Southdale Hospital, 6401 France Avenue South, 952-924-5000; Abbott Northwestern Hospital, 800 East 28th Street, 612-863-4000

Libraries: Linden Hills, 2900 West 43rd Street, 612-630-6750; Washburn, 5244 Lyndale Avenue South, 612-630-6500

Community Resources: Neighborhood Revitalization Program, 612-673-5140

Community Publications: *Southwest Journal*, 3225 Lyndale Avenue South, Minneapolis, MN 55408, 612-825-9205; *Southwest*

Journal Electronic Town Square, www.wcco.com/community/swjournal; *Linden Hills News*, 4037 Beard Avenue South, Minneapolis MN 55410, 612-926-2906

Transportation: **Bus Lines**: 4: Downtown/Bryant Avenue/ Southtown; 6: Downtown/Windom neighborhood/Bloomington; 28: Downtown/Xerxes Avenue/Southdale; numerous 35 routes run through southwestern neighborhoods onto I-35W; 47: Downtown/ Lyndale Avenue/Normandale Community College/U of M

NOKOMIS COMMUNITY

HALE, PAGE, DIAMOND LAKE
STANDISH-ERICSSON
FIELD, REGINA, NORTHRUP
KEEWAYDIN, MINNEHAHA, MORRIS PARK, WENONAH

Boundaries: **North**: 42nd Street, Hiawatha Golf Course; **West**: I-35W; **South**: Cross-town Highway 62; **East**: Hiawatha Avenue, 47th Avenue

"Say, if you'd begin to live, To Oleana you must go; The poorest wretch in Norway, becomes a Duke in a year or so." Those were the words of a song meant to lure Scandinavians to America. Oleana turned out to be a land fraud in Pennsylvania and many of the immigrants wound up here, in Minnesota. The first generation settled on "Snoose Boulevard" (Cedar-Riverside); the second generation built their sturdy post-depression bungalows here, in Nokomis, and lived in them for a lifetime.

Nokomis, with tree-lined blocks of pleasant yards and tidy houses is moderately priced, making it attractive to young singles and couples. Some luxurious Colonials line the curved parkways around Lake Nokomis; otherwise, what you'll find here are bungalows, mini-Tudors, and occasional one-story ranch houses. Brick apartment buildings dating to the 1920s can be found along larger streets such as Chicago Avenue and Cedar Avenue, and small commercial districts dot the area. Housing in this community is largely owner-occupied, with the local population a range of ages and pocketbooks. However, noise from Minneapolis/St. Paul International Airport, to the south, is definitely a factor to consider if you're looking at Nokomis. Federal grants are available for household sound insulation, but it is feared that construction of a new terminal and third runway will make the noise worse. Keep this in mind and ask pointed questions if you're house-hunting in this area.

On the other hand, the recreation amenities are excellent and close at hand. The heart of the community, Lake Nokomis, is an expansive body of water with more green space around it than the other lakes of South Minneapolis. Minneapolis' lake-parkway system winds through this community along Minnehaha Creek and around Lake Nokomis, leading to the public Hiawatha Golf Course and Lake Hiawatha. Baseball fields, open space and sparse wooded areas surround Lake Nokomis. Minnehaha Park is the annual venue for Svenskarnas Dag Scandinavian festival held near the end of June. For a description of Minnehaha Park and Minnehaha Falls, which are on the eastern edge of Nokomis, check **Lakes and Parkways**.

The **Hale**, **Page**, and **Diamond Lake** neighborhoods are located between Minnehaha Creek on the north, Highway 62 on the south, Cedar Avenue on the east and I-35W on the west. Most of the houses here have three bedrooms and were built as late as the 1960s. Some of the residents are original owners.

Standish and **Ericsson**, north and east of Lake Hiawatha from Cedar Avenue to Hiawatha, and from 36th Street down to Minnehaha Parkway, have small well-kept stucco bungalows and one and a half-story expansions with details like natural woodwork, hardwood floors and built-in buffets. There are new houses in the redevelopment area along Hiawatha Avenue, on the eastern edge of the neighborhoods. Hiawatha Park and public golf course, 612-724-7715, offers swimming, walking, and biking in the summer and groomed cross-country ski trails in winter. Sibley Field, off 40th Street, has a children's playground, sledding hill, and hockey and skating rinks. If you're interested in this part of town, be sure to check out the Standish-Ericsson Web site, (see below), which contains many photographs and information about churches, schools and garden clubs. Access to St. Paul is easy over the Ford Bridge, and future plans for the area include building the LRT corridor along the east side of these two neighborhoods.

In the center of Nokomis, bounded by I-35W and Cedar Avenue, **Field**, **Regina**, and **Northrop** consist mostly of small, two-bedroom pre-1940s stucco, brick and stone houses. Northrop in particular has some pretty, hilly streets (check out 12th, 13th and 14th) and a mix of well-kept, updated housing stock. This area is popular with young couples who are looking for an affordable alternative to Lake Harriet.

Finally, **Keewaydin**, **Minnehaha**, **Morris Park**, and **Wenonah** are spread out from the east shore of Lake Nokomis to Minnehaha Park. These neighborhoods have slightly newer housing, more renters, and they abut the airport.

Web Sites: www.standish-ericsson.org, www.ci.minneapolis.mn.us, www.tcfreenet.org

Area Code: 612

Zip Codes: 55406, 55407, 55409, 55417, 55419

Post Offices: Nokomis Station, 5139 34th Avenue South; Diamond Lake Station, 5500 Nicollet Avenue (all post office branches can be reached at 800-275-8777).

Police Precinct: 3rd, 3000 Minnehaha Avenue, 612-673-5703

Emergency Hospital: Abbott Northwestern Hospital, 800 East 28th Street, 612-863-4000

Library: Nokomis, 5100 34th Avenue South, 612-630-6700

Community Resources: Neighborhood Revitalization Program, 612-673-5140; Hiawatha Park and public golf course, 612-724-7715

Community Publication: *Southside Pride*, 3200 Chicago Avenue South, Minneapolis, MN 55407, 612-822-4662

Transportation: **Bus Lines**: 5: Downtown/Chicago Avenue/Mall of America; 7: Downtown/Minnehaha Avenue/International Airport; 14: Bloomington Avenue/Downtown/Brooklyn Park; 15: Southdale/ Hiawatha Avenue/Ford Parkway (St. Paul); 19: 28th Avenue South/ Downtown/Golden Valley; 22: 34th Avenue/42nd Street/Cedar Avenue

POWDERHORN COMMUNITY

POWDERHORN PARK
WHITTIER
LYNDALE
CENTRAL
CORCORAN

Boundaries: **North**: Franklin Avenue, Lake Street; **West**: Lyndale Avenue, I-35W; **South**: 38th Street, 42nd Street; **East**: Minnehaha Avenue

When the snow begins to fall, the rolling hills of Powderhorn Park become a well-used tobogganing area, and skaters take to the only outdoor speed-skating track in the Twin Cities. At the heart of Powderhorn's diverse community is this lovely park, a one square-mile reserve of hilly woods and wildflower-covered hills. There is a small lake that is home to egrets and great blue herons—a welcome expanse amid its urban surroundings. It's also the setting for May Day, Powderhorn Festival of the Arts, Shakespeare in the Park, July 4th fireworks and Friday night concerts. (See **A Twin Cities Year**.)

The park sits in marked contrast to some of the neighborhoods around it which are economically depressed rental areas with high levels of unemployment, crime, poverty and substandard housing. They include Central, Corcoran, Bryant and Bancroft, which span the distance between I-35W and Cedar Avenue to 42nd Street.

The exception to the area's general shabbiness is the **Powderhorn Park** neighborhood located between Chicago and Cedar Avenue, from Lake Street to 38th. Centrally located, with easy access to downtown, property values in this neighborhood are increasing, and many Powderhorn Park houses are getting a facelift. In fact, the neighborhood is hosting a national design competition called Little/LOTS to get architects to design houses for the narrow (40-foot) lots prevalent in this twelve by eight block neighborhood. One-third of the housing units here are duplexes.

Closer to downtown, **Whittier**, between Franklin and Lake Street from Lyndale to I-35W, is largely a rental area of run-down buildings interspersed with fixed-up old Colonials and Victorians on wide lots. The Washburn-Fair Oaks Mansion District along 22nd Street between 1st and 2nd avenues, near the Minneapolis Institute of Arts, is listed on the National Historic Register. More grand houses, some of the oldest homes in Minneapolis, are found along Blaisdell and Third avenues. Stephens Avenue is also home to a number of beautifully restored houses, and even an in-town bed and breakfast (see **Temporary Lodgings**).

Across Lake Street, the duplexes and apartments in **Lyndale**, south of Lake and east of Lyndale, are much like nearby neighborhoods in Uptown, although housing here is generally more affordable and incomes more modest. Now that the crime rate is going down, particularly in the southern portion, Lyndale's vision is to empower and enhance the community by making art and culture an integral and accessible part of community life. They have a good start with the pARTS photograhy gallery, Jungle Theatre and Bryant Lake Bowl.

Life is improving in other neighborhoods as well. In **Central**, just east of I-35 and south of Lake Street, gang activity has decreased significantly in recent years, and while clearly still a work in progress, the East Lake Street business district is also being redeveloped. Restaurants, shops and cafes at the corner of Lake Street and Lyndale Avenue (Lyn-Lake) mark the beginnings of Uptown, and the rest of Lake Street's old-style commercial district is being updated—a gun shop has been turned into the Midtown Cafe, and the Hispanic Mercado opened in the summer of 1999. Two complexes expected to have a great stabilizing impact on the Powderhorn community are the Great Lakes Center (old Sears building), which will bring government services, a transit center, offices and up-scale retail into the community, and the already completed YWCA fieldhouse and aquatic center at 22nd and Lake. It provides a place to run, play basketball and swim. Housing in the Central neighborhood includes the grand Queen Anne "Healy Block," between Lake Street and East 31st Street, along 2nd Avenue South. Once known as "crack alley," these historic houses have been rehabilitated, signaling a profound change in the neighborhood.

At the far east end of Lake Street, the **Corcoran** neighborhood has hopes that the adjacent Hiawatha LRT corridor will bring about renewal here as well.

Web Sites: www.lyndale.org, www.ci.minneapolis.mn.us, www.tcfreenet.org

Area Code: 612

Zip Codes: 55405, 55406, 55407, 55408, 55409

Post Offices: Powderhorn Station, 3045 Bloomington Avenue; Minnehaha Station, 3033 27th Avenue South; Lake Street Station, 110 East 31st Street (all post office branches can be reached at 800-275-8777).

Police Precincts: west of I-35W: 5th Precinct, 2429 Nicollet Avenue, 612-673-5705; rest of Powderhorn: 3rd Precinct, 3000 Minnehaha Avenue, 612-673-5703

Emergency Hospital: Abbott Northwestern Hospital, 800 East 28th Street, 612-863-4000

Library: Hosmer, 347 East 36th Street, 612-630-6950

Community Resources: Neighborhood Revitalization Program, 612-673-5140; pARTS Gallery, 711 West Lake Street, 612-824-5500; Powderhorn Park

Community Publications: *Common Sense*, 3537 Nicollet Avenue, Minneapolis, MN 55408, 612-824-9402; *Southwest Journal*, 3225 Lyndale Avenue South, Minneapolis, MN 55408, 612-825-9205

Transportation: **Bus Lines**: 4: Downtown/Lyndale Avenue/ Southtown; 5: Downtown/Chicago Avenue/Mall of America; 9: 4th Avenue/Downtown/Golden Valley; 10: Grand Avenue/Downtown/ Northeast Minneapolis; 14: Bloomington Avenue/Downtown/ Brooklyn Park; 18: Downtown/Nicollet Avenue/Bloomington; 19: Mall of America/Cedar Avenue/Downtown; 21: Lake Street 22: Cedar Avenue/Downtown; 23: 38th Street 47: Downtown/Lyndale Avenue/Normandale Community College; 94L: Lake Street/I-94/ Downtown St. Paul. Numerous I-35W routes board where the highway crosses Lake Street.

PHILLIPS COMMUNITY

Boundaries: North: I-94; **West**: I-35W; **South**: Lake Street; **East**: Hiawatha Avenue

The Phillips community in south-central Minneapolis has a complex history. Elegant victorian mansions, some of the largest in the city, are a sign of this neighborhood's past grandeur. Unfortunately, urban decay, due in part to construction of Interstate highways 35W and 94, has laid much of this area to waste. However, corporate and community activism in Phillips are resulting in some urban renewal and redirection, and a slight decrease in the crime rate. In Minneapolis' largest neighborhood (it spans 220-blocks), over 50 block clubs have been formed, and Phillips' residents are patrolling their blocks in an effort to take back their neighborhood. Vacant lots have been turned into community gardens. New housing has been built along the Hiawatha LRT corridor, and many youth programs have been initiated by community groups and churches. The Midtown Greenway will pass through Phillips, one block north of Lake Street, on its long run from France Avenue to the Mississippi. The community's sense of pride is exemplified by a graceful gateway sculpture built at Franklin and Chicago Avenues by Rafala Green.

Unfortunately, time has not been kind to the mansions of Park and Portland Avenues. Some of them have been converted into apartments, group homes, halfway houses and office spaces, others have been adapted for use by the cluster of hospitals and specialty clinics in Phillips, including Abbott Northwestern Hospital and Minneapolis Children's Medical Center. Perhaps the neighborhood's best-known landmark is the American Swedish Institute, a 33-room mansion that houses a museum of Swedish culture at 2600 Park Avenue. The Minneapolis American Indian Center and Art Gallery is at the corner of Franklin and Bloomington Avenues.

Phillips, like Central and Cedar-Riverside, is a culturally diverse area. The neighborhood, with over 70 non-profit community agencies, serves as a gateway to newly arrived immigrants. North African restaurants and food stores can be found a little north of the neighborhood on Cedar Avenue, and the new Hispanic Mercado at 15th and Lake serves the 9,000 Spanish-speaking people who live within its surrounding three miles.

Housing consists mainly of rentals in the form of duplexes and triplexes, many of which are in deteriorated condition. The latter part of 1997 saw average house prices in Phillips at around $53,000; this according to the Regional Multiple Listing Service. Newly built homes did better, selling for between $86,000 and $89,000.

Revitalization projects continue to bring new capital into Phillips. Park Avenue mansions are being renovated and converted into owner-occupied condominiums; new duplexes, condominiums, and green spaces are in the plans for the area bounded by 24th and 25th streets, between Chicago and Portland. Portland Place, an association development of 31 new houses and townhouses which places no income limitations on potential buyers, opened in the summer of 1999. Most recent revitalization efforts in Phillips are centered around a two-million square foot retail and office mall called Great Lakes Center, which is on the site of the old Sears building at 10th Avenue and Lake.

Web Sites: www.ci.minneapolis.mn.us, www.tcfreenet.org

Area Code: 612

Zip Codes: 55403, 55404, 55405, 55407, 55408

Post Offices: Powderhorn Station, 3045 Bloomington Avenue, Minnehaha Station, 3033 27th Avenue South. Lake Street Station, 110 East 31st Street (all post office branches can be reached at 349-4711).

Police Precinct: 3rd, 3000 Minnehaha Avenue, 612-673-5703

Emergency Hospital: Abbott Northwestern Hospital, 800 East 28th Street, 612-863-4000

Library: Franklin, 1314 East Franklin Avenue, 612-874-1667

Community Resources: American Swedish Institute, 2600 Park Avenue, 612-871-4907; Minneapolis American Indian Center, 1530 Franklin Avenue East, 612-813-1268

Community Publication: *The Alley*

Transportation: **Bus Lines**: 2: Franklin Avenue/U of M; 5: Downtown/Chicago Avenue/Mall of America; 9: 4th Avenue/ Downtown/Golden Valley; 14: Bloomington Avenue/Downtown/ Brooklyn Park; 19: Mall of America/Cedar Avenue/Golden Valley; 21: Lake Street; 22: Cedar Avenue/Park Avenue; 94L: Lake Street/I-94; numerous I-35W express routes board where the highway crosses Lake Street.

LONGFELLOW COMMUNITY

LONGFELLOW
SEWARD
COOPER, HOWE, HIAWATHA

Boundaries: **North**: I-94; **West**: Minnehaha Avenue; **South/East**: Mississippi River

Longfellow is the sliver-shaped bungalow community that flanks the gorge of the Mississippi River between I-94 and Minnehaha Falls Park, extending east to the Hiawatha LRT corridor. Longfellow is bisected by Lake Street and bordered by Hiawatha Avenue. Popular since the 1920s with working-class people, it is well-served by public transportation, and an LRT station on east Lake Street near 27th Avenue will make access to and from Longfellow even better.

The community has an industrial/commercial look along the Minnehaha/Hiawatha corridor where there is also a large concentration of multi-family rental housing. But residents still have easy access to nature— bike trails through the river gorge lead north and south; Minnehaha Falls Park is connected to the Grand Round system; and eventually the Midtown Greenway will cross Longfellow and Cooper neighborhoods.

It is actually hard to find a home in **Seward**, which at the end of the 1990s developed a hip reputation. Housing here ranges from deteriorated student digs that appear to be held together by colorful paint jobs, to two blocks of gentrified railroad workers' houses (circa 1880) located on Milwaukee Road, and now listed on the Historic Register.

A little farther south, a patchwork of homes in various stages of improvement characterize the **Cooper**, **Howe**, and **Hiawatha** neighborhoods. Houses in the blocks closest to the river have been upgraded substantially, and more modest homes farther back are also being renovated on a block-by-block basis. At the south end of Hiawatha, Minnehaha Parkway boasts larger homes with decorative details, but for architecturally unique dream-houses, look to the river and shop along Edmund Boulevard.

Much of Longfellow's housing is deemed worthy of rehabilitation, but may fall short of meeting the needs of modern families. Over half the houses in these neighborhoods are bungalows—two-bedroom, one-bath, single-story houses with built-in cabinets and expansion attics. Two-story, four-square houses built in the 1920s are the second-most predominant style. So popular is renovation of existing homes in this neighborhood that the Longfellow community commissioned a book, *The Longfellow Planbook: Remodeling Plans for Bungalows and Other Small Urban Homes*, which contains ideas for up-dating the area's predominant housing types. Plans have been reviewed and approved by the Minneapolis Inspections Division. The book can be purchased from the Longfellow Community Council (see below), for $18.50, or $10 for Longfellow residents.

A number of additional initiatives are being employed to improve these neighborhoods. Longfellow United for Youth and Families (LUYF), 612-721-7811, coordinates an after-school tutoring program and employs young people to remove graffiti. There are also active block patrols formed in response to safety concerns.

Web Sites: www.ci.minneapolis.mn.us, www.tcfreenet.org

Area Code: 612

Zip Codes: 55404, 55406, 55407, 55417

Post Offices: Minnehaha Station, 3033 27th Avenue South; Nokomis Station, 5139 34th Avenue South (all post office branches can be reached at 800-275-8777).

Police Precinct: 3rd, 3000 Minnehaha Avenue, 612-673-5703

Emergency Hospitals: Abbott Northwestern Hospital, 800 East 28th Street, 612-863-4000; Fairview-University Medical Center, 2450 Riverside Avenue, 612-672-6000

Library: East Lake, 2727 East Lake Street, 612-630-6550

Community Resources: Neighborhood Revitalization Program, 612-673-5140; Longfellow Community Council, 4151 Minnehaha Avenue South, Minneapolis 55406, 612-722-4529; Longfellow United for Youth and Families (LUYF), 612-721-7811

Community Publications: *Southside Pride*, 3200 Chicago Avenue

South, Minneapolis 55407, 612-822-4662; *Longfellow-Nokomis Community Messenger*, 1885 University Avenue West, St. Paul 55104, 651-645-7045; *Seward Profile*, 2600 East Franklin, Minneapolis 55406, 612-692-8561

Transportation: **Bus Lines**: 2: Franklin Avenue/U of M; 7: Downtown/Minnehaha Avenue/Mall of America; 8: Franklin Avenue/Downtown/Golden Valley; 20: 46th Avenue/Plymouth Avenue; 21: Lake Street; 23: 46th Avenue/38th Street

UNIVERSITY COMMUNITY

MARCY-HOLMES
COMO
UNIVERSITY OF MINNESOTA
CEDAR-RIVERSIDE (WEST BANK)
PROSPECT PARK
NICOLLET ISLAND

Boundaries: **North**: East Hennepin Avenue, I-35W; **West**: Nicollet Island, I-35W; **South**: I-94, East Bank of Mississippi; **East**: city limits

Gold and maroon rule in these diverse neighborhoods that are tucked in along the banks of the Mississippi. Access to the campuses of the University of Minnesota and Augsburg College is direct, and housing styles range, from the multitudes of student duplexes and apartments next to campus in **Marcy-Holmes** (west of I-35W), to the low-rent high-rises at Cedar-Riverside, to University Avenue's fraternity row, to the quieter neighborhoods of Prospect Park and Como. Due to the campus location, rents are not a bargain, although house prices are moderate. If you're a student looking for housing in Prospect Park, check bulletin boards for rental notices at Tower Grocery; and for Cedar-Riverside on the West Bank, check North Country Co-op at 1925 South 5th Street.

An area that is often recommended for off-campus housing is the **Como** neighborhood, a swath of modest (sometimes dilapidated) bungalows and tall, skinny two-stories. This neighborhood is home to Joe's Market and Deli at 1828 Como, one of the Twin Cities' last family-owned neighborhood groceries.

The perks of an academic community—lectures, concerts, the University Film Society—are easily accessible to people living nearby, and the University's Weisman Art Museum, on the East Bank, is the riverfront's most significant architectural landmark. **University of Minnesota's** Dinkytown, between 8th Street and University Avenue on the East Bank, is the main campus commercial district. It has plenty of cheap places to eat and many businesses named "Gopher" (for the University of Minnesota mascot). Bob Dylan (known locally as Robert Zimmerman from Hibbing, Minnesota) played at the "Twelve O'clock Scholar" here in the early sixties.

Limited University operated housing is available for families (with or without children) at two complexes: the Como Student Community at 1024 27th Avenue Southeast, 612-378-2434, and Commonwealth Terrace Cooperative on the St. Paul campus, 651-646-7526. These complexes feature excellent playgrounds and sponsor numerous activities for children. Intercampus buses serve both facilities, as does MCTO (see **Transportation**).

Across the river on the West Bank, **Cedar-Riverside** has gone through many incarnations from the "Snoose Boulevard" of Scandinavian immigrants at the turn of the century to the bohemian "New Town in Town" of the 1960s. Named for the crossing of the two streets, Cedar-Riverside has been a cultural center for over one hundred years, since the Danish immigrants built Dania Hall, a gathering place for Scandinavian singles, theatergoers and vaudeville entertainers. Sadly the hall burnt down during renovations in 2000. A creative element is still evident in the many music venues and small performance theaters which draw college students and music fans from all over the Twin Cities. The recently renovated Cedar Cultural Centre, 416 Cedar Avenue South, 612-338-2674, books culturally diverse acts from blues and folk to Celtic-rock. Cooperatively run vegetarian and ethnic restaurants thrive in this neighborhood filled with foreign accents. Most of the people who live here are college students or are connected with the University. Almost all the housing is rental, one-bedroom and built in the 1970s for a mobile population. The Riverside Plaza, a low-rent high-rise whose colored squares are visible from I-94, looms above the neighborhood. A residential area which includes mid-western square-style duplexes and apartments lies to the east of Cedar Avenue. Next door neighbor University of Minnesota provides escorts to people who are out on campus at night. Take this as your cue that security is a definite concern here.

Back on the East Bank along the river, between the University and St. Paul, **Prospect Park** is a place where security is not a huge concern. People who live in "the Park" say they live in a small town with an urban beat, a place where they can walk to work, to recreation, shopping, and community events, and probably recognize everybody along the way.

Residents here are 10 minutes by car from each downtown, and centrally located for travel to any place in the Twin Cities. Their strong sense of place probably has to do with the area's clear geographic boundaries: steep hills and the pointy green witch's hat water tower, which is visible from I-94. Once a year the whole neighborhood climbs to the top and is treated to a panoramic view of the cities all the way to the airport.

The area's civic history dates back to the late 1800s when it was a commuter suburb on the Minneapolis streetcar line. Today, imposing historic residences rub elbows with new condos and public housing on Prospect Park's meandering streets. Though there is a laissez-faire attitude toward landscaping, and the used auto parts business displays "found-art" sculptures, beautiful restoration is appreciated. Many of the homes date from the early 1900s up to the 1930s and feature art glass windows and other elegant details. Popular updates include turning butler's pantries into second bathrooms and putting in modern kitchens. While Prospect Park lacks a large grocery, it does have Tower Foods, a convenience store that doubles as a community meeting place. Quiet streets and tree-covered slopes give the neighborhood a tranquil character.

Another antique refuge with a view of the city skyline is just northwest of the university, out in the river. Forty-seven-acre **Nicollet Island** is a 19th century Victorian landmark settlement and park within the St. Anthony Falls Heritage Zone. Known as the "Mississippi Mile, the zone stretches from the Plymouth Avenue Bridge and Boom Island downstream to the I-35W bridge. A flood of restaurants line the "mile"—you can enjoy seafood at Anthony's Wharf, sushi at Kikugawa, and a stuffed jalapeno and cream cheese Tuggburger at Tugg's River Salon—and never have to leave Southeast Main Street. Most of Nicollet Island's 400 graceful stone houses were built between 1880 and 1910, and today they are being faithfully restored. Even if you decide not to move to this neighborhood, be sure to take the River City Trolley's narrated tour of the area, 612-673-5123. (See **Transportation**.)

Web Sites: www.ci.minneapolis.mn.us, www.tcfreenet.org

Area Code: 612

Zip Codes: 55455 (University of Minnesota), 55413, 55414, 55454, 55404

Post Offices: University Station, 2811 University Avenue SE; Dinkytown Station, 1311 SE 4th Street (all post office branches can be reached at 800-275-8777).

Police Precinct: 2nd, 1911 Central Avenue NE, 612-673-5702

Emergency Hospitals: University Hospital, Harvard Street at East River Parkway, 612-626-3000; Fairview-University Medical Center, 2450 Riverside Avenue, 612-672-6000

Libraries: Southeast, 1222 SE 4th Street, 612-630-6850; University libraries, administrative offices: 612-624-4520

Community Resources: Neighborhood Revitalization Program, 612-673-5140; The Cedar Cultural Centre, 416 Cedar Avenue South, 612-338-2674

Community Publications: *Southeast Angle*, 2600 East Franklin Street, Minneapolis, MN 55406, 612-692-8561; *Minnesota Daily*, www.daily.umn.edu

Transportation: Bus Lines: there are more than 30 U of M bus routes that run from many parts of the Twin Cities to campus. Call 612-626-7275 for routes and information. Most limited-stop and express buses to the University operate on weekdays only. Supersavers are on sale at the following campus locations: Coffman Union, the West Bank Skyway Store, the Williamson Hall Bookstore, the St. Paul Student Center and the Fairview-University Medical Center Ticket Office. Supersavers are sold at all MCTO stores and at over 130 outlets around town. They can also be purchased online at www.metrocouncil.org/transit.

NORTHEAST COMMUNITY

ST. ANTHONY EAST (HISTORIC ST. ANTHONY)
ST. ANTHONY WEST
BELTRAMI, NORTHEAST PARK
BOTTINEAU, SHERIDAN, MARSHALL TERRACE
COLUMBIA PARK
WAITE PARK, AUDUBON PARK
HOLLAND, LOGAN PARK
WINDOM PARK

Boundaries: **North**: 37th Avenue, NE; **West**: Mississippi River; **South**: Nicollet Island, Central Avenue, I-35W; **East**: city limits

"Nord'east" isn't all polka bars—it's also sturdy housing in relatively safe neighborhoods at affordable prices. Historically, the Northeast Community has been home to blue-collar workers of Polish, Ukrainian, Scandinavian, and German backgrounds, and the no-nonsense, roll-up-your-sleeves attitude of these early residents served to keep houses in this community in good repair.

Midwestern squares and small turn-of-the-century wood frame houses built before 1940 predominate in most of the neighborhoods. But the "Parks"—Waite, Audubon, Windom and Columbia—have newer houses and more white-collar workers, and are actually more like the suburbs they adjoin. Nearby, a stretch of parkway that runs from Hillside Cemetery through the community along St. Anthony Boulevard to the Mississippi River to the west, has many parks in which to play, unwind, or walk the dog. And Heaven knows there are plenty of places to pray: one block of Northeast is even listed in the Guiness Book of World Records for having four churches.

Music, bars and polka lounges also have been an important part of the community's history, and more recently, the visual arts have become prominent. St. Anthony East and Beltrami are home to many artists' studios, and Logan Park has set aside neighborhood redevelopment money to support the arts. Other neighborhood priorities include holding on to small local businesses, controlling heavy industry and reclaiming the riverfront. Where there are concentrations of deteriorated rental housing, safety is a concern. In response, many active residents are coming together, planning and writing grant proposals to improve the safety and attractiveness of the community, and are discussing creating a special service district to bring a mix of useful businesses and housing to Central Avenue, the main north-south thoroughfare.

Two blocks after crossing the river on Hennepin Avenue, Kramarczuk's East European Deli, which has done business on this corner since 1954, ushers you into the city's old working-class neighborhood of historic **St. Anthony East**, the birthplace of Minneapolis—not to be confused with the nearby suburb of St. Anthony. This wedge-shaped neighborhood, bordered by NE Washington Avenue, NE Central Avenue and NE Broadway, is home to many historical notes of interest including St. Anthony Falls, "discovered" by Father Louis Hennepin in 1680; the Pillsbury "A" mill, the beginning of "Mill City's" flour, lumber and textile industry; and dandelions, brought here by the first millwright's wife from her homeland. Architectural landmarks, the Russian Orthodox and Ukranian Orthodox churches, Surdyk's Liquors and Nye's Polonaise Room, serve as reminders of St. Anthony's booming business district of days gone by. Now, at the beginning of the new millennium, these businesses are again enjoying popularity, and East St. Anthony is thriving. Massive waves of redevelopment in the 1960s, '70s and '80s demolished many of the old houses that were replaced with multi-unit housing, including luxury high-rises where residents are treated to spectacular views of the river and the soaring music from Our Lady of Lourdes Catholic Church. Consistent with the Northeast tradition of homeownership, nearly all the housing is owner-occupied. For those who love the river, this is an ideal place to live, it's near Boom Island Park for river access, and only a 20-minute walk to offices downtown.

Next-door neighbor **St. Anthony West** also experienced the three waves of redevelopment, but came through it with some of its Victorians intact, as well as a suburban-style development of ramblers, split-levels and townhouses. This area is a Historic Garden District, and the demand for its vintage homes far exceeds the supply, resulting in most of St. Anthony West's residents living in some form of multi-housing such as duplexes or townhomes. The heart of this neighborhood is Boom Island Park, a 14-acre riverside park that features a day-use marina, playground and picnic area. Like St. Anthony East, this neighborhood is within walking distance of downtown, and biking distance of the University.

Heading north along Central Avenue, you'll see delis, polka lounges and supper clubs, as well as rows and rows of small, mid-western squares and bungalows. The **Beltrami** and Northeast Park neighborhoods, east of Central and south of Broadway, are picking up the pace. Some parents of university students are buying the tiny houses and duplexes for their children instead of paying room and board at school. Two-story plain frame houses built during the early 1900s make up the bulk of housing, but there are some more recently constructed (mid-1980s) houses to be found near the railroad tracks and along East Hennepin Avenue. Beltrami Park, off East Broadway, has a playground, pool, tennis and basketball courts and a baseball diamond. Now that the downtown warehouse area is in the midst of gentrification, some artists are choosing Beltrami for its less expensive studio space. This area is conveniently located to the university, Interstate 35W and to Northeast Park, where you'll find the Quarry shopping center with a Rainbow Foods, Target, Office Max, Petsmart, Home Depot, and Old Navy. The neighborhood of **Northeast Park**, just north of I-35W, is a small neighborhood, made up of quiet, dead-end streets. The Hillside Cemetery occupies a full third of this small neighborhood. Older homes in the area (1920s and '30s) are being bought by young families looking for starter homes with character, and some of its sturdy ramblers changed ownership for the first time in the 1990s.

Up the river, the rental working-class communities of Sheridan, Bottineau and Marshall Terrace may lack indoor recreation amenities like field houses and health clubs, but residents can still get their workouts biking the Grand Rounds or dancing the polka at Gasthof Zur Gemutlichkeit at 2300 University. **Bottineau** actually has some houses on the riverfront, and has become popular with artists. The California Building, at 20th and California, a 90,000-square-foot grain mill built in 1920, now houses 75 artists' studios. The **Sheridan** neighborhood is a good example of Northeast's unpretentious, working-class style. Plain, often large, and in good condition, these houses are being fixed, not gentrified. A good amount of small apartment buildings can also be found in Sheridan. **Marshall Terrace**, between 37th Street on the north and Lowry on the south, looks like it would be 100% industrial, until you get into it. Then you see plain turn-of-the-century houses on quiet streets. The houses are affordable and many are being purchased by parents of college students and young professionals. About one-quarter of the houses here are duplexes. For those concerned about living near an industrial zone, current residents say that NSP and the other industries that occupy the riverfront are generally good neighbors, and the bulk of their complaints are related to noise; though there is concern about the proposed Kondirator metal shredder to be located across the river. (See **Camden** in the **North Minneapolis** section of this chapter.) These neighborhoods have access to the river bike paths through West River Road.

Another well-kept Northeast secret is the upscale **Columbia Park** neighborhood, tucked away from industrial surroundings, between the city of Columbia Heights and Columbia Park and Golf Course. The northernmost part is made up of a narrow strip of streets extending from Main Street to Central Avenue. Columbia Boulevard, which runs north of the golf course looks very much like the south Minneapolis parkways, with the same type of housing—stucco and brick Tudors and two-story colonials. The curvy Architect Avenue, off Columbia Boulevard, west of Van Buren, is a particularly picturesque street, with houses designed by prominent Twin Cities architects over the course of the 1930s, '40s and '50s. Homes here are elaborate and well kept, with meticulous landscaping and mature trees that contribute to the park-like atmosphere.

Waite Park and **Audubon Park**, across Central from Columbia Golf Course, down to Lowry, are known as friendly, safe neighborhoods with well-kept houses. The streets are quiet, the topography is hilly and there is easy access to I-35W and 280. Houses with their 1940s charm and contemporary renovations, located in the vicinity of Johnson Street and St. Anthony

Boulevard, are popular with young professionals and their families.

South, down Central and across Lowry, the **Holland** neighborhood, with its steadily increasing property values, is often overlooked by those on their way to Logan Park. **Logan Park**, located about two miles from downtown Minneapolis is defined by Spring Street to the south, Central to the east, 5th Avenue to the north and Washington to the west. It's a small neighborhood that boasts large houses, including Victorians with dining rooms, built-in buffets and intact woodwork. With its four elementary schools and Edison High School all within a few blocks, this area especially appeals to young families. Commuters find it nice as well, with on and off ramps to I-35W only a few blocks away. The heart of this neighborhood is Logan Park, originally a decorative city square in the late 1800s, with flower beds and a Victorian fountain in the center, it is now a recreation area.

Windom Park is made up of a long strip of land running from Central Avenue, east to St. Anthony, between 18th Avenue and Lowry. Central Avenue is the main commercial corridor, and the new Quarry Shopping Center is on 18th Avenue. This end of Johnson Street has a mix of commercial and large residential rental units. The other major thoroughfare, Stinson, is a parkway that is included in the Grand Round. Craftsman and Tudor-style homes built in the 1920s and '30s are found along the parkway and to the east. Windom, the park, at the intersection of Johnson Street and Lowry Avenue, features a long, sloping hill that serves as a site for summer concerts and the annual Ice Cream Social, a carnival that attracts families from throughout the area.

Adjacent to the park is the magnet Pillsbury School, specializing in math, science, and technology for early childhood through grade six. As one of its projects, it is collaborating with classrooms all along the Mississippi River to explore their communities' connections to the river. Students are studying the culture and history of their unique part of the river and are collecting and analyzing scientific data related to river water quality.

Web Sites: www.neighborhoodlink.com.minneapolis/beltrami, www.windompark.org, www.ci.minneapolis.mn.us, www.tcfreenet.org

Area Code: 612

Zip Codes: 55413, 55418

Post Office: East Side Station, 1600 18th Avenue NE (all post office branches can be reached at 800-275-8777).

Police Precinct: 2nd, 1911 Central Avenue NE, 612-673-5702

Emergency Hospital: University of Minnesota Hospital, Harvard Street at East River Parkway, 612-626-3000

Libraries: Northeast, 2200 Central Avenue NE, 612-630-6900; Pierre Bottineau, 1224 Second Street NE, 612-630-6890

Community Resources: Neighborhood Revitalization Program, 612-673-5140; Beltrami Park, Boom Island Park, Logan Park, Windom Park

Community Publication: *Northeaster*, 2304 Central Avenue NE, Minneapolis, MN 55418, 612-788-9003

Transportation: Bus Lines: 1: Kenwood/East Hennepin Avenue/ Apache Plaza; 4: Downtown/Johnson Street NE/New Brighton; 10: South Minneapolis/Central Avenue/New Brighton; 18: 2nd Street NE/western neighborhoods; 24: Downtown/University Avenue NE/Coon Rapids; 25: Downtown/Johnson Street NE/Northtown; 27: Downtown/Marshall Street/Anoka; 29: Downtown/Central Avenue/Blaine; 32: Lowry Avenue NE/Rosedale; numerous routes take I-35W to Northern and Eastern suburbs.

NORTH MINNEAPOLIS AREA

CAMDEN COMMUNITY

MCKINLEY, FOLWELL, CLEVELAND
LIND-BOHANON
SHINGLE CREEK
VICTORY

Boundaries: **North**: 53rd Avenue North; **West**: Xerxes Avenue North; **South**: Lowry Avenue North; **East**: Mississippi River

Camden is comprised of industrial zones and diverse middle- to lower-income working-class areas. Almost 80% of the houses in Camden are single-family homes, primarily two-story wood-frames and bungalows, with some small stucco Tudors. Most houses were built between 1910 and 1930, and many are considered on the small side for today's families. Organizations like Habitat for Humanity, A Brush with Kindness, and Christmas in April are working to improve the housing stock here.

From east to west, between Dowling and Lowry, the southernmost neighborhoods, **McKinley**, **Folwell** and **Cleveland**, are areas of deteriorated housing. **Lind-Bohanon**, at the north city limits, between the Mississippi River and Humboldt, has a reputation for being a quieter neighborhood with a low resident turnover rate. Some families have lived in their houses here for two or three generations. In the Shingle Creek and Victory areas, homes are slightly more expensive and incomes are slightly higher when compared to the rest of Camden, although all of the neighborhoods are modest in comparison to the rest of Minneapolis. **Shingle Creek**, west of Humboldt and north of 49th Avenue, is made up of bungalows and ramblers built primarily in the 1950s after the lowlands were drained. The creek cuts diagonally through the neighborhood and creates a natural green space. **Victory**, west of Penn, between Dowling and the Shingle Creek neighborhood, contains vintage homes from the 1920s and '30s through the 1960s, some of which are being rehabilitated. There are several small apartment buildings along Thomas Avenue North, which is also a major bus route. Most home sales are to first-time buyers.

There's no shortage of places to walk or ride your bike in Camden. From Webber Park you can wander along a narrow swath of parkland that follows the Mississippi as far north as the city limits. Victory Memorial Drive is part of the Grand Round parkway and bike path circuit. The North Mississippi Regional Park in Lind-Bohanon provides the community's best access to the river.

There are several elementary schools within Camden's boundaries: Loring School (K-5), off Victory Memorial Drive in Victory neighborhood, is a magnet for Hmong bilingual students; Jenny Lind Community School is on Bryant Avenue North in Lind-Bohanon; and Shingle Creek Urban Environmental Center (K-5), at 50th and Oliver in the Shingle Creek neighborhood, describes itself as an earth-friendly school where students use the outdoors as an urban environmental laboratory. Civic projects intended to stabilize, revitalize and provide amenities for this community are uncertain because of what has been referred to as "the elephant sitting in the middle of the room," the Kondirator, which is a metal mill that shreds, compacts and separates metal scrap, appliances and car hulks. Residents are concerned about possible noise and air pollution and toxic runoff. For updated information about the Kondirator, check out Minneapolis' web site, www.ci.minneapolis.mn.us/citywork.

Web Sites: www.ci.minneapolis.mn.us, www.tcfreenet.org

Area Code: 612

Zip Codes: 55412, 55430

Post Offices: Lowry Avenue Station, 2306 Lowry Avenue North (all post office branches can be reached at 800-275-8777).

Police Precinct: 4th, 1925 Plymouth Avenue North, 612-673-5704

Emergency Hospital: North Memorial Medical Center, 3300 Oakdale Avenue North, Robbinsdale, 763-520-5200

Library: Webber Park, 4310 Webber Parkway, 612-630-6640

Community Resources: Neighborhood Revitalization Program, 612-673-5140; North Mississippi Regional Park, Webber Park

Community Publications: *Camden Community News*, P.O. Box 11492, MN 55411-1309, 612-521-3060, www.home-media.com/camdenews; *North News*, 2304 Central Avenue NE, Minneapolis 55418, 612-788-9003

Transportation: Bus Lines: 5: Downtown/Fremont Avenue N/Brooklyn Center/Mall of America; 22: Downtown/Lyndale Avenue N/Brooklyn Park; numerous 94 Express buses enter I- 94 at 49th Avenue North

NEAR NORTH COMMUNITY

HAWTHORNE
JORDAN
WILLARD-HAY, WILLARD HOMEWOOD
SUMNER-GLENWOOD
NEAR NORTH
HARRISON

Boundaries: **North**: Lowry Avenue; **West**: Xerxes Avenue; **South**: Bassett Creek; **East**: I-94, Mississippi River

The Northside of Minneapolis is one of the city's oldest neighborhoods and has been home to many different ethnic populations through the years. It is described by people who lived there in the 1950s and '60s as a wonderful place to grow up. These days, unfortunately, drive through the neighborhood and you'll see that the area is suffering. Unemployment is high, crime is a concern, and it is one of the few places in the city where property values are on the decline. However, the six neighborhoods that make up the Near North community are different in significant ways.

Hawthorne, located north of Broadway to Lowry, and east of Emerson Avenue to the Mississippi River, is separated from the Mississippi River industrial area by I-94. Over three-fourths of the houses in Hawthorne are over 75 years old, with six properties listed on the National Historic Register. One such, the 1886 Bremer School building located on Lowry Avenue North between Emerson and Fremont, has been converted into condominiums. The units have 12-foot ceilings and 9-foot windows. However, many of Hawthorne's old buildings have not fared so well, and have been demolished.

In **Jordan**, north of Broadway and west of Emerson, where there is a higher rate of home-ownership, there is a trend toward rehabilitating houses, rather than tearing them down. The same is true in **Willard-Hay**, south of Broadway, from approximately Penn Avenue to Xerxes. Willard-Hay, which has many dilapidated houses is the unlikely location of "the poor-man's Kenwood," otherwise known as **Willard-Homewood**, located south of Plymouth Avenue, abutting Theodore Wirth Parkway. This area of large, architecturally interesting Tudor, Spanish and Arts and Crafts style houses was one of the city's first planned developments. Most of the houses were built between 1905 and 1930. Residents left this neighborhood in the 1960s when north Minneapolis was the scene of racial rioting, and houses here have been at fire-sale prices ever since. You can get a lot of house for the money—sun porches, high ceilings, fireplaces, built-in bookcases and buffets, beamed ceilings, hardwood floors, front and back staircases and libraries. This is, however, a neighborhood for those who have a high tolerance for urban interactions.

The easternmost neighborhoods in this community, **Sumner-Glenwood** and **Near North**, are part of a broad redevelopment plan being undertaken by the City of Minneapolis. The result of the settlement of a 1995 lawsuit, known as "Hollman," this plan requires Minneapolis to demolish ghettos of public housing and replace them with mixed-income housing, including 750 subsidized rental units. While the long-term plan for Sumner-Glenwood may be promising, the current situation—razed buildings, empty lots, displaced residents, has been a source of frustration for many. There are almost no residential buildings left in Sumner-Glenwood, though there is a library. The historic 1915 Sumner library is a church-like sanctuary sitting amid vacant lots and the traffic roaring by on Highway 55. It houses the largest black history collection in Minneapolis.

Lovely reminders of Minneapolis' proud past, the so-called "painted ladies' can be found on the 1500 block of Dupont Avenue (past acres of chain-linked vacant lots where the projects have recently come down), just north of Plymouth Road. Here you'll find National Historic Register Victorians being restored and preserved.

More housing is being demolished in the **Harrison** neighborhood, which is just north of Bassett Creek to Highway 55, adjacent to the Bryn Mawr neighborhood. There is considerable dispute about whether the southern part of the Harrison neighborhood should remain residential or be zoned for light industrial use.

Web Sites: www.ci.minneapolis.mn.us, www.tcfreenet.org

Area Code: 612

Zip Codes: 55405, 55411

Post Offices: Loring Station, 18 North 12th Street; Lowry Avenue Station, 2306 Lowry Avenue North (all post office branches can be reached at 800-275-8777).

Police Precinct: 4th, 1925 Plymouth Avenue North, 612-673-5704

Emergency Hospitals: North Memorial Medical Center, 3300 Oakdale Avenue North, Robbinsdale, 763-520-5200; Hennepin County Medical Center, 701 Park Avenue, 612-347-2121

Libraries: North Regional, 1315 Lowry Avenue North, 612-630-6600; Sumner, 611 Emerson Avenue North, 612-630-6390.

Community Resources: Neighborhood Revitalization Program, 612-673-5140

Transportation: **Bus Lines**: 5: Downtown/Fremont Avenue North/Brooklyn Center/Mall of America; 14: Downtown/Broadway/ Brooklyn Park. 19: Mall of America/Downtown/Golden Valley; 20: Plymouth Avenue/Cedar-Riverside/Highland (St. Paul); 22: Downtown/Lyndale Avenue North/Brooklyn Park; 55: State Hwy 55; numerous express lines board at stops along I-94

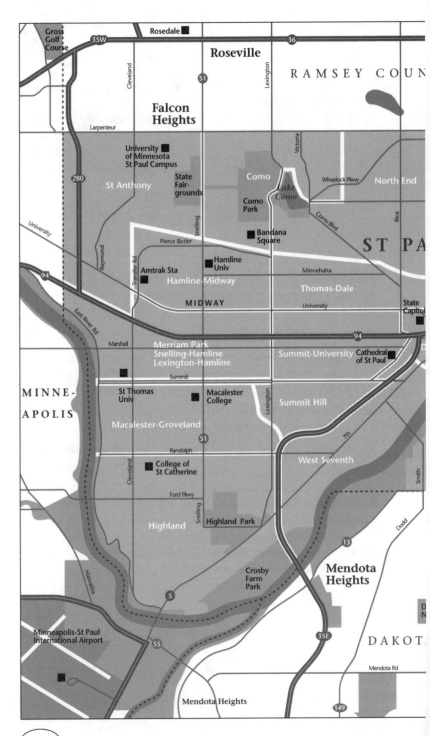

Gross Golf Course
Rosedale
35W
36
Roseville
Cleveland
51
Lexington
RAMSEY COUN

Falcon Heights
Larpenteur

280
University of Minnesota St Paul Campus
St Anthony
State Fair-grounds
Como
Victoria
Lake Como
Wheelock Pkwy
North End

University
Raymond
Transfer Rd
Snelling
Pierce Butler
Como Park
Bandana Square
Como Blvd
Rice

94
Amtrak Sta
Hamline Univ
Hamline-Midway
Minnehaha
Thomas-Dale
ST PA

East River Rd
MIDWAY
University
State Capitol

Marshall
Merriam Park
Snelling-Hamline
Lexington-Hamline
94
Summit-University
Cathedral of St Paul

Summit
St Thomas Univ
Macalester College
Lexington
Summit Hill

MINNE-APOLIS
Macalester-Groveland
7th
West Seventh
Smith

Cleveland
Randolph
51
College of St Catherine
Ford Pkwy

Snelling
Highland Park
Highland
13
Dodd

Crosby Farm Park
Mendota Heights

5
Hiawatha
D N

Minneapolis-St Paul International Airport
55
35E
DAKOT

Mendota Rd
Mendota Heights
149

44

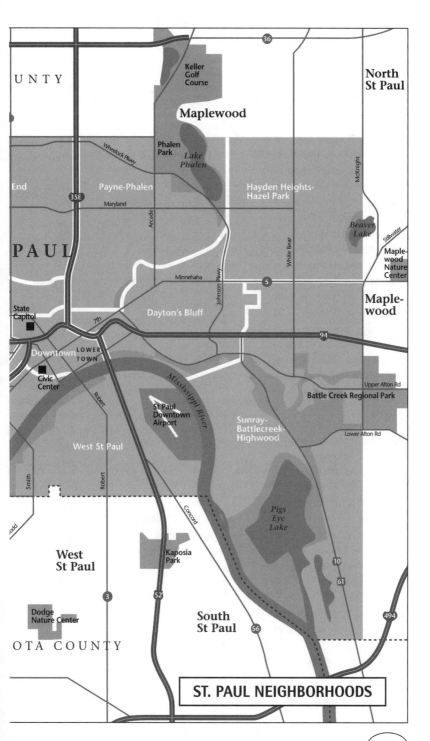

ST. PAUL NEIGHBORHOODS

ST. PAUL

While St. Paul was settled only slightly earlier than Minneapolis, it seems older because so much of early St. Paul survives: old, brick buildings, divided boulevards, established neighborhoods—even the trees are old. From the horse-drawn golden chariot on the state capitol's marble dome to Summit Avenue, the longest and best-preserved boulevard of Victorian mansions in the US, a stately 19th century elegance permeates much of St. Paul.

In addition to feeling older than Minneapolis, St. Paul's population and economy have always trailed Minneapolis, which actually is one of the reasons people like to live here—it feels more like a small town than a big city. St. Paul's downtown is compact and the streets are more wholly residential than the streets of Minneapolis. Grocery stores, restaurants, bookstores, and the many historical and cultural sites are easily accessible by foot from most neighborhoods.

A true sense of community is fostered within St. Paul's 17 neighborhoods (here called districts), assisted by district councils that work together with city government, giving neighborhoods a voice in city and state decisions. District councils are also active in civic beautification, community gardening, home improvement, recycling, and they work closely with the St. Paul Police Department on crime prevention. Call the district councils listed at the end of each neighborhood profile for more information about a specific neighborhood.

St. Paul's police force is organized into three districts, western (north and south), central and eastern. Each district has several neighborhood substations. The telephone numbers given with each neighborhood are for the stations from which officers prepare to go out on patrol. For information about crime in a particular neighborhood, call the St. Paul Crime Prevention Coordinator at 651-292-3625. This office will connect you with appropriate district councils. St. Paul's annual crime reports and maps of crime locations (STATMap) are posted on the internet at www.st.paul.gov/police or call 651-292-3501. The *St. Paul Pioneer Press* also has a web site to help you find out about crime in different parts of town, www.pioneerplanet.com/archive/crime.

DOWNTOWN DISTRICT

LOWERTON

Boundaries: **North**: University Avenue; **West**: Marion Street, Irvine Avenue; **South**: Kellogg Boulevard, Mississippi River; **East**: I-94, Lafayette Road

The beauty of living downtown is that most everything is within walking distance— although, since St. Paul is built on hills, people sometimes opt to take the bus up and then walk down. Bus service is convenient; you can take the bus anywhere within downtown for twenty-five cents (fifty-cents during rush hour). Or, use it to get to downtown Minneapolis, the Mall of America or the Rosedale Shopping Mall. In fact, immediate amenities are so accessible many downtown St. Paul residents don't own a car.

Downtown is dotted with high-rise apartment buildings containing both moderate-rent and luxury apartments. The State Capitol building and state offices are here, as are headquarters for a few large companies. Many of these offices are connected by skyways (enclosed breezeways that connect building to building). On weekdays these skyways bustle with restaurants and food-courts, coffee shops, grocery stores, a fresh fruit and vegetable stand, video rentals, a branch library and branch post office. Most of the shops are closed in the evenings and on weekends and holidays.

Downtown St. Paul is not a world-class shopping destination, but that may change. New street-level shopping will soon join the downtown Dayton's, and the city is landscaping the walkways and street corners, enhancing the charm of Old St. Paul.

In the 1970s, developers completed several high-rise apartments and renovations, including an overhaul of **Lowertown**, the city's unique artists' colony, located near the river, between Robert Street and Broadway, on the east side of downtown. With over 500 sculptors, potters, painters and performance artists, it's one of the largest concentrations of working artists of any city in the Midwest. Each April and October, the members of the Artists Collective open their studio doors for the St. Paul Art Crawls. Check www.lowertown.org or www.stpaul-artcrawl.org for more information. Site of one of St. Paul's two early river landings, this neighborhood contains large, old brick buildings that have been converted into offices, artists' lofts and apartments. This neighborhood also features a weekend farmers' market, from spring through fall. (See **Shopping for the Home**.)

Open space, while not as plentiful as elsewhere in the Twin Cities, is available in three small city parks tucked in amid the tall buildings, and a regional park on Harriet Island in the river. Rice Park is a formal square bordered by the Ordway Music Theatre, Landmark Center, and the grand old St. Paul Hotel. The ice sculpture contest is held here during the St. Paul Winter Carnival. Kellogg Park is a narrow strip of green space that runs between the edge of the river bluff and Kellogg Boulevard, from the Robert Street Bridge to the Wabasha Street Bridge. A popular setting for weddings, it includes sculptures depicting St. Paul's history. Mears Park is a beautifully landscaped square at 5th and Sibley that features a band shell, and is summer home to Shakespeare in the Park. Visit in the spring for a stunning display of thousands of tulips. Harriet Island Regional Park is a short walk across the Wabasha Bridge. The St. Paul Yacht Club is located here, as is the famous No Wake Cafe.

Historic and cultural sites and annual events abound in downtown, making it easy to entertain out-of-town visitors. People flock to events at the RiverCentre auditorium and convention center, the Ordway and Fitzgerald Theaters, the Science Museum of Minnesota, the Children's Museum, the Minnesota History Museum and to numerous festivals throughout the year. During the summer, on Friday and Saturday evenings, Kellogg Boulevard is closed off between Robert and Wabasha for antique car shows, complete with food vendors and live music. The car shows are an intimate *tête-à-tête* compared to the serious food-fest, the Taste of Minnesota, which is held over the Fourth of July weekend. Restaurants from all over the Twin Cities set up booths in front of the Capitol, live bands play throughout the park, and each evening ends in fireworks. There are more fireworks in January during the century-old St. Paul Winter Carnival, a major event that includes sled dog races, parades and a treasure hunt.

Web Sites: www.ci.stpaul.mn.us, www.tcfreenet.org

Area Code: 651

Zip Codes: 55101, 55102, 55107

Post Offices: Main Office, 180 East Kellogg Boulevard; Pioneer Station, 141 East 4th Street; Uptown-Skyway, 415 West Wabasha Street; Riverview Station, 292 Eva Street (all post office branches can be reached at 800-275-8777).

Police: Central District Patrol Team, 651-292-3563

Emergency Hospitals: St. Paul-Ramsey Medical Center, 640 Jackson

Street, 651-221-3456; HealthEast Street Joseph's Hospital, 69 West Exchange Street, 651-232-3000

Library: Central, 90 West 4th Street, 651-266-7000

Public School: St. Paul, District Office: 651-632-3701, www.stpaul. k12.mn.us

Community Resources: Capitol River Council, 445 Minnesota Street, Suite 524, 651-221-0488; Kellogg Park; Mears Park; Harriet Island Regional Park

Community Publications: *St. Paul Grand Gazette*, 651-699-1462; *St. Paul Pioneer Press*, 651-222-5011, www.pioneerplanet.com; *Minneapolis/ St. Paul Skyway News*, 612-843-5226, www.skywaynews.com

Transportation: Bus Lines: numerous city bus lines run through downtown, and you can get around downtown by bus on most major streets. Check a transit map (an MCTO store in the American National Bank building at 5th and Minnesota streets gives them out) or call 612-373-3333. Also, the Capital City Trolley runs shuttles around downtown; call 651-223-5600. Local Routes: 54 Express: 6th Street/International Airport/Mall of America; 94B, C, D Express: 6th Street/I-94/Downtown Minneapolis

SOUTHWEST DISTRICTS

St. Paul's counterpart to Kenwood in Minneapolis, the neighborhoods of the Southwest district have the ambiance of a library filled with leather-bound books: old, hefty, rich with historical detail—all first-rate. Variations include the more trendy east end of Summit, and the more academic west end, but the housing is basically the same, and all the people who live here have access to the restaurants and shops of Grand Avenue, one of St. Paul's great pleasures.

SUMMIT HILL DISTRICT

CROCUS HILL
SUMMIT AVENUE
SUMMIT HILL

Boundaries: **North**: Summit Avenue; **West**: Ayd Mill Road; **South/East**: I-35E

The mansions and historic buildings poised high on Summit Hill epitomize the grandeur and wealth of boom-era St. Paul. They are superior examples of many styles of turn-of-the century architecture and ornamentation. Summit's first mansion, built in 1862 at 432 Summit, caused a sensation by incorporating such modern features as steam heating, hot and cold water and gas lighting.

In the 1880s and 1890s the Crocus Hill and Grand Hill neighborhoods also became fashionable locations for wealthy families. **Crocus Hill** is still one of the Twin Cities' most desirable and eccentric neighborhoods. If you buy a house in this maze of cobblestone streets, it may come with a ghost, but your garage might be four blocks away. Crocus Hill, the street, is only half a block long, which is long enough, because house numbering is not consecutive. One, is the first house built on the street; but the second house, built at the opposite end of the street, is Four. In between are Twelve, Two, Eleven, Sixteen, and Four—Five is around the corner. Only two of the early 1880s houses remain; the rest were built between the 1920s and '40s. Crocus Hill, the neighborhood, extends to St. Clair, and, mercifully, its streets do employ sequential numbering.

All five miles of **Summit Avenue**, in the Summit Hill District, are protected, either as a national or local Historic District. There are some extraordinary buildings here, and the district has received national recognition for their careful preservation. Summit Avenue is St. Paul's power address. The Minnesota governor's residence is at 1006. (Free public tours are given on selected Fridays, May through October, call 651-297-8177.) Railroad baron James J. Hill's 45-room red sandstone mansion at 240 Summit Avenue was the largest in the Midwest when it was built in 1891. (It is open for tours Wednesdays through Saturdays, 651-297-2555.) Across the street is the Renaissance-style Catholic Cathedral of the Archdiocese of Saint Paul and Minneapolis, which looks across at the other domed building in town, the Minnesota State Capitol. The cathedral is host to many concerts, the most popular of which is the annual Christmas performance of Handel's "Messiah." F. Scott Fitzgerald was born in the neighborhood, and returned to write *This Side of Paradise* in a shabby-genteel red stone rowhouse on the corner of Summit and Dale. You can see these and many of the other historic buildings and gardens by joining one of the Minnesota Historical Society's guided walking tours, held every Saturday from May through September. Another tour called "These Old Houses" is held every other year on the first Sunday after Mother's Day, and is popular with locals and tourists alike. Needless to say the cost of housing near or along Summit Avenue is among the city's highest.

Step away from Summit Avenue and you'll find more than a museum that pays homage to the lavish excesses of the late 19th century. Residential opportunities abound in **Summit Hill**, and not everyone living here is a millionaire. The neighborhood's last housing boomlet, in the 1920s, included the building of many apartments, particularly along the streetcar lines on major thoroughfares like Grand Avenue. During the depression of the 1930s a lot of families found they could no longer afford to live in their expensive homes, and subsequently many single-family homes were converted into duplexes or rooming houses, which remain today, making up much of the housing in Summit Hill. While vacancy rates are low, it is possible to find an apartment with refinished hardwood floors, tall windows, and fireplaces. The least expensive apartments generally are found on Cathedral Hill. Also try the area south of Grand Avenue for more modest housing. People from all walks of life live here, including faculty, staff and students from nearby colleges.

Proximity to Grand Avenue, one of the Twin Cities' most attractive commercial districts, is another perk to living in Summit Hill. Grand Avenue is loaded with interesting restaurants, specialty stores, taverns and book-stores. The southwest districts' principal summer festival, Grand Old Days, attracts crowds from all over the Twin Cities. The street is closed off and its entire length becomes one long party, with live bands, food, beer, games, a parade and great people watching.

However, the area's popular shopping, coupled with the presence of so many apartments, has created three problems: burglaries, traffic and parking. Be assured the St. Paul police department is working on these issues. A word to the wise, don't park your car even for a minute in a space that requires a resident's sticker.

Web Sites: www.ci.stpaul.mn.us, www.tcfreenet.org

Area Code: 651

Zip Codes: 55102, 55105

Post Offices: Main Office, 180 East Kellogg Boulevard; Elway Station, 1715 West 7th Street (all post office branches can be reached at 800-275-8777).

Police: Western District Patrol Team, North: 651-292-3512, South: 651-292-3549

Emergency Hospital: United Hospital, 333 Smith Avenue North, 651-220-8000

Libraries: Central, 90 West 4th Street, 651-266-7000; Lexington, 1080 University Avenue West, 651-642-0359

Community Resource: Summit Hill Association, 860 St. Clair Avenue, 651-222-1222

Community Publications: *St. Paul Grand Gazette*, 651-699-1462; *St. Paul Pioneer Press*, 651-222-5011, www.pioneerplanet.com

Transportation: Bus Lines: 3: Grand Avenue/Downtown/3M Center; 17: Dale Street/Rosedale

SUMMIT–UNIVERSITY DISTRICT

SELBY-DALE
CATHEDRAL HILL

Boundaries: **North**: University Avenue; **West**: Lexington Parkway; **South**: Summit Avenue; **East**: Irvine Avenue, Marion Street

Not long ago, **Selby-Dale**, in the Summit-University neighborhood, was one of St. Paul's most notorious intersections, host to multiple porno shops and accompanying crime. Today it is in the process of being gentrified into one of St. Paul's most peaceful, if colorful, residential areas. A rainbow of dark green, deep blue and yellow houses mixed in with brownstone apartments surround the Selby-Dale corner, many restored to the glory of their golden days by the artists and hip young professionals who moved here in the 1990s.

Much like Summit Hill to the south, the Summit-University neighborhood contains many of the city's oldest buildings, including stone rowhouses, fortress-like Victorian woodframes, and, along Selby Avenue, many elegant 19th-century brick storefronts. The neighborhood survived being decimated in the 1950s when planners changed plans to route I-94 directly down one of its streets; and it survived the tumult of the 1960s when a bomb blew up the Selby-Dale police station and broke all the windows in the neighborhood.

Selby-Dale (the roads) create a clear-cut crossroad through the neighborhood. Selby, a main thoroughfare, has been lined with businesses and apartments since the 1880s. Dale acts as the dividing line between grand houses on the east in the area known as **Cathedral Hill**, and modest homes on the west that were built primarily in the 1960s. The streets near the cathedral are *the* place for young city hipsters who can find huge apartments with "character" (sometimes even fireplaces) at rents that are lower than in Uptown.

If you're in the market to buy, Selby-Dale is a great place to find a fixer-upper, especially if you like two-story frame houses with front porches and picture windows. Houses range from 700 square feet near Selby and Dale, to around 4,000 square feet in the blocks adjacent to Summit. Thanks to urban renewal, some houses now sit on a lot-and-a-half, with owners having purchased land when next-door derelict houses were torn down. Still, lots are small in proportion to the houses, and it's hard to garden because there's so much shade. Pocket gardens and boulevard gardens are popular, and they have the additional advantage of bringing people out onto the streets where they can keep an eye on what's going on.

Like the other neighborhoods surrounding Summit, shopping on Grand Avenue is within easy walking range, but some of the best local dining is to be found right on Cathedral Hill. Sweeney's at Dale and Ashland, has an old Irish pub atmosphere, and The Vintage serves excellent food accompanied by even better wine. The Mississippi Market natural food co-op, at the corner of Selby and Dale offers a fine selection of food in its deli.

The lack of a large open space in the area may be problematic for some. While people walk, run and bike the city streets—and the Twin Cities Marathon comes right down Summit—there is no place to play ball; in fact, the closest open area is along the Mississippi River. However, there are playgrounds every few blocks, and an unofficial off-leash dog area at Webster Park.

Prospective residents will want to be aware of the concentration of lower income housing in a section of Summit University, north of Selby. Numerous community initiatives and revitalization projects have been accomplished or are in the works. The area is now home to the Hallie Q. Brown Community Center, which provides day care services and other activities, and the well-known Penumbra Theater, 270 Kent Street, 651-224-3180, which features plays with African-American themes.

From the mansions of Summit Avenue to the business district along University Avenue, and from the historic neighborhood of Ramsey Hill/Cathedral Hill to the blocks of middle-class homes to the west, Summit-University is a diverse district. If you're accustomed to the usual security precautions that are necessary in an urban area, you may want to consider Summit-U.

Web Sites: www.ci.stpaul.mn.us, www.tcfreenet.org

Area Code: 651

Zip Codes: 55102, 55103, 55104

Post Office: Industrial Station, 1430 Concordia Avenue (all post office branches can be reached at 800-275-8777).

Police: Western District Patrol Team North, 651-292-3512; South, 651-292-3549

Emergency Hospital: United Hospital, 333 Smith Avenue North, 651-220-8000

Library: Lexington Branch, 1080 University Avenue West, 651-642-0359

Community Resources: Summit-University Planning Council, 627 Selby Avenue, 651-228-1855; Hallie Q. Brown Community Center, 270 Kent Street, 651-224-4601

Community Publications: *St. Paul Grand Gazette*, 651-699-1462; *St. Paul Pioneer Press*, 651-222-5011, www.pioneerplanet.com

Transportation: Bus Lines: 3: Grand Avenue/Downtown/3M Center; 16: Downtown Minneapolis/University Avenue/Downtown St. Paul; 17: Dale Street/Rosedale; 21: Downtown/Selby Avenue/Lake Street (Minneapolis); 22: St. Anthony Avenue/Downtown/Regions Hospital

MACALESTER-GROVELAND DISTRICT

Boundaries: **North**: Summit Avenue; **West**: Mississippi River; **South**: Randolph Avenue; **East**: Ayd Mill Road

Universities and colleges located in or near the Macalaster Groveland (Mac-Groveland) district: Macalaster College, the University of St. Thomas, St. Paul Seminary, The College of St. Catherine, and William Mitchell College of Law, give Macalester-Groveland a friendly, college-town feel.

Created in the 1880s when a group of Macalester College trustees bought a farm west of St. Paul and divided it into a campus and lots for houses, Macalester-Groveland has become one of St. Paul's epicenters, bustling with academic and commercial energy. Grand Avenue, the main east-west thoroughfare, includes specialty retail shops, restaurants, and interesting bistros. There are scores of places to eat, drink, and argue politics and religion along the length of the street, but a focal point of the academic spirit is Ruminator Books (previously Hungry Mind Bookstore), located just west of the Macalester campus. This literary masterpiece is host to frequent author readings, publishes a quarterly book review, and is adjacent to the gourmet restaurant, Table of Contents. Traffic on Grand Avenue is heavy, but slow enough to make living near the street tolerable.

Once a farm, then a commuter suburb, the history of Mac-Groveland has resulted in an interesting mixture of housing sizes, prices and designs, with rents and house prices among the highest in St. Paul. The best time to look for an apartment is in late spring to early summer when students move out and sublets and leases become available.

More than three-fourths of Macalaster Groveland's homes were built before 1940, and range from two- and three-bedroom homes on the east end, to luxurious Mississippi River-front residences. On and near Grand Avenue, two- to four-story brick apartments from the 1920s are interspersed with the brick storefront cafés and retail businesses that make Grand Avenue St. Paul's most lively commercial district. Architectural styles range from 19th century Tudor-style cottages and meticulous Arts-and-Crafts bungalows to contemporary designs from the 1960s. Roomy homes with front porches line the curvy streets skirting Macalester College. Bordering the neighborhood to the north are the impressive houses of Summit Avenue (read more about this elegant boulevard in the description of **Summit Hill**). Residential streets in Macalester-Groveland are attractive and tranquil, lined with mature oaks and maples.

The bluffs and the Mississippi River gorge lie at the western end of the neighborhood. Land adjacent to the St. Paul Seminary is relatively wild and picturesque, and miles of river walking or bike riding are accessible from Mac-Groveland by the river parkway. If you settle here, you'll thank Bishop Thomas Grace of St. Thomas University for preserving the natural habitat along the river.

Web Sites: www.ci.stpaul.mn.us, www.tcfreenet.org

Area Code: 651

Zip Code: 55105

Post Office: Elway Station, 1715 West 7th Street (all post office branches can be reached at 800-275-8777).

Police: Western District Patrol Team, North: 651-292-3512, South: 651-292-3549

Emergency Hospital: United Hospital, 333 Smith Avenue North, 651-220-8000

Library: Merriam Park, 1831 Marshall Avenue, 651-642-0385

Community Resources: Macalester-Groveland Community Council, 320 South Griggs Street, 651-695-4000

Community Publications: *St. Paul Grand Gazette*, 651-699-1462;

St. Paul Pioneer Press, 651-222-5011, www.pioneerplanet.com

Transportation: Bus Lines: 3: Grand Avenue/Downtown/3M Center; 4: Mall of America/Snelling Avenue/Rosedale; 7: Smith Avenue/ Downtown/Signal Hills; 14: Ford Plant/Randolph Avenue/Downtown; 94H and J: Highland Park/Snelling Avenue South/Downtown Minneapolis

MERRIAM PARK, SNELLING–HAMLINE, LEXINGTON–HAMLINE DISTRICTS

Boundaries: **North**: I-94, Cleveland Avenue, University Avenue; **West**: City limits at 33rd Avenue, Mississippi River; **South**: Summit Avenue; **East**: Lexington Parkway

Merriam Park's identity derives not only from the atmosphere of its scenic riverfront and well-kept homes, but also from the interesting people who live here. From the long-distance racer who trains by running a marathon everyday to the president of the University of Minnesota, Merriam Parkers treasure their neighbors as well as their neighborhood's aura of urbane wilderness.

Bordered by the magnificent gorge of the Mississippi to the west and by the mansions of Summit Avenue to the south, Merriam Park is conveniently located midway between downtown Minneapolis and St. Paul. It includes Desnoyer Park, Iris Park, Merriam Park, and Shadow Falls located on or near the Mississippi River.

Although it is in the center of urban activity today, once upon a time Merriam Park was one of the Twin Cities' first suburbs, located a couple of trolley stops outside of early St. Paul. Colonel John Merriam, who in the 1880s owned much of the neighborhood's bluff land, envisioned the creation of a rural village built on large estates separated by abundant parkland. Merriam built himself a luxurious house and sold lots to those who would agree to his requirement that homes built on this land cost at least $1,500—a sizable amount at the time.

Traces of Merriam Park's exclusive beginnings are still apparent along the Mississippi, where turn-of-the-century Tudor and Arts-and Crafts style houses line streets shaded by mature, graceful trees. The green and fittingly groomed land surrounding the Town and Country Club, located along the river north of Marshall Avenue, adds to Merriam Park's air of grandeur. During winter, the country club's gates are left open for cross-country skiers.

It seems every style of architecture is represented here, from opulent Queen Annes, Gothic and Italiante styles reflecting Victorian taste, to colonial revivals, Dutch colonials, Tudors, American foursquares, and prairie style homes. Built to last, these homes exhibit solid construction and craftsmanship and loving attention to detail. Housing is mixed from small to large, with many of the biggest houses clustered in the vicinity of Marshall Avenue.

Generally you'll find housing to be less expensive than in Highland, with houses near the University of St. Thomas campus occupied by students and university related folk. And there's been a recent influx of young families moving into the two- and three-bedroom 1900s stucco and wood houses that line many of the streets of Merriam Park.

The northernmost part of **Snelling-Hamline**, located to the east of Merriam Park between Snelling and Hamline, was decimated by the construction of I-94. However, the southern streets near Summit are now being rehabilitated. Here you can find old brownstone apartments, a few new duplexes, and some single-family houses. The neighborhood pub, O'Garra's at Snelling and Selby, has a micro-brewery and offers music that ranges from an Irish jam session on Sunday nights to rock in O'Garra's Garage.

Further east, **Lexington-Hamline** also straddles I-94 between Lexington and Hamline Avenues from University to Summit. South of I-94, most people live in single family houses, while those north of I-94 live in high-rise apartments. Lex-Ham, as it is known, is a neighborhood noted for its 19th and early 20th-century houses, its community enthusiasm, as well as St. Paul Central High School and Concordia College. Farm-in-the-City uses the facilities of Concordia University and the community schools and parks to provide garden-based summer programs for children and community garden plots.

The major cross streets, Cretin, Selby, Marshall, Snelling, and Lexington, are busy and commercial, and add to the general convenience of the district. Events at the University of Minnesota and University of St. Thomas and other campuses in the area are only a walk, bike or bus ride away, and residents can easily stroll to many of the restaurants, shops and conveniences of Grand Avenue to the south. (For more about Grand Avenue, see **Shopping for the Home**.) Coffeehouses, bakeries and specialty shops are found on Marshall and Cleveland and other Merriam Park street corners, and the Midway Shopping Center, also nearby at University and Snelling Avenues, offers staples at discount stores and supermarkets.

Merriam Park Community Center, 2000 St. Anthony Avenue, is a symbol of the neighborhood to many Merriam Park residents. The center has evolved over the years, and offers a variety of services to area families, including a preschool for 3, 4 & 5 year olds, adult community education programs, recreation, a community food shelf, seniors programs and "The Wordsmiths" toastmasters club.

Though not over-endowed with neighborhood parks and play-grounds, life here offers the open splendor of the Mississippi bluffs. A pleas-ant hike along the river begins at Merriam Park, goes south to the Ford Parkway Bridge, then across the river and back up to the Marshall Avenue Bridge. Don't miss the color extravaganza in October.

Web Site: www.ci.stpaul.mn.us, www.tcfreenet.org

Area Code: 651

Zip Code: 55104

Post Office: Industrial Station, 1430 Concordia Avenue (all post office branches can be reached at 800-275-8777).

Police: Western District Patrol Team, North: 651-292-3512; South, 651-292-3549

Emergency Hospital: Fairview-University, 2450 Riverside Avenue (Minneapolis), 612-672-6000

Library: Merriam Park, 1831 Marshall Avenue, 651-642-0385

Community Resources: Merriam Park Community Council (West), 1573 Selby Avenue, 651-645-6887; Snelling-Hamline Community Council (Central), 1573 Selby Avenue, #319, 651-644-1085; Lexington-Hamline Community Council (East), 1160 Selby Avenue, 651-645-3207; Town and Country Club, 2279 Marshall Avenue, 651-646-7121; Farm in the City; Merriam Park Community Center, 2000 St. Anthony Avenue, 651-298-5766

Community Publications: *St. Paul Grand Gazette*, 651-699-1462; *St. Paul Pioneer Press*, 651-222-5011, www.pioneerplanet.com

Transportation: Bus Lines: 3: Downtown/Grand Avenue/3M Center; 4: Mall of America/Rosedale/Snelling Avenue; 7: Downtown/Signal Hills/Mendota Heights; 16: University Avenue; 21: Lake Street (Minneapolis)/Marshall Avenue/Downtown; 22: Downtown/Regions Hospital/Redeemer Arms Highrise

HIGHLAND DISTRICT

EDGCUMBE/MONTCALM

Boundaries: North: Randolph Avenue; **West/South**: Mississippi River; **East**: I-35W, Homer Street from West 7th Street to Shepard Road

Highland Park is a neighborhood where moving up doesn't necessarily mean moving out, and subsequently selling a house here is much easier than finding one to buy. Housing ranges from original farmhouses and two-bedroom ramblers to in-town estates with spectacular views of the Mississipi River, to fabulous high-rises with penthouses and all possible amenities.

The south and west sides of the district are embraced by the river which runs in a gorge far below these hills. The houses on Mississippi River Boulevard are not actually on the water, but have views of the river across the parks and parkways. Near the Ford Plant off Ford Parkway, which crosses the river into the Hiawatha neighborhood of Minneapolis, you will find small 1950s and '60s ramblers in good condition, laid out on grid streets. More substantial brick and stucco homes on correspondingly larger lots line Mt. Curve Boulevard and Highland Park Golf Course. The architect-designed houses in the **Edgcumbe/Montcalm** neighborhood near the golf course have their own river views, and near the College of St. Catherine, well-kept rental duplexes and apartment buildings are in high demand.

Highland's main commercial area is centered around Highland Village, located on the eastern end of Ford Parkway. This shopping destination has it all—bookstores, department stores, a movie theater and restaurants. Sibley Plaza and Grand Avenue are nearby. (Read more about Grand Avenue in the descriptions of **Summit Hill** and **Macalester-Groveland**.) O'Shaughnessy Auditorium at the College of St. Catherine is the St. Paul home of the Minnesota Orchestra and provides an intimate performance venue for a wide variety of dance groups and other performances. Highland also hosts an annual art fair that draws artists from all over the country.

The other major perk of living in Highland is its proximity to green space and wilderness areas. Highland Park is a hilly expanse with a municipal golf course, outdoor swimming pools and cross-country ski trails. On the wild side, Hidden Falls and Crosby Farm Regional Park adjacent to the southern end of Highland, offer walking and biking trails through the woods. The confluence of the Mississippi and Minnesota Rivers, which includes Minnehaha Falls, the Fort Snelling State Park, and the Minnesota River National Wildlife Refuge are just across the Ford Bridge.

Web Sites: www.ci.stpaul.mn.us, www.tcfreenet.org

Area Code: 651

Zip Code: 55116

Post Office: Elway Station, 1715 West 7th Street (all post office branches can be reached at 800-275-8777).

Police: Western District Patrol Team, North: 651-292-3512, South: 651-292-3549

Emergency Hospital: United Hospital, 333 Smith Avenue North, 651-220-8000

Library: Highland Park, 1974 Ford Parkway, 651-292-6622

Community Resources: Highland Area Community Council, 1978 Ford Parkway, 651-695-4005; O'Shaughnessy Auditorium, 2004 Randolph Avenue, 651-690-6700

Community Publications: *St. Paul Grand Gazette*, 651-699-1462; *St. Paul Pioneer Press*, 651-222-5011, www.pioneerplanet.com

Transportation: Bus Lines: 4: Snelling Avenue/Rosedale/Mall of America; 7: Downtown/Signal Hills/Mendota Heights; 9: Downtown/Highland Park/Maplewood/Oakdale; 14: Ford Plant/Randolph Avenue/Downtown; 54 Express: Downtown/Minneapolis-St. Paul International Airport/Mall of America; 94H and J: Highland Park /I-94W/Downtown Minneapolis

WEST SEVENTH DISTRICT

IRVINE PARK
LEECH/MCBOAL, CLIFF STREET

Boundaries: **North**: I-35E; **West**: I-35E, Homer Street; **South**: Mississippi River; **East**: West Kellogg Boulevard

Just to the west of downtown is St. Paul's old Uppertown, named for being the location of the "upper" of St. Paul's two boat landings. Known also as West Seventh, Fort Road (because it leads to Fort Snelling) or the West End, this is St. Paul's historic heart and soul. This is where old "Pig's Eye" Parrant set up his still and founded the city of "Pig's Eye" which we know as St. Paul. This is also where many of St. Paul's earliest residents stepped off riverboats to begin making their homes on the frontier.

While the houses of West Seventh were not built on as grand a scale as the homes along Summit Avenue, many of them are older and at least as historic. Amid streets laid out around elegant Irvine Park at Walnut Street and Ryan, you'll find such treasures as stone houses built before the Civil War, Pioneer-era Greek Revivals, restored red brick row houses, and lap-sided Victorian Queen Annes. This National Historic District is also the setting for Governor Alexander Ramsey's stone, two-story Second Empire house at 265 Exchange Street which, together with its surrounding English garden, is open for hourly tours and holiday dances.

As St. Paul expanded, West Seventh Street became the destination of workers arriving from Europe in search of jobs on railroads and in grain mills. Earlier residents moved "up the hill" to Summit in the first of many flights away from the docklands. By the late 1800s, there were so many Czechs living in the neighborhood that Czech composer Antonin Dvorak stopped in at the now refurbished CSPS Hall while on his music tour across America. Poles, too, began moving to the neighborhood in the late 19th century, and their Saint Stanislaus Catholic Church still stands on Superior Street. Eventually, these immigrants moved as well. As is often the case with many urban areas, the large old houses became too big to manage for the working classes who lived there, and were divided up for flophouses and more disreputable purposes. Many of them, including a house designed by state capitol architect Cass Gilbert, became so derelict they had to be torn down.

Another part of the history of West Seventh has literally been washed away. As early as the 1850s, Italian families built houses along the levee below 7th Street (the site of today's Shepard Road). Their community, with its flocks of chickens and community ovens, was evacuated after it was inundated by a series of floods. Cossetta's Restaurant on West 7th, was moved up from the flood plain and has an awning reminding us all that it is "just a piece of the levee." What it really is, is a slice of Italy where you can buy genuine pancetta and every kind of pasta.

Finally, in the 1970s, when all of West Seventh was close to being bulldozed for an industrial park, a group of residents stepped in, rolled up their sleeves and formed the West 7th/Fort Road Federation. Their efforts resulted in the area's designation as a Historic District, and the subsequent renovation of six to eight houses per year.

Today's West Seventh district is a convenient location that offers a variety of starter home possibilities (particularly if you are not afraid of rehabbing) as well as condos, duplexes and townhouses. Besides **Irvine Park**, this 2.5 mile long ribbon of neighborhood includes **Leech/McBoal** and

Cliff Street neighborhoods at the end of the High Bridge. South of West 7th and west of Smith Avenue, a stretch of simple, affordable Victorians are poised on the steep precipice of the Mississippi bluff, and farther back, blocks of modest Midwestern squares mixed with brick workers' cottages and a few Victorian brick houses offer quick access to Grand Avenue shopping up the hill. All have not been rehabbed, however, and there are pockets of poverty and economic distress.

The bedrock that creates the river channel and underlies this neighborhood sometimes makes rehabilitation of houses and upgrading of utilities difficult, but the river itself is a source for neighborhood recreation. The bike trail along Shepard Road offers a bird's eye view of the Mississippi; and Crosby Farm Park, off Gannon Road at Shepard Road, is a bluff and floodplain forest complete with a boardwalk running through its marsh and a network of hiking and biking trails.

To meet the residents' need for affordable child care, there are several non-profit child care organizations in the West Seventh District. RAP/Headstart, 651-298-5537, is available to qualifying families. The Salvation Army runs a latchkey program, 651-224-4316. The Community Center, 651-298-5493, runs a kids' club for 5- to 10-year-olds. All are free or sliding-fee programs.

Visitors come to West Seventh for the antique shops at the east end of the street and the fine dining at Forepaugh's, located in a mansion on Exchange Street in Irvine Park, 651-224-5606. At the opposite end of the spectrum, the region's classic diner, Mickey's Diner at 36 West 7th, 651-222-5633, serves pancakes, burgers and fries 24-hours a day.

Web Sites: www.ci.stpaul.mn.us, www.tcfreenet.org

Area Code: 651

Zip Codes: 55102, 55116

Post Offices: Main Office, 180 East Kellogg Boulevard; Elway Station, 1715 West 7th Street (all post office branches can be reached at 800-275-8777).

Police: Central District Patrol Team, 651-292-3563

Emergency Hospital: United Hospital, 333 Smith Avenue North, 651-220-8000

Library: Central, 90 West 4th Street, 651-266-7000

Community Resources: West Seventh Fort Road Federation, 974 West 7th Street, 651-298-5599; Community Center, 651-298-5493

Community Publications: *St. Paul Grand Gazette*, 651-699-1462; *St. Paul Pioneer Press*, 651-222-5011, www.pioneerplanet.com

Transportation: Bus Lines: 3: Grand Avenue/Downtown/3M Center. 9: Downtown/Highland Park/West 7th Street/Maplewood Mall/Oakdale. 14: Ford Plant/West 7th Street/Hillcrest Center/Downtown. Numerous routes run on I-35E, including the 54 Express to the Minneapolis-St. Paul International Airport and Mall of America.

NORTHWEST ST. PAUL
(West of I-35E and North of University)

ST. ANTHONY PARK DISTRICT

NORTH ST. ANTHONY PARK
SOUTH ST. ANTHONY PARK
MIDWAY WEST (ENERGY PARK DRIVE)

Boundaries: **North**: city limits; **West**: city limits; **South**: I-94, B.N. Railroad; **East**: Cleveland Avenue, Snelling Avenue

With St. Anthony Park lying directly east of the University neighborhoods in Minneapolis many U of M affiliated residents live here as a pleasant alternative to being closer to the main U of M campus. The St. Anthony Park District's neighborhoods also border the University of Minnesota's St. Paul campus, the Luther Seminary, and the Minnesota State Fair Grounds. Also here, the St. Anthony Park United Church of Christ which plays host to the popular Music in the Park Series (see **Cultural Life** for more details). Tame hills and mature trees provide a park-like setting for a variety of stolid brick apartments and stately old homes in these neighborhoods. The lovely curved streets were laid out in the 1870s by landscape architect Horace Cleveland. His idea was to build a community of large rural estates adapted to the natural contours of the land, thus creating the meandering streets and oddly-shaped parks and greenways that make up St. Anthony Park.

Although St. Anthony Park still offers the original tranquillity its designer sought, the city has long since risen up around the neighborhood. The Burlington Northern Railroad is an industrial/commercial corridor that divides the district into northern and southern halves. **North St. Anthony Park** is an affluent twist of wooded residential streets containing larger Colonials and variations of Midwestern-squares, the majority of which were built between 1900 and 1929. Many of the newer buildings are apartments, where university faculty and students make up a good number of the residents. Heading south on Raymond Avenue, under the railroad-bridge and past the large warehouse district, **South St. Anthony Park** is a more modest area made up mostly of single-family homes. Bungalows and Midwestern-square style houses predominate here.

Two small commercial districts containing numerous locally-owned businesses are within walking distance of most homes in the St. Anthony Park District, Como-Carter, and University-Raymond. At the west end of Como, and often credited with putting St. Anthony on the map, are the Luther Northwestern Theological Seminary and the surrounding shopping area that includes Micawbers Bookstore, Muffuleta Restaurant and The Bibelot Shop. Raymond Avenue is the site of several small cafes and restaurants, as well as a grocery co-op.

Following the eastern "arm" of the neighborhood, **Midway West** (Energy Park Drive) is a mixed-use strip of development that went up in the 1980s and includes apartment complexes, office space and the Municipal Stadium, home of the St. Paul Saints Northern League baseball team. Although the Saints are a minor league team, their games are quite popular, due in part to their wacky promotions, such as free back rubs during games and the famed pig who carries out new balls.

As befits a neighborhood of professional and academic households, a Carnegie library, endowed in 1917 by "the patron saint of libraries," Andrew Carnegie, is the neighborhood centerpiece. St. Anthony also has its own band, and is home to the Music in the Park Sunday Concert Series. The highlight of the year is a 4th of July celebration that starts with a morning run, features a neighborhood bike/trike/lawnmower brigade parade and a patriotic speech contest, and ends with an evening concert and dance.

Several small parks provide children's playgrounds, tennis courts, winter skating rinks and picnic tables. Access to the trails and parks along the Mississippi River is gained from city streets

While St. Anthony Park is distinctly residential, major employers located near or within the district include the University of Minnesota, Luther Seminary, H.B. Fuller Company, and the Waldorf Corporation.

Web Sites: www.sap.org, www.ci.stpaul.mn.us, www.tcfreenet.org

Area Code: 651

Zip Codes: 55104, 55108, 55114

Post Office: Industrial Station, 1430 Concordia Avenue (all post office branches can be reached at 800-275-8777).

Police: Western District Patrol Team North, 651-292-3512; South, 651-292-3549

Emergency Hospital: University of Minnesota Hospital, Harvard Street at East River Parkway, 651-626-3000

Library: St. Anthony Park, 2245 Como Avenue, 651-642-0411

Community Resources: St. Anthony Park Community Council, 890 Cromwell Avenue, 651-649-5992; Municipal Stadium, 1771 Energy Park Drive, 651-644-6659

Community Publications: *St. Paul Grand Gazette*, 651-699-1462; *St. Paul Pioneer Press*, 651-222-5011, www.pioneerplanet.com

Transportation: Bus Lines: 4: Snelling Avenue/Rosedale/Mall of America; 5: Downtown/Como Avenue/Signal Hills; 12: Downtown/ Roseville; 16: Downtown Minneapolis/University Avenue/Downtown St. Paul; 95E: Downtown Minneapolis/Bandana Square/Downtown St. Paul; 105: Raymond Avenue/U of M St. Paul campus/Rosedale/ Northwestern College; certain U of M #52 routes run from many parts of the Twin Cities to the St. Paul campus on weekdays, call 612-625-9000. A Park & Ride lot is at Eustis and Como avenues.

HAMLINE–MIDWAY DISTRICT

Boundaries: **North**: Burlington-Northern Railroad; **West**: Cleveland Avenue; **South**: University Avenue; **East**: Lexington Parkway

Living next to a major commercial thoroughfare such as the Midway section of University Avenue can be considered a plus or minus, depending on your point of view. While it's nice to be able to walk to a bakery or to a performance at Ginkgo Coffeehouse, the commercial character of the neighborhood may not be right for you, particularly if you have children.

Located just east of Saint Anthony Park and in the middle between Minneapolis and St. Paul, Hamline-Midway is a swath of moderate to low-priced houses adjacent to St. Paul's Midway, one of the Twin Cities' busiest corridors of discount grocery and department stores. University Avenue was an early route between the two Twin Cities—first by horse-drawn carriage, then electric streetcar, then by car. As the cities grew toward each other, the Hamline-Midway neighborhood emerged haphazardly as a checkerboard of mixed residential and commercial uses. Much of the housing stock went up before 1940, although pleasantly landscaped residences lining the narrow streets immediately surrounding the university were built as late as 1960.

Derelict housing to the east and south of the university is a concern, and in recent years, bank robberies, restaurant hold-ups and murder have all taken place in this area. The western end of University Avenue is an industrial area containing warehouses, processing plants, some office buildings and the Amtrak passenger train station. The other center of activity in the neighborhood is Hamline University, a private college on Snelling Avenue.

Web Sites: www.ci.stpaul.mn.us, www.tcfreenet.org

Area Code: 651

Zip Code: 55104

Post Office: Industrial Station, 1430 Concordia Avenue (all post office branches can be reached at 800-275-8777).

Police: Western District Patrol Team North, 651- 292-3512; South, 651-292-3549

Emergency Hospital: Fairview-University, 2450 Riverside Avenue, 612-672-6000 (Riverside Campus); 420 SE Delaware Street, 612-273-3000 (University Campus)

Library: Hamline Branch, 1558 Minnehaha Avenue West, 651-642-0293

Community Resource: Hamline-Midway Coalition, 1564 Lafond Avenue, 651-646-1986

Community Publications: *St. Paul Grand Gazette*, 651-699-1462; *St. Paul Pioneer Press*, 651-222-5011, www.pioneerplanet.com

Transportation: Bus Lines: 4: Snelling Avenue/Rosedale/Mall of America; 7: Downtown/Signal Hills/Mendota Heights; 22: St. Anthony Avenue/Regions Hospital/Downtown

THOMAS-DALE (FROGTOWN) DISTRICT

Boundaries: **North**: B.N. Railroad; **West**: Lexington Parkway; **South**: University Avenue; **East**: I-35E

Nobody knows for sure where the name—Frogtown—comes from, although chances are it has to do with the neighborhood's earliest aquatic residents. In the 1880s, when Germans first settled here to be near rail yard jobs, they called their marshy new home, Froschburg, or Frog City, probably for their croaking companions outside, although the debate over the name rages on. Today, the marshes, with their frog choruses, are long gone.

Located northwest of the Capitol, the houses of Thomas-Dale/Frogtown are modest, consisting of worker cottages built by the earliest residents and newer two-story Midwestern-squares and ramblers. Some of the lots are narrow, apparently the result of subdivisions by enterprising residents. Over half of the housing is pre-1940, and many of the cottages are over one hundred years old. Habitat for Humanity, the Twin Cities Builders Outreach Foundation and other civic organizations have rehabilitated and replaced some of the deteriorated housing stock, and artists have brightened up the district's color palette. Today Thomas-Dale is mostly a Vietnamese business district with scores of restaurants and bilingual services along eastern University Avenue. The neighborhood's striking monument to the area's early European workers is the Church of St. Agnes, with its 200-foot high onion dome roof and featuring performances of chamber music and the works of Mozart.

Though the neighborhood is still beset by poverty, crime and overcrowded housing, Thomas-Dale is a St. Paul Police Department "Weed and Seed" site. The goal: to "weed" out violent crime, drug use and gang activity from targeted high-crime neighborhoods, and to prevent crime from recurring by "seeding" the area with a wide range of programs and services from both public and private entities. Overall, this area is recommended to newcomers only if they are accustomed to the energy of an urban neighborhood.

Web Sites: www.ci.stpaul.mn.us, www.tcfreenet.org

Area Code: 651

Zip Codes: 55103, 55104

Post Offices: Rice Street Station, 40 Arlington Avenue; Industrial Station, 1430 Concordia Avenue (all post office branches can be reached at 800-275-8777).

Police: West of Rice Street: Western District Patrol Team North, 651-292-3512; South, 651-292-3549; East of Rice Street: Central District Patrol Team, 651-292-3563

Emergency Hospital: St. Paul-Ramsey Medical Center, 640 Jackson Street, 651-221-3456

Library: Lexington Branch, 1080 University Avenue, 651-642-0359

Community Resource: Thomas-Dale Planning Council, 369 University Avenue, 651-298-5068

Community Publications: *St. Paul Grand Gazette*, 651-699-1462; *St. Paul Pioneer Press*, 651-222-5011, www.pioneerplanet.com

Transportation: Bus Lines: 5: Inver Grove Heights/Como Boulevard/State Fairgrounds/Downtown; 7: Downtown/Thomas Avenue/Signal Hills/Mendota Heights; 8: Downtown/Jackson Street/Inver Hills College; 12: Downtown/ Rice Street/Roseville; 16: Downtown Minneapolis/University Avenue/Downtown St. Paul; 17: Dale Street/Rosedale; 95E: Downtown/Bandana Square/Downtown Minneapolis

COMO DISTRICT

Boundaries: North: Hoyt Avenue, Larpenteur Avenue; **West**: Snelling Avenue; **South**: B.N. Railroad, Como Park, West Maryland Avenue; **East**: Lexington Parkway, Dale Street

When it's minus 25 degrees, and the rest of the folks in the Twin Cities are fantasizing about someplace warm, all Como residents have to do is step next door to the tropical park inside the glimmering glass Victorian Conservatory of Como Park. With one million visitors each year at the zoo alone, Como rates as the most used park in the seven-county metro area. Easily accessible to residents by bike or foot, most of Como's attractions are free, although there are modest entrance fees to visit the conservatory, use the pool, or play golf.

Known as St. Paul's Garden District, the park also features miles of trails, a Japanese garden, a band shell and extensive picnic grounds. Throngs of picnickers enjoy summer evenings much as they did at the turn-of-the-century when they rode out to the lake in horse-drawn omnibuses.

While the neighborhood surrounds the park and Lake Como, none of the homes are lakeside, although many of them enjoy lake and park views. The oldest houses were built on the lake's west side, some of them as summer villas for visitors from the South. A row of impressive 19th-century Victorians overlook the southern shore of Lake Como. Later waves of building in the 1940s, '70s and '80s added Craftsman homes with sun-porches as well as moderately-priced bungalows close to Snelling Avenue. Today, about one-third of the houses are less than thirty years old. Two-thirds of the homes in the district are owner-occupied.

On the western edge of this neighborhood lies the Minnesota State Fairgrounds, which is viewed alternately as an asset and a liability. A perennial controversy at State Fair time has to do with those residents who allow fairgoers to park in their yards. While this brings in extra cash for some, it also clogs traffic and turns the usually tranquil neighborhoods into noisy parking lots for almost two weeks each August.

Shopping is close by: Midway shopping area, to the south, has banks, groceries and discount stores; Rosedale Shopping Center and the shopping centers along Highway 36 are to the north in Roseville.

Web Sites: www.district10.comopark.com, www.comopark.com, www.ci.stpaul.mn.us, www.tcfreenet.org

Area Code: 651

Zip Codes: 55103, 55108, 55117

Post Offices: Como Station, 2286 Como Avenue Rice Street Station; 40 Arlington Avenue East (all post office branches can be reached at 800-275-8777).

Police: Western District Patrol Team North, 651-292-3512; South, 651-292-3549

Emergency Hospital: United Hospital, 333 Smith Avenue North, 651-220-8000

Library: Hamline Branch, 1558 Minnehaha Avenue West, 651-642-0293

Community Resource: Como Community Council, 1556 Como Avenue, 651-644-3889

Community Publications: *St. Paul Grand Gazette*, 651-699-1462; *St. Paul Pioneer Press*, 651-222-5011, www.pioneerplanet.com

Transportation: Bus Lines: 5: Downtown/State Fairgrounds/Inver Grove Heights; 12: Downtown/Rosedale/Roseville; 17: Dale Street/Rosedale; 95E: Downtown Minneapolis/Bandana Square/Downtown St. Paul

NORTH END DISTRICT

SOUTH OF MARYLAND AVENUE
NORTH OF MARYLAND AVENUE

Boundaries: North: Larpenteur Avenue; **West**: Dale Street, Lexington Parkway; **South**: B.N. Railroad; **East**: I-35E

Heading north from the State Capitol on Rice Street, you cross the railroad tracks and enter the city's North End District, a mix of residential and light industrial properties. The North End District is bisected by Maryland Avenue and the streets **south of Maryland** include an intact working-class enclave of small Victorian wood frames built by rail yard and mill workers at the end of the 19th century. **North of Maryland** there is a more suburban feel with curving streets, larger lots and houses built in the 1930s, '40s and '50s. There are many large apartment buildings, and North End housing is fairly evenly divided between single- and multi-family dwellings.

The neighborhood's older, blue-collar section centers around two large cemeteries. Pre-Civil War Oakland Cemetery, east of Rice Street, is a designated historic site where many of St. Paul's early statesmen, including founding father Henry Sibley, are buried. Calvary Cemetery is west of Como Avenue. Besides the Victorian houses, many sturdy Midwestern squares and small worker cottages line the streets. Newer North End housing includes a small single-family development overlooking Lyton Park. The Lewis Park development offers townhomes and barrier-free apartments. The northern stretch of residences surrounding Wheelock Parkway, extending to the east toward Lake Phalen, makes up the neighborhood's more affluent section. Here, large pre-1940 Midwestern-squares and Colonials are interspersed with more recently built split-levels. Wheelock Parkway winds through the North End, following the edge of a sheer bluff overlooking another cemetery (Elmhurst) and the plain below. The tracts here of recently built houses and rolling hills have more in common with the surrounding suburb of Maplewood than with St. Paul. Convenient shopping is available on thoroughfares, including Rice Street, and Maplewood Mall is a short drive north on White Bear Avenue.

Web Sites: www.ci.stpaul.mn.us, www.tcfreenet.org

Area Code: 651

Zip Codes: 55101, 55103, 55117

Post Office: Rice Street Station, 40 Arlington Avenue East (all post office branches can be reached at 800-275-8777).

Police: west of Rice Street: Western District Patrol Team, North: 651-292-3512; South: 651-292-3549; east of Rice Street: Central District Patrol Team, 651-292-3563

Emergency Hospital: St. Paul-Ramsey Medical Center, 640 Jackson Street, 651-221-3456

Library: Rice Street Branch, 995 Rice Street, 651-558-2223

Community Resources: District 6 Planning Council, 1053 North Dale Street, 651-488-4485; North End Area Revitalization (N.E.A.R.) Inc., 651-488-1039; Neighborhood Housing Agenda Committee, 651-222-2111

Community Publications: *St. Paul Grand Gazette*, 651-699-1462; *St. Paul Pioneer Press*, 651-222-5011, www.pioneerplanet.com

Transportation: Bus Lines: 5: Inver Grove Heights/State Fairgrounds/Downtown; 8: Downtown/Jackson Street/Inver Hills College; 12: Downtown/Rice Street/Roseville; 17: Dale Street/Rosedale; 95E: Downtown St. Paul/Bandana Square/U of M/Downtown Minneapolis

EAST ST. PAUL AREA

According to the St. Paul Police Annual Report, the East St. Paul areas, known as East Consolidated, are "weed and seed" sites in which law enforcement activities include extra patrols targeting problem properties and illegal activities. The FORCE Unit works in this area to eliminate illegal activities by gang members. Please keep this in mind while considering the following communities.

PAYNE-PHALEN DISTRICT

Boundaries: **North**: Larpenteur Avenue; **West**: I-35E; **South**: Grove Street, B.N Railroad; **East**: Johnson Parkway, McAfee Street

Payne-Phalen suffers from rising crime rates, absentee landlords and deteriorating housing. A September 1999 report from the Community Revitalization Center for Urban and Regional Affairs at the University of Minnesota states that "the greatest concentration of crime along St. Paul's East Side is located south of Maryland and east of Edgerton along Arcade Street and Payne Avenue"—the very center of the Payne-Phalen neighborhood. That said, those considering housing here will find houses that are simpler and smaller than the opulent spreads that surround Minneapolis' lakes. Even houses along Wheelock Parkway are distinctly low-key. You will be close to excellent recreation amenities, however. Lake Phalen is surrounded by a substantial expanse of rolling hills, a golf course, tree-shaded bluffs and a paved running path. In the summer you can rent sailboats and in the winter, the park offers cross-country ski lessons.

Residential areas around Lake Phalen are in many ways similar to the North End: modest two-story frame houses; bungalows and Midwestern-squares (as well as a scattering of unique turn-of-the-century Victorian houses) are found on the southern end, and rows of larger Colonials and bungalows line the gradual slope toward Lake Phalen.

Web Sites: www.ci.stpaul.mn.us, www.tcfreenet.org, www.esndc.org

Area Code: 651

Zip Codes: 55101, 55106

Post Offices: Dayton Bluff Station, 1425 Minnehaha Avenue; Seeger Square Station, 886 Arcade Street (all post office branches can be reached at 800-275-8777).

Police: Eastern District Patrol Team, 651-292-3565

Emergency Hospital: St. Paul-Ramsey Medical Center, 640 Jackson Street, 651-221-3456

Library: Arlington Hills, 1105 Greenbrier Street, 651-793-3930

Community Resource: District 5 Planning Council, 1014 Payne Avenue, 651-774-5234

Community Publications: *St. Paul Grand Gazette*, 651-699-1462; *St. Paul Pioneer Press*, 651-222-5011, www.pioneerplanet.com

Transportation: Bus Lines: 8: Downtown/Signal Hills/Inver Hills; 11: Downtown/Maplewood Mall/Inver Hills; 14: Downtown/Hillcrest/Ford Plant; 15: Downtown/Mahtomedi/Century College; a Park & Ride lot is at Larpenteur Avenue and Arcade Street.

DAYTON'S BLUFF DISTRICT

Boundaries: North: Grove Street and B. N. Railroad; **West**: Lafayette Road and State Highway 3; **South**: Warner Road; **East**: US Highway 61, Birmingham Street, Hazelwood Street, Johnson Parkway

Sitting high on Dayton's Bluff, overlooking I-94, are charming restored houses and Metropolitan State University's main campus. This was St. Paul's first upscale neighborhood. From the bluff, there is a spectacular view of the cityscape below.

This terraced neighborhood was developed in the 1850s by land speculator Lyman Dayton who built a house on this land, hence the name, Dayton's Bluff. Today many Victorian "painted ladies" still stand here, some rehabilitated, some not. Cupolas, dormers, gables, turrets, parapets and pediments are common architectural elements in this historic area. In addition, there are numerous smaller square wood frames built by workers who moved here in the 1880s.

Residents have worked hard to beautify this neighborhood. Gardens have been planted, billboards removed, and the work continues. Gauger Park is the setting for community socials, small outdoor theater and musical performances and neighborhood festivals. At the southern end of Dayton's Bluff is a steep hilltop with a breathtaking view of the Mississippi River Valley and both downtowns. As early as 1,000 B.C. the Hopewell Indians chose this area as a burial site, leaving behind a series of oval-shaped burial mounds along the edge of the bluff. The overlook, with the six gravesites that remain, is now Indian Mounds Park, complete with walking paths, picnic areas and playgrounds.

Dayton's Bluff Neighborhood Housing Services offers low-interest loans for homes in the Dayton's Bluff neighborhood. For information, call 651-774-6995.

Web Sites: www.ci.stpaul.mn.us, www.tcfreenet.org

Area Code: 651

Zip Codes: 55101, 55106

Post Offices: Dayton's Bluff Station, 1425 Minnehaha Avenue; Main Office, 180 East Kellogg Boulevard (all post office branches can be reached at 800-275-8777).

Police: Eastern District Patrol Team, 651-292-3565

Emergency Hospital: St. Paul-Ramsey Medical Center, 640 Jackson Street, 651-221-3456

Libraries: Arlington Hills, 1105 Greenbrier Street, 651-793-3930; Sun Ray Branch, 2105 Wilson Avenue, 651-292-6640

Community Resource: Dayton's Bluff Center for Civic Life, 281 Maria Avenue, 651-772-2075

Community Publications: *St. Paul Grand Gazette*, 651-699-1462;

St. Paul Pioneer Press, 651-222-5011, www.pioneerplanet.com

Transportation: Bus Lines: 3: Downtown/East 3rd Street/3M Center; 9: Downtown/Highland Park/East 7th Street/Maplewood/Oakdale; 12: Rosedale/East 6th Street/Downtown; 49: Downtown/Burns Avenue/Sun Ray Center/Ramsey County Correctional Facility

HAYDEN HEIGHTS/HAZEL PARK/HILLCREST DISTRICTS

Boundaries: **North**: Larpenteur Avenue; **West**: Hazelwood Street, Johnson Parkway, McAfee Street; **South**: East Minnehaha Avenue; **East**: McKnight Road

Driving up the gradual slope of Minnehaha Avenue and crossing White Bear Avenue, one comes upon a plateau of small- to mid-sized post-1940s Cape Cods and ramblers, sometimes on curving streets, shaded by relatively young trees. This is Hayden Heights/Hazel Park/Hillcrest, which, together with several other small subdivisions, comprises the northeastern corner of the city. It is a residential area with a mix of young families and retirees. Hillcrest Country Club, in the neighborhood's northeastern corner, occupies almost a quarter of the acreage in Hayden Heights. Some houses face the golf course's meticulously groomed grounds, and many others benefit from the quiet roads that parallel the course. When compared to many of St. Paul's other neighborhoods, there is a dramatic difference between this area's post-World War II suburban-style homes and the older housing that predominates in much of the rest of the city. While home values are only slightly higher here than in Payne-Phalen and Dayton's Bluff, the small, well-tended yards have more in common with the upscale suburb of Maplewood next door than with most of St. Paul.

Maplewood, surrounding this district to the north and east, is the relatively affluent suburban home to 3M Company's international headquarters. Hayden Heights/Hazel Park residents enjoy some of the commercial amenities of living next to this well-off suburb, including Maplewood Mall, a large indoor shopping center to the north, and Maplewood Bowl, an entertainment center that hosts live music shows. Hayden Heights/Hazel Park has several small parks, and Lake Phalen is close enough to the neighborhood for easy visits. (See **Washington County** for more about Maplewood.)

Residents say that crime is a concern in this district.

Web Sites: www.ci.stpaul.mn.us, www.tcfreenet.org

Area Code: 651

Zip Codes: 55106, 55119

Post Office: Eastern Heights Station, 1910 Suburban Avenue (all post office branches can be reached at 800-275-8777).

Police: Eastern District Patrol Team, 651-292-3565

Emergency Hospital: St. Paul-Ramsey Medical Center, 640 Jackson Street, 651-221-3456

Library: Hayden Heights Branch, 1456 White Bear Avenue North, 651-793-3934

Community Resource: District 2 Community Council, 2169 Stillwater Avenue, 651-731-6842

Community Publications: *St. Paul Grand Gazette*, 651-699-1462; *St. Paul Pioneer Press*, 651-222-5011, www.pioneerplanet.com

Transportation: Bus Lines: 9: Downtown/Maplewood Mall/Oakdale; 12: Downtown/Rosedale/Roseville; 14: Downtown/Maryland Avenue/Hillcrest Center/West 7th/Ford Plant; 20: Maplewood Mall/White Bear Avenue/Sun Ray Center

SUNRAY/BATTLE CREEK/HIGHWOOD DISTRICTS

Boundaries: **North**: Minnehaha Avenue; **West**: Hazelwood Street, Birmingham Street, Warner Road; **South**: Mississippi River, city limits; **East**: McKnight Road

If you're looking for open space, the wide expanse of Sunray/Battle Creek/Highwood has it. Making up St. Paul's southeastern corner, much of this area consists of the wetlands of Pig's Eye Lake Park and Battle Creek Park, as well as a railroad and industrial zone that occupies a slice of land along State Highway 61. Two-thirds of the houses here have been built since the 1970s, and run along grid streets and cul-de-sacs in the north, and on large lots in the south. Large apartment and condominium complexes were built on the northern and central streets in the 1970s. As a result of the recent construction and low density, the neighborhood has the newer look of nearby Maplewood and Woodbury. The exception to this suburban appearance is the northwestern corner of Sunray, which is made up of simple, turn-of-the-century bungalows and Midwestern-squares, much like those in adjacent Dayton's Bluff.

Many Sunray/Battlecreek/Highwood residents are professionals; others work in service and retail jobs. The neighborhood is youthful—you'll find youngsters galore—and mobile. Prices for the tidy houses, condos, and townhouses are above average for St. Paul, comparable to house values in Como, but well below the most expensive Twin Cities neighborhoods. Houses also tend to be less expensive than in the nearby suburban communities of Maplewood and Woodbury.

Sunray/Battle Creek/Highwood is close to shopping centers along I-94, among them the Sun Ray Shopping Center and the Horizon Outlet Center, a mall containing more than fifty factory outlet stores. Ample hiking and biking areas can be found along the rocky ravines of Battle Creek Park and at other green spaces in the neighborhood. Across State Highway 61 from Battle Creek, Pig's Eye Lake Park is home to nesting great blue herons, egrets and cormorants.

Web Sites: www.ci.stpaul.mn.us, www.tcfreenet.org

Area Code: 651

Zip Codes: 55106, 55119

Post Office: Eastern Heights Station, 1910 Suburban Avenue (all post office branches can be reached at 800-275-8777).

Police: Eastern District Patrol Team, 651-292-3565

Emergency Hospital: St. Paul-Ramsey Medical Center, 640 Jackson Street, 651-221-3456

Library: Sun Ray Branch, 2105 Wilson Avenue, 651-292-6640

Community Resource: District 1 Community Council, 2090 Conway Street, Room 126, 651-292-7828

Community Publications: *St. Paul Grand Gazette*, 651-699-1462; *St. Paul Pioneer Press*, 651-222-5011, www.pioneerplanet.com

Transportation: Bus Lines: 3: Downtown/Sun Ray Center/3M Center; 12: Downtown/Rosedale/Roseville; 20: Maplewood Mall/White Bear Avenue/Sun Ray Center; 49: Downtown/Sun Ray Center/3M Center/Ramsey County Correctional Facility; numerous 94 routes run along I-94 to eastern suburbs.

SOUTH OF THE MISSISSIPPI RIVER

WEST ST. PAUL

Boundaries: North/West/East: Mississippi River; **South**: Annapolis Street

Cross the arching Smith Avenue High Bridge, and you're in another world—St. Paul's West Side, a world filled with the strains of mariachi bands and the seductive rhythms of salsa music. If you can't tell by the murals and brightly painted benches, you can tell by the lively mix of restaurants and ethnic markets (including the only Lebanese-Mexican deli in the world) that you are in one of the most diverse neighborhoods in the Twin Cities. For over one hundred years, Neighborhood House, the local outreach program, has opened its arms to waves of immigrants, first from Russia and Lebanon, now from Latin and Central America, Africa, Mexico and Cambodia. At Neighborhood House the newly-arrived learn to speak English and are assisted with their transition to American life. The vibrant flux of new immigrants has turned this drab industrial area into a technicolor melting pot guaranteed to overcome any case of winter blues.

Separated from the rest of St. Paul by the Mississippi River, West St. Paul actually lies directly south of downtown. The bluff area was once a sprawling farm, and the earliest buildings here are farmhouses and workers' cottages dating from the mid-19th century. Many of the other houses are Midwestern squares and variations on bungalows, intermingled with newer split-levels and new townhouses. More than half the housing was built before 1940, and includes a smattering of renovated Victorians. The blocks west of Smith Avenue directly across from Cherokee Park hold stately, larger Colonials, Tudors and bungalows. Many of these properties are expected to appreciate as St. Paul continues to develop its riverfront.

Robert Street, which runs north-south, is a commercial district where you can find everything from housewares to used cars. Concord Street from the Lafayette Bridge to Plato Boulevard is the Latino strip. Check out the margaritas at Boca Chica and the cherry empanadas at El Burrito. La Placito's peaceful courtyard is the setting for lively music, plays and lectures. On the far eastern side of the neighborhood, on the flats across the river from downtown, Holman Field, a small airplane landing strip used mostly by private aviation and the Minnesota Air National Guard, is only slightly less quiet.

Even if you don't move here, be sure to visit during Cinco de Mayo (in May), when the whole neighborhood turns into one big street carnival. Or come over for one of the productions of Teatro del Pueblo. While you're here, stop in at the Riverview Branch Library. On the National Historic Register, this

Carnegie library has a special section for Spanish-speaking patrons.

Set atop a steep sandstone bluff, Cherokee Park offers an awesome panorama of river barges and downtown St. Paul. This is a place for solitude, and an occasional glimpse of the river's wildlife. Bird watchers can spot herons and egrets riding updrafts over the bluff's edge and, once in a great while, a bald eagle perched on a branch or soaring overhead. Below the bluffs are the sandstone walls and marshy river flats of Lilydale Park, which contain small caves created by eons of percolation and erosion. At the turn of the century, some of the caves were used by Yoerg's Brewery for cold storage of product, which was subsequently marketed as "Yoerg's Cave-Aged Picnic Beer." Nearly all of the cave openings are now barred up because of cave-ins and other accidents, but the foundations of the brewery, the ruins of an old brick foundry, and the massive cottonwoods standing along the Mississippi flats still make for interesting exploring.

For a preview of this neighborhood, listen to Radio Rey, 740 A.M. Its programming in Spanish and Hmong audibly reflects the diversity of the area.

Web Sites: www.ci.stpaul.mn.us, www.tcfreenet.org

Area Code: 651

Zip Code: 55107

Post Office: Riverview Station, 292 Eva Street (all post office branches can be reached at 800-275-8777).

Police: Central District Patrol Team, 651-292-3565

Emergency Hospitals: St. Paul-Ramsey Medical Center, 640 Jackson Street, 651-221-3456; HealthEast Street Joseph's Hospital, 69 West Exchange Street, 651-232-3000

Library: Riverview Branch, 1 East George Street, 651-292-6626

Community Resources: West Side Citizens' Organization, 625 Stryker Avenue, 651-293-1708; Cherokee Park; Lilydale Park

Community Publications: *St. Paul Grand Gazette*, 651-699-1462; *St. Paul Pioneer Press*, 651-222-5011, www.pioneerplanet.com

Transportation: Bus Lines: 5: Downtown/State Fairgrounds/Stryker Avenue/Inver Grove Heights; 7: Downtown/Smith Avenue/South Robert Street/Mendota Heights; 8: Downtown/South Robert Street/Inver Hills; 11: Dowwntown/Little Canada/Concord Street/Inver Hills; 29: Downtown/Riverview Industrial Park; 95 U of M: West St. Paul Park & Ride/U of M/Downtown Minneapolis.

MINNEAPOLIS SUBURBS

BLOOMINGTON

RICHFIELD
EAST BLOOMINGTON
EDINA
WEST BLOOMINGTON

Boundaries: **North**: I-494; **East**: Minnesota River; **South:** Minnesota River; **West**: Town Line Road

Like yin and yang, the two disparate halves of Bloomington fit together to form the state's third-largest city. The eastern half, known locally and in the classifieds as East Bloomington, has flat streets laid out in grids, and a large proportion of property that is zoned for business and commercial/industrial uses. When you go shopping at Mall of America, you are in East Bloomington. The western side of the city, which is largely residential, more affluent and hilly, is known locally, as West Bloomington. When you're driving on I-494 and see the ski jump just south of the freeway, you are in West Bloomington. The two halves of Bloomington are treated separately below.

RICHFIELD AND EAST (HALF OF THE CITY OF) BLOOMINGTON

Boundaries: *Richfield:* **North**: 62 Crosstown; **East:** Minneapolis-St Paul International Airport; **South**: I-494; **West**: Xerxes Avenue; area: 7 square miles; *East Bloomington*: (the eastern half of the City of Bloomington) **North**: I-494; **East**: Minnesota River; **South**: Minnesota River; **West**: approximately Penn Avenue

In 1945, the city of Minneapolis stopped at Mother's Lake where the 62 Crosstown is now. The villages of Richfield and Bloomington were out in the country, about five miles south of downtown Minneapolis, and fields of vegetables and a poultry farm occupied the land where Mall of America now sits. But, at the end of WW II, returning veterans and their growing families needed homes, and so residential development of the area commenced, the result, modest ramblers on small, flat lots. And, when Richfield was finished, they moved across what is now the I-494 "strip" of shopping, restaurants and bars to the farm fields of Bloomington, giving birth to the

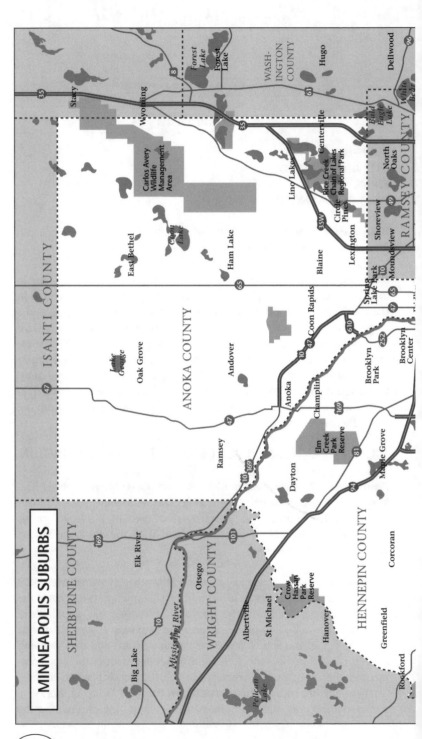

MINNEAPOLIS SUBURBS

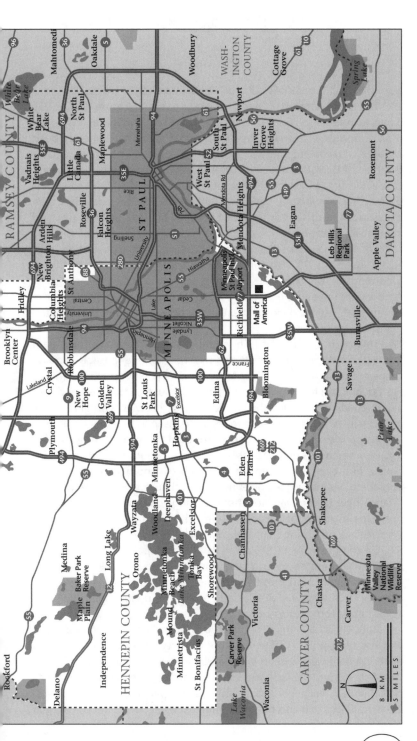

second ring of Minneapolis' suburbs and the state's third-largest city.

The grid-style streets, Cape Cods and small ramblers are with us still, along with some 1970s split-levels and a few old farmhouses. While the bulk of homes in this area are "maturing," many have already been replaced with contemporary housing or "transformed" into more valuable commercial real estate. Executive-level homes may be found around Wood Lake in Richfield and along the river bluffs in East Bloomington. Most houses, however, run around 1,500 to 2,000 square feet, have detached one-car garages, and sell for under $150,000. Because of their size and affordability, these houses go quickly, often to young, single professionals.

The housing in these communities is dense, and the populations now stand at about 40,000 for Richfield and 90,000 for the City of Bloomington. Many people who live here work either at the Mall of America or in one of the 25 hotels close by. Despite having a number of commercial, retail and industrial areas, neither Richfield nor Bloomington has a real downtown.

This region, south of Minneapolis, abuts Minneapolis-St. Paul International Airport, and is affected by airplane noise, possibly capping property values. And while the Metropolitan Airports Commission (MAC) has bought and torn down more than 400 houses in this area, and provided sound-insulation in others, residents fear that MAC's programs have stalled-out. When looking here for housing, keep in mind that noise is a serious problem, and the airport's proposed north-south runway may make some houses uninhabitable. Both Bloomington and Richfield do have a number of programs in place to assist homeowners who are upgrading or replacing the older housing. Richfield, for example, will help finance new buyers, and for those looking to remodel, will supply a "remodeling advisor." Each January the city holds the "Street of Possibilities Remodeling Fair" at the Richfield High School.

Despite the noise, Richfield and East Bloomington are desirable areas, particularly to renters, due in part to its central location along freeways 494 and 35W. About one-third of the housing units are rentals, and vacancy rates are low. You will find apartments, double bungalows and single family homes to rent here as well.

Both cities have many recreation facilities. Richfield's **Wood Lake Nature Center** is a 149-acre nature preserve with walking paths and floating boardwalks and an excellent interpretive center located at 735 Lake Shore Drive, 612-861-9365. Young children love the nature center's Half-Haunted Halloween which features face painting and the Trick-or-Treat Trail. Richfield also has a community center, an ice arena, two golf courses and a 50-meter city pool featuring a 29-foot-high double water-slide. The east half of Bloomington boasts **Knott's Camp Snoopy** at the Mall of America and the **Minnesota Valley National Wildlife Refuge,** 38155 East 80th Street, 952-335-2323, a floodplain and forest along the Minnesota River.

Richfield is served by Independent School District #280. It has about 4,500 students in three elementary schools, one intermediate school, one junior high and one high school. Bloomington is served by Independent School District #271, 952-885-8454.

RICHFIELD

Web Site: www.ci.richfield.mn.us

Area Code: 612

Zip Code: 55423

Post Office: 825 West 65th Street, 800-275-8777

City Hall: 6700 Portland Avenue, 612-861-9700

Police/Fire non-emergency: 612-861-9800

Hospital: Fairview Southdale, 6401 France Avenue, 952-924-5000, www.fairview.org

Libraries: Augsburg Park, 7100 Nicollet Avenue, 612-869-8863; Southdale Regional Library, 7001 York Avenue, 612-830-4900, www.hennepin.lib.mn.us

School: District #280, 612-798-6000, www.richfield.k12.mn.us

Community Publication: *Richfield Sun Current*, 612-829-0797, www.mnsun.com

Chamber of Commerce: 612-866-5100

BLOOMINGTON

Web Site: www.ci.bloomington.mn.us

Area Code: 952

Zip Codes: 55420, 55425, 55431

Post Offices: 9641 Garfield Avenue South, 800-275-8777

City Hall: 2215 West Old Shakopee Road, 952-948-8700

Police/Fire non-emergency: 952-948-3900

Hospital: Fairview Southdale, 6401 France Avenue, 952-924-5000, www.fairview.org

Libraries: Southdale Regional Library, 7001 York Avenue, 952-830-4900; 8801 Portland Avenue South, Bloomington, 952-888-3369, www.hennepin.lib.mn.us

School: District #271, 952-885-8454, www.bloomington.k12.mn.us

Community Publication: *Bloomington Sun Current*, 612-829-0797, www.mnsun.com

Bus Transportation: Richfield and East Bloomington are webbed with bus routes too numerous to cover here. Most routes go through the Southtown Transit Center, Southdale Shopping Center or Mall of America. **Express Route 46** serves Normandale Community College. For bus schedules and route information call the **MCTO**, 612-373-3333 or visit www.metrotransit.org.

EDINA AND WEST (HALF OF THE CITY OF) BLOOMINGTON

Boundaries: *Edina*: **North**: St. Louis Park and Hopkins; **East:** France Avenue north of 54th Street, Xerxes south of 54th Street; **South**: I-494; **West**: Washington Avenue and Highway 169; area: 16 square miles; *West Bloomington*: **North**: I-494; **East:** Penn Avenue; **South**: Minnesota River; **West**: Town Line Road

The upscale ambiance of Edina and West Bloomington exists in marked contrast to the more working-class atmosphere of easterly neighbors Richfield and East Bloomington. Still, Edina and West Bloomington also exhibit an enormous diversity of housing.

Although there is no official boundary line, somewhere between Penn Avenue and France Avenue the apartment buildings, hotels and 1940s tract housing of East Bloomington give way to curved streets, 1970s, '80s and '90s splits-levels, ranches and colonials with multi-car garages, and residents who tell you that they live in West Bloomington. Custom-built homes grace these hilly streets, particularly around Hyland Lake Park Reserve and Hyland Hills Ski Area, and along the Minnesota River Bluffs. Fast-growing West Bloomington looks very much like an extension of Edina to the north—mostly residential, big houses, two- and three-car garages, meticulous landscaping. While both Edina and West Bloomington have significant percentages of rental housing, the units tend to be clustered in park-like townhome settings with tennis courts and walking trails. One Edina high-rise complex, Edinborough Park, off France Avenue and I-494, has an indoor park with real trees and an indoor ice-skating rink.

In the City of Bloomington, 25% of the land is set aside for parks and nature areas, mostly located in the west half of the city. The parkland includes 208 lakes and ponds, 14 miles of shoreline along the Minnesota River, the Nine Mile Creek Watershed, which includes several parks and nature areas, Hyland Lake Park Reserve, the Hyland Hills Ski Area and Ski School (see **Sports and Recreation**), and the Minnesota Valley National Wildlife Refuge (see **Lakes and Parkways**). While West Bloomington's open spaces tend toward the wild side, in Edina you'll find groomed parks and carefully tended golf courses in each of its four-corners.

Much is made of Edina and its affluent residents' supposed high-flying lifestyle. But, in many ways, Edina is more mystique than fact. While many residents really are corporate kings and prominent professionals, at least one fourth of Edina's population is retired and over age 65, and while Edina does have houses that sell for well over one million dollars, it also has over 500 subsidized apartment units, as well as condominiums and townhouses, located near the freeways and major arteries. And, a nice selection of single-story ramblers dating from the 1950s and '60s can be found here. Look for them west of France Avenue in the vicinity of Pamela Park, around Highway 100 and the 62 Crosstown, east of France Avenue, or bordering Hopkins close to the Blake School in the northwest corner of town. These are particularly popular with young families and seniors. (For those who like fixer-uppers, the northwest corner even has some houses that date from the early 1900s.)

More typical of what's considered Edina, however, are the $500,000 to one million dollar-plus houses in plush neighborhoods. The 1920s to 1940s historic-revival stone, brick and stucco houses surrounding the Edina Country Club are listed on the National Register of Historic Places. These houses are large in proportion to their lots and this pattern has served as the template for much of the rest of Edina's development. The classic styles of these homes offer formal rooms like first-floor libraries and dining rooms. Braemar, Indian Hills and the area around the Interlachen Country Club are also ritzy, but have newer houses, 1950s to 1970s, and tend toward lavishly remodeled sprawling ramblers and two-story colonials nestled beneath canopies of mature trees.

With very little open land available for development, Edina's current building boomlet is taking place on top of the hill above Ridge Road off Highway 169 and also in the vicinity of Dewey Hill just north of I-494. Want to know what the most expensive piece of Edina real estate was in 1999? A 1972 contemporary in Indian Hills priced around two million dollars. 1972!

Bloomington and Edina are both known for their shopping, though Edina's reputation is more up-market. Fiftieth and France—the closest thing Edina has to a downtown—is a cluster of boutiques, groceries and excellent restaurants (see **Shopping for the Home**). Southdale/The Galleria/Centennial Lakes malls, along France Avenue, are home to everything from multi-plex movies to home furniture.

Finally, for those who do the *New York Times* crossword puzzle, Edina is the answer to the clue, "Five-letter suburb of Minneapolis."

EDINA

Web Site: www.ci.edina.mn.us

Area Code: 952

Zip Codes: 55343, 55410, 55416, 55424, 55435, 55436, 55439

Post Office: 3948 49 1/2 Street

City Hall: 4801 West 50th Street, 952-927-8861

Police non-emergency: 952-826-1600

Fire non-emergeny: 952-826-0330

Hospital: Fairview Southdale, 6401 France Avenue, 952-924-5000, www.fairview.org

Libraries: Southdale Regional Library, 7001 York Avenue, 952-830-4900; 4701 West 50th Street, Edina, 952-922-1611; www.hennepin.lib.mn.us

School: District #273, 952-928-2530

Community Publication: *Edina Sun Current*, 612-829-0797, www.mnsun.com

WEST BLOOMINGTON

Web Site: www.ci.bloomington.mn.us

Area Code: 952

Zip Codes: 55437, 55438

Post Office: 6101 West Old Shakopee Road

City Hall: 2215 West Old Shakopee Road, 952-948-8700

Police/Fire non-emergency: 952-948-3900

Hospital: Fairview Southdale, 6401 France Avenue, 952-924-5000, www.fairview.org

Libraries: Southdale Regional Library, 7001 York Avenue, 952-830-4900; Penn Lake, 8800 Penn Avenue South, Bloomington, 952-884-3667; 4701 West 50th Street, Edina, 952-922-1611; www.hennepin.lib.mn.us

School: District #271, 952-885-8454, www.bloomington.k12.mn.us

Community Publication: *Bloomington Sun Current*, 612-829-0797, www.mnsun.com

Bus Transportation: for bus schedules and route information, call the **MCTO**, 612-349-7000 or visit www.metrotransit.org.

BE-Line Route 88: Southdale, Southtown, Mall of America, Appletree Square; **BE-Line Route 89**: Southdale, Normandale Community College, Oxboro Plaza, Mall of America; **Express Route 87**: Downtown Minneapolis, Edina, Valley View Road, Cahill Road, Highwood Drive; **Minneapolis Route 4**: Downtown Minneapolis, NE Minneapolis, Johnson Street NE, Apache Plaza, New Brighton, South Minneapolis, Lyndale Avenue South, Bryant Avenue South, West 50th Street, Opus II, Penn Avenue South, Southtown; **Express Route 35B**: Downtown Minneapolis, East and West 46th Street, West 50th Street, Edina, Chicago, Avenue, East 52nd Street, Cedar Avenue

MINNETONKA, HOPKINS, EDEN PRAIRIE

MINNETONKA

Boundaries: **North**: Ridgemont Avenue; **East**: St. Louis Park, Hopkins and Edina; **South**: 62 Crosstown; **West**: Woodland, Deephaven, Shorewood; area: 8 square miles

The city of Minnetonka barely touches Lake Minnetonka at Gray's Bay, so it isn't the lake that has fueled the city's growth—it's jobs.

Work has always brought people here. Historically, farmers didn't have use for the low wetlands or high, hilly ground surrounding the lake. They wanted flat land. So they located their farms and villages back from the water in what is now Minnetonka. They did use Minnehaha Creek to power the sawmill they built in 1852 in the historic area known today as

Minnetonka Mills. The lovely original Victorians are no longer here, but you will find homes dating from the 1960s and '70s...and '80s...and '90s. The building boom seems to have no end and continues in areas previously believed to be un-buildable.

By and large, Minnetonka's neighborhoods have been constructed on wooded lots with rolling terrain, and an effort has been made to preserve the city's natural assets. Many neighborhoods are built around wetlands, and land ownership here involves following wetlands policies, which may affect the way you may use your yard.

Rising taxes and rapidly increasing market values, particularly for new homes, are chasing some long-time residents out, gilding Minnetonka's reputation as a move-up market capable of challenging Edina. In 1990, the average value of a newly constructed home was $159,000; by 1999 even a townhome was difficult to find in that price range. For Minnetonka's most affordable housing, check in the neighborhoods that were built circa 1970: Scenic Heights Holiday Road, many neighborhoods south of Minnetonka Boulevard, or off of Excelsior Boulevard. Minnetonka is also a city in which you can find less expensive homes scattered among the new stucco starter castles. For those looking for reasonably-priced rentals or condominium apartments, look around Ridgedale Shopping Center, Cedar Lake Road in the north, or highways 101 and 7 in the southern portion of the city. For temporary housing, try The Cliffs, near Ridgedale, 952-545-2500.

Settle anywhere in Minnetonka and you won't be far from a playground or park. Among the city's many sport and recreation amenities are **Shady Oak Lake's** swimming beach, which boasts a zero depth water play area and canoe and paddle-boat rentals; **Minnetonka Ice Arena**, which offers public skating, lessons and competitive adult hockey leagues; and two city-owned sports and fitness clubs for residents. Though there are many parks, **Purgatory Park** off Excelsior Boulevard, is particularly good for walking the dog.

Minnetonka is served by three school districts. Minnetonka School District #276, which serves most of the city, emphasizes both academics and athletics, and is believed by many to be particularly good for high-achievers. Children in the northernmost sections attend Wayzata District #284 (see **Wayzata** section of this chapter), and neighborhoods east of I-494 (more or less) are in the Hopkins #270 school district. Hopkins is the district believed by many to be the best in the state for its music program, and it is highly regarded for its warm interaction with students and parents alike. If you are moving here with children who are already in school, Hopkins and Wayzata have excellent reputations for integrating new students, especially teenagers, into the school community. If you fall in love with a house that is not in your preferred school district, you do have an alternative besides private school; it's called "popping" (Parent Option Plan) to a district outside of where you live. Both school districts have to agree to the plan, but many people have done it and have been happy with the results. Call the State Department of Children, Families and Learning for more information, 651-582-8701.

Major international employers such as Cargill, Carlson Companies, Fingerhut and General Mills, and the massive Ridgedale shopping area, as well as numerous smaller businesses provide white-collar jobs. In fact, Minnetonka's labor force grew by nearly 30% in the 1990s. The Metropolitan Council predicts that the job growth will continue, forecasting that Minnetonka will be among the top three cities in the state with respect to job creation, well into the 21st Century.

Web Site: www.ci.minnetonka.mn.us

Area Code: 952

Zip Codes: 55305, 55343, 55345

Post Office: 14702 Excelsior Boulevard, 800-275-8777

City Hall: 14600 Minnetonka Boulevard, 952-939-8200

Police non-emergency (daytime): 952-939-8500

Fire non-emergency (daytime): 952-939-8595

Hospital: Methodist, 6500 Excelsior Boulevard, St. Louis Park, 952-993-5000, www.healthsystemminnesota.com

Library: 12601 Ridgedale Drive, 952-847-8800; 17524 Excelsior Boulevard, 952-949-4690; www.hennepin.lib.mn.us

Schools: Hopkins School District #270, 952-988-4000; Minnetonka School District #276, 952-470-3400; Wayzata School District #284, 952-745-5000

Community Publications: *Minnetonka, Lakeshore Weekly News,* 612-375-9222, www.weeklynews.com; *West Minnetonka/Deephaven Sun Sailor,* 952-829-0797, www.mnsun.com

Bus Transportation: bus service is built around commuter service and routes that connect at Ridgedale Shopping Center or the Plymouth Road Transit Center. For routes and schedules call the **MCTO**, 612-349-7000, or access www.metrotransit.org.

Minneapolis Route 12: Downtown Minneapolis, Excelsior Boulevard, St. Louis Park, **Methodist Hospital**, Hopkins, Opus II, Minnetonka, Glen Lake Area; **Minneapolis Route 63**: Downtown Minneapolis, Louisiana Avenue Transit Center, Minnetonka, Cedar Lake Road, County Road 73, Ridgedale Center; **Minneapolis Express Route 64**: Downtown Minneapolis, Excelsior Boulevard, St. Louis Park, Methodist Hospital, Hopkins; **Minneapolis Express Route 67**: Downtown Minneapolis, St. Louis Park, Minnetonka Boulevard, Knollwood Mall Area, Minnetonka; **Minneapolis Express Route 70**: Downtown Minneapolis, Louisiana Avenue Transit Center, Highway 7, Hopkins, Shorewood, Tonka Bay; **Express Route 71**: Downtown Minneapolis, Plymouth Road Transit Center, Minnetonka, Deephaven, Excelsior

HOPKINS

Boundaries: **North**: St. Louis Park and Minnetonka; **East**: St. Louis Park and Edina; **South**: Edina and Minnetonka; **West**: Minnetonka; area: 4 square miles

At one time Hopkins was the center of a thriving truck farming community, and while it still calls itself the Raspberry Capital and hosts the Raspberry Festival every July, it now grows industries. SuperValu foods, Honeywell, NAPCO International and Alliant Techsystems are major corporations with manufacturing and distribution facilities in Hopkins. The plants and the railroad tracks that serve them do not make for a beautiful city, yet Hopkins has some beautiful neighborhoods and the downtown is undergoing a revitalization program that is packing people in—for the arts, no less!

The recently built **Hopkins Center for the Arts**, 1111 Main Street, is home to **Stages Theatre Company**, 952-979-1111, www.stagestheatre.org, a wonderful training ground for young actors, as well as art galleries which showcase local artists and students. Across the street, a former car dealership is now everybody's favorite movie theater with several screens and $2 tickets ($1 on Tuesdays). Around this core, several restaurants have been added, and the accompanying throngs are bringing a tangible vibrancy and exuberance to Hopkins' streets.

The streets in downtown Hopkins, south of Highway 7, are laid out in grids and lined with small bungalows, apartments and townhomes, both rental and owner-occupied. Downtown amenities are typical: a library, city hall, post office, a public safety department, large bank/office complexes, and a large ball field. For ideas about how to update the simple Cape Cods and ramblers that line these streets, residents may purchase a copy of *Cape Cods and Ramblers: A Remodeling Planbook for Post WWII Houses* for $10 at the city hall.

If you are looking for a larger home, built on curving streets, look around the Oak Ridge Country Club north of Highway 7. **Drillane** is a 1960s development of well-maintained, custom-built brick ramblers and split-levels set on hilly, wooded lots. **Knollwood/Cottage Downs/Wilshire Walk**, across the street, is an immaculate upscale neighborhood of large distinctive houses with two- and three-car garages, arranged around central ponds.

On the north side of Oak Ridge golf course, off Minnetonka Boulevard and Hopkins Crossroads, the 1950s ramblers and Cape Cods of **Belgrove** sit at the ends of longish driveways on densely shaded large lots that curve along Minnnehaha Creek. Virtually all of the houses in this well-maintained neighborhood have been remodeled, with some newer homes mixed in. Another charming neighborhood, **Interlachen Park**, is on the east side of town, south of Excelsior Boulevard and east of the Blake School. Here you'll find modest well-kept ramblers and split-levels with two-car garages on grid-like streets close to Highway 7. And, as you travel deeper into this neighborhood that abuts Meadowbrook Golf Course and Interlachen Country Club, the area becomes heavily wooded with large brick and stucco two-story Tudors and colonials spread out beneath mature trees.

In addition to its varied and affordable housing, possibly the best thing going in Hopkins is good schools. The Blake School is an outstanding college-preparatory day school. Hopkins School District #270 serves the city of Hopkins, a large part of Minnetonka, about half of Golden Valley, and portions of Edina, Eden Prairie, St. Louis Park, and Plymouth, with a total K-12 student population of about 9,000. Gatewood Elementary, which is actually in Minnetonka, was named an International Peace Site in 1994 and has been host to students from ten different countries. In 1992-93, one of Gatewood's fifth-grade teachers was named Minnesota Teacher of the Year. This district is known for its ability to work with children who have special needs and is enthusiastically recommended by parents who have transferred into it. (See **Child Care and Schools**.)

Hopkins is the trailhead for the Southwest LRT biking and hiking trail going west to Lake Minnetonka, Carver Park Reserve and Victoria or south to Chanhassen, Lake Riley and Chaska.

An affordable place to rent or buy a home and a convenient commute to Minneapolis, Hopkins is one of the few suburbs that offers a real, and now thriving downtown.

Area Code: 952

Zip Codes: 55305, 55343, 55345

Post Office: 9190 South First Street, 800-275-8777

City Hall: 1010 South First Street, 952-935-8474

Police/Fire non-emergency: 952-938-8885

Hospital: Methodist, 6500 Excelsior Boulevard, St. Louis Park, 952-993-5000, www.healthsystemminnesota.com

Library: 22 11th Avenue North, 952-930-2740; www.hennepin.lib.mn.us

School: Hopkins School District #270, 952-988-4000

Community Publication: *Hopkins/East Minnetonka Sun Sailor*, 952-829-0797, www.mnsun.com

Bus Transportation: for routes and schedules call the **MCTO**, 612-373-3333, or access metrotransit,org.

Minneapolis Express Route 70: Downtown Minneapolis, Louisiana Avenue Transit Center, Highway 7, Hopkins, Shorewood, Tonka Bay

EDEN PRAIRIE

Boundaries: **North**: 62 Crosstown; **East**: City of Bloomington, Town Line Road; **South**: Minnesota River; **West**: Chanhassen at Chanhassen Road and Dell Road; area: 36 square-miles

Plan: what one intends to do or achieve ... In 1968, when Eden Prairie consisted of a few streets of houses off Highway 5 and County Road 4, with working farms nearly everywhere else, committees of city residents drafted the Eden Prairie Comprehensive Guide which planned Eden Prairie's future development and committed it to a balance of business, parks, homes and shopping facilities. It was just in time. People flocked to the rolling farm fields and cow pasture lakes of this southwestern Hennepin County suburb, and Eden Prairie soon became the most rapidly growing city in Minnesota. It stayed at the top for ten straight years from 1980 to 1990.

Home to the Minnesota Vikings, many corporations and several upscale neighborhoods, Eden Prairie's commitment to balance includes development of life cycle and affordable housing. (Life cycle housing is housing that meets people's needs through all the different stages of life.) One of Eden Prairie's goals is to have 25% rental housing stock by the year 2010, and a total of 43% multiple family housing. Much of Eden Prairie's residential development has occurred in several Planned Unit Developments (PUDs), with many of the most affordable rental and multi-housing units located in southeast Eden Prairie in the **Preserve**, a 1970s development that includes a commercial area as well as single-family homes, town homes, condominiums and apartments. Nearby recreational amenities include a natural swimming pool, tennis courts, trails, and a community center and library. The **Edenvale** PUD in the north-central section of the city incorporates residential, commercial and industrial uses. With a population of 5,500, Edenvale includes a golf course, trails and parks. Other PUDs are **Bluffs East** and **West** in the southeast corner of the city, **Hidden Glen** in the northwest corner, **Red Rock Ranch** on the southeast shore of Red Rock Lake, and **Fairfield** in the southwest. **Bearpath**, the newest Eden Prairie development is an exclusive gated, golf-course community. A stunning piece of property, with a cranberry bog, ponds and lakes, Bearpath has expensive single-family homes as well as maintenance-free golf villas, twinhomes and townhomes.

Several apartment complexes are located near Eden Prairie Center. For descriptions, rental rates and telephone numbers of the large rental complexes, check out www.ci.eden-prairie.mn.us/rentalcomm on the city's helpful web page or call the city hall. They can also help you with housing issues or landlord problems (see number below).

Eden Prairie, with its social conscience and practical attitude, also provides chore and maintenance services to seniors, and at the other end of the age range, the city, together with the school district, local volunteers, and a variety of agencies, participates in Project Hope. This group effort pairs young, single-parent families with mentors who help them work toward achieving economic self-sufficiency by completing school and finding steady employment.

With little open land left for development, and a population right around 65,000, Eden Prairie's growth is slowing. But this is not just a Twin Cities' bedroom community like many of the other suburbs; it is home to over 1,500 businesses including Eaton Corporation and GE Capital. The carefully planned mix of commercial and residential property is starting to pay off as the city expects to be a metro area leader in employment growth well into this millennium.

To meet the transportation needs of its workforce, Eden Prairie has joined with Chaska and Chanhassen to develop Southwest MetroTransit, a system that offers express commuting for those who work in Minneapolis as well as reverse commuting that brings workers out from the Twin Cities to area jobs. (See **Transportation** section below.)

To serve its high proportion of young families, Eden Prairie offers many resources. Eden Prairie School District #272 serves most of the city, although some areas along the northern edge are in the Minnetonka or Hopkins school districts. District #272 has pioneered innovative programs including the "Freshman Academy" to help students transition into the high school, and they offer a separate school for kindergarten students. Eden Prairie youth athletics are supervised by parent volunteers, and include baseball, basketball, volleyball, hockey, soccer, swimming and more. The **Community Resource Center,** 8080 Mitchell Road, 952-975-0444, was established to connect families and individuals with education, counseling, recreation, health care, housing, employment, transportation, and day care services, volunteer opportunities and much more.

A recent city survey showed that 70% of Eden Prairie's families have access to the internet, so much of the city's communication with residents is delivered via the city's web page, www.ci.eden-prairie.mn.us.

Because of Eden Prairie's commitment to affordable, high-density housing, the city has retained more than 10,000 acres of parks, public right-of-way and open space. A community sports complex with hockey and skating rinks, as well as beaches, fishing piers, community gardens, and paved bike trails are among the many amenities the city offers. Also available to Eden Prairie residents, an antique lodge conference center set in a nature preserve on the shore of Starring Lake.

Agriculture, Eden Prairie's link to the past, is still practiced here but on a very limited basis and mostly along the Minnesota River or in the southwestern corner of the city. Woodbear Stable on Eden Prairie Road still has horses and room to ride them; you'll find a seasonal roadside produce stand on the corner of Eden Prairie Road and Pioneer Trail; and Halla Nursery still operates on Highway 101. But these are mere remnants of the city's not-so-distant agricultural past. In many ways, the highway is king now. Girded by I-494, highways 169 and 212, and Highway 5, the arteries that caused Eden Prairie's wildfire growth are now giving rise to Eden Prairie's most serious problem yet—traffic congestion.

Web Site: www.ci.eden-prairie.mn.us

Area Code: 952

Zip Codes: 55343, 55344

Post Offices: 8725 Columbine Road; Little Red gas section, County Road 4 at Duck Lake Trail; Jerry's New Market, 9589 Anderson Lakes Parkway

City Hall, 8080 Mitchell Road, 952-949-8300, TDD 952-949-8399, 24-Hour Prairie Line, 612-949-8561

Police non-emergency: 952-949-6200

Fire non-emergency: 952- 949-8361

Hospital: Fairview Southdale, 6401 France Avenue, 952-924-5000, www.fairview.org

Library: Hennepin County Library, 479 Prairie Center Drive, 952-829-5460, www.hennepin.lib.mn.us

School: District #272, Eden Prairie Schools, 8100 School Road, Eden Prairie, Minnesota 55344, 952-975-7000, www.edenpr.k12.mn.us

Community Publication: *Eden Prairie News*, 952-934-5045, www.edenprairienews.com; *Eden Prairie Sun Current*, 952-829-0797, www.mnsun.com

Bus Transportation: the Southwest Station is at the southwest intersection of Highway 5 and Prairie Center Drive; parking lot access is from Technology Drive. For the latest information, call SW Metro Transit at 952-949-2BUS. For complete bus schedules call the **MCTO** at 612-349-7000 or visit www.metrocouncil.org and go to Southwest Metro Transit. You can buy a bus pass electronically on this site by charging it to your credit card.

Airport Park and Fly Service: hourly service is provided daily, 6:30 a.m. to 8:30 p.m., from Southwest Station in Eden Prairie to Minneapolis/St. Paul International Airport; 24-hour advance reservations are required for service to the airport, 952-827-7777. Parking at SW Station is free. Pick-up times are scheduled at 30 minutes past the hour with arrival at the airport at 10 minutes past the hour. Cost is $15 per person with advance purchase of tickets at Southwest Station. The cost is $17 when tickets are purchased from the driver. Tickets can be purchased at Southwest Station during regular business hours 5:30 a.m. to 6:30 p.m. Catch the return shuttle at the airport's Ground Transportation Center, one level below baggage claim. Shuttles depart every 30 minutes daily 6:00 a.m. to 10:00 p.m. from the Scheduled Shuttle/Hotel Shuttle loading area. Tickets may be purchased at the Express Shuttle USA desk or directly from the driver.

Vanpools to St. Paul: Service to downtown St. Paul and the Capital area, Monday-Friday, from Southwest Station in Eden Prairie costs $2.86 per day. Call 952-974-3102.

Service to Mall of America and the Airport: buses run approximately every ninety-minutes, daily, to and from the Mall of America and Airport from Southwest Station. The bus stop at the Mall of America is located at the lower level on the east side at Gate 2. The bus stop at the airport is located on the upper level roadway, adjacent to the parking lot.

Dial-A-Ride Service: the bus can pick you up in the front of your building and take you anywhere in Eden Prairie, Chanhassen, and Chaska, Monday-Friday 6:00 a.m. to 7:00 p.m. and Saturday, 9:00 a.m. to 5:30 p.m. Reservations are required, 952-949-2BUS.

Connecting Service to Popular Destinations: Dial-A-Ride can connect customers at Southwest Station in Eden Prairie to: Southdale, Downtown Minneapolis, Mall of America, Minneapolis/St. Paul International Airport.

Service to Southdale & Minneapolis: hourly midday service to/from Southdale and downtown Minneapolis from Southwest Station, Monday-Friday. At Southdale, the bus stops at the lower level entrance at Carousel Lane. In downtown, the bus drops off passengers along 2nd Avenue and picks up passengers along Marquette Avenue.

Commuter Service to Minneapolis and Reverse Commuter Service: SouthWest MetroTransit provides express service to commuters going into Minneapolis to work or coming out to Eden Prairie/Chanhassen/Chaska to work, and evening returns.

ST. LOUIS PARK

Boundaries: **North**: Interstate 394; **East**: Minneapolis at France Avenue; **South**: Edina and Hopkins; **West**: Highway 169 and Hopkins; area: 7,000 acres

The spirit of St. Louis Park is ecumenical in every way. The residents, businesses and neighborhoods are diverse: Jewish school, Catholic school, and Indian restaurants. In 1990 the local library added a Russian language collection to assist the new Russian families being brought into the community by local synagogues.

Fully-developed, St. Louis Park only added 1,000 residents between 1980 and 1998. In recent years it has issued twice as many commercial building permits as residential. With a high proportion of single-family and multi-family rental units, the median rent is on the low side for the Twin Cities' market. Still, the range of housing is probably the most diverse in the Twin Cities. Low-cost, modest 1940s ramblers and 1-1/2-story expansions built for the soldiers coming home from World War II can be found in many areas, in addition to the expensive homes along Minnehaha Creek and the golf courses. Custom-built homes from the 1950s along Minnehaha Creek in the western end of town were sited to take advantage of creek views. A green-way running alongside the creek is ideal for walking. Garages here are double, but many will not accommodate two of today's large vans or sport utility vehicles.

North of Cedar Lake Road, **Westwood Hills** is a 1960s and newer development of executive homes adjacent to the **Minneapolis Golf Club** and **Westwood Hills Nature Center**, a great place to walk your dog or bike through woods. Bird watching is possible near the marsh. On the east side of St. Louis Park's other golf course, **Meadowbrook**, you will find smaller single-story and 1-1/2 story wood and brick houses circa 1950 situated on hilly, heavily wooded lots.

East of Highway 100, **Minikahda Vista**, in the southeast corner of town, borders yet another golf course, the Minikahda Club, which is actually in Minneapolis. Houses here were built in the 1920s and '30s, about the same time as neighboring Linden Hills in Minneapolis. Though this is one of St. Louis Park's oldest neighborhoods, it is one of the most desirable for those looking for houses with character. Large brick and stone two-story Tudors, with three-season porches and fireplaces, sit on gently rolling lawns and quietly appreciate. In the tight market of 1999, a majority of the homes for sale here sold at or above their asking prices, with those closest to Edina fetching the most.

One of the most interesting housing options in St. Louis Park is the **Monterey Co-Housing Community** at 2925 Monterey Avenue South, 952-930-7554, www.jimn.org/mococo. Located on 2 1/4 acres of woods and lawn, this collaborative community is home to 15 families or households who live in apartments in the Common House or townhouses on the grounds. The Common House includes a large living room, library/den, dining room, kitchen, and wood shop.

As a first-ring suburb, St. Louis Park's residents are closer to Minneapolis amenities like the Chain of Lakes than many Minneapolis residents, and shopping and health care are close by, as well. Miracle Mile shopping center and Methodist Hospital/Health System Minnesota, one of the country's largest multi-specialty clinics, are both on Excelsior Boulevard near Highway 100.

St. Louis Park's Recreation Center, which offers an ice arena and an aquatic park (among other things), is also located near Highway 100 at 3700 Monterey Drive. Tall water slides, body flumes, lap lanes, sand play areas (castles and volleyball), sundecks and locker rooms create a popular facility that is open to residents of St. Louis Park, Minnetonka and Golden Valley. Call 952-924-2567 for membership information. About 14% of the city is set aside for trails and open space. The **Cedar Lake Bike Trail** which parallels the Burlington Northern track features a pair of wide, paved, mostly flat one-way paths for biking and skating. The trail runs from downtown Minneapolis at Glenwood and 12th, through the Bryn Mawr neighborhood and ends in St. Louis Park at Highway 100.

There are several organizations that provide services to the Jewish community here, among them: the **Jewish Community Center-Greater Minneapolis**, 4330 Cedar Lake Road, 952-377-8330 and the **Jewish Newcomers-Shalom,** Minneapolis, 5901 Cedar Lake Road, 952-593-2600.

St. Louis Park is served by St. Louis Park School District #283 as well as by several private schools, including Minneapolis Jewish Day School, 4330 Cedar Lake Road, 952-374-5650, a K-6 elementary school; and Benilde-St. Margaret's, a (7-12) Catholic junior high and high school, 2501 South Highway 100, 952-927-4176.

Major employers in St. Louis Park include: Health System Minnesota, Travelers Express, St. Louis Park Public Schools, Sandoz Nutrition and Musicland Group. Bus transport is easy from the Louisiana Avenue Transit Station to downtown Minneapolis, and there are many routes that run through Knollwood Shopping Center, Methodist Hospital, or along Minnetonka Boulevard and Excelsior Boulevard as well.

Finally, no description of St. Louis Park would be complete without mentioning its landmark, the 100 year-old concrete "smokestack" on Highway 7, near Nordic Ware, that is actually the nation's first concrete grain elevator.

Web Site: www.stlouispark.org

Area Codes: 952

Zip Codes: 55426, 55416

Post Office: 2700 Louisiana Avenue South, 800-275-8777

City Hall: 5005 Minnetonka Boulevard, 952-924-2500

Police/Fire non-emergency: 952-924-2618

Hospital: Methodist, 6500 Excelsior Boulevard, St. Louis Park, 952-993-5000, www.healthsystemminnesota.com

Library: 3240 Library Lane, 952-929-8108; www.hennepin.lib.mn.us

School: St Louis Park District #283, 952-928-6790, www.stlpark.k12.mn.us

Community Publication: *St. Louis Park Sun Sailor*, 952-829-0797, www.mnsun.com

Bus Transportation: numerous routes run through St. Louis Park. For routes and schedules call the **MCTO**, 612-373-3333, or access www.metrotransit.org

LAKE MINNETONKA COMMUNITIES

WAYZATA
ORONO, MAPLE PLAIN, MEDINA, LONG LAKE
DEEPHAVEN, WOODLAND
EXCELSIOR, GREENWOOD, SHOREWOOD
MOUND
PLYMOUTH
MAPLE GROVE

Lake Minnetonka, (the "Big Water" in the native Dakota language) is located twenty miles west of Minneapolis. It has 110 miles of shoreline and was inhabited by Native American tribes for millennia before the lake was "discovered" by soldiers from Fort Snelling in about 1820. Ancient Indian burial mounds are visible in several places, particularly along the north shoreline off Highway 15. Wayzata has a street named Indian Mound, that probably is built on top of an Indian mound, as is the city of Mound.

The late 1800s were boom years for Lake Minnetonka. Rail lines reached Wayzata in 1867 bringing visitors from all over the country. To accommodate the sightseers, grand hotels were built in Wayzata, Deephaven, Excelsior, Minnetonka Beach and Tonka Bay. According to a tourist brochure, they boasted "long luxurious porches with easy chairs" and "entrancing views (which) cast a Circes' spell over time." The summer visitors played tennis, sailed, and participated in amateur theatricals. Excelsior put on pageants, at what is now the Excelsior Commons, that featured galloping horses and wagons and included nearly every person and animal who lived in the village.

Turn of the century steamboats ferried visitors on tours of the lake; one, the City of Saint Louis was a 160 foot side-wheeler that is said to have carried 1,000 passengers. Excelsior had a casino overlooking the lake at the north end of Water Street, and Big Island was the site of an amusement park.

Within a quarter of a century, Lake Minnetonka was literally transformed from an Indian hunting ground into a fashionable tourist destination. Within another quarter of a century many of the resorts had burned down and the summer cottage era had begun.

Today, 100 years later, Lake Minnetonka is again a playground. Cruise boats offer tours of the lake. Excelsior has bed and breakfasts (see **Quick Getaways** chapter). Day-trippers visit the antique stores, dine at the many restaurants, and swim at the beaches. The lake provides world-class sailing, scuba diving, bass fishing, power-boating and water-skiing. In winter, ice several feet thick is safe for cross-country skiing, ice boating, ice fishing and snow-mobiling. A few people "swim" here even in winter—every January the Lung Association sponsors cold-water dipping, and a local diving club scuba dives beneath the ice.

Wayzata, Excelsior and Mound are the commercial centers for the surrounding bedroom communities of Orono, Minnetrista, Minnetonka Beach, Spring Park, Tonka Bay, Shorewood, Greenwood, Deephaven and Woodland. Long Lake, Medina and Maple Plain, three cities that do not have any lakeshore, are still included among the Lake Minnetonka communities, or spoken of collectively as "Wayzata." Extension of the metropolitan sewer line to Lake Minnetonka in the 1970s gave birth to a building boom that continues today. "The Lake" has become an extremely desirable place to live.

WAYZATA

Boundaries: **North**: Plymouth, Medina; **East**: Minnetonka city limits; **South**: Lake Minnetonka; **West**: Orono city limits; area: 3.2 square miles

With wooded hills and Lake Minnetonka lapping at its doorsteps, Wayzata, pronounced "Y-zeta," (it's a Sioux word meaning "north shore") satisfies people's desire to get away from it all, while still living only a 20-minute commute from the Twin Cities.

The city of Wayzata has 4,000 residents and is located 12 miles west of Minneapolis, at the northeast end of Lake Minnetonka. But, when people refer to Wayzata, they are usually talking about the general area of Wayzata: Orono, Long Lake, Maple Plain, Medina, Minnetonka Beach, Deephaven and Woodland. This entire area is known among Realtors as a "transferee area" because so many corporate families whose jobs move them to Minneapolis choose to live here.

In the 1800s, the railroad was key to the growth of the area. It carried well-to-do passengers daily between Minneapolis and Wayzata, linking them with The Lady of the Lake and other streetcar boats, which transported them farther to their weekend retreats and grand hotels. Today, the Minnehaha, a restored streetcar boat, picks up passengers at the Wayzata Depot and takes them across the lake to Excelsior, five miles away, May to September. The railroad, which is active, is still a factor in life here. The train depot, built on Lake Street in 1906, is home to the Historical Society, and outdoor concerts for boaters and picnickers take place here on Wednesday nights in the summer.

Though the resort era ended in the late 1800s, its legacy continues as I-394 brings tourists out to Wayzata's dense selection of classy shops, restaurants and recreation amenities. In particular, Wayzata's antique stores attract collectors from all over the country (see **Shopping for the Home**).

Though the Wayzata area has one of the highest average home sale prices in the Twin Cities, it does offer a full range of housing, including rentals. Expensive condominiums with commanding views, small homes, businesses and rental apartments are all to be found in the central business district that includes City Hall, the fire station, the library, post office, and St. Bartholomew Catholic Church and school. While not the prettiest, this part of town does have two things that are rare in the western suburbs—sidewalks and city water. Across Wayzata Boulevard, the northern half of this neighborhood offers tidy Cape Cods lining quiet streets in a neighborhood that is rapidly being gentrified by singles and young families. As it extends west and north this quarter becomes **North Ferndale/Far Hills**. Many of these spacious homes were built in the 1970s.

The east end of Wayzata is pricey, being on the lake, near the yacht club, but includes the **East Circle Drive** neighborhood which is one of the best bargains around. Here older Cape Cods and ramblers sit on small lots mixed with apartments. A few of them enjoy lake views without carrying the burden of lakeshore taxes. A number of young families and singles live here. The principal drawback is that this neighborhood is everybody's favorite shortcut, though stop signs on every block are helping to solve that problem. East of Highway 101, off McGinty Road, **Holdridge** and Minnetonka's **Gray's Landing** are known for their cul-de-sacs of recently built executives' homes, artistically dispersed around marshes and Gray's Bay, a part of Lake Minnetonka which offers powerboat, but not sailboat, access to the main lake.

Located at the west end of town is Wayzata's premier neighborhood, **Ferndale**. View this neighborhood from the lake, and you will see vast houses with manicured lawns sloping down to the water. Back from the lake, immaculately-tended architect-designed homes on the gently curving streets of Highcroft/Peavy Lane, look like they're dressed up to go to Grandmother's house for Sunday dinner. A number of families with children live here, adjacent to the Highcroft (Pre K-5) campus of the Blake Schools, a fine college- preparatory private school whose other campus is located in Hopkins. If it's sailing you love, Harrington Road has a perfect view of the regattas which are usually held off this shore. There is a variety of housing here, including some older, smaller homes.

Wayzata likes to think of itself as a city for all seasons, and its recreation possibilities mirror this attitude. The city maintains an extensive public beach and boat dock complex for residents at the west end of Lake Street and, in winter, plows fairways out on the ice for the **Chilly Open** golf tournament. Other public facilities include tennis courts and hockey rinks at the middle school; a tiny meditation park on Minnetonka Avenue across from the post office; and **Life Time Fitness Center/Plymouth Ice Center**, 612-509-5250, a pool/ice arena/fitness center actually located inside the city of Plymouth. This center is the unique product of a public-private partnership between the cities, the Wayzata school district, and a health club. Private recreation facilities include two country clubs on the edge of town and the **Wayzata Yacht Club**, 952-473-0352.

Minnesota's most exclusive country club, **Woodhill**, is tucked into lush wooded hills at the western edge of the city off Highway 15. It is surrounded by gracious country homes on large plots of land. This is the beginning of Minnesota's horse country, which extends to the north and west through Orono, Long Lake, Hamel, Maple Plain and Medina.

ORONO, MAPLE PLAIN, MEDINA, LONG LAKE

Orono (www.ci.orono.mn.us), west of Wayzata out highways 12 and 15; **Maple Plain**, out Highway 12; and **Medina**, off Highway 55, boast large estates, hobby farms and working farms. Orono has a vast amount of lakeshore frontage, with many 1980s and '90s developments of custom-built homes. While there is some industrial/commercial property and less expensive housing along the highways, most of the landscape is rolling and agricultural. But while the town of **Long Lake** just west of Wayzata Country Club, does have many smaller, older, more affordable houses in town, most of the area is very "silver spoon." The **Twin City Polo Club**, 763-479-4307, is here, as are **Norenberg Garden Park**, 612-559-6700, and the **Minnetonka Center for the Arts**, 952-473-7361, which has classes for adults and children.

DEEPHAVEN, WOODLAND

South of Wayzata, down Highway 101, Woodland, and **Deephaven** (area. 2.3 square miles), are quiet residential villages on the lower lake. Houses in these communities are large, set in grounds of one plus acres—that is, until you get to the neighborhoods of Groveland Assembly Ground in Woodland, and **Deephaven Park** and **Cottagewood** in Deephaven, which offer smaller houses built close together on lots originally staked-out for tent camping. One old house on Cottagewood Avenue has been featured in *Better Homes and Gardens* magazine, and you'll find the little red 1893 Cottagewood Store pictured on local Christmas cards. Recently some of the older, smaller homes have been torn down and replaced with contemporary houses complete with triple garages that have the effect of walling the lake views off from the street. The neighborhood of Deephaven Park, on St. Louis Bay, has fared better. Here the waterfront is used for tennis courts, a swimming beach and boat docks; and the field-stone foundations offer nostalgic glimpses of the past when a grand hotel and its surrounding summer cottages stood here. Other historic neighbor-hoods include **Walden**, **Chimo**, and **Northome/Cedarhurst**, where houses have been built on properties that used to be large estates. Off the lake, there are relatively more affordable neighborhoods: **Fairhomes** and the houses around St. Therese Church, at the north end of town, **Heathcote** in the middle and **Rosedale/Hooper Lake Road** at the south end. For those who live away from the lake, Deephaven has public docks and mooring buoys, but the waiting list is many years long.

Deephaven has long been the kind of place where you can start walk-ing in front of a mansion, but when you turn the corner you're in a lane where somebody is building a boat bigger than his little house, though, with the development that is occurring in both Deephaven and Woodland, those days may be coming to an end.

Deephaven is an outdoor kind of town. Boats bob on Carson's and St. Louis bays and the Minnetonka Yacht Club's fine sailors are world famous. Recreation facilities include four sets of tennis courts, a paddleball court, three main swimming beaches, three parks, hockey rinks, baseball diamonds and the Southwest LRT (hiking, biking and ski) Trail. Deephaven has sewer, but not city water, consequently it only has a small commercial area along Minnetonka Boulevard near Highway 101.

Tiny **Woodland** (area, .8 square miles), has no businesses; no commercial property; no sidewalks; and, except for the closely-packed, modest **Groveland Assembly Ground** near Highway 101, no sewer or water. It is one of the smallest municipalities in the Twin Cities, with 190 houses sitting atop Breezy Point, a fist of land that juts out into the eastern end of the lake. People here vote at someone's home and the mayor usually runs unopposed. Though quaint would not be the adjective to describe this small town—Sunday gawkers head here to look at the multi-million-dollar estates, including a medieval re-creation and the Norwegian consulate.

Families with school age children are drawn to this area by more than the desire to live at a good address—Wayzata School District #284 gets five stars from parents for its academic and sports programs, and for how well it succeeds at integrating new students. Nearby Orono School District #278 is small and personal with an excellent music program, and Minnetonka School District #276 has a reputation for working well with gifted students. (See **Child Care and Schools**.)

For those who are interested in local history, resident Ellen Wilson Meyer has written three books about Lake Minnetonka: *Happenings Around Deephaven, Happenings Around Wayzata,* and *Happenings Around Excelsior;* and the Excelsior-Lake Minnetonka Historical Society has published *Picturesque Lake Minnetonka* which features nostalgic glimpses of the good old days.

WAYZATA

Web Site: www.wayzata.org

Area Code: 952

Zip Codes: 55331, 55357, 55359, 55391

Post Offices: 229 Minnetonka Avenue South, Wayzata, 952-473-4253; located in the Coffee 101 shop, 17623 Minnetonka Boulevard, Deephaven, 952-404-1868

Wayzata City Hall: 600 Rice Street, 952-473-0234

Police non-emergency: 925-404-5340

Fire non-emergency: 925-473-0234

Hospital: Methodist, 6500 Excelsior Boulevard, 952-993-5000, www.healthsystemminnesosta.com

Library: 620 Rice Street, 952-475-4690; www.hennepin.lib.mn.us

School: Wayzata #284, 952-745-5000; Orono #278, 952-449-8300

Community Publication: *Wayzata/Orono/Plymouth/Long Lake Sun Sailor*, 952-829-0797, www.mnsun.com

Motor Vehicle License: 952-404-5320

DEEPHAVEN, WOODLAND

Web Site: www.cityofdeephaven.org

Area Code: 952

Zip Codes: 55331, 55391

Post Offices: 229 Minnetonka Avenue South, Wayzata, 800-275-8777; located in the Coffee 101 shop, 17623 Minnetonka Boulevard, Deephaven, 952-404-1868; 545 First Street, Excelsior and 7730 Laredo Drive, Chanhassen, 800-275-8777

Deephaven/Woodland City Hall: 20225 Cottagewood Road, Deephaven, 952-474-4755

Police non-emergency: 952-474-7555

Fire non-emergency: 952-474-3261

Library: 341 2nd Street, Excelsior, 952-474-8760; 620 Rice Street, Wayzata, 952-475-4690; www.hennepin.lib.mn.us

School: Minnetonka School District #276, 952-470-3400

Community Publication: *Deephaven Sun Sailor*, 952-829-0797, www.mnsun.com

Bus Transportation: For routes and schedules call the **MCTO**, 612-373-3333, www.metrotransit.org. Number 75 buses run several times a day to Minneapolis. Number 74 buses provide commuter service, morning and evening rush hours, non-stop to downtown Minneapolis, in 19 minutes. The **Park & Ride** lot is located at Wayzata Boulevard at Barry Avenue. They start leaving Wayzata at 6:45 a.m. and begin returning about 4:30 p.m. The **Wayzata Trolley** provides free service departing from The Depot (on Lake Street) and circulating through the commercial district. The trolley does not operate in the winter.

EXCELSIOR, GREENWOOD, SHOREWOOD

Boundaries: *Excelsior*: **North**: Lake Minnetonka; **East**: Shorewood and Greenwood; **South**: Shorewood; **West**: Shorewood; area: 1 square mile; *Greenwood*: **North**: Shorewood and Deephaven; **East**: Shorewood; **South**; Shorewood and Excelsior; **West**: Excelsior and Lake Minnetonka; *Shorewood*: **North**: Deephaven, Greenwood, Excelsior, Tonka Bay, Lake Minnetonka; **East**: Minnetonka, Deephaven; **South**: Chanhassen, Victoria; **West**: Minnetrista

Excelsior is a quaint and enchanting enclave. In fact, Excelsior is so aesthetically appealing that many artists and writers have made it their home, including the world famous fresco artist Mark Balma.

It wasn't always so cute. It languished residentially, as just another running-down village with a glorious past, until the 1990s when a local woman started renovating the old houses and painting them pink. That got everybody going, and now the center of Excelsior boasts a mix of mostly small, cottagey houses, many of which have been supplied with new craftsman details. The rehabilitation efforts are paying off for anybody who wants to sell their Excelsior home, but not many do. The city's many long-time residents feel a great deal of affection for their town. They stay for generations and make a point of shopping locally in the pedestrian-friendly business district.

Like many other lake communities, Excelsior's first success came as a resort town in the 1800s, and unlike most other lake communities, many of Excelsior's homes and apartments are affordable. About half the city's residential units are rental apartments. Senior citizens, particularly, live in apartments in the town proper; but there are large complexes on the other side of Highway 7. Also south of Highway 7 you'll find smaller 1970s brick ramblers and two-story frame houses built in the vicinity of Galpin Lake and St. John the Baptist Catholic Church.

Recreation here revolves around the Commons, or village green. It has a swimming beach, children's playground, tennis courts, tour boats, the city docks and a high promontory from which one can see to Wayzata, five miles away. (For more information about Excelsior see **Quick Getaways**.)

Excelsior is abutted on the east by .3 square mile **Greenwood**. Most of the houses in Greenwood are on the lake, either circling St. Alban's Bay or on a short strip of shoreline on the main lake that is oriented toward the west, offering beautiful sunsets. Some winterized summer cottages remain, but expensive new houses are replacing many. Much of Greenwood is characterized by small lots and houses set very close together. You will find recently-built large two-story houses set farther apart on lots with lake views along Lyman Boulevard. The **Old Log Theater**, 952-474-5951, is the heart of the village, offering hilarious British comedies and serving as the neighborhood meeting place. For recreation, Greenwood has one small park on Meadville Street, which has a playground and tennis court. The Southwest LRT trail passes through the village, paralleling the lake. Greenwood contracts with Deephaven (see above) for a city clerk and police protection, and contracts with the Excelsior Volunteer Fire Department for fire protection.

Shorewood is an entirely different kind of place. Big, sprawling and comprised of all the land no other city wanted in the rush to incorporate during the 1950s, it stretches for six miles along parts of both sides of Highway 7 going west from Minnetonka to Minnetrista. Shorewood has a lengthy stretch of lakeshore and includes three islands, **Spray**, **Enchanted,** and **Shady Island,** which can only be reached from the north side of the lake. Homes in Shorewood range from moderately priced to very expensive. Three of the upscale neighborhoods are **Christmas Lake**, south of Highway 7, on the east end of Shorewood, **Boulder Bridge** on Lake Minnetonka in the west, and **Waterford**, south of Highway 7 at Old Market Road near Christmas Lake. Built in the 1980s, Waterford offers executive-level two-story homes and has its own city water system. (Only about one-third of Shorewood has city water; all has sewer.) Going west out Highway 7, there are more moderately priced neighborhoods of much smaller houses, circa 1970, with much bigger yards, built around Lake Minnewashta to the south, and Minnewashta Elementary school to the north.

Shorewood residents use Excelsior's "downtown" as their own, but there are four strip malls and service areas within Shorewood: Highway 7 near Vine Hill, Highway 7 at Highway 41, and on Highway 19 going toward Navarre. Incorporated in the 1960s, Shorewood was able to make joint power agreements with the surrounding cities and shares many services including South Lake Minnetonka Police and the Excelsior Fire Department. There are five parks in Shorewood, offering playgrounds, tennis courts, ball fields and ice-skating. It is also situated along the Southwest LRT trail.

Shorewood is the one city around the lake that has open land, and has expressed an interest in providing new affordable and life cycle housing (housing for people through all the different stages of their lives). Unfortunately, with land prices skyrocketing and a dearth of public transportation and public support, it has only been moderately successful.

"Not in my backyard" is a popular refrain here. It's been difficult to convince residents to give up the protection of low-density zoning. It does make for interesting council meetings.

Major employers are Northern States Power Company and the Minnetonka Country Club.

Web Sites: www.excelsioronline.com, www.ci.shorewood.mn.us

Area Code: 952

Zip Code: 55331

Post Offices: 7730 Laredo Drive, Chanhassen; 545 1st Street Excelsior, 800-275-8777

Excelsior City Hall: 339 3rd Street, 952-474-5233,

Greenwood City Hall: 20225 Cottagewood Road, Deephaven, 952-474-4755

Shorewood City Hall: 5755 Country Club Road, Shorewood, 952,474-3236,

Police/Fire non-emergency: South Lake Minnetonka Public Safety, 952-474-3261

Hospital: Methodist, 6500 Excelsior Boulevard, 952-993-5000, www.healthsystemminnesota.com

Library: 343 Third Street, Excelsior, 952-474-8760, www.hennepin.lib.mn.us

School: Minnetonka School District #276, 952-470-3400

Community Publication: *Excelsior/Shorewood/Chanhassen Sun Sailor*, 952-829-0797, www.mnsun.com

Bus Transportation: For routes and schedules call the **MCTO**, 612-373-3333, www.metrotransit.org. **Minneapolis Express Route 70**: Downtown Minneapolis, Louisiana Avenue Transit Center, Highway 7, Hopkins, Shorewood, Tonka Bay; **Minneapolis Express Route 71**: Downtown Minneapolis, Plymouth Road Transit Center, Minnetonka, Deephaven, Excelsior

MOUND

Boundaries: **North**: Minnetrista; **East**: Spring Park; **South**: Lake Minnetonka; **West**: Minnetrista; area: 4 square miles

Mound, located at the west end of Lake Minnetonka, about ten miles west of Wayzata on Highway 15, covers approximately 17 miles of shoreline around Cook's Bay in Upper Lake Minnetonka. Named for the ancient Indian mounds that are located within the city limits, Mound was also a turn of the century resort destination with three fine hotels, including Hotel Buena Vista. Today Mound has a large commercial area and feels more like a working city than either Wayzata or Excelsior. Generally speaking, this end of the lake is far more affordable than the east end, but the commute to the Twin Cities on two-lane Highway 15 is a killer. Housing in Mound generally consists of single-family homes, but there are some apartments. While some turn-of-the-century lake cabins have been modernized, many of Mound's homes were built during the housing boom of the 1970s.

Web Site: www.cityofmound.com

Area Code: 952

Zip Code: 55364

Post Office: 5501 Shoreline Drive, 800-275-8777

City Hall: 5341 Maywood Road, 952-472-0600

Police non-emergency: 952-472-0621

Fire non-emergency: 952-472-0600

Hospital: Waconia Ridgeview Medical Center, 500 South Maple Street, Waconia, 952-442-2191, www.ridgeviewmedical.org

Library: 2079 Commerce Boulevard, 952-473-4105

School: Westonka District #277, 952-491-8000

Community Publication: *Mound, The Laker*, 952-472-1140

Bus Transportation: For routes and schedules call the **MCTO**, 612-373-3333, www.metrotransit.org.

Express Route 75: Downtown Minneapolis, Louisiana Avenue Transit Center, I-394 & County Road 73 Park & Ride, Ridgedale, Long Lake, Mound; Route 78: Mound, Spring Park

PLYMOUTH

Boundaries: **North**: Maple Grove; **East**: Highway 169; **South**: Ridgemont Avenue, Luce Line Hiking and Biking Trail; **West**: Ferndale Road/Brockton Lane; area: 36 square miles

Plymouth, 10 miles northwest of Minneapolis, maintained its rural character well into the 1970s, much longer than most Twin Cities suburbs, though today agriculture is a thing of the past. With a diverse economic base and a population of over 62,000, Plymouth supplies the Twin Cities with more than 48,000 jobs. Interstate-494, highways 169 and 55, and county roads 6 and 9, run through the city, making it attractive to corporations. Major industries include manufacturing and distributing, printing, telecommunications and computer related industries. Major shopping is minutes away at Ridgedale.

Plymouth's stated goal is to provide its residents with a strong economic base, preserve the natural environment, and foster respect for individuals. Resources have been committed to preserving open space, and the city now has 70 miles of trails and about 40 parks, ranging from small neighborhood playgrounds to the large community playing fields by Parker's Lake. Year-round recreation programs for all ages have something for everyone, from ballroom dance to community garden plots to rock climbing. The **Plymouth Life Time Recreation Center**, 763-509-0909, includes an ice arena, pool complex and fitness center. **Plymouth Creek Center**, 763-509-5280, on 34th Avenue between Plymouth Boulevard and Fernbrook Lane, has an inflatable dome field house, a walking-jogging track and a ballroom.

The city works hard to make this a supportive environment for all ages. McGruff Trucks, driven by public works and park maintenance workers, offer safe havens for children who find themselves in need of assistance. The police department sells bike helmets at cost and the fire department sends their fire engines into the parks to do safety education. For seniors, Plymouth Towne Square has 97 units with subsidized rent for low-income residents. For first time home buyers, Plymouth participates in programs offered by the Minnesota Housing Finance Agency, 763-509-5413.

Plymouth has been involved in a planned development process since 1973, which has created pockets of industrial/commercial development along main roads, and a wide range of available housing, both owner-occupied and rental. The neighborhoods of **Alterra** and **Pintail** off Vicksburg Lane are townhome areas; **Fox Run** between Vicksburg and

and Dunkirk contains recently built, two-story wood and brick, single-family houses with triple garages. Older neighborhoods contain a mix of ramblers, bungalows, 1970s split-levels, and two-story houses with double garages—these on more rolling and wooded lots than new developments. Many of the new neighborhoods look like gated communities—without the gate.

The city's newsletter, *The Plymouth News*, and the "City Recreation Booklet" are mailed to all residents and businesses, keeping them informed of upcoming events and elections. Cable Channel 37 broadcasts city announcements and provides gavel-to-gavel coverage of city council and Planning Commission meetings. Cable 12 News also covers local government. Local cable service is being upgraded in order to provide more channel choices, better reception and two-way high speed internet access and digital telephone service.

People like to live in Plymouth. It's safe. It has many resources for families, and most day to day necessities and services are available only a few minutes' drive away. It seems surprising, then, that it does not have is its own schools. Instead, it is served by four highly-regarded school districts: Wayzata #284, Robbinsdale #281, Osseo #279, and Hopkins #270 (see **Child Care and Schools**).

Web Site: www.ci.plymouth.mn.us

Area Code: 763

Zip Codes: 55446, 55447

Post Office: 3300 Plymouth Boulevard, 800-275-8777

City Hall: 3400 Plymouth Boulevard, 763-509-5000

Police/Fire non-emergency: Plymouth Public Safety Bldg., 3400 Plymouth Boulevard, 763-509-5000

Hospital: North Memorial, 3300 Oakdale Avenue North, 763-520-5200, www.northmemorial.com

Library: 15700 36th Avenue North, 763-551-6000

Schools: Wayzata #284, 952-745-5000; Robbinsdale #281, 763-504-8000; Osseo #279, 763-391-7000; Hopkins #270, 952-988-4000

Community Publication: *Plymouth News*

Bus Transportation: **Dial-A-Ride** is a shared, curb-to-curb transit service operated for Plymouth residents and visitors on a will-call basis. Transportation is provided throughout the Plymouth area and to Ridgedale Shopping Center, the Golden Valley Center, New Hope K-Mart and the Wayzata Bay Center. Connections can be made to downtown Minneapolis and other metro locations at Ridgedale. Rides can be reserved between 8 a.m. and 5 p.m. Monday-Friday, call 763-559-5057. Give the day, time, and place you need to go. Standing orders can also be registered for repetitive trips. The cost is $2 for each one-way ride, or $1.50 if the ride is reserved at least 24 hours in advance. Dial-A-Ride's operating hours are Monday-Friday from 6 a.m. to 10 p.m. and Saturdays from 9 a.m. to 5 p.m. If it is necessary to cancel a ride, call 763-509-5519 as soon as possible to free the service for another passenger. For information on connecting with other Metro Transit services, call 612-373-3333.

Express Route 75: Downtown Minneapolis, Louisiana Avenue Transit Center, I-394 and County Road 73 Park & Ride, Ridgedale, Long Lake, Mound; **Route 91AB**: Plymouth Road Transit Center, Dunkirk Land, Vicksburg Lane, Xenium Lane; **Minneapolis Express Route 672**: Downtown Minneapolis, Plymouth Road Transit Center, Carlson Towers, Wayzata Transit Center; **Minneapolis Express Route 674**: Downtown Minneapolis, Wayzata, Long Lake, Orono; **Minneapolis Express Route 71**: Downtown Minneapolis, Plymouth Road Transit Center, Minnetonka, Deephaven, Excelsior

MAPLE GROVE

Boundaries: **North**: 109th Avenue North; **East**: Highway 169; **South**: 62nd Avenue North; **West**: Highway 101; area: 36 square miles

The steam shovels are digging in Maple Grove even as you read this book. The city is going from open land and half a dozen residential centers along I-494 to a real city with a new downtown and proposals for mixed-use developments, new industrial zones, a private school, office buildings and retail shopping centers. Practically every big Twin Cities developer was in Maple Grove during the summer of 1999 with a proposal. Many of the projects slated for land north of I-694 or west out I-94 going toward St. Cloud. Some redevelopment is also being suggested in the southern quarter of the city along I-494.

In 1950, Maple Grove's population was under 2,000. Twenty years later, the population was nearly 40,000 with most of the growth centered on Fish Lake, Eagle Lake, Rice Lake, Mud Lake, and I-494. By 1999 the population exceeded 50,000 and it isn't expected to quit until the population nearly doubles again by 2020, making Maple Grove one of, if not *the* fastest growing community in the metro area for the next 20 years. Additional fire stations, more schools and other city services are being planned to keep pace with residential and commercial development. In fact, Maple Grove is building itself a whole new downtown, complete with a library, retail shops, rental townhomes, a city hall with a public safety wing, and a regional mall. The new downtown, referred to as the Arbor Lakes Development, is located just north of interstates 94 and 694, in the Arbor Lakes gravel-mining area.

In addition to Maple Grove's civic construction, parents will find that children of all ages have been worked into the expansion equation. To that end, there is a **TrueRide Skate Park** for skateboarders and in-line skaters at the Community Center. The police department runs a 30-hour Police Academy for residents and students over age 16, which teaches how the police department operates and the realities of law enforcement. Volunteers who are at home during the day provide McGruff safe houses for children who find themselves in frightening situations. **Maple Grove Community Center**, 763-494-6200, offers child care, the Maple Maze indoor playground, meeting rooms, gymnasium, ice arena, indoor pool, senior center and teen center. The city operates a swimming beach at **Weaver Lake**, and there are two Hennepin County parks here that have trails, camping and swimming and picnic grounds. Call **Elm Creek Park Reserve** at 420-5511 or **Fish Lake Regional Park** at 420-3423 for information.

The community is served by two separate school districts. Osseo district #279 covers most of the Maple Grove area and serves almost 22,000 students, making it the fifth largest school district in Minnesota. Wayzata district #284 provides service to the southern one-eighth of the city. Information about Osseo's schools is broadcast on Cable Channel 40.

Major corporations at this writing include SciMed Life Systems, Norstan Communications, World Aerospace, Braun Medical, Gannett, REO Plastics and Tenant Corporation.

Web Site: www.ci.maple-grove.mn.us

Area Code: 763

Zip Codes: 55311, 55369

Post Offices: 13500 Grove Drive North, 800-275-8777

City Administration: 8001 Main Street, 763-494-6000

Police non-emergency: 763-494-6100

Fire non-emergency: 763-494-6080

Hospital: North Memorial, 3300 Oakdale Avenue North, 763-520-5200, www.northmemorial.com

Library: 8351 Elm Creek Boulevard, 763-420-8377, www.hennepin.lib.mn.us

Schools: Osseo Independent School District #279, 763-391-7000, www.osseo.k12.mn.us; Wayzata District #284, 952-476-3100, www.wayzata.k12.mn.us

Bus Transportation: **Maple Grove Transit**, 763-494-6010, operates white buses with a maple leaf logo that provide rush hour express service to and from downtown Minneapolis, Monday-Friday. You can catch a bus anywhere along its route by simply flagging it down. Bus routes are marked with directional signs. One-way express service costs $2.00; discount tickets are available. Bus schedules are available at City Hall, Cub Foods and the Hennepin County Service Center.

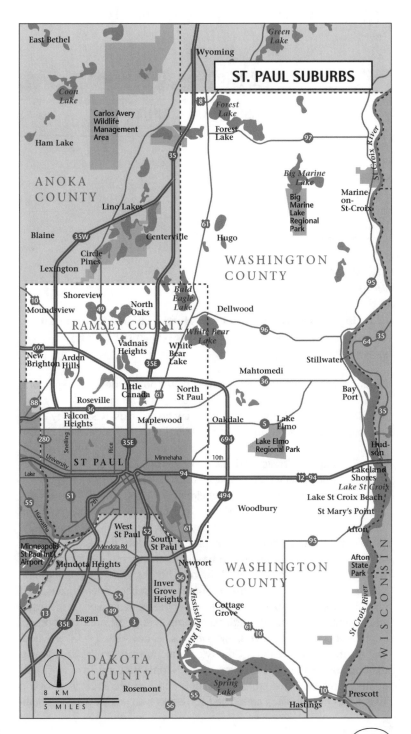

ST. PAUL SUBURBS

East Bethel

Wyoming

Green Lake

Coon Lake

Carlos Avery Wildlife Management Area

Forest Lake

Forest Lake

97

St Croix River

Ham Lake

35

ANOKA COUNTY

Big Marine Lake

Big Marine Lake Regional Park

Marine-on-St-Croix

Lino Lakes

Blaine

35W

Centerville

61

Hugo

WASHINGTON COUNTY

95

Lexington

Circle Pines

Shoreview

Bald Eagle Lake

Dellwood

96

64 35

10

Moundsview

49

North Oaks

White Bear Lake

RAMSEY COUNTY

Stillwater

New Brighton

694

Vadnais Heights

White Bear Lake

35E

Mahtomedi

36

Bay Port

35

Arden Hills

Little Canada

61

North St Paul

88

Roseville

36

Maplewood

Oakdale

5

Lake Elmo

Hud-son

Falcon Heights

280

Snelling

Rice

35E

694

Lake Elmo Regional Park

University

ST PAUL

Minnehaha

10th

94

Lakeland Shores

Lake

55

51

7th

494

12-94

Lake St Croix Beach

St Mary's Point

Lake St Croix

Hiawatha

Woodbury

Afton

West St Paul

52

South St Paul

61

Minneapolis-St Paul Int'l Airport

Mendota Rd

Mendota Heights

Newport

95

WASHINGTON COUNTY

Afton State Park

56

13

55

Inver Grove Heights

Mississippi River

35E

Eagan

149

3

Cottage Grove

61

10

St Croix River

WISCONSIN

N

DAKOTA COUNTY

Rosemont

Spring Lake

55

10

Prescott

8 KM

5 MILES

56

Hastings

115

ST. PAUL SUBURBS

WASHINGTON COUNTY

AFTON
BAYPORT
COTTAGE GROVE
FOREST LAKE
HUGO
LAKE ELMO
MAHTOMEDI
OAKDALE
STILLWATER
WOODBURY

Washington County Boundaries: **North**: Chisago County; **East**: St. Croix River; **South**: Mississippi River; **West**: Ramsey County; area: 424 square miles

Picture rows of corn growing next to new housing developments with freshly laid sod, and you're visualizing parts of Washington County, surrounding St. Paul. With nearly 50,000 new households expected by 2010, this is the fastest growing county in Minnesota. It has developed from farmland to suburb at breakneck speed because of its proximity to downtown St. Paul and, ironically, because of its rural, open-to-the-skies landscape, of which nearly three-fourths was still vacant in 1990.

The county is made up overwhelmingly of single-family and owner-occupied houses, though new townhomes are being built, mainly in Woodbury and Mahtomedi. Woodbury is also the location of most of the rental units. Generally homes are set on expansive lots, necessary for private septic systems in a county which has limited access to the metropolitan sewer (MUSA) line. In spite of all the new houses, these undulating hills, lakes and forests are still home to hunters, horseback riders, bikers, bird watchers, and record-book fishing. Many of the residents work at the small- and mid-sized medical and high-tech companies in the area, or at one of Minnesota's largest employers, 3M, which is headquartered in Maplewood.

Alarm over Washington County's headlong rush to urbanization was the impetus for the 1991 creation of the Minnesota Land Trust (MLT). Its goal: to preserve agricultural and scenic space in the already-sprawling Twin Cities metropolitan area. The MLT works with landowners, local officials and developers on a wide range of projects, from helping developers cluster units in the least environmentally sensitive areas of a subdivision to integrating open space into commercial and institutional settings. These principals are being applied with debatable success in certain parts of Washington County, particularly in the new construction of Lake Elmo/ Stillwater, Cottage Grove and Woodbury. To learn more, contact the Minnesota Land Trust at 651-647-9590 or www.mnland.org.

One perennial complication of suburban sprawl is education. Children in Washington County attend classes in eight school districts. If you have children and this concerns you, take care to determine where your children will go to school, and keep in mind that attendance boundaries are sometimes redrawn as populations change.

With miles of frontage on the St. Croix National Scenic Riverway (see **Quick Getaways**), and numerous lakes, the landscape of Washington County is an inviting area, filled with opportunities for diverse experiences: trips down the rivers; scuba diving in the clear waters of **Square Lake Park** north of Stillwater, 651-430-8370; and horseback riding at **Lake Elmo Park Reserve**, 651-430-8370, which includes an equestrian center and over 20 miles of trails. Call ahead for reservations. Comprehensive information and directions to all Washington County's parks are available online at www.co.washington.mn.us/parks.

Washington County Government Center, 14949 62nd Street North, Stillwater, Minnesota 55082-0006, 651-439-3220, www.co. washington.mn.us, open Monday-Friday (except recognized holidays), 8 a.m. to 4 p.m.

Washington County Law Enforcement Center, 15015 62nd Street North, Stillwater, Minnesota 55082-3801, Non-Emergency Telephone 651-439-9381, open Monday-Friday (except recognized holidays), 8 a.m. to 4:30 p.m.

Fire: each city contracts for its own fire protection, often with volunteer fire departments

Hospital: Lakeview Hospital, 927 West Churchill Street, Stillwater, 651-439-5330, www.lakeview.org

Washington County Library Branches: Lake Elmo, 651-777-5002; Marine on St. Croix, 651-433-2820; Newport, 651-459-9631; Oakdale, 651-730-0504; Park Grove, 651-459-2040; Valley, 651-436-5882; Wildwood, 651-426-2042; and Woodbury, 651-731-1320; visit the Washington County Library web page at www.washington.lib.mn.us

Washington County School Districts: District #200 Hastings, 651-437-6111; #622 North St. Paul/Maplewood/Oakdale, 651-748-7622; #624 White Bear Lake, 651-653-2700; #831 Forest Lake Area, 651-982-7000; #832 Mahtomedi, 651-407-2000; #833 South Washington County, 651-458-6300; and #834 Stillwater, 651-430-8200

Despite Washington County's development, the spaces are not all filled in, and if the MLT is successful, the area will continue to offer wide-open spaces mixed with contained office, retail, and residential sections. Washington County is made up of 24 distinct cities. Following are brief profiles of some of these communities.

AFTON

Boundaries: North: I-94; **East**: St. Croix River; **South**: 60th Street; **West**: Highway 18 (formerly Highway 95); area: 36 square miles

If you dream of living in a small village, Afton (population about 3,000) may be the spot. It's the best of all worlds: friendly neighbors, a broad range of housing styles set in a village-like atmosphere, and only a 30-minute commute to St. Paul. The charm here is natural: the St. Croix River, the lush floodplain forest, the rolling fields and country meadows. Enough to make your heart sing.

Afton's small business district, made up of marinas, restaurants, shops and services, many housed in buildings left over from the 19th Century, lines Highway 21 (St. Croix Trail). There are no shopping centers, no strip malls. There is the 12-room Afton House Inn, 651-436-8883, which is listed on the National Historic Register, and whimsical Squire House Gardens, 651-436-8080, which sells everything floral, from china to statuary.

As the village streets extend into the country, they lead to newer houses on large lots of one- to five-acres, sometimes more. Concerned about the possibility of sprawling, unchecked development, the residents of Afton cracked down, and new development is being carefully planned to preserve the area's rural feeling. Five-acre lots are the minimum and all subdivisions are required to have contiguous open space.

Afton is a major recreation area, offering the **Afton Alps Golf and Ski Area**, 651-436-1320, one of the largest ski hills in Minnesota, and **Afton State Park**, 651-436-5391, located along the St. Croix River flyway—a great place to hike, camp and watch hawks, Bald Eagles and other birds of prey.

Area Code: 651

Zip Code: 55001

Post Office: 3343 St. Croix Trail, 800-275-8777

Afton City Hall, 3033 South St. Croix Trail, 651-436-5090

Police non-emergency: Washington County, 651-439-9381

Fire non-emergency: Lower St. Croix Volunteer Fire Department, 651-436-7033

Hospital: Lakeview Hospital, 927 West Churchill Street, Stillwater, 651-439-5330 or www.lakeview.org

Schools: South Washington County District #833, 651- 458-6300; Stillwater District #834, 651-430-8200

BAYPORT

Boundaries: **North**: Oak Park Heights; **East**: St. Croix River; **South**: Lakeland Township; **West**: Highway 21; area: 1,200 acres

During Prohibition, the tiny, unassuming town of Bayport had an unsavory reputation as a bootlegger's hideaway. Today Bayport is the home of the Minnesota Correctional Facility (its second largest employer), though you'll find residents to be no more criminally minded here than they are in the next town. Bayport's largest employer, Andersen Corporation, has a long-standing tradition of local philanthropy, which helped fund the Bayport library, city hall, and the volunteer fire department.

Bayport's business district on Highway 95 gets a lot of traffic. The elementary school and most of the village's businesses are on this highway which parallels the river and leads to Stillwater, two miles north, or to I-94, three miles to the south.

The 3,600 employees at Andersen Corporation actually outnumber the city's residents. This strong industrial base provides jobs close to home and accounts for the city's reputation as a community of affordable, mostly single-family detached housing. Bayport is fully developed with a large proportion of the houses here built before 1940. Rental and multi-housing units are limited. Newly constructed homes around the park in **Barker's Alps** are being filled by transplants from the city who've been lured by the river, creating a more cosmopolitan air in this traditionally blue-collar town. For now, however, the social life still revolves around taverns and fish fries, Easter egg hunts and American Legion baseball, and even the newer residents hope that it stays this way. One word of caution: houses sell fast here, often by word of mouth, with little or no advertising. "For sale" signs barely go up, if they go up, before the transaction is closed.

Visit the **Bayport State Wildlife Management Area** off Highway 21, 651-296-5200. It has open water all year, so it's always a great place to watch waterfowl.

Web Site: www.cityofafton.net

Area Code: 651

Zip Code: 55003

Post Office: 209 North 3rd Street, 800-275-8777

City Hall: 294 North Third Street, 651-439-2530

Police Non-emergency: 294 North 3rd Street, 651-439-7116

Fire Non-emergency: 651-439-6992

Hospital: Lakeview Hospital, 927 West Churchill Street, Stillwater, 651-439-5330, www.lakeview.org

Library: 582 North 4th Street, 651-439-7454

School: Stillwater District #834, 651-430-8200

Bus Transportation: call 612-373-3333 for route and schedule information or access www.metrotransit.org.

St. Paul Express Route 294: Downtown St. Paul, Oakdale, 3M, Imation, Lake Elmo, Stillwater, Oak Park Heights, Bayport

COTTAGE GROVE

Boundaries: **North**: Woodbury; **East**: Highway 95 (Manning); **South**: Mississippi River; **West**: St. Paul Park and Grey Cloud Township; area: 34.6 square miles

Cottage Grove is said to be the birthplace of Minnesota agriculture, and descendants of the original settlers still farm here. Early surviving landmarks include two "old villages"—**Old Langdon School Village**, at Jamaica Avenue and West Point Douglas Road, and **Old Cottage Grove**, at 70th and Lamar—that date back to the 1850s. Old Cottage Grove has one home on the National Register of Historic Places and three that are on the city's register of historic landmarks.

Cottage Grove was a quiet place until the 1960s, when Orrin Thompson Homes started the bedroom-community development which brought the population to nearly 30,000 by 1999. Houses that sold in the 1960s and '70s for as little as $10,000, in 1999 sold for up to $142,000, which is less than many houses in neighboring suburbs, making them good starter homes. Recent construction, however, tends to be in the $150,000 to $250,000 price range. Newer developments include **Sandy Hills**, **Hidden Valley**, **Hidden Lakes**, **River Acres** and **West Draw**.

While the fertile soil sustains working farms in Cottage Grove, it is the Mississippi and St. Croix river scenery that is attracting new residents. The river valleys also provide space in which to cross-country ski and ride horses, and **Cottage Grove Ravine Regional Park** off Point Douglas Road is the location of dramatic wooded ravines that are popular for hiking and bird-watching. For golfers, **River Oaks Municipal Golf Course** boasts splendid views of the Mississippi River. Call 651-438-2121 for tee times.

Most commercial development in Cottage Grove is in the downtown portion of the city along Highway 61, where you'll find Rainbow Foods, Cub Foods, Snyder Drug, K-Mart and Target.

Bailey Nurseries and 3M are among the city's largest employers.

Web Site: www.cottage-grove.org

Area Code: 651

Zip Code: 55016

Post Office: 7130 East Point Douglas Road, 800-275-8777

City Hall, 651-458-2800, TDD 651-458-2897

Police non-emergency: 651-458-2811

Fire non-emergency: 651-458-2809

Hospital: United, 333 North Smith Avenue, St. Paul, 651-220-8000

School: South Washington County District #833, 651-458-6300

Bus Transportation: call 612-373-3333 for route and schedule information or access www.metrotransit.org.

St. Paul Express Route 362: Downtown St. Paul, Warner Road, Highway 61 Park & Ride lots, Cottage Grove east of Highway 61; **St. Paul Express Route 364**: Downtown St. Paul, Warner Road, Highway 61 Park & Ride lots, Cottage Grove west of Highway 61, St. Paul Park, Newport

FOREST LAKE

Boundaries: **North**: 240th Street North; **East**: New Scandia; **South**: 180th Street North; **West**: Anoka County; area: 36 square miles

Forest Lake used to be considered "Up North" but now, located 25 miles north of the Twin Cities up I-35, it's viewed as a reasonable commute. This fast-growing community fans out from the city of Forest Lake and spreads over parts of Washington, Anoka and Chisago counties. Forest Lake serves as the hub for the area, with shopping malls, major grocery chains, churches, a radio station and two newspapers, the *Forest Lake Times* and *Forest Lake Press*.

The mix of property here is urban, rural and agricultural. Homebuilders have a choice of city or lake lots, hobby farms or estates. This is a lively real estate market with many new houses under construction. Though you can spend nearly a million dollars on a house here, you can also move in for under $100,000. Check the *Times,* 651-464-4601, www.ecm-inc.com, and *Press,* 651-407-1234 for real estate listings.

Recreation revolves around water sports on **Forest Lake**, as well as hunting, fishing and cross-country skiing in 23,800-acre **Carlos Avery Wildlife Management Area,** 651-296-5290. Downhill skiing is close by at **Wild Mountain** at Taylors Falls, 651-257-3550, 800-447-4958, www.wildmountain.com, and **Trollhagen** in Dresser, Wisconsin, 800-826-7166.

Area Code: 651

Zip Code: 55025

Post Office: 78 6th Avenue SW, 800-275-8777

Forest Lake City Hall: 220 North Lake Street, 651-464-3550

Forest Lake Township City Hall: 651-464-4348

Police non-Emergency: 651-464-5877; after 4:30 and weekends, 651- 439-9381

Fire non-emergency: 220 North Lake Street, 651-464-2244

Hospital: Fairview Lakes Regional Medical Center, 5200 Fairview Boulevard, Wyoming, MN 55092, 651-982-7000, www.fairview.org

Library: 220 North Lake Street, 651-464-4088,

School: Forest Lake Area District #831, 651-982-7000

Forest Lake License Center, 1432 South Lake Street (Northland Mall); open Monday, Wednesday, Friday 8:00 a.m. to 4:30 p.m., Tuesday and Thursday, 8:00 a.m. to 6:00 p.m., 651-430-8280. The following licenses can be purchased here: Drivers Licenses & Renewals, Motor Vehicle License Plates/Stickers, Boat/Snowmobile/ATV Licenses/Decals, Park Permits, Cross Country Ski Licenses, Game & Fish Licenses, Marriage Licenses, Passports and Passport Photos.

HUGO

Boundaries: North: 180th Street; **East**: Keystone; **South**: 120th Street; **West**: Elmcrest; area: 36 square miles

Native Americans used to harvest rice from Hugo's many lakes and wetlands. Because of the area's high water table, flooding can be a problem here for residents.

While Hugo may or may not be named for French writer Victor Hugo, this rural community located fifteen miles north of St. Paul is the second-fastest-growing city in Washington County. With about 7,000 residents in 1999, the population is expected to double by 2002!

The lakes and fields have historically attracted outdoorsmen, hunters and fishermen, horse and cattle ranches. To preserve the country look, the city has adopted policies that encourage cluster housing and field preservation.

Hugo does have some multiple-family housing units, but rentals are scarce. Most homes are single family detached, owner-occupied and have been built since 1970. By metro standards, Hugo's housing is considered affordable and therefore attractive to young families. There are also executive-level developments such as **Duck Pass, Dellwood Ridge, White Oak Ridge**, and **White Oaks Heights. Woods of Bald Eagle** on Bald Eagle Lake offers homes in the $250,000 to $500,000 range on large 2- to 8-acre lots. Some hobby farms of 5- to 10-acres are still available for people who really want the country life. Municipal sewer and water service are only available in the southwest quadrant of the city.

Hugo's children are split among four school districts. Within Hugo there are two elementary schools located on opposite sides of the city, one in downtown and the other off County Road 7 in the southeast corner.

As for shopping, the downtown has the basic necessities, a hardware store and several restaurants. Major retail stores are located nearby in White Bear Lake and Forest Lake.

Web Site: www.ci.hugo.mn.us

Area Code: 651

Zip Code: 55038

Post Office: 5615 150th Street, 800-275-8777

City Hall: 5524 Upper146th Street North, 651-429-6676

Police non-emergency: Washington County, 15015 62nd Street North, Stillwater, 651-439-9381

Fire non-emergency: 5323 140th Street North, Hugo, 651-429-6366

Hospitals: HealthEast St. John's Hospital, 1575 Beam Avenue, Maplewood, 651-232-7000, www.healtheast.org; Fairview Lakes Regional Medical Center, 5200 Fairview Boulevard, Wyoming, MN 55092, 651-982-7000, www.fairview.org

Schools: Forest Lake District #831, 651-982-8100; Mahtomedi District #832, 651-407-2000; Stillwater District #834, 651-351-8340; White Bear Lake District #624, 651-653-2700

LAKE ELMO

Boundaries: **North**: Highway 36; **East**: Manning; **South**: I-94; **West**: Ideal Avenue and Oakdale; area: 26 square miles

Lake Elmo and its neighbor Baytown Township are either an egregious example of urban sprawl or sublime havens that preserve the rural lifestyle, depending on how you look at large houses spaced far apart on acreage.

Only recently has the city encouraged housing development designed to control the sprawl. One development, **Fields of St. Croix** on Highway 5, between the Washington County Fairgrounds and Stillwater High School, includes the **Natural Harvest Farm**, 651-351-1038, farm-crew@bitstream.net, which grows organic produce for its shareholders. Other open-space developments include **Tanner Ridge, Homestead, Hamlet on Sunfish Lake,** and **Parkview Estates**. Development here is fast paced. In an effort to preserve space, contain sprawl, and retain the village-like feel, newly built subdivisions have homes clustered on no more than half the land in each development, with the rest preserved as open space. Such preservation is made necessary in a city with sewer and water available in only three small areas: the commercial zone at I-94 and County Road 13; the "Old Village" business district; and Lake Jane, where there are contamination issues from an old abandoned landfill.

At first glance, Lake Elmo looks like an unlikely resort. The town is as plain as apple pie, but the landscape is rich: grasslands, prairies, meadows, orchards, woodlands, open water, marshes and swamps make for a hospitable wildlife habitat. Lake Elmo is a superb fishing lake and is where the state record tiger muskie was caught in 1999.

Unfortunately, the "Old Village" of Lake Elmo has not fared as well. The business district is somewhat derelict with only a few businesses left. But the Lake Elmo Inn has a popular restaurant, and handsome older houses on Lake Elmo Avenue overlook the lake.

There is no multi-family housing here. Lake Elmo's major housing boom occurred in the 1970s when new construction doubled the number of residential units and increased the population by 50%. Since the 1980s, housing valued at $100,000 or less has declined, while the percentage of homes valued at $200,000 plus has increased dramatically.

Three school districts serve Lake Elmo, but an elementary school and a junior high school are within the city limits. City park facilities include baseball fields, skating rinks and playgrounds. Lake Elmo Park Reserve's two-acre chlorinated swimming pond is a family favorite with a sandy bottom and gradual drop-off.

Web Site: www.lakeelmo.org

Area Code: 651

Zip Code: 55042

Post Office: 3469 Lake Elmo Avenue, 800-275-8777

City Hall: 3800 Laverne Avenue North, 651-777-5510

Police non-emergency: Washington County, 651-439-9381

Volunteer Fire Department non-emergency: 3510 Laverne Avenue, 651-770-5006

Schools: Stillwater District #834, 651-351-8340; Mahtomedi District #832, 651-407-2000; Maplewood-North St. Paul-Oakdale District #622, 651-748-7622

Hospital: Lakeview Hospital, 927 West Churchill Street, Stillwater, 651-439-5330, www.lakeview.org

Bus Transportation: Call 612-373-3333 for route and schhedule information or access www.metrotransit.org

St. Paul Express Route 294: Downtown St. Paul, Oakdale, 3M, Imation, Lake Elmo, Stillwater, Oak Park Heights, Bayport

MAHTOMEDI

Boundaries: **North**: Dellwood and Grant; **East**: Ideal Avenue; **South**: I-694 and Pine Springs; **West**: Highway 120; area: 2,500 acres

Mahtomedi (pronounced "Ma Toe Mee Dee"), a turn of the century resort town on a lake which had an amusement park, was to St. Paul what Excelsior was to Minneapolis: a summer resort for escapees from the heat of the cities. But the merry-makers had such a good time on the giant slide that dropped them into the cooling waters of White Bear Lake or dancing to the music of Guy Lombardo in the pavilion, that they decided to winter-ize their cottages and stay year 'round. A few of the old buildings are still standing and the old Mahtomedi Hotel is now a private home on Quail Street. Those interested in history should read *Mahtomedi Memories*, a book of reminiscences about the city's past, co-authored by local historians.

The presence of its landmarks has preserved Mahtomedi's summer resort ambiance despite the rapid growth and development that took place in the 1970s. Because the whole city has municipal sewer and water, it is fully built out, with a population of about 7,500 in 1999. It is basically residential with a small industrial area along I-694. One-fourth of the hous-es in Mahtomedi were built before 1940. Recent construction consists of townhomes in the southwest, which recently acquired sewer and water.

Housing here is considered affordable, with many units in the $120,000 and under range; but there are rapidly increasing numbers of homes priced at $200,000 and up.

Area Code: 651

Zip Code: 55115

Post Office: 2223 Fifth Street, White Bear Lake, 800-275-8777

City Hall: 600 Stillwater Road, 651-426-3344

Police non-emergency: Washington County, 651-439-9381

Fire non-emergency: Call City Hall, 651-426-3344

School: Mahtomedi District #832, 651-407-2000

Library: Wildwood Branch/South Washington County Library System, 651-426-2042

Hospital: HealthEast St. John's, 1575 Beam Avenue, Maplewood, 651-232-7000, www.healtheast.org

Bus Transportation: call 612-373-3333 for route and schedule information or access www.metrotransit.org.

St. Paul Route 15: Downtown St. Paul, Forest St., Hillcrest Center, White Bear Lake, Mahtomedi, Maplewood Mall, Century College.

OAKDALE

Boundaries: **North**: I-694; **East**: Lake Elmo; **South**: I-94; **West**: Geneva Avenue (also known as Trunk Highway 120 and Century Avenue); area: approximately 7,000 acres

Oakdale, once a quiet farm-belt, now a thriving suburban community, lies just east of St. Paul. In 1990 it was among the fastest-growing cities in the Twin Cities metropolitan area, growing to 26,000 by 1999. Today, the city is fully developed, and its population is expected to stabilize at around 30,000.

Named for the large groves of oak trees that sheltered this landscape before oak wilt struck in the 1970s, the city has changed significantly over the last 30 years, while still retaining some of its small-town feel. Neighborhood housing includes snug ramblers laid out on suburban-style curbless streets. Drive through, and you'll see children—in the yards, at the parks playing ball, and in-line skating. In fact, Oakdale is starting to experience some of the problems and crime associated with a younger demographic, and the city has responded by instituting curfews, a crime alert network, and McGruff safe houses for children.

While Oakdale lacks a defined downtown or major shopping mall, **Walton Park Recreation Area**, 651-730-2700, with a tot lot, ball fields and band-shell, has emerged as a community gathering place, as has Tartan High School (named for local employer, 3M).

In addition to 3M facilities, Hubbard Broadcasting's US Satellite Broadcasting Co. is located in Oakdale. The presence of these two corporations and the area's recent industrial and commercial development is good news for the local workforce. It's expected that Oakdale will have a workforce of 9,000 to 10,000 people early in this millennium.

Web Site: www.ci.oakdale.mn.us

Area Code: 651

Zip Code: 55128

Post Office: 1175 Gershwin Avenue, 800-275-8777

City Hall: 1584 Hadley Avenue North, 651-739-5086

Police non-emergency: 1584 Hadley Avenue North, 651-738-1022

Fire non-emergency: Station #1, 6279 50th Street, 651-777-8886; Station #2, 6633 15th Street, 651-731-8886

Library: 1010 Heron Avenue North, 651-730-0504

Hospital: HealthEast St. John's, 1575 Beam Avenue, Maplewood, 651-232-7000, www.healtheast.org

School: District #622 Maplewood-North St. Paul-Oakdale, 651-748-7622

Community Publication: *North St. Paul, Ramsey County Review*, 612-777-8800

Cable Television: Channel 16 broadcasts City Council meetings, Planning and Park Commission meetings, Environmental Management Commission meetings, the "Oakdale Update" Show, the Oakdale Fire Department "Fire Time" Show, and many other programs of local interest.

Bus Transportation: call 612-373-3333 for route and schedule information or access www.metrotransit.org.

St. Paul Route 12: Downtown St. Paul, Rice Street, Falcon Heights, Rosedale, Lauderdale, East 6th Street, Oakdale, Roseville, Stillwater, Oak Park Heights Prison

St. Paul Express Route 294: Downtown St. Paul, Oakdale, 3M, Imation, Lake Elmo, Stillwater, Oak Park Heights, Bayport

STILLWATER

Boundaries: **North**: Highway 96; **East**: St. Croix River; **South**: Highway 36; **West**: Manning; area: 7 square miles (the Stillwater vicinity encompasses a much larger area).

On the way to Stillwater via Highway 36, you'll pass fast-food joints, chain stores and innumerable cul-de-sac developments. Who would guess that at the end of the four-lane highway, lies a town that's on the National Register of Historic Places—Victorian "painted ladies," with cupolas, gazebos, leaded glass windows and all.

This old lumbertown, which bills itself as the birthplace of Minnesota, celebrates its 19th-century past with antique shops, romantic bed and breakfasts, Lumberjack Days and paddle-wheeling up and down the St. Croix. But be advised, if it's one of the old houses you want you'll probably have to get in line. Tourists are always knocking on residents' doors saying, "If you ever want to sell..."

Fortunately, there are a lot of other not-quite-so-old homes on Stillwater's streets: nearly 2,000 of its houses were built before World War II. Gone, however, are the days when people covered up the walnut floors with wall-to-wall carpeting and converted the big houses into duplexes and triplexes. New owners are converting them back to single-family use. In fact, you'll find conversation with Stillwater locals tends to revolve around where to go for architectural artifacts and what brand of varnish stripper works best. Keep in mind that these houses, though old, are not cheap. In fact, the number of rental and affordable housing units, both in town and farther out, continues to decline.

If you prefer newer construction, 1970s housing units built on pleasant cul-de-sacs sell in the $150,000 to $200,00 price range. Brand new houses are going for much, much more—anywhere from $250,00 to over a million dollars. New developments are being built at breakneck speed and offer amenities like clustered homes, central parks and gazebos. The concept is called "new urbanism"—diminishing the size of private spaces that encourage alienation and separation and increasing public spaces to foster community interaction. **Liberty on the Lake**, off Highway 36, and **Legends** have houses built in the styles that reference the older homes of Stillwater; **The Fields of St. Croix**, near the high school, resembles a New England town.

Local sporting events and cultural opportunities are well attended by area residents, and the **St. Croix Valley Recreation Center**, 651-430-2601, offers a field house, ice arena, walking track, and golf, hockey and soccer programs. The Stillwater high school orchestra has been ranked #1 in the state; and then there is football...

Web Site: www.ci.stillwater.mn.us

Area Code: 651

Zip Codes: 55082, 55083

Post Office: 102 3rd Street North, 800-275-8777

City Hall: 216 North Fourth Street, 651-430-8800

Police non-Emergency: Washington County Law Enforcement Center, 15015 62nd Street North, 651-351-4900

Fire: emergency only, 911

Hospital: Lakeview Hospital, 927 West Churchill Street, 651-439-5330, www.lakeview.org

School: Stillwater District #834, 651-351-8340

Library: 223 North Fourth Street, 651-439-1675

Community Publications: *Stillwater Courier News*, 651-430-3037; *Stillwater Evening Gazette*, 651-439-3130

Stillwater License Center: 651-430-6176 (recorded message), open Monday, Tuesday, Thursday, Friday, 8:00 a.m. to 4:30 p.m.; Wednesday, 8:00 a.m. to 7:30 p.m.; Saturday, 8:00 a.m. to 11:30 a.m. (except holiday weekends). Drivers license tests: written test, Wednesdays only, 8:00 a.m. to 11:15 a.m. and 12:30 p.m. to 3:45 p.m. Road test, 1520 West Frontage Road (River Heights Plaza); by appointment only, 651-639-4058.

Bus Transportation: call 612-373-3333 for route and schedule information or access www.metrotransit.org.

St. Paul Express Route 294: Downtown St. Paul, Oakdale, 3M, Imation, Lake Elmo, Stillwater, Oak Park Heights, Bayport

WOODBURY

Boundaries: **North**: I-94; **East**: St. Croix River; **West**: I-494, I-694; **South**, Cottage Grove; area: 36 square miles

If you've lived in Woodbury for ten years, you're an old-timer; and if you've lived here since the late 1970s when the first developer struck out across the farm fields, you can call yourself a founding father, or mother.

Since the 1970s when the upscale Evergreen development was built to lure 3M executives over from Maplewood, Woodbury, located a mile southeast of St. Paul, has been transformed from a sleepy rural township of 3,000 residents into Minnesota's fastest growing city. In 1999 the estimated population was over 40,000. It is the city's goal to provide flexible housing options that will enable citizens to live here throughout their lives. Consequently, those looking to buy in Woodbury can choose from single- and multi-family homes priced from $100,000 to a million dollars; housing stock that includes 1960s ramblers and split levels, contemporary townhomes, and newly built single-family homes in exclusive golf course communities.

Woodbury is being developed around existing open space including three golf courses, 20 city parks, a recreation trail that runs through the city, and a string of small lakes. Because Woodbury has been receptive to allowing high-density building in order to hold down the cost of land and therefore the cost of housing, there are a large number of rental units available, many of them three-or four-bedroom.

Woodbury does not have an established downtown, only large-scale malls. But it isn't letting the lack of a downtown keep it from doing some small-town things, including a **farmers' market** on Sunday mornings in the city hall parking lot, the **Woodbury Youth Orchestra**, **Shakespeare in the Park**, and **Woodbury Days**. To connect online with Woodbury's businesses and activities, check "Neighborly Necessities," www.sowashco.com/welcome.

Criticisms of Woodbury include its winding, twisting streets which make it difficult to get around; trails that don't go anywhere; and the lack of a community gathering place. Word has it that there are plans for a YMCA, library, shopping center and indoor park, all linked by a bike trail.

Woodbury's population growth touched off a parallel explosion in jobs. Major employers include 3M, State Farm Insurance, Rivertown Trading, and other high tech and manufacturing companies, retailers, schools, and the Woodbury Health Care Center. Combined, these companies have made Woodbury into a place where you can both live and work—unusual in a region where many experience long commutes.

But, while growth has been good for residents in many ways, it has put a strain on municipal services and schools. Three school districts serve Woodbury. Be sure to check with the school district offices to see where your children will go; attendance is based on boundaries that vary to meet enrollment needs.

Web Site: www.ci.woodbury.mn.us

Area Code: 651

Zip Codes: 55125, 55129

Post Office: 7595 Currell Boulevard

City Hall: 8301 Valley Creek Road, 651-714-3500

Police: Woodbury Public Safety, non-emergency, 651-739-4141

Fire non-emergency: 651-714-3700

Hospital: HealthEast St. John's Hospital, 1575 Beam Avenue, Maplewood, 651-232-7000

Library: Washington County Library-Woodbury Branch, 2150 Radio Drive, 651-731-8487

Schools: South Washington County District #833, 651-458-6300; Stillwater District #834, 651-351-8340; North St. Paul/Maplewood/Oakdale District #622, 651-770-4600

Community Publications: *The Woodbury Bulletin*, 651-730-4007; *Woodbury News*, 651-730-0000; *Woodbury/Maplewood Review*, 612-777-8800

License Center: 8301 Valley Creek Road, 651-714-3780; renew a Minnesota drivers' license here or purchase automobile tags, but if you're moving from another state, you must take a written test administered in Stillwater on Wednesdays; call 651-430-6189. The test is administered at the license substation at 1600 University Avenue in St. Paul, 651-642-0808.

Bus Transportation: call 612-373-3333 for route and schedule information or access www.metrotransit.org.

St. Paul Route #351 provides rush hour express service to downtown St. Paul from the Park & Ride at Christ Episcopal Church, 7305 Afton Road. There are four trips each morning and four each evening between Woodbury, Maplewood and downtown St. Paul. The **#350 bus** provides limited stop service between southern Maplewood and downtown St. Paul. **Local circulator service:** small buses pick up riders throughout local neighborhoods and connect at the Park & Ride with #351 and other local routes. **Number 301** serves Tamarack Apartments and the Park Hills neighborhood; **#302** circulates in Royal Oaks, along Tower Drive, Lake Road and Woodlane Drive; **#303** serves the Colby Lake area.

Reverse Commute Service: **#352** provides express service from downtown St. Paul to Rivertown Trading in the morning and return service in the afternoon. **Number 351** also provides express service from downtown St. Paul to the Park & Ride in the morning and connects with #304 serving State Farm Insurance and Rivertown Trading. SuperSaver discount passes are available. Call 651-349-7681, for a SuperSaver order form.

Information about transit service in Woodbury, including route maps and schedules, is available at Woodbury City Hall and the Transit Store in downtown St. Paul. For those who need flexible, personalized service, **Dial-A-Ride** offers personal handicapped-accessible service, much like a taxi, for $1.50 per trip. Dial-A-Ride operates its small buses within the city or to nearby shopping centers between 8 a.m. and 4:15 p.m. on weekdays. Reservations required. Call 651-735-RIDE (7433) weekdays between 8 a.m. and 5 p.m. Dial-A-Ride does not operate on weekends or holidays.

RAMSEY COUNTY

MAPLEWOOD
WHITE BEAR LAKE

MAPLEWOOD

Boundaries: **North**: County Road D, I-694; **East**: North St. Paul at Ariel Street and Oakdale, and Woodbury at Century Avenue; **South**: St. Paul at Larpenteur Avenue and Newport at Bailey Road; area: 19 square miles

Maplewood is a first ring suburb that wraps around the east and north sides of St. Paul like a puzzle piece. In a city that has developed constantly since World War II, housing styles vary greatly. You'll find examples of every era's popular housing types, most of which have been well-preserved, some updated. More recent construction tends to run to townhomes. The city's newest neighborhoods are located in a six-mile long, one-mile wide leg that extends southward alongside Woodbury and Oakdale, and resemble those suburbs, with more contemporary and upscale housing units available. Approximately one-third of Maplewood's housing units are townhouses and condominiums.

Bracketed by major interstates: 94, 694, 494, 35E, and by highways 61 and 36, Maplewood is in the heart of vast shopping and big business. Maplewood Mall is the center of an extensive commercial area that has grown up around it. Headquartered here, 3M is one of Minnesota's largest employers and best-known international corporations.

Maplewood and Ramsey County have been purchasing parcels of open land and wetlands as they have become available. Consequently, Maplewood has many two- to five-acre neighborhood parks and playgrounds as well as the **Maplewood Nature Center**, 651-738-9383; **Keller Golf Course**, 651-484-3011; **Goodrich Golf Dome**, 651-777-0500, and adjacent **Aldrich Arena**, 651-777-2233, and **Goodrich Golf Course**, 651-777-7355. Mountain bikers should head for **Winthrop**

Street Mountain Biking Area in Battle Creek Park, with its over 5.5 kilometers of challenging mountain biking trails in hilly, wooded terrain. This is also a thrilling cross-country ski trail in the winter. (See **Sports and Recreation**.) For information and maps contact the **Parks and Recreation Department** at 651-748-2500. Also, maps and directions to Maplewood's parks are available online at www.co.ramsey.mn.us/parks. Indoors, the **Maplewood Community Center**, 2000 White Bear Avenue, 651-779-3540, offers swimming lessons and is a great spot for birthday parties. The Gateway Trail bike path can be easily accessed from the community center's parking lot.

Children in Maplewood attend schools in three school districts. Be sure to find out which school district serves the neighborhood you're considering.

Web Site: www.ci.maplewood.mn.us

Area Code: 651

Zip Codes: 55119, 55109, 55117

Post Offices: 2523 7th Avenue East, North St. Paul; 40 Arlington Avenue East, St. Paul; 1175 Gershwin Avenue North, Oakdale, 800-275-8777

City Hall: 1830 East County Road B, 651-770-4500

Police non-emergency: 651-777-8191, 770-4590

Fire non-emergency: 651-779-4945

Hospital: HealthEast St. John's Hospital, 1575 Beam Avenue, 651-232-7000, www.healtheast.org

Library: 1670 Beam Avenue, Maplewood, 651-777-8146

Schools: North St. Paul/Maplewood/Oakdale District #622, 651-770-4600; Roseville District #623, 651-635-1600; White Bear Lake District #624, 651-775-6000

Community Publication: *Woodbury/Maplewood Review*, 612-777-8800

Bus Transportation: call 612-373-3333 for route and schedule information or access www.metrotransit.org.

St. Paul Route 9: Downtown St. Paul, Highland Park, Ft. Snelling, East and West 7th Street, North St. Paul, Maplewood Mall, Oakdale; **St. Paul Route 11**: Downtown St. Paul, Arkwright Street, Little

Canada, St. John's Hospital, Maplewood Mall, Concord Street, Inver Hills; **St. Paul Route 15**: Downtown St. Paul, Forest Street, Hillcrest Center, White Bear Lake, Mahtomedi, Maplewood Mall, Century College; **St. Paul Express Route 35C**: Downtown St. Paul, Maplewood Mall, White Bear Area, White Bear Lake, Vadnais Heights; **Minneapolis Express Route 36**: Downtown Minneapolis, Maplewood Mall, White Bear Lake

WHITE BEAR LAKE

Boundaries: North: Hugo; **East**: Washington County; **South**: I-694; **West**: Centerville Road; area: 12 square miles

White Bear Lake has a racy past. A turn-of-the-century haven for wealthy families from St. Paul, it became a hideout for gangsters in the 1930s, and Zelda and Scott Fitzgerald boozed it up here during Prohibition. In fact, they created such a rumpus, they were asked to leave. Fitzgerald, a St. Paul native, is said to have used it as the setting for *Winter Dreams*.

Following recent renovations, the pedestrian-friendly downtown looks more like a turn-of-the century summer resort than ever. Ornate lamp posts and old-fashioned store fronts evoke images of those indolent years and invite visitors to linger and browse in the unique shops. (See **Shopping for the Home**.)

Over the past 50 years this one-time summer resort has developed into a bedroom community with a mix of homes, some that rival Summit Avenue's mansions, while others are modest and cottagey, more typical of Up North. The lakeshore is where you'll find the most lavish homes, and while the historic lakeside retreats designed by Cass Gilbert and other famous architects have been protected, other less famous houses have been razed and replaced. Many newcomers, attracted by golf and sailing, choose to live close to the **Dellwood Country Club**. White Bear Lake is also home to many tracts of 1960s split-levels and ramblers, and about one-third of its housing is rental or multi-family.

Anti-business sentiments were strong until the mid-1980s, when rising property taxes prompted the city to expand its tax base—several business-es quickly moved in. Smart Carte, a manufacturer of airport baggage-cart systems is located here, as is the established (here since the late 1800s) Johnson Boat Works.

The **White Bear Yacht Club** (and golf course) is actually in **Dellwood**, which curves around the northeastern shore of White Bear

Lake. Other lakeshore communities include: **Bellaire, Cottage Park, White Bear Township, Mahtomedi** and **Birchwood**. Current lake issues include Eurasian milfoil weed and contamination. There is also concern that development in the lake's recharge area to the north and west will draw down White Bear's water level.

White Bear's early reputation as a health and recreation resort persists with relaxation and amusement still revolving around the water. **Tamarack Nature Center**, 651-407-5350, is a 320-acre park preserve located within **Bald Eagle-Otter Lakes Regional Park** in White Bear Township. Its floating dock serves as an observation platform where you can view heron, turtle, mink and muskrat. **Manitou Ridge Golf Course**, 651-777-2987, built off McKnight Road on one of the highest points in Ramsey County, has some long holes with panoramic views of the metropolitan area and is open in the winter for cross-country skiing. Swimming beaches and two public launches are located at **White Bear Lake County Park**. White Bear is also home to the **Lakeshore Players**, 651-429-5674, the oldest continuously operating community theater in the state.

The city is served by the White Bear School District #624.

Web Site: www.whitebearusa.com

Area Code: 651

Zip Code: 55110

Post Office: 2223 5th Street, 800-275-8777

City Hall: 4701 Highway 61, 651-429-8526

Police non-emergency: 651-429-8551

Fire non-emergency: 651-429-8568

Hospital: Regions, 640 Jackson Street, 651-221-3456, www.health-partners.com

Library: 4698 Clark Avenue, 651-407-5302

School: White Bear Lake #624, 651-773-6100

Community Publication: *White Bear Lake, White Bear Press, 651-407-1200*

Bus Transportation: call 612-373-3333 for route and schedule information or access www.metrotransit.org.

St. Paul Route 15: Downtown St. Paul, Forest Street, Hillcrest

Center, White Bear Lake, Mahtomedi, Maplewood Mall, Century College; **St. Paul Express Route 35AB**: Downtown St. Paul, North St. Paul, White Bear Lake, Birchwood, South Shore Area; **St. Paul Express Route 35C**: Downtown St. Paul, Maplewood Mall, White Bear Area, White Bear Lake, Vadnais Heights **Minneapolis Express Route 36**: Downtown Minneapolis, Maplewood Mall, White Bear Lake; **North Suburban Express Route 270**: Downtown St. Paul, White Bear Lake; **North Suburban Express Route 271**: Downtown St. Paul, White Bear Lake, Centerville, Lino Lakes

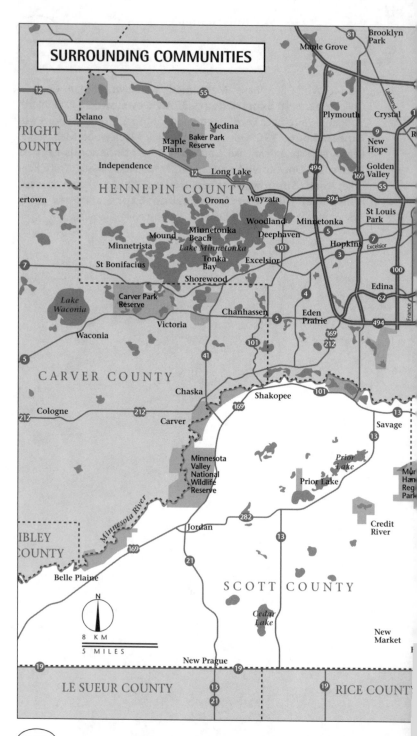

SURROUNDING COMMUNITIES

Maple Grove

Brooklyn Park

Delano

Medina

Plymouth

Crystal

WRIGHT COUNTY

Maple Plain

Baker Park Reserve

New Hope

Independence

Long Lake

Golden Valley

HENNEPIN COUNTY

Wayzata

ertown

Orono

Minnetonka

St Louis Park

Mound

Minnetonka Beach

Woodland

Deephaven

Minnetrista

Lake Minnetonka

Tonka Bay

Hopkins

Excelsior

St Bonifacius

Excelsior

Shorewood

Edina

Lake Waconia

Carver Park Reserve

Chanhassen

Eden Prairie

Victoria

Waconia

CARVER COUNTY

Chaska

Shakopee

Cologne

Carver

Savage

Minnesota Valley National Wildlife Reserve

Prior Lake

Prior Lake

Mu Han Reg Park

Credit River

Minnesota River

Jordan

SIBLEY COUNTY

Belle Plaine

SCOTT COUNTY

N

8 KM

5 MILES

Cedar Lake

New Market

LE SUEUR COUNTY

New Prague

RICE COUNTY

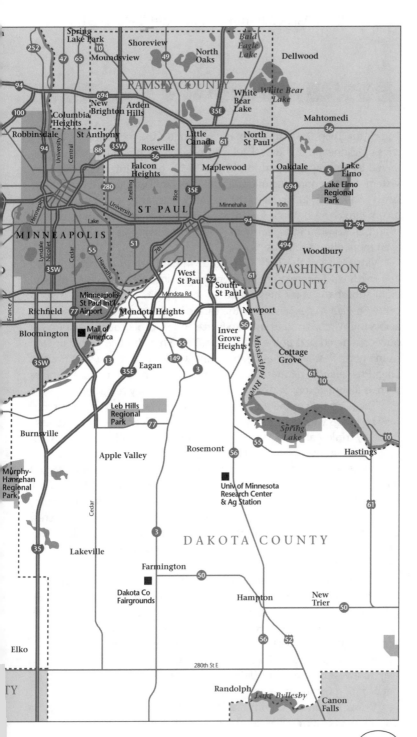

SURROUNDING COMMUNITIES

Today, the Twin Cities are much more than just the metropolitan boundaries of Minneapolis and St. Paul. The post World War II baby boom followed by the rapid expansion in the 1960s of the Interstate highway system, led to enormous migration of new families into what had been farms and forests. In fact, over the past fifty years or so the metro area has grown into an amorphous expanse that includes more than eighty distinct suburban communities, some of them now serving as mini-centers for even more distant suburbs.

Virtually all of the Twin Cities' growth has been in the suburbs, and two-thirds of Minnesota's population growth since 1990 has taken place in eight suburban Twin Cities counties. The appetite for new land is voracious; St. Paul has expanded to the east in Washington County, and even across the Wisconsin state line into Pierce and St. Croix counties, which are now considered part of the metro area. There has also been rapid growth to the northwest in Plymouth and Maple Grove, and to the southwest in Eden Prairie and Chanhassen. More established inner-ring communities such as Bloomington, St. Louis Park and Golden Valley remain vital.

The attraction of the surrounding communities is obvious: larger lots, new buildings with floor-plans that meet the needs and desires of today's families, triple garages. There are both brand-new suburbs and established ones: Apple Valley was little more than farm fields thirty years ago whereas Anoka, an old river city, has a historic downtown and elegant Victorian houses. Furthermore, the monotony of the post World War II bedroom communities has, in many places, given way to vibrant suburbs that offer a variety of services, reasonable dining options, and even trendy coffee shops. The newest suburbs, like Maple Grove, try to provide a mix of housing and workplaces that keep people close to home and able to walk, bike or take a bus to local services.

One important consideration to keep in mind as you choose where to live is the question of transportation. If you don't own an automobile, mass transit is next to non-existent in many outlying communities—although some of the suburbs are served by metro bus lines, and Park & Ride lots can connect you to city buses. Check **Transportation** for more information.

Subscriptions to community newspapers (sent by mail) are a good way to investigate an area before arriving. Check www.mnnewspaper-net.org for more information.

Below are phone numbers and city web sites to call for information on suburban communities not profiled in this book.

SOUTHERN SUBURBS

- Apple Valley, 952-932-2500
- Burnsville, 952-895-4400, www.ci.burnsville.mn.us
- Eagan, 651-681-4600, www.cityofeagan.com
- Inver Grove Heights, 651-450-2500, www.ci.inver-grove-heights.mn.us
- Lakeville, 952-469-4431, www.ci.lakeville.mn.us
- Mendota Heights, 651-452-1850
- Prior Lake, 952-447-4230, www.cityofpriorlake.com
- Rosemount, 651-423-4411, www.ci.rosemount.mn.us
- Savage, 952-882-2660, www.cityofsavage.org
- Shakopee, 952-445-3650, www.ci.shakopee.mn.us
- South St. Paul, 651-554-3200, www.southstpaul.org
- West St. Paul, 651-552-4100

WESTERN SUBURBS

- Chanhassen, 952-937-1900, www.ci.chanhassen.mn.us
- Chaska, 952-448-2851, www.chaska.com
- Golden Valley, 763-593-8000, www.ci.golden-valley.mn.us

NORTHERN SUBURBS

For a map of this area, see page 80.

- Andover, 763-755-5100, www.ci.andover.mn.us
- Anoka, 763-421-6630
- Arden Hills, 651-633-5676
- Blaine, 763-784-6700, www.ci.blaine.mn.us
- Brooklyn Center, 763-569-3300
- Brooklyn Park, 763-493-8000, www.brooklynpark.org
- Champlin, 763-421-8100, www.ci.champlin.mn.us
- Circle Pines, 763-784-5898, www.ci.circle-pines.mn.us
- Columbia Heights, 763-706-3600, www.ci.columbia-heights.mn.us
- Coon Rapids, 763-755-2880, www.ci.coon-rapids.mn.us
- Crystal, 763-531-1000, www.ci.crystal.mn.us
- Dayton, 763-427-4589, www.ci.dayton.mn.us
- Falcon Heights, 651-644-5050
- Fridley, 763-571-3450, www.ci.fridley.mn.us
- Ham Lake, 763-434-9555, www.ci.ham-lake.mn.us

- Lino Lakes, 651-982-2400
- Little Canada, 651-484-2177
- Mounds View, 763-717-4000, www.tcfreenet.org/org/moundsview
- New Brighton, 651-638-2100, www.ci.new-brighton.mn.us
- New Hope, 763-531-5110, www.ci.new-hope.mn.us
- Robbinsdale, 763-537-4534, www.ci.robbinsdale.mn.us
- Roseville, 651-490-2200, www.roseville.mn.us
- Shoreview, 651-490-4600, www.ci.shoreview.mn.us
- St. Anthony, 612-789-8881, www.ci.saint-anthony.mn.us
- Vadnais Heights, 651-429-5343, www.ci.vadnais-heights.mn.us

EASTERN SUBURBS

- Hastings, 651-437-4127, www.ci.hastings.mn.us
- North St. Paul, 651-770-4450

THERE ARE PLACES WHERE TWIN CITIES' STREETS FOLLOW A PERFECT grid, and places where streets are laid out at crazy angles with no sense to east, west, north or south. The convolutions are due primarily to the Mississippi River winding through both downtowns, oblivious to the needs of city planners. City boundaries, where streets occasionally change names, add additional confusion. Suburban communities often follow Twin Cities' street patterns, but not always. For the full picture, you'll need to accompany this guide with a map. Even better is a hefty street atlas, which offers page-by-page micro-views of every metropolitan block accompanied by an index of all streets, such as *Hudson's Street Atlas of the Greater Twin Cities*. With one in hand, keep the following things in mind:

MINNEAPOLIS

- Street addresses are uniformly divided in hundreds, block by block. Numbers increase moving outward from the Mississippi River on the north side and from Nicollet Avenue on the south side.
- Downtown streets are laid out diagonally to the compass (the pesky Mississippi!) so try not to let compass directions throw you off. Because of their orientation to the river, numbered streets and those running parallel to them are labeled north or south, dividing at Hennepin Avenue.
- South Minneapolis (south of Grant Street) is straightforward and easy to understand. Numbered streets run east-west, with ascending numbers going southward. Avenues for the most part run north-south, and have numbers east of Nicollet Avenue and proper names west of Nicollet, which means, in South Minneapolis, the higher the numbered street, the further south it is; the higher the num-

bered avenue, the further east it is.

- In the University of Minnesota neighborhood, numbered streets generally run east-west, while numbered avenues run north-south. Streets and avenues here are labeled Southeast.
- In Northeast Minneapolis numbered avenues run east-west, with numbers ascending northward. North-south streets are numbered heading east from the river until 6th Street. East of 6th the streets are named chronologically after US presidents, from Washington to Coolidge.
- In North Minneapolis numbered avenues run east-west, with numbers ascending northward. North-south streets have ascending numbers as you go west from the Mississippi, until 7th Street. West of 7th streets have proper names.

ST. PAUL

Governor Jesse Ventura got into trouble for suggesting that St. Paul was laid out by tipsy Irishmen, but there are many who live here who would agree.

- Along with St. Paul's old-world charm comes a somewhat confusing street system. St. Paul's street numbers don't always follow tidy increments of one hundred for every block; they may change from 100 to 200 in the middle of the block so . . . get out that atlas.
- West of Downtown, the north-south dividing line is Summit Avenue. Street numbers increase going westward from Downtown.
- Downtown, Wabasha Street is the division between east and west. The Mississippi River is the north-south marker.
- East of Downtown the north-south dividing line is Upper Afton Road. Street numbers increase going eastward from Downtown.

FROM CITY TO CITY

- University and Franklin avenues keep their names going from St. Paul to Minneapolis, but Marshall Avenue in St. Paul becomes Lake Street in Minneapolis, and St. Paul's Ford Parkway becomes 46th Street in Minneapolis. Don't worry too much, there are only a handful of these streets to remember. The river breaks up most of them.
- Some suburbs, especially inner ones, number their streets according to the grid of the Twin Cities. Other older or far-flung suburbs, such as Wayzata, are laid out on their own grids. The simple advice: don't expect address numbers in the 'burbs and cities to match up.

All in all, the Twin Cities are no more difficult to navigate than any other middle-aged American city with local geographical quirks. Take a few trips to different parts of town and it won't be long before you're tooling around like a native.

T HE TWIN CITIES IS CONSISTENTLY RANKED ONE OF THE MOST affordable, large metropolitan areas by the National Association of Home Builders. But, with a median sale price averaging over $130,000, and rising, it is a sellers' market here. The suburbs and the most desirable in-town neighborhoods are appreciating rapidly. Some south-west Minneapolis neighborhoods have gained 30 to 40% in assessed value since 1993, and the North Loop neighborhood has increased over 100% since 1997. So if it's important to you to locate in one of the hot areas, either for the quality of schools or ease of commuting, expect to pay a premium. And, if you are looking for a starter home, you may need to be flexible about your choice of neighborhood. As for apartments, the short supply and low vacancy rates throughout the Twin Cities is accom-panied by escalating rents and stiff competition for available units.

Whatever type of housing you choose, the **Neighborhood Revitalization Program** in Minneapolis, 612-673-5140, is an excellent resource, offering assessments of neighborhoods and will even put you in touch with area residents. You can also call the police precinct that patrols your neighborhood of interest. The numbers are listed at the end of each neighborhood profile.

The best advice when house or apartment hunting is to visit prospec-tive neighborhoods—have breakfast at a local restaurant, and walk around, don't just drive. Find out if services and conveniences you are accustomed to having are available nearby. Pay attention to your comfort level. Check on traffic and noise levels at different times of the day and night. If you are put off by the overhead noise of airplanes taking off and landing (as in South Minneapolis, Richfield, East Bloomington, and west-ern St. Paul) or by strangers roller-blading on your street (around the city lakes), factor these into your decision about where to live.

Also consider the commute. Twin Cities' roads are less congested than Los Angeles or Chicago, but more clogged than Boston or New York (1996 ranking of the 25 largest US metropolitan areas, done by the Texas Transportation Institute). Test drive your route at rush hour, morning and night, to find out what you might be getting into. Ride-sharing is often an option. Call **Metro Commuter Services**, 651-602-1602, for information on van and car pools, or check the on-going online discussion about commuting and other transportation issues at www.startribune.com/gettingthere. After decades of wrangling, Light Rail Transit (LRT) is on its way! A 12-mile LRT line, connecting downtown Minneapolis with the Minneapolis-St. Paul International Airport and the Mall of America in Bloomington, is scheduled to open sometime in 2003. Finally, some people are able to commute by bus, but the usefulness of buses depends entirely upon where you live and where you need to go. Information about the Twin Cities' 900 bus routes can be accessed on the internet at www.metrocouncil.org. This same web site also allows you to compare the cost of driving alone to work each day with the cost of taking a bus or carpooling. See **Transportation** for more details.

RENTING

In 1999, the overall Twin Cities vacancy rate was about one percent, although especially desirable neighborhoods such as Uptown have vacancy rates that are even lower. Consequently landlords now are charging $20 to $50 per rental application. According to Apartment Search Profiles, in the spring of 1999 the cost of a two-bedroom unit averaged $660 per month in St. Paul, $754 in Minneapolis, and over $800 in the western suburbs. To calculate current averages, keep in mind that rent is increasing at an annual rate of almost six-percent.

If possible, use Minnesota's climate to assist your apartment search; many people choose not to move around in the winter, creating more vacancies in the summer. Begin looking around the first of June, and you might be lucky enough to find a handsome, turn-of-the-century brick apartment with hardwood floors and tall windows, perhaps even in Uptown or near Summit/Grand, two of the most popular neighborhoods for newcomers.

In many ways, the Twin Cities are a "big small town" which means you can easily find an apartment on your own. Should you decide to do your own footwork, check this guide's neighborhood descriptions to learn about the types of housing in different parts of town.

DIRECT ACTION

Look everywhere—on bulletin boards at cafes, laundromats, and on college campuses. If you are single, on a tight budget, and don't mind sharing, answer "Roommate Wanted" ads. If you're connected to a college, check its housing referral service. **University of Minnesota's Housing Office**, Comstock Hall East in Minneapolis (612- 624-2994) and Coffey Hall in St. Paul (651-624-3731), can fix you up, or check the *Minnesota Daily* classifieds (see below). "Roommate wanted" notices are often found on the bulletin board in the main hallway of the basement of Blegen Hall and along the wall in the building attached to the St. Paul Central Library. Other such notices are posted at scattered locations throughout the University. Another good tip is to walk or drive around, looking carefully— some apartments are only advertised by a sign in the window.

NEWSPAPER CLASSIFIEDS

- **Star Tribune** has the most comprehensive metro-area listings. Get it Saturday night at a convenience store to plan out a Sunday hunt. You can access the classifieds online at www.startribune.com/homezone.
- **St. Paul Pioneer Press** is the better resource for St. Paul and the eastern metro area. The Sunday edition has the most listings. Access the classifieds at www.pioneerplanet.com.
- **City Pages** is a free alternative weekly, available at businesses metrowide. The listings are not extensive, but worth checking, and it also lists sublets; www.citypages.com.
- **Minnesota Daily** is the University of Minnesota newspaper. To place an ad, call 612-627-4140 or check www.daily.umn.edu/classifieds.

Often free, neighborhood newspapers can be found at businesses and newsstands throughout the Twin Cities. See **Skyway News** for listings in and near the downtowns and the **Sun** newspapers in the suburbs. Also, many suburbs have their own newspapers for sale at area convenience stores.

OTHER MEDIA

A few companies publish free guides to large apartment complexes, condos and townhouses, which are available at metro businesses, especially grocery stores, bus stops and newsstands. The best known is **Living Guide** *of the Twin Cities*, which has a useful cross-referenced index of amenities and features for the rental complexes that they list. They'll mail it to you free of charge; call 612-858-8960 or 800-413-5784. **Apartment Search Profiles** gathers data and publishes a quarterly report on average rents, vacancies and significant trends for seventeen rental districts representing the greater Twin Cities area. Call 800-989-8780 and they will send you their brochure.

APARTMENT SEARCH FIRMS

Many landlords contract with rental agents or apartment search firms to find tenants for their units. A search firm can be convenient if you have a limited amount of time to find a place to live. Agents are willing to fax you information, refer you to rental properties, or arrange appointments for you to view available units. When talking to a rental agent, be specific about your needs, this way you will not waste time considering places that aren't right for you. The following are some of the largest and most well-known apartment search firms. The property owners typically pay their fees, so the service to the tenant is free with one exception noted below:

- **Apartments.com**, www.apartments.com, has apartments plus short term listings as well as video tours and a furniture rental center.
- **Apartments by Rent Net**, www.rent.net, offers 360-degree online visuals.
- **Apartment Mart**, Minneapolis: 612-927-4591, St. Paul: 651-224-9199
- **Apartment Referral, Inc.**, 800-899-5665
- **Apartment Search**, 800-989-4005, www.apartmentsearch.com
- **Find-A-Home, Inc.**, 612-869-3177 or 612-571-6040, lists bungalows, houses, hobby farms (everything but apartments) within a 75-mile radius of the Twin Cities. It is free to landlords and charges a $95 registration fee to prospective tenants.
- **Park Avenue of Wayzata**, 612-475-1700, lists townhouses and condominiums in the western suburbs.

TEMPORARY HOUSING/SUBLETS/SHARING

If finding a long-term place to live is proving difficult, you may want to consider taking a short-term sublet. Many such sublets are available in May, when students begin to leave town with time remaining on their leases, or during the winter when the "snowbirds" move to warmer climates. But remember, most leases say that a tenant can sublet only if the landlord agrees to it—and that permission should be in writing. (The original tenant remains responsible for unpaid rent and damage done to the apartment by the new tenant.) Apartment search firms can be put to work to find a short-term place to stay, and the *Living Guide of the Twin Cities* (see **Other Media** above) has several short-term listings. The USWest Yellow Pages includes short-term rentals under "Hotels and Other Accommodations." Check online at www.qwestdex.com. The *Minneapolis Star-Tribune* lists corporate/relocation short term rentals in its classified section, and *Citypages* has ads for sublets and roommates. Check the **Temporary Lodgings** chapter for additional temporary alternatives. Of course, as a last resort, there's always your friend's couch.

EXTRA INFORMATION FOR RENTERS

Your apartment search will be easier if you keep a few things in mind. First, ask yourself how much space you really want to pay for. If you're alone, a studio or efficiency might be most cost-effective. Studios generally are found in downtown Minneapolis and St. Paul and in 2000, the average rent was about $535. A one-bedroom generally will cost $150 more than a studio, a second bedroom adds another $150, and add a third bedroom and you're looking at an approximate total cost of $1,100 to $1,200. If you do require a three-bedroom apartment, the bulk of these units can be found in the southern and western suburbs.

In Minnesota, an important question to ask is who will be paying for heat. If it's you and not the landlord, you could be adding a substantial amount to your cost of living during the cold months, depending on the size and insulation of the apartment. You can find out the average cost of heating for an apartment by calling the gas or electric company that provides service to that building (most likely Northern States Power or Minnegasco—see the **Getting Settled** chapter). For residential customers who are unable to pay their utility bills Minnesota has developed the Cold Weather Rule, which, while it does not prohibit shut-offs, does provide some protection against having one's heat source disconnected between October 15 and April 15. Local utilities or the Consumer Affairs Office of the Minnesota Public Utilities Commission (651-296-0406 or 800-657-3782) can supply more information.

Another consideration when choosing a place to live is the availability of parking. Off-street parking is especially desirable in the winter—your car will start in the morning, you won't have to scrape off ice and snow, and you won't have to move your car for the city snowplow. City streets are plowed according to several different plans, but no matter the schedule, if your car is parked on a street in the way of the snowplow, you will be towed, and be assured it will be expensive and time-consuming to get your car out of the impound lot. (See **Snow Emergency Parking** in **Getting Settled**.)

CHECKING IT OUT

You're on your way to the day's first rental appointment, you haven't had breakfast, the old college friend you're staying with is getting restless, your back is aching from a bad night's sleep, and twenty other people are waiting outside as you drive up—you panic, take a quick glance around, like what you see, and grab an application. Three months later you're wondering how you landed in such a dump. To avoid this scenario, tour each apartment with a clear idea in your head of what you are looking for. Beyond these personal likes and dislikes, there are some specific things to check for as you view a prospective apartment:

- Is the apartment on the first floor? If so, does it have burglar bars? First-floor apartments are easy targets for break-ins.
- Are the appliances clean and in good working order? Test all of the stove's burners. Does the kitchen sink have one or two basins? Is the counter space sufficient?
- Is heat included in your rent? If not, ask for recent heat bills to get a sense of how much you can expect to pay in addition to rent.
- Check the windows to make sure they open, close and lock. Check for operable storm or double- or triple-paned windows. If you have single panes of glass, it's going to be cold near your windows in the winter. If you still like the apartment, you can cover the windows with plastic to insulate your apartment until spring, but this takes some work.
- Do the windows, especially the bedroom windows, open onto a busy street or alley? Alleys are especially notorious for late night car horns and loud early morning trash removal.
- Are there enough closets? Are the closets big enough to accommodate your belongings? Is there private storage in a secure area?
- Is there adequate water pressure for the shower, the sink and the toilet? Turn them on and check. Flush all toilets and check for leaks or unusual noises.
- Check the number of electrical outlets. In older buildings it is common to have one or two outlets per room. Are there enough outlets for all your plug-in appliances?

- Are there laundry facilities in the building? Is there a laundromat within walking distance?
- How close is the building to public transit and the grocery store?
- Is there a smoke detector as well as a carbon monoxide detector in the apartment? While landlords are only required by law to provide smoke detectors, carbon monoxide detectors are a good idea.
- Visit the actual unit you'll be renting, not "one just like it" in the same complex.
- Make sure that the landlord or building manager has a phone number and is available at any time. It's also a good idea to check with a tenants' group (see below for listings) to find out if a prospective landlord/manager has a history of complaints against him/her.
- Check with the city's housing inspection department for past code violations and current citations. Minnesota law requires that landlords disclose any outstanding inspection orders for which a citation has been issued for violations that threaten the health or safety of tenants. However, a landlord has not violated this requirement if the time allowed to make the repairs has not run out, or it is less than 60 days past the deadline for making repairs. The **Minneapolis Housing Services Office**, 612-673-3003, the **St. Paul Housing Information Office**, 651-266-6000, or your city's inspections department can give you current status information. Landlords who rent units built before 1978 also must disclose any known lead-based paint and include a warning in the lease. The **National Lead Information Center**, 800-424-5323, can provide information and a copy of the Environmental Protection Agency's pamphlet "Protect Your Family from Lead in Your Home."
- Watch for discrimination. In Minnesota, it's illegal to deny housing based on race, religion, age or any other personal basis. Minneapolis specifically prohibits discrimination based on sexual orientation. However, Fair Housing laws may not apply to owner-occupied complexes of four or fewer units.

For more assistance with your investigations of prospective apartments, we suggest The *Savvy Renter's Kit* written by Ed Sacks. It comes complete with a renter's checklist.

STAKING A CLAIM

When viewing prospective apartments, take along appropriate documentation. This usually includes job and bank account information, personal references, the name and telephone number of your previous landlord, and your checkbook to nail down your dream apartment. Many landlords use tenant screening services and the information they receive is used to approve or deny your tenancy. If a landlord uses the service's information to deny rental, increase your security deposit, or increase your rent, he/she must give you written notice of the adverse action. Then you can request a free copy of the report and challenge any inaccuracies. If a reinvestigation by the screening service does not resolve the dispute, then you have a right to add an explanation of the problem to your file.

LEASES, SECURITY DEPOSITS, AND TAX REFUNDS

The terms of a rental agreement are stated in a lease. Lease agreements should be in writing. Be sure you understand everything in a written lease before you sign it, and get a copy for your files. Remember that a lease is a legally binding agreement and that a tenant does not have the right to break a lease, even for good reasons like moving or buying a home. Following are some clauses you should challenge before signing or avoid:

- Unannounced entry—Minnesota has enacted a law forbidding a landlord to enter an apartment without permission or reasonable notice (24 hours) except in emergencies.
- Responsibility for repairs without compensation. If you agree to perform any maintenance on your apartment, you can negotiate a rent decrease. Make sure it's in writing.
- Escalation and acceleration clauses—some leases permit an owner to raise the rent during a lease period (escalation). Other lease language may state that upon missing a month's rent, you are immediately liable for the rest of the lease amount, which could be thousands of dollars (acceleration). These kinds of clauses are legal, but you may not want to rent from someone who proposes them. Pay attention and read the fine print.
- Late charges—if your lease does not include information about late charges, then your landlord may not impose them, except for the filing and service fees related to unlawful detainer that are permitted by law.

As for security deposits, a landlord may require a deposit of any amount in order to pay for damage the tenant might do to the unit. The amount of this deposit may be increased at any time during a month-to-month lease. However, the security deposit must be returned with interest within 21 days after the end of the tenancy, or the landlord must provide a written explanation as to why it is being withheld. As of May 1, 2001, Minnesota Statute Section 504.20 requires an interest payment of four-percent. If a landlord does not refund the deposit, with interest, or if the tenant is dissatisfied with the landlord's reason for keeping the deposit, the tenant can take the matter to court in the county where the rental property is located. The law allows that the tenant may be awarded up to $200 in punitive damages if the landlord is found to have acted "in bad faith."

Minnesota law also gives tenants the chance to get some of their money back in the form of a partial refund for the property taxes they pay indirectly through their rent. To claim your credit, file a property tax refund form (M-1PR) and certificate of rent paid (which your landlord will give you by January 31 of each year) with the Minnesota Department of Revenue. For answers to your questions, call 651-296-3781 or 800-652-9094.

LANDLORD PROBLEMS

An excellent resource for learning your rights and responsibilities as a renter is *The Tenants Rights Handbook*, the product of a joint effort by three Minnesota consumer groups. It's free with membership, or may be purchased by non-members for $7 ($8.50 by mail) from the tenants' unions listed below. These tenants' unions are invaluable resources if you should have a problem with your landlord. The Minnesota Attorney General's office also offers several free booklets: "Landlords and Tenants: Rights and Responsibilities" and the "Homebuyer's Handbook," among them. These may be accessed on the internet at www.ag.state.mn.us or they will be sent to you upon request to the Attorney General's office (see number below).

- **State of Minnesota Attorney General**, 651-296-3353, 800-657-3787, www.ag.state.mn.us, offers information on buying a house or renting, and direct assistance with respect to consumer complaints; free booklets.
- **Minnesota Department of Human Rights**, 190 East 5th Street, St. Paul, MN 55101, 651-296-5663, 800-657-3704, TDD, 651-296-1283, enforces and administers the Minnesota Human Rights Act which protects people against discrimination in housing and other areas.
- **Minnesota Tenants Union**, 1513 Franklin Avenue East, Minneapolis 612-871-7485; pay-per-call hotline 900-225-8888.
- **Minnesota Multi-Housing Association Hotline**, 612-858-8222, a non-profit organization of owners, developers, and managers of multi-family housing can answer questions with respect to tenants' and property owners' rights and responsibilities.

- **First Call for Help** (24 hours), funded by the United Way, this is a general information number which can provide housing assistance with respect to lists of available rental housing, advice on landlord issues, loan programs, transitional housing, and referrals to other resources. East Metro (St. Paul, Ramsey, Washington, and Dakota counties) 651-224-1133, West Metro (Minneapolis, Hennepin, Anoka, Carver, and Scott counties) 612-335-5000.
- **Landlord-Tenant Information Help Line**, 612-341-9003, 10:30 a.m. to 5 p.m., weekdays, provides information and resource services to landlords and tenants including a tenant apartment information kit and move-in package. There is a charge for some of the printed materials.
- **Minneapolis Housing Services**, 612-673-3003, 8 a.m. to 4:30 p.m., weekdays.
- **St. Paul Housing Information Office**, 651-266-6000, 8 a.m. to 4:30 p.m., weekdays.
- **St. Paul Tenants Union**, 500 Laurel Avenue, St. Paul, 651-221-0501, offers services for a yearly membership fee (sliding scale based on ability to pay $7-$18).
- **Dispute Resolution Center**, 974 West Seventh Street, St. Paul, 651-292-7791, serves Ramsey County and the east metro area.
- **North Hennepin Mediation Program, Inc.**, Brooklyn Center, 763-561-0033, is a free service in northern and northwestern Hennepin county.
- **West Suburban Mediation Center**, Hopkins, 952-933-0005, is free to residents of the western and southern suburbs.

RENTER'S INSURANCE

Get it. Generally a building owner's insurance covers damage to the building, not your personal possessions. Renter's insurance, however, does provide relatively inexpensive protection against theft, water damage, fire and, in many cases, personal liability. Insurance companies that sell homeowner's insurance also sell renter's insurance.

You will probably be happier, should you have a disaster, if you have a replacement policy, instead of a cash-value policy—clothes, electronics, and other personal belongings can quickly depreciate down to nothing, but they may be expensive to replace. Before settling on the best policy, take an inventory of your possessions by making a list, taking photos, or videotaping *all* of your valuables. This will give you an idea of how much insurance you need as well as valuable documentation should you need to prove losses; and it will help you decide if you need to purchase a rider to cover especially valuable articles like antiques or jewelry. Be sure to store this documentation in a secure place outside of your home, perhaps in a bank safe deposit box or with a friend.

BUYING

Minnesota loves homeowners! Yes, property taxes are high, but if you live in the house you buy, the state will offset some of your tax burden by giving you a homestead property tax credit and by allowing you to deduct mortgage interest payments from your taxable income, thereby reducing the amount of income taxes you have to pay. The state even allows you to deduct interest from other loans if you are willing to use your home as collateral.

Homes come in many forms, from traditional, single-family detached houses to multiple ownership situations: cluster homes, condos, townhouses, patio homes, and co-ops. **Cluster homes** are detached houses built close together with shared outdoor grounds, recreational facilities, and maintenance costs. **Condominiums** are buildings in which you purchase a unit, and all the land and facilities are jointly owned by the condo community. In a **townhouse** situation you purchase the structure and the land under it. A patio home is similar to the townhouse, however, in addition to purchasing the unit and the land under it, it will also come with a small yard. **Cooperatives** are buildings in which you own a share in the corporation that owns the building, with a housing unit reserved for each shareholder's use. A multiple housing complex, sometimes referred to as association housing, is managed by a board of the homeowners, which collects dues and assessments for maintenance and repairs.

Good questions to ask about association housing are:
- What percentage of the units are owner-occupied?
- How much are the association dues and projected assessments?
- What are the rules and regulations?
- Is the development professionally managed?
- Have there been any lawsuits involving the association in the past five years?

These and many other issues are covered in the "Condominium/

Townhome Guide," published by Re/max Real Estate (800-878-8404). The guide provides information about different styles of housing, associations, and comprehensive checklists to use to evaluate developments.

When scouting for a house, don't forget the cold climate! Energy costs are high here for both heating and cooling. And, while houses built since the energy crisis of the 1970s may have very tight, energy efficient construction, they may also have problems with moisture and poor indoor-air-quality (carbon monoxide, radon). The newest houses solve this problem with balanced mechanical ventilation systems and sealed-combustion appliances that do not draw air from inside the home.

Older houses can also be remodeled and/or made more energy efficient to meet modern families' needs. Two locally produced books have been created to assist those with older homes. *The Longfellow Planbook: Remodeling Plans for Bungalows and Other Small Urban Homes* can be purchased from the Longfellow Community Council, 4151 Minnehaha Avenue South, Minneapolis 55406, 612-722-4529, for $18.50, $10 for Longfellow residents. *Cape Cods and Ramblers: A Remodeling Planbook for Post-WW II Houses* will help you time-tune houses from the 1940s, '50s and '60s. Residents of Blaine, Brooklyn Park, Columbia Heights, Coon Rapids, Crystal, Fridley, Golden Valley, Hopkins, Mounds View, New Brighton, New Hope, Robbinsdale, Richfield, Roseville and St. Louis Park can purchase the book for $10 from their city halls. Those who live outside those communities can get a copy for $15 from the City of Brooklyn Park, 763-424-8000. Online, www.homebuildingresource.com offers house plans, remodeling ideas, financing and a guide to building products.

Upon signing a standard purchase agreement, the seller is required to disclose only certain problems and environmental hazards like lead paint. When inspecting a prospective home, be sure to keep your eyes open for roof and structural damage caused by ice dams which may form if a house is not adequately insulated and ventilated—this is a common problem in Minnesota. It is wise to protect yourself by having a professional roof/mechanical systems inspection prior to purchase. Professional residential inspectors can be found in the Yellow Pages under "Home and Building Inspection," or ask your realtor for a recommendation. There is a free pamphlet available from the **American Society of Home Inspectors** (800-743-ASHI or www.ashi.com). Ask for document #1029.

If you're thinking of building, then "location, location, location" is as important here as it is anywhere. Land prices within the Twin Cities are skyrocketing, particularly in coveted, fast-growing localities such as Woodbury, Eden Prairie and Lakeville. On Lake Minnetonka, people are even buying houses and tearing them down just to get the lots! In general, the most expensive suburbs lie to the west and southwest of Minneapolis and to the north and northeast of St. Paul. And, of course, lakeshore property sells at a premium, and you pay higher property taxes to live on it. For those willing to live a 40 minute drive away from the Twin Cities, in communities where the cul-de-sacs meet the cornfields, such as Waconia, Chisago City, Northfield, or Hudson, Wisconsin, land prices are much more reasonable—though the environmental costs with respect to the loss of farmland and long car commutes are certainly high.

Building a new home in the Twin Cities may require the additional expense of drilling a well and adding a septic system. While there is a lot of water around, many municipalities do not provide it. Be sure to check this out even in established suburbs. (An example: the cities around Lake Minnetonka have sewer service, but they don't all have municipal water.) Well water here, by the way, is likely to be full of iron, requiring the installation of water softeners and high-tech filter systems, all of which add to the cost of a house.

While you are looking for that perfect lot, keep in mind that you will have to comply with strictly enforced local zoning restrictions as well as the most stringent building code in the nation. In fact, the latest revision of the building code, which addresses energy consumption and air-quality issues, is estimated to add $6,000 to $10,000 to the price of a new home, though much of this can be recouped in lower energy costs and higher resale value. Call the **Builders Association of the Twin Cities** (651-697-1954) for information about building a new home, or the **Builders Association of Minnesota** (651-646-7959) for more information on the building code. The clerk or the building inspector of the city you're interested in will be able to provide information with respect to local zoning ordinances. (See **Useful Phone Numbers and Web Sites**.) The **Minnesota Department of Public Service's Energy Information Center** provides free information on conservation and renewable energy, 651-296-5175, 800-657-3710, www.dpsv.state.mn.us. If you're here in the spring or fall, the trademarked Parade/Preview of Homes sponsored by the Builders Association of the Twin Cities (see above) will give you the opportunity to scout locations, check out the latest home designs and construction techniques, and connect with the builders themselves.

Finally, the challenge when buying or building a house is always to find a property that meets your needs while it maximizes your potential resale price. To that end, you need to know that attached three-car garages, mud rooms, fireplaces, second bathrooms, three-season porches and flat driveways (or steep driveways with built-in heating coils to melt the ice) are considered desirable features in the Twin Cities market; swimming pools, however, are often a detriment.

PURCHASE AGREEMENTS, CREDIT, MORTGAGES, INSURANCE

The purchase agreement is a legally binding document between the buyer and seller that states the price and all the terms of a sale. It is the most negotiable and variable document produced in the home-buying process. It is also the single most important. Minnesota does not regulate purchase agreements, but it does require the inclusion of certain disclosure statements, and federal regulations require the disclosure of lead paint and asbestos. Among other things, the purchase agreement is the document to which a buyer may attach contingencies. Such contingencies can protect you, the buyer, from being legally bound by the purchase agreement if, for example, you cannot sell the house you live in now, the house you are buying does not pass its mechanical and structural inspection, the seller is not able to give you possession by a certain date, or you cannot qualify for a loan.

Lenders suggest that you pre-qualify for your loan—to that end, meet with your potential lender to determine the amount of possible financing. Go prepared with documents that pertain to your finances and check your credit report to make sure it is accurate *before* meeting with a loan officer. You can check your credit report with all three national credit bureaus listed here. You will need to provide your name, address, previous address, and Social Security number with your request. Check with each company for specific instructions, or contact all three online at **www.icreditreport.com**. Some credit bureaus will give you a free copy of your report, while others may charge up to $8. Reports are free, if you've been denied credit based on your credit report within the last 30 days.

The National Credit Bureaus are:

- **Experian** (formerly TRW), P.O. Box 2104, Allen, TX 75002-2104, 888-397-3742
- **TransUnion Corporation**, P.O. Box 390, Springfield, PA 19064-0390, 800-916-8800
- **Equifax**, P.O. Box 105873, Atlanta, GA 30348, 800-685-1111

When qualifying for a mortgage, the rule of thumb is that most people (depending on their existing debt load) can afford a home that is two and one-half times their annual gross income, or monthly payments of about 28% of their gross income. The **Attorney General's Home Buyer's Handbook** (800-657-3787, www.ag.state.mn.us) contains information about Veteran's Administration (VA), Federal Housing Administration (FHA), and conventional mortgages as well as a Loan Qualification Worksheet to help you figure out what you can afford. Another possibility when acquiring a house is signing a contract for deed (CD) and paying the seller directly.

Major banks and mortgage-lending institutions usually have web sites. Norwest, a large Twin Cities lender can be accessed at www.norwest.com. See **Money Matters** for additional sites. E-Loan at www.eloan.com and Computer Loan Network at www.clnet.com function like a mortgage broker.

Housing assistance is available for those in need. The **US Department of Housing and Urban Development** (**HUD**) has opened a talking, interactive kiosk that looks like an ATM machine on the first level of the Minneapolis Public Service Center, 250 South 4th Street. Called "HUD Next Door," the kiosk helps consumers buy homes, find rentals, access HUD properties that are for sale and figure out how much they can afford to spend on housing. This service also is available on the internet at www.hud.gov. The **Minnesota Housing Finance Agency**, 651-296-8215, 612-370-3000, is sometimes able to make loans at below-market interest rates to first-time buyers or those with moderate incomes. The **Northside Residents' Redevelopment Council**, 612-335-5923, sells rehabilitated homes in north Minneapolis neighborhoods to moderate-income buyers, and the **Richfield Housing and Redevelopment Authority**, 612-861-9760, sponsors several programs for first-time home or lower-income buyers. Also contact the city and county where you want to live—there may be incentive programs for moving into their area.

Once your loan is approved, your lender will require you to buy **homeowner's insurance** to protect their investment (your home). Be sure the policy you choose covers the house, its contents, and outbuildings. You'll also want to protect yourself in case of liability. Policies vary, so check restrictions and exclusions carefully to make sure you have the coverage you need. A basic homeowner's policy includes: liability insurance to protect you if someone is injured on your property; property protection which insures your house and personal belongings against damage or loss; and living expense coverage that will pay for you to live elsewhere while repairs are being made. You may also need the following: mortgage insurance, which is required by many lenders as well as the FHA to cover them if you default on your loan; and title insurance, which protects the lender in case the legal title to the property isn't clear. It doesn't protect you though, so, in addition, you may want to buy an owner's title insurance policy, or get an attorney's opinion on your title. If the seller has purchased title insurance in recent years, you may be able to get the same title company to issue you a new policy at a lower cost, so be sure to ask for a re-issue credit.

Some of the major insurance companies in the area are:

- **Allstate** (www.allstate.com)
- **American Family Insurance** (www.amfam.com)
- **Farmers Insurance Group** (www.farmersinsurance.com)
- **St. Paul Fire and Marine Insurance Company** (www.stpaul.com/fire-and-marine)
- **State Farm** (www.statefarm.com)

Consumer tips for buying insurance are available from Qwest (612-586-6000, press 3436 for homeowners' insurance). You can check on specific companies and agents by calling the **Minnesota Department of Commerce**, 651-296-4026, or its **Division of Enforcement**, 651-296-2488.

WORKING WITH REALTORS

You certainly can find a home without going through a real estate agent, but if you decide to work with one, there are a few things you should know. Even if an agent takes you to see a home, he or she is actually representing the seller, not you. If you want an agent who will act on your behalf, you will need to hire a buyer's broker. This person will not give information about you and what you can afford to the seller and will negotiate the lowest possible price for you.

Some of the real estate firms in the Twin Cities are listed below:

- **Century 21**, Blaine: 1633 NE Highway 10, 612-786-8702; Coon Rapids: 2437 NW Coon Rapids Boulevard, 612-755-5050, 11499 NW Martin Street, 612-757-4240; Edina: 4536 France Avenue South, 612-925-3901; Eden Prairie: 16395 Wagner Way, 612-975-9900; Spring Lake Park: 1633 NE Highway 10, 612-786-8702; Woodbury: 1750 Weir Drive, 651-739-0044; Eagan: 1570 Century Point, 651-454-3410; Stillwater: 1940 South Greeley Street, 651-439-1797; Forest Lake: 179 South Lake Street, 651-464-5400
- **Coldwell Banker Burnet**, www.coldwellbanker.com; over 25 offices in the metro area, check the White Pages for a location near you.

- **Counselor Realty, Inc.**, www.counselor-realty.com; offices in the western and northwestern suburbs: Spring Lake Park: 7766 NE Highway 65, 612-786-0600; Wayzata: 36225 South Highway 101, 612-473-9500; Anoka: 3200 NW Main Street, 612-566-4111; Brooklyn Park: 7001 78th Avenue North, 612-566-4111; Edina/Bloomington: 5810 West 78th Street, 612-921-0911
- **Edina Realty**, 24-hour hotline, 612-858-5858
- **Johnsen-Bormes Realtors**, 18300 Minnetonka Boulevard, Deephaven, 952-473-3839
- **Prudential Real Estate**, offices metro wide, main office: Edina, 4901 West 77th Street; check www.prureinfo.com or call 612-835-4499 for an office near you.
- **Remax**, www.Remax.com, over 25 offices, check the White Pages for a location near you.

The **Minneapolis Area Association of Realtors**, 612-935-8313, can give you more information about licensed real estate agents in different localities.

ONLINE RESOURCES—HOUSE HUNTING

If you want to get an idea of the market before arriving in the Twin Cities, you may want to subscribe online to one of the city newspapers for a month. Check their sites (listed below) for subscription details. For additional community newspapers, log on to www.mnnewspapernet.org. If you're in the market to buy a home before relocating here, look into the last four web sites listed below. From them you can link to listings of homes, look up realtors, and even download photos. Also, look up realtors' individual web sites through keywords such as "realty," "Minneapolis," and so on. **Bankrate.com** lists current mortgage rates.

- *Citypages*, www.citypages.com/classifieds
- *Star Tribune*, www.startribune.com/homezone
- *St. Paul Pioneer Press*, www.pioneerplanet.com
- *Minnesota Daily*, www.daily.umn.edu/classifieds
- **Realtor.com** is the homepage for the national association of Realtors. It has a large on-line database of home listings and offers virtual tours of listed property.
- **go.com** has property listings, information on Realtors and neighborhoods, roommate referrals, loan and relocation information, and comparison price checks.

- **Homeadvisor.com** is Microsoft's answer to home buying on the web. It includes nationwide home listings, relocation tips, financing a new home, and selling.
- **Virtual Realty**, www.mnrealty.com

See **Moving and Storage** for more sites related to relocation.

BEFORE YOU CAN START YOUR NEW LIFE IN THE TWIN CITIES, YOU and your worldly possessions have to get here. How difficult that will be, depends on how much stuff you've accumulated, how much money you're willing or able to spend on the move, and where you're coming from.

TRUCK RENTALS

The first question you need to answer: am I going to move myself or will I have someone else do it for me? If you're used to doing everything yourself, you can rent a vehicle and head for the open road. Look in the Yellow Pages under "Truck Rental" and call around and compare. Below we list four national truck rental firms and their toll-free numbers and web sites. For the best information you should call a local office. Note that most truck rental companies now offer "one-way" rentals (don't forget to ask whether they have a drop-off/return location in or near your destination) as well as packing accessories and storage facilities. Of course, these extras are not free and if you're cost conscious you may want to scavenge boxes in advance of your move and make sure you have a place to store your belongings upon arrival. Also, if you're planning on moving during the peak moving months (May through September), call well in advance of when you think you'll need the vehicle. A month at least.

Once you're on the road, keep in mind that your rental truck may be a tempting target for thieves. If you must park it overnight or for an extended period (more than a couple of hours), try to find a safe place, preferably somewhere well-lit and easily observable by you, and do your best not leave anything of particular value in the cab.

- **Budget**, 800-428-7825, www.budget.com
- **Penske**, 800-222-0277, www.penske.com

- **Ryder**, 800-467-9337, www.ryder.com
- **Uhaul**, 800-468-4285, www.uhaul.com

Not sure if you want to drive the truck yourself? Commercial freight carriers, such as **Consolidated Freightways** and **ABF** offer an in-between service: they deliver a 28 foot trailer to your home, you pack and load as much of it as you need, and they drive the vehicle to your destination (usually with some commercial freight filling up the empty space). Available through their web sites at www.cfmovesu.com and www.upack.com.

MOVERS

Surveys show that most people find movers through the **Yellow Pages**. If that's too random for you, probably the best way to find a mover is through a personal recommendation. Absent a friend or relative who can point you to a trusted moving company, you can try the **internet**; just type in "movers" on a search engine and you'll be directed to dozens of more or less helpful moving related sites. For long distance or interstate moves, the **American Moving and Storage Association's** site, www.moving.org, is useful for identifying member movers both in Minnesota and across the county. In the past, *Consumer Reports* (www.consumerreports.org) has published useful information on moving. Check out a recent *Consumer Reports* index to find any articles or surveys they may have published to aid you in your search. Members of the **AAA** can call their local office and receive discounted rates and service through AAA's Consumer Relocation Service.

Disagreeable moving experiences, while common, aren't obligatory. To aid you in your search for a hassle free mover, we offer a few **general recommendations**:

- Make sure any moving company you are considering hiring is licensed by the appropriate authority. For intrastate moves, the mover should have a Household Carrier Permit granted by the Office of Motor Carrier Services. You can look at their web site, www.dot.state.mn.us or call 888-472-3389 (select option "2"), to confirm a carrier's license. If yours is an interstate move, make sure the carrier has a Department of Transportation MC ("Motor Carrier") or ICC MC number that should be displayed on all advertising and promotional material as well as on the truck. With the MC number in hand, contact the Department of Transportation's Federal Motor Carrier Safety

Administration at 202-358-7028 or check www.fmcsa.dot.gov, to see if the carrier is licensed.

- If someone recommends a mover to you, get names (the salesperson or estimator, the drivers, the loaders). To paraphrase the NRA, moving companies don't move people, people do.
- Before a move takes place, federal regulations require interstate movers to furnish customers with a copy of *Your Rights and Responsibilities When You Move*, prepared by the old Interstate Commerce Commission. If they don't give you a copy, ask for one.
- Once you've narrowed it down to two or three companies, ask a mover for references, particularly from customers who did moves similar to yours. If a moving company is unable or unwilling to provide such information or tells you that they can't give out names because their customers are all in the federal Witness Protection Program . . . perhaps you should consider another company.
- Check with the Better Business Bureau (www.bbb.org) in the state where the moving company is licensed, as well as that state's Consumer Protection Office, to find out if any complaints have been filed against a prospective mover.
- Even though movers will put numbered labels on your possessions, you should make a numbered list of every box and item that is going in the truck. Detail box contents and photograph anything of particular value. Once the truck arrives on the other end, you can check off every piece and know for sure what did (or did not) make it. In case of claims, this list can be invaluable. Even after the move, keep the list; it can be surprisingly useful.
- Be aware that during the busy season (May through September), demand can exceed supply and moving may be more difficult and more expensive than during the rest of the year. If you must relocate during the peak moving months, call and book service well in advance of when you plan on moving. A month at least. If you can reserve service way in advance, say four to six months early, you may be able to lock in a lower winter rate for your summer move.
- Whatever you do, *do not* mislead a salesperson about how much and what you are moving. And make sure you tell a prospective mover about how far they'll have to transport your stuff to and from the truck as well as any stairs, driveways, obstacles or difficult vegetation, long paths or sidewalks, etc. The clearer you are with your mover, the better he or she will be able to serve you.
- You should never have to pay for an estimate and you should request

a written "not to exceed" quote. This means that you will not be charged more than the guaranteed price, and if your shipment is lighter than the salesperson estimated, you may even be charged less. A caveat, however: if your shipment is much heavier or much more difficult than the salesperson estimated, the driver may cry foul and require an adjustment to the quote at the point of origin. If a potential problem is not taken care of at the point of origin, the delivering driver may protest the shipment and require a "backweigh" and an adjustment to the quote on the other end. To avoid such a hassle, see the preceding recommendation.

- Remember that price, while important, isn't everything, especially when you're entrusting all of your worldly possessions to strangers. Choose a mover you feel comfortable with.
- Think about packing. Depending on the size of your move and whether or not you are packing yourself, you may need a lot of boxes, tape and packing material. Mover boxes, while not cheap, are usually sturdy and the right size. Sometimes a mover will give a customer free used boxes. It doesn't hurt to ask. Also, *don't* wait to pack until the last minute. If you're doing the packing, give yourself at least a week to do the job, two or more is better.
- Above all, ask questions and if you're concerned about something, ask for an explanation in writing.
- Listen to what the movers say; they are professionals and can give you expert advice about packing and preparing. Also, be ready for the truck on both ends—don't make them wait. Not only will it irritate your movers, but it may cost you. Understand, too, that things can happen on the road that are beyond a carrier's control (weather, accidents, etc.) and your belongings may not get to you at the time or on the day promised. (See note about insurance below.)
- Treat your movers well, especially the ones loading your stuff on and off the truck. Offer to buy them lunch, and tip them if they do a good job.
- Ask about insurance, the "basic" 60 cents per pound industry standard coverage is not enough. If you have homeowner or renter's insurance, check to see if it will cover your belongings during transit. If not, consider purchasing "full replacement" or "full value" coverage from the carrier for the estimated value of your shipment. Though it's the most expensive type of coverage offered, it's probably worth it. Trucks get into accidents, they catch fire, they get stolen—if such insurance seems pricey to you, ask about a $250 or $500 deductible. This can reduce your cost substantially while still

giving you much better protection in the event of a catastrophic loss. Irreplaceable items such as jewelry, photographs or key work documents should be transported by yourself.

- Be prepared to pay the full moving bill upon delivery. Cash or bank/cashier's check may be required. Some carriers will take VISA and MasterCard but it is a good idea to get it in writing that you will be permitted to pay with a credit card since the delivering driver may not be aware of this and may demand cash. Unless you routinely keep thousands of dollars of greenbacks on you, you could have a problem getting your stuff off the truck.
- Finally, before moving pets, attach a tag to their collar with your new address and phone number in case your pet accidentally wanders off in the confusion of moving.

Those moving within the Twin Cities with minimal belongings probably won't need a huge truck to complete the task. If you (and all of your friends) are not inclined to load and unload a rented truck, you may want to consider hiring one of the following local movers:

- **A-1 Moving**, 952-926-7017, www.a-1moving.com
- **Harco Moving and Storage Inc.**, 612-571-6227, www.harcomoving.com; hauls locally and statewide.
- **Sorensen's Apartment Movers**, 763-525-8883
- **Two Men and a Truck**, 612-894-8606, www.twomen.com/locations

ROAD RESTRICTIONS

A special consideration when you're timing a move or building a house in Minnesota is road restrictions. From March 1 to May 1, when the roads are heaving and thawing, the state, counties and cities all restrict the weight of the vehicles that may drive here. For example, many residential streets are closed to vehicles weighing more than four tons per axle. This affects both construction equipment and moving vans. In fact, large moving vans often have to park at some distance from an address and actually complete the move using smaller, lighter vehicles. Local contractors are accustomed to working around the road restrictions, but if you're moving from out of state be sure to bring this to your mover's attention. For more information about road restrictions for the state of Minnesota, call 651-406-4701.

STORAGE

If your new pad is too small for all of your belongings or if you need a temporary place to store your stuff while you find a new home, self-storage is the answer.

Probably the easiest way to find storage is to look in the **Yellow Pages**. Check under "Storage—Household & Commercial" for complete listings. If you want to call to reserve a storage unit before your move you can check Qwest's online Yellow Pages, www.qwestdex.com, try www.storagelocator.com, or check the listings below for full service storage operations in the Twin Cities. When looking for a unit, price, convenience, security, fire sprinklers, climate control, and accessibility are all considerations. Ask, too, how a storage company bills and whether a deposit is required.

Keep in mind that demand for storage surges in the prime moving months (May through September) . . . so try not to wait until the last minute to rent storage. Also, if you don't care about convenience, your cheapest storage options may be outside the Twin Cities. You just have to figure out how to get your stuff there and back.

A word of warning: unless you no longer want your stored belongings, pay your storage bill and pay it on time. Storage companies may auction the contents of delinquent customers' lockers.

A few area storage companies include:

- **AAA Midway Inside Storage**, 1400 Selby Avenue, St. Paul, 651-642-1661
- **Brooklyn Park Mini Storage**, 4224 83rd Avenue North, Minneapolis, 763-561-3011
- **EZ Mini-Storage**, 10 locations: 3601 Hiawatha Avenue, Minneapolis, 612-722-1111; St. Louis Park, 952-546-4744
- **Minikahda Mini Storage**: 1441 Hunting Valley Road 1, 651-641-0101 (U of M and Midway); 300 North 5th Street, Minneapolis, 612-332-1332; 3200 France Avenue South, St. Louis Park, 952-929-0929; 10830 Greenbrier Road, Minnetonka/Hopkins, 952-545-5500; 1200 North Concord Street, South and West St. Paul, 651-450-1202; 2356 University Avenue West, St. Paul, 651-917-0707
- **Minnesota Mini-Storage**: I-494 and France Avenue, Edina/Bloomington, 952-835-0580; Highway 5 and Eden Prairie Road, Eden Prairie (West), 952-934-6848; Highway 212 and Shady Oak Road, Eden Prairie (East), 952-944-1448; I-94 and Lyndale, Richfield/Bloomington, 612-1861-5300; Highway 7 and Vine Hill Road,

Minnetonka/Shorewood, 952-474-2123; I-494 and Highway 55, Plymouth/Wayzata 763-553-1545; Highway 81 and Zachary Lane, Maple Grove, 763-493-9339; Highway 10 and Sunfish Lake Boulevard, Anoka, 763-712-1985; I-494 and Lake Street, Woodbury, 651-578-8788; 1144 South 7th Street, Hopkins, 612-931-0942
- **Secure Mini Storage**: 3245 Hiawatha Avenue South, Minneapolis, 612-721-4748; 246 Eaton Street, St. Paul, 651-227-2700; 849 Terrace Court, 651-772-2554; 5710 Memorial Avenue North, Stillwater, 651-439-0250; 415 West Marie, West St. Paul, 651-455-3720; 9640 Hudson Road, Woodbury, 651-731-0807

CHILDREN

Studies show that moving, especially frequent moving, can be hard on children. According to an American Medical Association study, children who move often are more likely to suffer from such problems as depression, worthlessness and aggression. Often their academic performance suffers as well. Aside from not moving more than is necessary, there are a few things you can do to help your children through this stressful time:

- Talk about the move with your kids. Be honest but positive. Listen to their concerns. To the extent possible, involve them in the process.
- Make sure the child has his or her favorite possessions with them on the trip; *don't* pack "blankey" in the moving van.
- Make sure you have some social life planned on the other end. Your child may feel lonely in your new home and such activities can ease the transition.
- Keep in touch with family and loved ones as much as possible. Photos and phone calls are important ways of maintaining links to the important people you have left behind.
- If your child is of school age, take the time to involve yourself in their new school and in their academic life. Don't let them fall through the cracks.

For younger children, there are dozens of good books on the topic. Just a few include, *Alexander, Who's Not (Do You Hear Me? I Mean It!) Going to Move* by Judith Viorst; *The Moving Book: A Kid's Survival Guide* by Gabriel Davis; *Goodbye/Hello* by Barbara Hazen, *The Leaving Morning* by Angela Johnson; and the *Little Monster's Moving Day* by Mercer Mayer.

For older children, try: *Amber Brown is Not a Crayon* by Paula Danziger; the *Kid in the Red Jacket* by Barbara Park; *Hold Fast to Dreams* by

Andrea Davis Pinkney; *Flip Flop Girl* by Katherine Paterson and *My Fabulous New Life* by Sheila Greenwald.

A moving kit recommended by the Parents Choice Foundation in 1998, "Goodbye-Hello: Everything You Need to Help Your Child When Your Family Moves" might be particularly useful for those with children in the 4-12 age group. In addition to a booklet for parents, the kit includes a child's wall calendar, change of address post cards, a moving journal, markers and more. Visit firstbooks.com or call 503-588-2224 to order any of the above resources.

For general guidance, read *Smart Moves: Your Guide through the Emotional Maze of Relocation* by Nadia Jensen, Audrey McCollum and Stuart Copans (Smith & Krauss)

CONSUMER COMPLAINTS—MOVERS

If you have a problem with your mover that you haven't been able to resolve directly, you can file a complaint with the state's **Office of Motor Carrier Services** at 888-472-3389 (select option "2") or go to www.dot.state.mn.us. If yours was an interstate move, your options are limited in terms of government help. Once upon a time, the Interstate Commerce Commission would log complaints against interstate movers. Today, you're pretty much on your own. The Federal Motor Carrier Safety Administration recommends that you contact the Better Business Bureau in the state where the moving company is licensed as well as that state's consumer protection office to register a complaint. If satisfaction still eludes you, start a letter writing campaign: to the state Attorney General, to your congressional representative, to the newspaper, the sky's the limit. Of course, if the dispute is worth it, you can hire a lawyer and seek redress the all-American way.

TAXES

If your move is work-related, some or all of your moving expenses may be tax-deductible—so you may want to keep those receipts. Though eligibility varies, depending for example, on whether you have a job or are self-employed, generally, the cost of moving yourself, your family and your belongings is tax deductible, even if you don't itemize. The criteria: in order to take the deduction your move must be employment-related, your new job must be more than 50 miles away from your current residence, and you must be here for at least 39 weeks during the first 12 months after your arrival. If you take the deduction and then fail to meet the requirements, you will have to pay the IRS back, unless you were laid off through no fault of your own or transferred again by your employer. Consulting a tax expert for guidance with IRS's rules in respect to moving is probably a good idea. However, if you're a confident soul, get a copy of IRS Form 3903 (www.irs.gov) and do it yourself!

ONLINE RESOURCES—RELOCATION

- Apartments.com, www.apartments.com, includes short-term rentals and furniture rental
- Apartment Search.com, www.apartmentsearch.com, provides free help finding an apartment.
- www.erc.org, the Employee Relocation Council, a professional organization, offers members specialized reports on the relocation and moving industries
- www.firstbooks.com, relocation resources and information on moving to Atlanta, Boston, Chicago, Los Angeles, New York, Philadelphia, San Francisco and the Bay Area, Seattle, Washington, DC, as well as London, England
- www.homeadvisor.com, realty listings, buying and selling, relocation advice, and more
- www.homefair.com, realty listings, moving tips, and more
- www.homestore.com, renting, buying, selling, and building; home improvement, and more
- www.moverquotes.com, comparison shop for mover quotes
- www.moving.com, a moving services site: packing tips, mover estimates, etc.
- www.moving-guide.com, movers and moving services
- www.moving.org, members of the American Moving and Storage Association
- www.rent.net, apartment rentals, movers, relocation advice and more
- www.springstreet.com, apartment rentals, moving tips, movers, and more
- United Rentals, www.unitedrentals.com
- www.usps.com, relocation information from the United States Postal Service

O PENING A BANK ACCOUNT IS ONE OF THE FIRST THINGS YOU will need to take care of upon arriving. Many landlords and rental agents will not accept a tenant who does not have a checking account, so its probably wise to keep your old bank account for at least a short time after moving.

BANK ACCOUNTS AND SERVICES

When choosing a bank, consider convenience, proximity to home or work, banking hours, services required, interest rates and fees. Twin Cities' banks have been consolidating at a fast pace, so there are not as many big-bank choices as there used to be. On the other hand, smaller, more community-based banks are springing up all the time, perhaps due to consumers' desire for personal service. The first four financial institutions listed below are large and have branches throughout the Twin Cities, the rest of the list are smaller community banks.

- **Firstar**, 612-784-5600; 24-hour banking, 612-784-5100, www.firstar.com
- **Norwest**, 612-667-9378, TTD, 651-205-8839, www.norwest.com
- **US Bank**, 612-US-BANKS, www.usbanks.com
- **Twin Cities Federal (TCF) Savings and Loan**, 612-823-2265 (has branch offices in some Cub Foods stores), www.tcfbank.com
- **Anchor Bank**: Wayzata, 952-473-4606; Plymouth, 763-559-9336; Eden Prairie, 952-942-7522
- **The Bank Chanhassen**, 952-937-2265
- **Cherokee State Bank**: St. Paul: 607 Smith Avenue South, 651-227-7071; 985 Grand Avenue, 651-292-9200; Randolph at West 7th, 651-290-6965; 175 Concord, 651-290-6115; North Oaks, 651-483-3559
- **Citizens Bank**: St. Louis Park, 952-926-6561; Robbinsdale, 763-588-2715

- **First State Bank of Eden Prairie**, 952-944-6262; Calhoun Square, 612-825-2211
- **Franklin National Bank**, Plymouth, 763-550-0500
- **National City Bank**, Minneapolis and Edina, 612-904-8000
- **Premier Banks**: Bloomington, 952- 888-5678; Maplewood, 651-777-7700; White Bear Lake, 651-426-7800; www.premierbanks.com
- **Western Bank**: Edina, 952-857-1707; Maplewood, 651-290-7844; Minneapolis, 651-290-7888; Oakdale, 651-290-7844; St. Paul, 651-290-8100
- **Northeast Bank**: Minneapolis, 612-379-8811; Columbia Heights, 612-788-9351; Coon Rapids, 763-784-3533
- **Richfield Bank and Trust**: St. Paul, 651-222-1406; Minneapolis, 612-677-0272; Bloomington/Eden Prairie, 952-944-6993; Burnsville, 952-435-3036; Chanhassen, 952-906-9545; Edina, 952-869-2445; Richfield, 612-798-3400
- **Ridgedale State Bank**: Minnetonka, 952-544-2444; Nicollet Mall, 612-332-8890
- **State Bank of Long Lake**, 952-473-7347

CHECKING ACCOUNTS

Call around to ask about special promotions for opening new checking accounts—banks regularly offer such perks as free checks or, better yet, free checking. A popular option most banks now offer is the debit card. You can use it to withdraw money from your checking account at an automated teller machine (ATM), or you can make purchases with it directly, as with a credit card, again, the money comes directly from your checking account. Some banks also connect the debit card to a line of credit as overdraft protection. Debit cards are quickly becoming the way to bank, with banks encouraging people to use the cards instead of tellers for simple deposits and withdrawals. That aside, if you're coming from a large urban area, you'll probably be pleasantly surprised at how readily most Twin Cities merchants still accept personal checks.

To open an account, most banks require a minimum deposit (depending on the type of account you want, some have minimums as low as $50), current photo identification and your Social Security number.

SAVINGS ACCOUNTS

You may also want to open a savings account at the same time you line up your checking account. Most banks will take care of both at the same time. But, with the lines between banks, savings and loans, insurance companies and brokerage houses blurring, many banks are now active in a variety of financial arenas, and, in lieu of a simple savings account, may offer you a number of financial products, including CDs, money market accounts and stock funds. If these are relevant issues to you, it may be worth asking about them when deciding upon where to open your account.

ONLINE BANKING

Many area banks offer online banking. You can easily track account activity, pay all of your bills automatically or even apply for a loan, all from the comfort of your own home. You'll also have 24-hour-a-day access to your account and never have to write another check, lick an envelope or buy a stamp. Services vary from bank to bank; some charge a fee for automatic bill paying features. See above under **Bank Accounts and Services** for area banks' web addresses.

When investigating online banking you will find that each bank provides a demonstration that covers all online banking activities and explains what services are offered, how these services are accessed (whether by internet or specialized banking software) and the cost of added features. Information is encrypted at the highest security level available to assure the privacy of your account information. As an added bonus, many financial institutions insure your account against online theft. As with any services offered online, there are a few precautions you can take to maintain your account's security: never give out your password, never use e-mail to send confidential information, and change your password regularly. To open an online account you will need to have a preexisting account.

Two national internet banks that may be worth investigating are www.netbank.com and www.telebank.com. Both advertise significantly higher interest rates than their so-called "brick and mortar" competitors. While this form of banking is not for those who love the service and physical presence of a traditional bank, the internet age has arrived, and many are embracing what's sure to become banking's future.

CREDIT UNIONS

Your place of work or your alma mater may offer membership in a credit union, which could be the best deal of all. They offer almost all the same products that banks do (even travel planning), with fewer fees.

According to Credit Union Online, in 1999 the average credit union credit card fee was seven percent, and the average car loan interest rate was a full point below bank rates. Your employer will be able to tell you if you are eligible for membership through your office. Some Minnesota credit unions serve people who work or live in specific areas. The **Pioneer Plus Federal Credit Union** serves people who live or work in Washington County, 651-578-8737, 651-578-8880, and **Como Northtown Community Credit Union**, 651-488-2535, serves those who live or work between Snelling and Dale, from University to Larpenteur. To locate a credit union near you, call the **Minnesota Credit Union Network**, 612-854-3071. **CUOnline**, www.cuonline.com, is another web resource for and about credit unions that includes a list of participating Minnesota credit unions.

CREDIT CARDS

For those who want a credit card, you can call or apply online:
- **VISA and MasterCard**: your bank probably offers both. The Northwest Airlines WorldPerks VISA card earns frequent flyer miles with every purchase, 800-327-2881.
- **American Express**, 800-THE-CARD, www.americanexpress.com
- **Diner's Club**, 800-2DINERS, www.dinersclubus.com
- **Discover**, 800-347-2683 (or apply at Sears stores), www.discover-card.com
- **Department store credit card** applications can be obtained at the checkout counter, and stores frequently offer immediate discounts if you apply for a card at the checkout. The most well known local department store is Dayton's, with several locations metro-wide. Department store cards are easy to qualify for and can be used to establish a credit history if you have none.

A word of warning to credit card users: the biggest revenue sources for credit card issuers are penalty charges for late credit card payments. If you want to avoid high finance charges, check to see what your grace period is—the period between the end of a billing cycle and the payment due date during which no interest is charged, if the account balance is paid off in full. Try to pay off your balance within this period. In some cases, however, grace periods have been eliminated altogether. This is most often the case on cards issued with rewards programs, such as university cards. But you don't have to be late with your payment to pay more to use your credit card. Some companies actually start charging you interest from the date of your purchase. Another method for calculating finance charges compounds interest daily instead of monthly. Called "daily periodic rate" billing, this may only squeeze a few extra pennies out of you, but they're still your pennies. The billing method, which has the potential to be most costly to consumers, is called "two-cycle average daily balance" billing. This is a complicated form of billing which totals charges for two months and divides them by the number of days to calculate an average daily balance; the finance charge is applied to the resulting amount only if the cardholder has not already been charged interest on the earlier month. In other words, if you usually pay off your balance when the bill comes and carry a month-to-month balance only occasionally, watch out! Since credit card issuers are always coming up with new ways to improve their profits, be sure to read the fine print in your contract, and don't necessarily be taken in by low interest rates. For additional consumer information access **CardWeb**, www.cardweb.com, or the **Consumer Action Organization**, www.consumer-action.org.

If you need credit counseling, **Consumer Credit Counseling**, 430 Oak Grove Street, Suite 204, Minneapolis, is a full-service financial counseling agency with offices in several locations, which can also help you to repair your credit rating. Call 612-874-8164.

CREDIT REPORTS

The Fair Credit Reporting Act gives you the right to check your credit reports to make sure they are accurate—many consumers have found errors. If you're unsure of your credit report profile, it may be a good idea to check your reports with all three national credit bureaus listed here. You will need to provide your name, address, previous address, and Social Security number with your request. Check with each company for specific instructions or contact all three online at **www.icreditreport.com**. Some credit bureaus will give you a free copy of your report, while others may charge up to $8. Reports are free if you've been denied credit based on your credit report within the last 30 days.

The national credit bureaus are:

- **Experian** (formerly TRW), P.O. Box 2104, Allen, TX 75002-2104, 888-397-3742
- **TransUnion Corporation**, P.O. Box 390, Springfield, PA 19064-0390, 800-916-8800
- **Equifax**, P.O. Box 105873, Atlanta, GA 30348, 800-685-1111

TAXES

Minnesota has a reputation for being a high-tax state, making taxes and weather the bane of Minnesotans' existence. If you are relocating to a job in the Twin Cities from another city or state, and are here for at least 39 weeks during the first 12 months after your arrival, you may be eligible to deduct moving expenses from your federal return. If you take the deduction and then fail to meet the requirement, you will be required to pay the IRS back, unless you were laid off through no fault of your own or transferred again by your employer. See **Moving and Storage** for more information.

INCOME TAXES

As a resident here, you will have to pay both federal and state income taxes. For federal forms and information contact:
- **Federal Tax Forms**, 800-829-FORM (or stop by a public library or post office) or download them from the internet, www.irs.ustreas.gov
- **Federal Teletax Information System**, 800-829-4477, TTY, 800-829-4059 (for recorded federal tax information) or www.irs.ustreas.gov.
- **Internal Revenue Service**, 316 North Robert Street, St. Paul, 800-829-4477 (for recorded help on federal taxes) or www.irs.ustreas.gov for Web help.

The state income tax is based on federal adjusted income plus or minus state modifications. There are three rates that increase with income: 6%, 8% and 8.5%. To obtain Minnesota state income tax forms and to ask questions call the **Minnesota Department of Revenue**, 10 River Park Plaza, St. Paul, 651-296-3781. The forms are also available at libraries and post offices during tax season or online at www.taxes.state.mn.us.

SALES TAX

The state sales tax (on everything except food and clothing) is 6.5% with an additional .5% being collected within the city of Minneapolis. Due to budget surpluses in 1999 and again in 2000, the state refunded a percentage of its sales tax collections to taxpayers.

PROPERTY TAXES

Property taxes are different for each city and county and include levies to support school districts, watershed districts, mosquito control and other services. Generally you can expect to pay between one and three percent of the market value of your property in taxes each year. The previous year's property taxes will be stated on a home's listing sheet. To find out about property taxes in the community you are considering, call the city hall or, since school district levies account for the bulk of property taxes, call your local school district.

Information is also posted on the following Web sites:
- **Hennepin County**: www.co.hennepin.mn.us
- **Minneapolis**: www.ci.minneapolis.mn.us
- **Minneapolis Schools**: www.mpls.k12.mn.us
- **Ramsey County**: www.co.ramsey.mn.us
- **St. Paul**: www.stpaul.gov
- **St. Paul Schools**: www.stpaul.k12.mn.us

STATE PROPERTY TAX REFUNDS

Minnesota offers tenants a renter's property tax refund. Your landlord is required to send you the Certification of Rent Paid (CRP) form no later than January 31. You then have nearly seven months (until August 15th) to fill out your half—the M1PR form—and send both to the state for a refund of the portion of your rent that went to property taxes. The refund may not amount to much, but it's usually worth filing. Homeowners are eligible for a "Homestead" tax credit on the property in which they live. The Minnesota Department of Revenue, listed above, can answer questions about property tax refunds.

CONSUMER PROTECTION

If you have a problem with your bank, first try to resolve the matter by bringing it to the attention of a senior bank officer. It's in their interest to resolve a conflict to the customer's satisfaction. If the problem is still not taken care of to your satisfaction, there are state and federal agencies that handle consumer complaints against banks. The first resource to call, for advice and referral elsewhere, is **Minnesota's Department of Commerce**, Office of Enforcement, 133 East 7th Street, St. Paul, 651-296-2488, www.state.mn.us/govtoffice. You can also file a complaint with one of the following regulatory agencies:
- **Board of Governors of the Federal Reserve System**, 202-452-3693

- **Federal Consumer Information Center** catalogue, 888-8-PUEBLO or www.pueblo.gsa.gov
- **Comptroller of the Currency**, 202-874-4700, 800-613-6743 or www.occ.treas.gov
- **Federal Deposit Insurance Corporation**, 202-942-3100
- **The Office of Thrift Supervision**, 202-906-6000; e-mail, public.info@ots.treas.gov; consumer complaints, 800-842-6929 or e-mail consumercomplaints@ots.treas.gov
- **The National Credit Union Administration**, 703-518-6300
- **Office of the Comptroller of the Currency**, 800-613-6743
- **Federal Trade Commission**, 202-326-2222

N OW THAT YOU'VE LANDED A PLACE TO LIVE AND OPENED A checking account, you're probably wondering: what will it take to get life back to normal? Among the first things you'll have to do is set up phone service, electricity and gas accounts, and perhaps cable TV as well. Try to arrange for your utilities a day or two before you move in, particularly your telephone. With this book and a phone, you can do most of your setting up from the comfort of a moving box. (You may want to go ahead and find a chair; some of these people ask a lot of questions.) Also included in this section is a list of broadcast media, so you can surf the dials while you're on hold. For online information about municipal services visit each city's Web site. (See **Neighborhoods**.)

UTILITIES

TELEPHONE

You may want to do this one first, even weeks in advance of your arrival. If you know where you'll be living, the phone company will assign you a phone number which you can then use to arrange for other services. With the recent merger of USWest and Qwest, local phone service in both Minneapolis and St. Paul is now provided by Qwest. The charge for installation of basic service is $18.35. For those needing inside wire work or additional jacks, the charge is $95.35. If you do not have a previous credit history with Qwest, a service deposit will be required. The monthly line charge is $14.90 with an added "federal access charge" of $4.35. For service call **Qwest**, 800-244-1111; TTY: 800-223-3131; or check www.qwest.com.

AREA CODES

Effective February 27, 2000, the region served by the 612 area code was split into three area codes: 612, 763, and 952. The 612 area code was kept by Minneapolis, Richfield, St. Anthony, and the Fort Snelling area. The new 763 area code serves suburbs to the north and northwest of Minneapolis, including: Becker, Blaine, Brooklyn Center, Buffalo, Cambridge, Circle Pines, Coon Rapids, Delano, Elk River, Fridely, Golden Valley, Isanti, Lexington, Medina, Monticello, Mounds View, Plymouth, Princeton, St Francis, and Waverly. The new 952 area code serves the suburbs to the south and southwest of Minneapolis: Apple Valley, Belle Plaine, Bloomington, Burnsville, Edina, Elko, Hamburg, Hopkins, Lakeville, Mayer Minnetonka, Mound, New Prague, Norwood, Orono, St. Louis Park, Watertown, and Wayzata.

St. Paul and most of the metro east side, and Dakota County use 651; suburbs north of I-394 and the west side of Anoka County use 763; and suburbs south of I-394 and west of Minneapolis use 952.

LONG DISTANCE SERVICE

You may want to arrange separately for long-distance service from among the multitude of long distance carriers. Call around for the best deals. Carriers frequently advertise very low per-minute rates, but be sure to read the fine print. If you have to pay $5.95 a month to get the five-cent per minute deal, and you don't make many long distance calls, it may make more sense for you to use a pre-paid calling card—or even your cell phone for long distance. For help comparing long distance and wireless calling plans, visit the **Telecommunications and Research and Action Center (TRAC)** (not affiliated with the communications industry), www.trac.org or call them at 202-263-2950. The TRAC site also provides directory assistance via the internet.

Sometimes consumers find that their long distance service provider has been changed without their consent, a practice known as "slamming." For more information about this and other consumer protection issues, see the **Consumer Protection** section of this chapter.

Major Long Distance Service Providers include:
- **At&T**, 800-222-0300, www.att.com
- **Cable & Wireless,** 888-454-4264
- **MCI/WorldCom**, 800-950-5555, www.wcom.com
- **US Sprint**, 800-877-7746, www.sprint.com
- **Verizon,** 800-343-2092

CELLULAR PHONE AND PAGING SERVICES

There are as many pricing plans as there are makes and models of pagers and cell phones. Sprint's Free and Clear and AT&T's Digital One-Rate are flat-rate cell-phone plans which sell you a set number of minutes per month. These minutes can be used for any call, any time, anywhere, however you do have to pay for unused minutes. Many people who have flat-rate plans use their cell phones for long distance calling. As digital phones are becoming more popular, the market is changing rapidly, so your best bet is to call around and determine for yourself which service and pricing structures best meet your needs. The Web can make it easier; **Wireless Dimensions**, www.wirelessdimension.com helps you compare service plans in your area, and **the Cellular Telecommunications Industry Association's** consumer-resource page, www.wow-com.com/consumer, offers helpful consumer tips. TRAC (see **Long Distance** above) is a consumer organization that publishes charts, comparing plans and prices: www.trac.org, 202-263-2950. Following are the metro area's largest cellular, Personal Communication Services (PCS) and paging service providers:

- **AT&T** Wireless Services, 800-IMAGINE, www.att.com/wireless
- **Aerial**, 888-AERIAL1, www.aerial1.com
- **AirTouch Cellular**, 800-AIRTOUCH, www.airtouch.com
- **Nextel**, 800-NEXTEL9, www.nextel.com
- **elect Wireless**, 612-333-1300, www.selectwireless.net
- **Skytel**, 800-858-4338
- **Sprint PCS**, 800-480-4PCS, www.sprintpcs.com
- **Qwest Wireless**, 800-ACCESS2, www.qwest.com

PREPAID CELLULAR SERVICES

With only slightly higher rates and no 12-month contract or monthly fees, prepaid cellular phone service is catching on with those in need of mobile phone service. Already a big hit in Europe, and available from **Pre-Paid Wireless** sales outlets in the Twin Cities, 651-221-9775, simply purchase a phone which comes with a card representing a certain financial value ranging from $15 to $100. Activate the card, and, when the money runs out, the card is easily replenished with a payment. Most of the outlets for this service are pawnshops and check-cashing services.

ONLINE SERVICE PROVIDERS

Minnesota has many local internet service providers. Just make sure the provider you choose furnishes technical support and has enough phone lines and equipment to handle the number of accounts it services:

- **Bitstream**, 612-321-9290, www.bitstream.net
- **Fishnet**, 612-338-3474, www.fishnet.com
- **Minnesota WaveTech**, 612-721-0355, www.wavetech.net
- **Onvoy**, 651-362-5880, www.onvoy.net
- **Qwest Megabit DSL Service**, 877-669-MEGA, www.megaspeed.com
- **Skypoint**, 612-417-0227, www.skypoint.com
- **Twin Cities Internet**, 612-377-8707, www.tcinternet.net
- **Vector Internet Services**, 612-288-9900, www.visi.com
- **Winternet**, 612-333-1505, www.winternet.com

NATIONAL ONLINE SERVICE PROVIDERS

When considering a national internet service provider, be sure to find one that will connect you through a local call instead of long distance. Getting connected during peak demand hours is often a problem, and some large providers bump you off after you've been online only a short time.

- **America Online**, 800-827-6364
- **AT&T WorldNet**, 800-967-5363
- **Compuserve**, 800-848-8199
- **Microsoft Network**, 800-426-9400
- **MindSpring Enterprises**, 800-719-4332
- **Prodigy**, 800-776-3449
- **Sprint Internet Passport**, 800-359-3900

ELECTRICITY AND NATURAL GAS

Northern States Power (**NSP**) supplies both electricity and gas to virtually the entire Twin Cities metropolitan area. You can arrange for both services with one telephone call, 800-895-4999, TTY/TDD 800-895-4949. Service can be connected with only a few days' notice, but NSP recommends that you put in your order two weeks in advance. NSP offers "Budget Helper" a 12-month plan to help even out your monthly energy payments. No deposit is required, but a processing charge of $10, plus state and city taxes, will appear on your first month's bill. Those who live in the southern metro areas may opt to buy their service from: **Dakota County Electric** (Eagan, Apple Valley and Burnsville), 651-463-7134, www.dakotaelectric.com, or **Minnesota Valley Electric** (Jordan), 952-492-2313. Electric service is also supplied to some sections of Ramsey County by **Anoka Electric**, 763-421-1343.

To locate buried cables and gas lines call Gopher State One Call, 651-454-0002.

For service problems call: Electric Outages: 1-800-895-1999; Gas Odor or Gas Leak Emergency: 1-800-895-2999.

CONSUMER PROTECTION—UTILITY COMPLAINTS

Try to resolve any billing or other disputes with your phone, gas or electric company on your own. But if a problem persists, the people to call are the officials at the **Minnesota Public Utilities Commission**. Their consumer affairs office telephone number is 651-296-0406, or check www.puc.state.mn.us. Another agency that oversees the fair pricing and reliable service of utilities in the state of Minnesota is the **Minnesota Department of Public Service**, 651-296-5120, www.dpsv.state.mn.us.

If you have been "slammed" (had your long distance carrier changed without your permission) or "crammed" (had calls you didn't make added to your bill), call Qwest or your authorized long distance carrier to have the incident investigated. If you are "slammed" you do not have to pay the bill from the company that did the "slamming," if you act within 30 days. The state attorney general's office can also assist you; call 651-296-3353. You may also file a complaint with the **Federal Communications Commission** electronically at www.fcc.gov or call 888-225-5322. To file a complaint with the **Federal Trade Commission**, call 202-382-4357, or file online at www.ftc.gov.

SEWER AND WATER

Of the municipalities in the Twin Cities metropolitan area, 123 out of 187 have municipal water supply systems, which serve a total of about 2 million people. Another 250,000 people, particularly homeowners around Lake Minnetonka in the west and White Bear Lake and the St. Croix River in the East, get water from their own private wells. Residents of St. Paul and Minneapolis are supplied with treated water from surface sources such as the Mississippi River and the St. Paul chain of lakes; the other 1.4 million use water supplied from the groundwater system via municipal wells.

If you are renting an apartment, sewer and water are probably included in your rent. If you are a homeowner or renting a house, call your local city hall to establish service. According to the Metropolitan Council, Minnesota's regional service provider and planning agency, the average charge for water in the region is $1.63 per 1,000 gallons—or ten cups for a penny. For Minneapolis, call the Utility Billing Office, 612-673-1114, for general information and questions about water, sewer and solid waste billing. A budget plan is available, For water emergencies, call 612-673-5600. St. Paul residents are billed once every three months. Call 651-266-6350 for billing and general information. Water emergencies are handled at 651-917-4777. If the house you are buying has a private well, be sure to have it inspected and tested for bacteria and hardness. A rotten-egg smell may indicate that you have iron bacteria growing in your well and plumbing, a common problem, but one that can be hard to solve. In such circumstances, chances are good that the water is safe to drink but you will need a water softener and pre-filter. Local water softener companies are:

- **Culligan Water Conditioning**, Minnetonka, 952-933-7200
- **Culligan Water Conditioning**, St Paul, 651-451-2241
- **Eco Water System**, 800-808-9899, www.ecowater.com
- **Servisoft and Miracle Water Conditioning**, 952-935-5105
- **Twin City Lindsay**, 952-941-2117

For home delivery of bottled water, see **Drinking Water** in **Shopping for the Home**.

GARBAGE AND RECYCLING

If you're in an apartment, you can probably skip this section, but if you're renting or buying a house, you'll need to arrange for garbage pick-up, and possibly recycling.

In Minneapolis, the city hauls residential garbage and recyclable materials and provides trash containers for each house. Haulers will take one or two large items, such as discarded furniture, per pick-up. And, if you've got more garbage than your trash container will hold, just make sure it's bagged and tied, and the haulers will probably take it. Garbage collection/recycling for a single-family home generally costs $16 per month including a monthly recycling credit.

In St. Paul recycling pick-up is provided, but each household must hire a garbage service. (If you are renting the landlord may already have made arrangements.) Rates vary from company to company and depend on the volume of the trash container you choose. City officials believe this system cuts down on waste, and it does get you to root out those recyclables in order to reduce your load. Disposal of large objects must be arranged separately with your hauler.

For specific information about what can be recycled, how to pack it, and when to put it out, call your city hall. In St. Paul, recycling is paid through property taxes; in some other cities, people who recycle are given a cheaper garbage rate. For Minneapolis and St. Paul garbage and recycling information call the numbers below:

- **Minneapolis Solid Waste and Recycling**, 612-673-2917
- **St. Paul Neighborhood Energy Consortium**, 651-633-3279 or 651-644-7678

COMPOSTING SITES

Bring your grass, leaves and small brush to the following locations:

- **Ramsey County**: North side of Pierce-Butler Route at Pryor; Pleasant Avenue just south of St. Claire; corner of Frank and Sims; and Winthrop just south of London Lane.
- **Hennepin County**: 630 Malcolm Avenue, Minneapolis, 612-331-4610; Maple Grove Yard Waste, west of County Road 121 on 101st Avenue North, 763-420-4886

DRIVER'S LICENSES, STATE IDS, & AUTOMOBILE REGISTRATION

DRIVER'S LICENSES, STATE IDS

You have 60 days from the date you move to Minnesota to obtain a Minnesota driver's license. The minimum age to receive a driver's license is 16. If you have a valid out-of-state license only a written test and eye exam are required. Take your current driver's license and another form of ID, such as a passport or birth certificate, with you to the licensing station. If you changed your name when you got married, take your marriage certificate as well. If your current license is no longer valid, or you are not a licensed driver yet, you will be required to pass a behind-the-wheel driving test. The cost for a license is $18.50.

To obtain a state identification card, take one form of identification, such as a passport or birth certificate to a licensing center (see below). The cost is $12.50.

Information regarding vehicle and driver licenses and state ID cards may be obtained by contacting the **Minnesota Department of Public Safety**, 445 Minnesota Street, St. Paul, 651-296-6911, www.dps.state. mn.us/dvs. Examining stations are located throughout the metro area, call to schedule a driving test:

- **Anoka**, 530 West Main Street, 763-422-3401
- **Chaska**, 418 South Pine Street, 952-448-3740
- **Hastings**, 427 Vermillion Street, 651-437-4884
- **North Metro/Arden Hills**, Highway 8 and West County Road 1, 651-639-4057
- **South Metro/Eagan**, 2070 Cliff Road, 651-688-1870
- **West Metro/Plymouth**, 2455 Fernbrook Lane, 763-341-7149
- **Sub-station/St. Paul**, written test only, 1472 University Avenue, 651-642-0808
- **Forest Lake**, 1432 South Lake Street, Stillwater, 651-430-8280
- **Stillwater**, 1520 West frontage Road, Stillwater, 651-430-6176
- **Woodbury**, 8301 Valley Creek Road, Woodbury, 651-714-3780

AUTOMOBILE REGISTRATION

You have 60 days from the time you move here to register your car with the state of Minnesota. After two months you can be hit with a fine, so it pays to get this done as quickly as possible. You can register your vehicle at one of the county service centers or licensing centers (above) or, for members, at the Automobile Association of America (AAA), 952-927-2600. Take your car's certificate of title, proof of insurance, and your personal identification. Motor vehicle licenses must be renewed each year. The registration tax depends on the value of your car; it will be no less than $35 a year, and could be as much as several hundred dollars (ouch!). Once you're registered, you should receive an annual renewal notice several weeks before your registration expires. For information call:

- **Department of Public Safety**, 651-296-6911,www.dps.state. mn.us/dvs
- **Hennepin County Service Centers**, 612-348-8240; Government Center, 300 South 6th Street, Minneapolis; Brookdale, 6125 Shingle Creek, Brooklyn Center; 13720 Grove Drive, Maple Grove; 12601 Ridgedale Drive, Minnetonka; 7009 York Avenue, Edina

AUTOMOBILE SAFETY

In Minnesota, approximately one-third of all traffic deaths involve alcohol. Consequently, the state has strengthened its intoxication laws and judges have toughened their sentencing. Minnesota now has "zero tolerance" for underage drinking and driving. Anyone under the age of 21 convicted of operating a motor vehicle after having consumed any amount of alcohol, will have his/her driving privileges suspended for 30 days. A second conviction will result in driving privileges being suspended for six months.

It is illegal to operate a motor vehicle in Minnesota while under the influence of alcohol and/or a controlled substance. Convictions for driving while impaired (even with blood alcohol levels as low as .04) can result in fines, jail sentences, loss of driving privileges and possible confiscation of your vehicle.

Another law to promote public safety is mandatory seat belt use, and use of federally approved "child passenger restraint systems" (children's car safety seats) is required for all children under the age of four. The car safety seat must bear a stamp of approval from the Federal Department of Transportation. A noteworthy site for tips on properly installing car seats is www.safekids.org.

In the Twin Cities, traffic congestion and poor weather often combine to create hazardous driving conditions. Radio station KBEM-FM 88.5 provides live traffic reports sponsored by a partnership between the Minnesota Department of Transportation (MN/DOT) and the Minneapolis Public Schools. Television station KVBM, Channel 45, also broadcasts Traffic Television weekdays from 6 a.m. to 8:30 a.m. For recorded traffic reports, call 612-586-6000, code 8859. MN/DOT also provides real-time traffic information on the internet, where you can view incident and road construction information, as well as ramp meter status and a traffic congestion map. The web address is www.twincities.sidewalk.com. Click on the "Trafficview" button.

PURCHASING AN AUTOMOBILE

For internet car-shoppers, the following sites may prove useful: **RateNet**, www.rate.net, and **Bank Rate**, www.bankrate.com, survey a variety of lenders and show the ten best rates in your area. *Consumer Reports* offers a comprehensive "New Car Price Service" that tells you all the information you need to know about a car before you walk into a dealer showroom. Your $12 report will include the "invoice" price, the "sticker" price, invoice and sticker prices for all options, national rebate information and more. Call 800-933-5555 or log onto their web site, www.consumerreports.org. Go to the **Kelley Blue Book** site, www.kbb.com for listings of used car values. The **Office of the Attorney General** offers a consumer information handbook that may be of interest to those in the auto market, whether leasing or buying. Call 651-296-3353 or try www.ag.state.mn.us/home/consumer/cars/TheCarHandbook.

CONSUMER PROTECTION—AUTOMOBILES

If you are looking for a new car, Minnesota has a lemon law that covers new vehicles that have been purchased or leased in the state. The law defines a "lemon" as a vehicle that continues to have a serious defect, which substantially impairs its use, value, or safety after a reasonable number of attempts to repair it. A "reasonable number of attempts" is defined as four attempts to repair the same defect or one attempt to repair a serious safety defect which could result in death or serious bodily harm. A car that you have been unable to use, due to warranty repairs, for 30 or more cumulative business days may also be covered by this law. For more information contact the **Minnesota Attorney General**, www.ag.state.mn.us, 651-296-3353 or 800-657-3787. In any case, if you report the defect within the warranty time period, the manufacturer must repair, refund or replace the defective vehicle. If, after a reasonable number of attempts, the manufacturer is unable to repair the defect you may go to court or go through a manufacturer's arbitration program to seek a full refund of the car's purchase price.

For those interested in purchasing a used car, Minnesota has a used car warranty law requiring used car dealers (not private sellers) to provide basic warranty coverage for cars that cost more than $3,000. The terms of this warranty vary according to the age and mileage of the car. A car that does not meet the warranty guidelines will be marked "as is" on the window sticker, meaning that the seller has no obligation to fix any problems that arise. For used car warranty details, call 651-296-3353 or 800-657-3787 or visit www.ag.state.mn.us.

Check the **US Department of Transportation's Auto Safety Hotline** for information about vehicle recalls and crash test information, 800-424-9393 or www.nhtsa.dot.gov. Check with the **Minnesota Department of Public Safety**, 651-296-2977 to see if a dealer is licensed (only licensed dealers must follow consumer-protection guidelines such as providing warranties). The department can also tell you how many complaints, if any, have been filed against the dealer in the last year.

Generally, more than three complaints is considered excessive. The **Better Business Bureau**, 651-699-1111 or 800-646-6222, also files complaints against local businesses. The Minnesota attorney general's office, 651-296-3353 or 800-657-3787, www.ag.state.mn.us, can tell you what legal action has been taken against a dealer, if any. To determine if the title is clear on a Minnesota-owned vehicle, make a written request to the Minnesota Department of Public Safety, 445 Minnesota Street, St. Paul, 55101. To search the title of a vehicle owned outside of the state, call Carfax, 888-422-7329 or www.carfax.com. There are charges for title searches no matter who does them.

AUTOMOBILE INSURANCE

Minnesota requires that you carry a minimum of $30,000 insurance per person and $60,000 per accident for bodily injury; $10,000 for property damage liability; $40,000 for personal injury protection; and $25,000 per person and $50,000 per accident for uninsured/underinsured motorist coverage. Premiums vary depending on your driving record, age, sex, age, make of your vehicle, etc. Some of the major insurance companies in Minnesota include **AAA**, 952-927-2518; **Allstate**; **American Family**, www.amfam.com; **Farmers Insurance Group**; and **State Farm**, www.statefarm.com. Check the Insurance listings in the Yellow Pages to locate agents near you.

PARKING RAMPS & LOTS

Parking in Minneapolis is tight, and you might have to look for a while to find parking at the price you want to pay. The city operates 15 ramps, nine lots, and thousands of street meters. For those who find a parking space on the street, take the meter seriously. An expired meter will get you a ticket and may get your car towed. For those needing to prioritize cost over convenience, you can expect cheaper rates on the city's periphery; parking at open air lots costs less than ramps; and parking at municipal properties beats parking at privately-owned lots and ramps. If you're determined to commute into downtown every day by car, consider purchasing a monthly ramp pass. The costs at this writing ran from $107.50 on the fringe to $250 a month at the courthouse. A number of office buildings offer parking underneath including: the IDS building, Hennepin County Government Center and Marquette Plaza. The difficulty and expense of parking in Minneapolis is as good a reason as any to take the bus or carpool.

In downtown St. Paul, one can often find on-street parking, and there are several ramps and open air lots. Convenient ramps are attached to RiverCentre, the St. Paul Hotel and the Minnesota History Center. Parking is harder to find around the state capitol. All downtown St. Paul ramps are privately owned, but they also offer monthly passes. Call around to find the best deal.

- **Minneapolis Parking Information**, 612-673-2411; Monthly & Event Parking, 612-338-7275; Permits, Critical Areas, 612-673-2411
- **St. Paul Parking Information**, 651-266-6200

For information on parking at the University of Minnesota, including rates and maps, contact the **University Parking Services** office, 612-626-PARK.

RESIDENTIAL PARKING PERMITS

In Minneapolis, St. Paul, and most of the surrounding suburbs there are designated Critical Parking Areas. Residents in these areas are given, or can buy, stickers that permit them to ignore the parking restrictions on their streets. In Minneapolis, stickers cost $10 a year and there is a limit of two stickers per person. Some cities, such as Deephaven, give one free parking permit to each household and charge for second and third permits.

SNOW EMERGENCY PARKING

Winter in the Twin Cities means ice and snow. Those moving here from a more southerly clime should pay particular attention to yet another peculiar aspect of life in the North: the "snow emergency." This is when Minneapolis, St. Paul and many of the suburbs restrict on-street parking in order to accomplish necessary plowing. Snow emergency rules require that you move your car from one side of the street to the other in some municipalities, or stay off certain streets entirely in others. After plowing is finished, restrictions may be lifted unless more snow is forecast. To find out if a snow emergency has been declared, call the relevant snow emergency number below or tune in to WCCO-AM Radio 830 or any local television or radio news broadcast. Look for this season's snow emergency rules in the mail, sometime in the fall, or check your community's web site under parking restrictions. In Minneapolis, snow emergency brochures can also be picked up at Tom Thumb stores, or you can check up-to-the-minute plowing schedules on the city's hotline at 612-348-SNOW or by clicking on the snow icon on the city's homepage, www.ci.minneapolis.mn.us. To request snow plowing or sanding in Minneapolis call 612-673-5720. In St. Paul, watch for "Night Plow Route" signs. These are the sides of streets that will be plowed between 9 p.m. and 6 a.m. the first night after a snowfall. The unsigned sides of streets are usually plowed the next night. St. Paul snow emergency information can be obtained by calling 651-266-PLOW or visiting the city's web site at www.stpaul.gov.

Don't worry that you might somehow miss the relevant information—it's all over the airwaves. But do take it seriously. The parking restrictions are strictly enforced and cars are tagged and towed quickly and unceremoniously. One last piece of advice: Don't go off on vacation and leave your car parked on a street—any street. Standing in a three-hour line at the impound lot is not a fun way to end a vacation. See **Surviving Winter** for more winter related tips.

TOWED VEHICLES

Ugh! Hope you never need these numbers. The **Minneapolis Impound Lot** is at 51 North Colfax Avenue. For directions and information call 612-673-5777 (have your license plate number ready, or provide the last four numbers of your car's serial number). The impound lot is open 6 a.m. to 3 a.m. daily. The regular towing fee is $70. The heavy-duty towing fee is $125. Storage costs $10 per day, and is assessed at midnight. The impound lot will accept a check, cash or a credit card. Identification is required. To report a stolen car in Minneapolis, call 612-673-5743.

The **St. Paul Impound Lot** is at 830 Barge Channel Road, 651-292-6005. This lot is open 24 hours a day. The charge for a normal tow is $74.90, if you pay cash; if you pay by check or credit card, there is an additional $3 service charge. Storage is $12 a day, assessed at midnight. To report a stolen car in St. Paul, call the police department's general number at 651-291-1111.

PET LAWS & SERVICES

Dogs in the Twin Cities metro area must be licensed and vaccinated. Call your city hall for information about your city's pet ordinances. To find a veterinarian, nothing beats word-of-mouth and a get-acquainted visit. In Minnesota, heartworm medication is given May-November, and to control ticks and fleas, many pet owners use a monthly externally applied systemic flea and tick medication such as Top Spot or Bio-Spot. Those who intend to take their pets to Wisconsin or rural areas or Up North should consider vaccinating their pets against lyme disease.

Help locating a veterinarian can be obtained by calling **the Minnesota Veterinary Medical Association**, 651-645-7533, whose membership includes 900 licensed veterinarians throughout the state. Listed below are several emergency veterinary clinics in the metropolitan area:

- **Affiliated Emergency Veterinary Services:** 1615 Northwest Coon Rapids Boulevard, Coon Rapids, 763-754-9434; 4708 Olson Memorial Highway, Golden Valley, 763-529-6560; 7717 Flying Cloud Drive, Eden Prairie, 952-942-8272
- **University of Minnesota Veterinary Hospitals**, 1365 Gartner Avenue, St. Paul; small animals, 612-625-1919; 24-hour emergency, 612-625-9711

Two national organizations that offer medical coverage for pets are **Veterinary Pet Insurance**, 800-872-7387, www.petinsurance.com; and **Pet Assure**, a Pet HMO, 888-789-7387, www.petassure.com.

For those who want to adopt a pet, a local animal shelter is a good place to begin. If choosing a kitten or puppy, it will come with its first vaccinations and a discount coupon to have it spayed or neutered. Area shelters include:

- **Animal Humane Society**, 845 North Meadow Lane, Golden Valley, 763-522-4325; Lost and Found, 763-522-7130
- **Humane Society of Ramsey County**, 1115 Beulah Lane, St. Paul (by the Como Park Zoo), 651-645-7387
- **Minnesota Valley Humane Society**, 1313 East Highway 13, Burnsville, 952-894-5000
- **St. Croix Animal Shelter**, 9785 Hudson Road, Woodbury, 651-730-6008

For those who want to adopt a purebred dog, most breed clubs include rescue groups that are dedicated to finding loving homes for abandoned dogs of their specific breed. A good place for the internet inclined is the **American Kennel Club's** web site, www.akc.org/breeds/rescue, which provides links to the national breed clubs' rescue organizations. The **Dog Zone**, www.dogzone.com/rescue, lists rescue organizations by state. Many people have found that retired racing greyhounds make sensible, adaptable family pets. For information call the **National Greyhound Adoption** network, 800-446-8637. If you're not on the net, ask your vet or the local humane society for referrals to local breed rescue organizations.

Once you get your pet, it will definitely require training and exercise. For training clubs and off-leash parks in the Twin Cities area see the **Dogs** section of the **Sports and Recreation** chapter of this book.

What to do when going out of town without Fido? Call a pet service. For those in the southwest metro area try **Pampered Paws**, 952-906-0303. Boarding kennels that come highly recommended by Twin Cities pet owners are **Paws, Claws and Hooves Pet Boarding**, 10500 Great Plains Boulevard, Chanhassen, 952-445-7991; and **The Dog House Boarding Kennels**, 3505 West Wayzata Boulevard, Orono, 952-473-9026. In Hopkins, day care can be found at **Cloud Nine Training and Daycare for Dogs**, 8 12th Avenue South, 952-939-9174, dfalk@mindspring.com. Agility Training is available at **Dogworks Agility Training Center**, 6338 Carlson Drive, Eden Prairie, 612-835-6670, dogworksinc@aol.com. For other boarding suggestions, check with your vet and other pet owners. Pet sitters and boarding facilities are found under "Pet Boarding and Sitting" and "Kennels" in the Yellow Pages.

VOTER REGISTRATION

Naturally, you'll want to join in Minnesota's lively political tradition by voting. In 1998, Minnesotans elected Jesse Ventura, the state's most colorful governor ever. Perhaps you caught him in his purple boa singing "Werewolves of Minnesota" at his inaugural party. If you'd like a portrait of the Guv painted on black velvet, they're auctioning them off over at eBay.com.

To register to vote, you must be a United States citizen, 18 years old, and neither legally incompetent nor a convicted felon deprived of rights. You must have lived in Minnesota for at least 20 days. You can register when you apply for your driver's license, or at your county courthouse, city hall or government center. Or, easier yet, you can register by mail using the Minnesota Voter Registration Form located in the government pages in your telephone book. Mail it, at least 20 days prior to the next election, to the Secretary of State, 180 State Office Building, 100 Constitution Avenue, St. Paul, 55155-1299. If you don't have time to register in advance, you can just go to your polling place on Election Day and register there. Take a driver's license or identification card that shows your new address, or a neighbor who can vouch for your residency. College students may use a student fee statement, student picture ID card, or registration card showing their address in the precinct. You need not register a party affiliation, and primaries are open. After you register, you may vote in all elections. A postcard will be sent to you confirming your registration and telling you where to vote. Call the Secretary of State for more information, 651-215-1440.

You'll notice references in the news to the "DFL" and the "IR" which are the Democratic Farmer-Labor and Independent Republican Parties. These aren't upstart third parties, they're the state's Democrats and Republicans. The DFL was formed in the 1940s, when Minnesota's Democrats (led by Hubert Humphrey) merged with the populist Farmer-Labor Party. At about the same time, Minnesota's Republicans added "Independent" to their name in the hope of attracting more independent voters. Following are additional numbers to call for polling locations or registration information:

- **Hennepin County Voter Registration**, 612-348-5151, www2.co. hennepin.mn.us
- **Ramsey County Voter Registration**, 651-266-2171
- **Washington County Auditor**, 651-430-6175
- **DFL State Office**, 651-293-1200
- **IR State Office**, 651-222-0022
- **Reform Party**, 612-939-6601
- **Secretary of State** public information line, 651-296-2805, www.sos.state.mn.us
- **League of Women Voters**, 651-224-5445, www.lwvmn.org

For those interested in going online to review and compare local and national candidates in upcoming elections try these sites: www.politics1.com; Women's Voting Guide, www.womenvote.org; and Project Vote Smart, www.vote-smart.org.

LIBRARY CARDS

Minnesota has been generous in the funding of libraries. Minneapolis, St. Paul, and surrounding counties all have separate library systems, but they are connected: once you get a card at one library system, you can use it to get a card at another one; you can search for a book and have it delivered from one system to the other; and you can even check out a book from one system and return it to the other. The library systems are online, so you can scan for titles, place requests, and check your borrowing records from home. To get a card, you'll need to visit a library in person with identification and, if you don't yet have a Minnesota driver's license, a piece of mail with your new address. Check the **Neighborhoods** chapter of this book

for the library nearest you. Call the following libraries if you have questions:
- **Hennepin County Libraries**, 12601 Ridgedale Drive, Minnetonka, 952-541-8530, www.hennepin.lib.mn.us
- **Minneapolis Central Public Library**, 300 Nicollet Mall, 612-630-6000, www.mpls.lib.mn.us
- **Ramsey County Library**, 4570 Victoria Street, Shoreview, 651-486-2200, www.ramsey.lib.mn.us
- **St. Paul Central Public Library**, 90 West 4th Street, 651-266-7000; New Cards, 651- 266-7030, www.stpaul.lib.mn.us.
- **Washington County Public Library**, 2150 Radio Drive, Woodbury, 651-731-8487, www.washington.lib.mn.us.

PASSPORTS

Anyone traveling outside the country, even a newborn child, needs a valid passport. Besides passport offices, forms can be obtained from travel agents, libraries, printed off the internet from the **Bureau of Consular Affairs**, http://travel.state.gov, or by calling 900-225-5674, ($1.95 per minute). In addition to passport offices, applications are processed at main post offices (see addresses below) and county offices. Do so at least 30 days in advance of your planned departure.

For those who have never had a United States passport before and are 13 years old or older, or who are renewing a passport that was issued more than 12 years ago, or had a previous passport lost or stolen, applications must be made in person. Bring your social security number; one proof of citizenship, such as a certified county or state copy of your birth certificate or most recent passport or naturalization papers; one additional form of identification, such as a current valid driver's license, identification card, or previous United States passport; and two passport photographs. You may have passport pictures taken at most commercial photography studios, but vending machine photos are not generally accepted. Both Hennepin (Minneapolis) and Ramsey (St. Paul) counties offer convenient systems to take your photo and process your passport at the same time. There is a charge of $7.50 for the photo. Although a Social Security number is not required for issuance of a passport, the Internal Revenue Code requires that passport applicants provide this information, and you can be fined up to $500 for failing to provide your number. The fee for a passport for an applicant age 16 or older is $60, and it is valid for ten years. The fee for a passport for an applicant age 15 or younger is $40, and it is valid for five years. If paying by cash, you will need to take the exact amount. Some passport offices accept major credit cards (VISA, MasterCard, American Express and Discover) and debit cards; call first to find out.

Customers can expect to receive their passports within 25 business days. For those needing a passport immediately, a trip to the Chicago passport agency may be necessary. You must have an appointment. Call 312-341-6020, 24 hours a day, seven days a week to schedule an appointment. Besides the regular proofs of citizenship and identity, you must also bring proof of immediate travel (airline ticket, confirmed itinerary or a letter from your employer for business travel). Passports can also be expedited by mail; call a local passport office for details or use a passport expediting service. These are listed under "Passport and Visa Services" in the Yellow Pages.

If your passport is lost or stolen, report the loss when you apply in person for your replacement passport. If you are abroad, report the loss immediately to local police and the nearest US embassy or consulate. Remember to write your current address in pencil in the space provided in your passport so that, if it is found, it can be returned to you.

To check on the status of your pending passport application, order application forms or get information, call the **National Passport Information Center** at 888-362-8668.

Passport agencies and acceptance facilities can be found at:

- **Dakota County Information & Service Center**, 14955 Galaxie Avenue, Apple Valley, MN 55124, 952-891-7570, (Monday & Friday, 8:00 a.m. to 4:30 p.m.; Tuesday, Wednesday, Thursday, 8:00 a.m. to 6:00 p.m.)
- **Hennepin County Government Center**, 300 South 6th Street, Minneapolis, MN 55487, 612-348-8241, (Monday-Friday, 8:00 a.m. to 4:30 p.m.)
- **Hennepin County Service Center-Ridgedale**, 12601 Ridgedale Drive, Suite 108, Minnetonka, MN 55343, 952-348-8241 (Monday-Friday, 9:00 a.m. to 6:00 p.m., Saturday, 9:00 a.m. to 2:00 p.m.)
- **Hopkins Post Office**, 910 First Street South, Hopkins, MN 55343-9998, 800-275-8777 (Monday-Friday, 9:30 a.m. to 4:00 p.m.)
- **Uptown Station Post Office**, 415 North Wabasha Court, St. Paul, MN 55102, 800-275-8777 (Monday-Friday, 9:00 a.m. to 4:00 p.m.)
- **Ramsey County Department of Vital Services**, Courthouse, 15 West Kellogg Boulevard, Room 110, St. Paul, MN 55102, 651-266-8265 (Monday-Friday, 8:00 a.m. to 4:00 p.m.)
- **Stillwater License Center** (Washington County), 1520 West Frontage Road, Stillwater, MN 55082, 651-430-6176 (Monday-Friday, 8:00 a.m. to 4:00 p.m.)

- **US Post Office - Seeger Square Station**, 886 Arcade Street, St. Paul, MN 55106-9998, 800-275-8777 (Monday-Friday, 9:00 a.m. to 2:30 p.m.)
- **US Post Office - Como Finance Station**, 2286 Como Avenue, St. Paul, MN 55108-9998, 800-275-8777 (Monday-Friday, 9:00 a.m. to 4:00 p.m.)
- **US Post Office - West St. Paul Finance Unit**, 3 Signal Hills Center, West St. Paul, MN 55118-9998, 800-275-8777 (Monday-Friday, 9:30 a.m. to 4:00 p.m.)

VISAS

If you need a visa, you must obtain it from the consular office of the country you are planning to visit. The addresses of foreign consular offices in the United States are in the Congressional Directory in the library. In the Midwest, many of the consular offices are located in Chicago. Before you send your passport through the mail to a consular office, be sure to sign it in ink and pencil-in your current address and daytime telephone number in the spaces provided. This will help the post office return it to you if it gets separated from its envelope in the mail. Some countries also require immunizations. For detailed health information for international travel, talk to your physician or contact the **Centers for Disease Control and Prevention**, 877-FYI-TRIP, www.cdc.gov.

Minnesotans often travel to Canada—Voyageurs National Park is half in Minnesota and half in Canada, and Winnipeg is a popular long-weekend destination. While visas and passports are not necessary to cross the Canadian border, a proof of United States citizenship and a photo ID are required. Anyone with a criminal record (including a Driving While Intoxicated charge) should contact the Canadian Embassy or nearest consulate before going.

TELEVISION

CABLE

Getting settled, for most people, now includes setting up cable TV or satellite service. Minneapolis and St. Paul are served by two separate companies while a host of providers cover the suburbs. (For suburban cable information, call your city hall.) Since each cable company has been granted a monopoly by city government, we've included Minneapolis' and St. Paul's consumer contact number for cable service complaints.

MINNEAPOLIS AND SUBURBS
- **Paragon Cable**, 612-522-2000
- **Minneapolis Office of Client Services** (complaints) 612-673-2910
- **Triax Cablevision**, 800-332-0245; customer service, 800-422-1273

ST. PAUL AND SUBURBS
- **Media One**, 651-222-3333; Customer Service, 612-533-8020
- **St. Paul Office of Cable Communications**, 651-266-8870

SATELLITE SERVICE

- **Primestar Satellite**, 651-228-3956

TV STATIONS

For old-fashioned broadcast (free) TV, the Twin Cities offer the national networks, plus independents and a few newcomers, such as Warner Brothers and Paramount Network. Of course, if you've ordered cable, the channels will differ from those given here.
- **Channel 2** KTCA-TVPBS
- **Channel 4** WCCO-TVCBS
- **Channel 5** KSTP-TVABC
- **Channel 9** KMSP-TVUPN
- **Channel 11** KARE-TVNBC
- **Channel 17** KTCI-TVPBS
- **Channel 23** KMWB-TVWarner Brothers
- **Channel 29** WFTC-TVFox
- **Channel 41** KPXM-TVIndependent

RADIO

Here's a brief guide to what's available on the radio airwaves in the Twin Cities.

ADULT CONTEMPORARY
KSTP94.5 FM
KTCL97.1 FM

ALTERNATIVE ROCK
KUOM770 AM
KXXR93.7 FM
KZNR (ZONE)105.1, 105.3, 105.7 FM

WRQC100.3 FM
KMJZ104.1 FM

BIG BAND/NOSTALGIA
KLBB1400 AM
WLOL1470 AM

BLACK COMMUNITY NEWS
KMOJ89.9 FM

CHILDREN'S PROGRAMMING
KDIZ1440 AM

CHRISTIAN/RELIGIOUS
KTIS900 AM, 98.5 FM
KKMS980 AM
WWTC1280 AM
KYCR1570 AM
WCTS1030 AM
KNOF95.3 FM
WLKX95.9 FM

CLASSICAL
KSJN99.5 FM
WCAL89.3 FM

COMMUNITY TALK
KFAI90.3, 106.7 FM

COUNTRY
WIXK1590 AM, 107.1 FM
KEEY102.1 FM
KWOM1600AM
KARP96.3 FM

EASY LISTENING
WLTE102.9 FM

JAZZ, TALK, TRAFFIC
KBEM88.5 FM
KSMM1530 AM

HISPANIC
WMIN740 AM

NATIONAL PUBLIC RADIO NEWS, INFORMATION
KNOW91.1 FM
WMNN1330 AM

NEWS, TALK, WEATHER, COMMUNITY UPDATES
WCCO830 AM
KSTP1500 AM

OLDIES
KQQL107.9 FM
WEZU1220 AM
KDWA1460 AM

POP, TOP 40S
KDWB101.3 FM

ROCK
KQRS92.5 FM

SOUL
KSGS950 AM

SPORTS
WDGY630 AM
KFXN690 AM
KFAN1130 AM

LOCAL NEWSPAPERS & MAGAZINES

Whether your interest is in theater, restaurants, or parenting, there is a local (and probably free) newspaper or magazine for you. The **Star Tribune**, 612-673-4000, www.startribune.com, and **St. Paul Pioneer Press**, 651-222-5011, www.pioneerplanet.com, are the two major news dailies. For an edgier read, try **City Pages**, 612-375-1015, www.citypages.com, a free alternative weekly available at businesses metro-wide, which covers the local arts/entertainment scene, offering its own take on everything from politics to the personals. The **Minnesota Daily** covers the University of

Minnesota's news and sports, www.daily.umn.edu. The **Sun** community newspapers, www.mnsun.com, and a number of other neighborhood and special-interest, feature-driven weeklies are always available next to grocery store entrances. Latest editions usually hit the newsstands on Wednesdays.

Two local glossies, **Mpls/St. Paul Magazine**, www.mspmag.com, and **Minnesota Monthly**, which is published on behalf of Minnesota Public Radio (MPR), www.mnmo.com, are great guides to life in the Twin Cities. They include reviews about area restaurants, trends, recreation, environmental issues, music, the arts, people profiles, shopping, lifestyles, getaways and children's activities. The *Minnesota Monthly* also contains MPR's program guide. The Twin Cities offer a multitude of parenting magazines and newspapers, probablay the most popular is **Twin Cities Parent**, call 800-820-3199 or check out its web site at www.tcparent.com. Free at coffee-houses, co-ops and bagel bars, **Minnesota Parent**, www.parent.com, describes itself as an "eclectic journal of family living" and contains essays as well as useful parenting information.

Two publications specializing in news for "minorities" are **Insight News**, www.insightnews.com, 612-588-1313, a free newspaper serving Minnesota's growing African-American community; and **Minnesota Women's Press**, 651-646-3968, www.womenspress.com, also free, and published every other Wednesday. Both of these can be found a co-ops and coffee shops.

For those interested in the moves and shakes of local finance and commerce, **CityBusiness**, 612-288-2100, www.amcity.com/twincities will keep you informed about the who's and the what's.

For gay, lesbian, transgender and bisexual publications, see the **Helpful Services** chapter.

FINDING A PHYSICIAN

Most people who live, work or go to school in the Twin Cities are enrolled in an HMO or managed care health plan. Even if you are not covered as part of a group, you may find that you are limited in your choice of physicians to your health plan's or insurer's list of providers. Health plans usually have resources to assist you in finding a provider, or ask around—there is no substitute for word of mouth. Lacking that, however, the **Neighborhood Health Care Network** provides medical and dental referrals, 651-489-CARE.

If objectively comparing performances and results among doctors and hospitals makes you feel better, there are services that will help:

HealthGrades, www.healthgrades.com, provides information about health plans, doctors and hospitals. Locally, **Mpls/St. Paul Magazine** lists outstanding Twin Cities' doctors each year. While these profiles make for interesting reading, they have been criticized for missing some top physicians. Other medical web sites that may be of interest include the **Mayo Clinic**, just down the road in Rochester, www.mayo.edu; and the **federal government's** easy to use and comprehensive site, www.healthfinder.gov. To determine if a doctor is board certified in a specialty area, check with the **American Board of Medical Specialties** at 800-776-2378, www.certifieddoctor.org. In the state of Minnesota **complaints** against health care providers—physicians, technicians, psychiatrists, etc.—are handled by the **Minnesota Board of Medical Practice**. Contact them at University Park Plaza, 2829 University Avenue SE, Suite 400, Minneapolis 55414, 612-617-2130, webmaster@bmp.state.mn.us.

See the **Health Care** chapter for more information on state and local health programs and clinics.

SAFETY & CRIME

When you consider at the number of violent crimes reported in the Twin Cities, you see why Minneapolis-St. Paul residents talk about the great quality of life here. Outside of East St. Paul, the crime rate in the Twin Cities, which is never as high as other US metropolitan centers, is declining, particularly in Minneapolis. Perhaps more significantly, few of these crimes appear to be stranger-on-stranger (although that's not true for less serious acts such as theft). Recent studies show that Twin Cities residents, in general, are less concerned now about crime than they were a few years ago. Having said that, the feeling of safety is different for each person. It's important to trust your instincts, not numbers. When out and about, especially at night, be sure to walk with a purpose; keep clear of abandoned/deserted areas; ride in the front of the bus, next to the driver; strap your purse across your chest and conceal your valuables. If you park around the Minneapolis chain of lakes while you go for a stroll, lock anything of value in your trunk—even small change. Smash and grabs occur in this area. Don't forget, though, that you've moved to Minnesota, a place that's still well behind the ever more violent times of the rest of the country, despite what *Fargo* may have led you to believe. The police suggest taking the following steps for you to feel safe in your new home:

- Experience your new neighborhood. Talk with your neighbors, local businesses, and others.

- Contact the neighborhood association (see the **Neighborhoods** chapter) and learn about the concerns of neighborhood residents.
- Call the local police precinct and ask for safety/security information before you choose a neighborhood. Telephone numbers are listed in the **Neighborhoods** chapter of this book.
- Prevent! Both Minneapolis and St. Paul offer programs on personal safety and methods of avoiding crime on the street. Police volunteers will explain simple and inexpensive ways to secure your home. Find out (at the numbers below) if there is a block or apartment club you can join. If there isn't one, consider volunteering to start one. Police and block clubs together resolve problems such as drug houses, noise at night, abandoned property or other potentially difficult situations. For more information in Minneapolis call **Community Crime Prevention/SAFE**, 217 South 3rd Street, 612-673-3015; in St. Paul call the **FORCE Unit** (Community Resources), 100 East 11th Street, 651-292-3712. **Safetynet**, http://freenet.msp.mn.us/conf/safetynet, is host to an online discussion devoted to safety and crime prevention in Twin Cities neighborhoods. Residents, block club leaders, and community activists meet here to share tools, techniques, and experiences. Anyone is welcome to participate in the discussion.

KNOWING WHERE TO GO FOR A SPECIFIC SERVICE IS PARTICULARLY important when you first move. The following information, which includes particulars about renting furniture, hiring a house cleaner, pest control, shipping services, and consumer protection might make your life a little easier.

At the end of this chapter is a section on gay and lesbian services in the Twin Cities area.

RENTAL SERVICES

In keeping with the business adage "find a need and fill it," just about anything you can imagine can be rented, from pagers, televisions and stereos to furniture, wedding wear and steamrollers. If you don't own everything you need to set up housekeeping, have no fear—someone has it and they're ready to rent.

A word of caution, generally it's much more cost effective to buy than to rent. Even buying on credit is typically better than a rent-to-own situation. Many of the complaints made to the State Attorney General's Office and Better Business Bureau involve rent-to-own businesses. If you have a problem, call the Minnesota Attorney General's Office of Consumer Assistance, 651-296-3353; or 800-657-3787; TTY 651-297-7206; TTY toll free, 800-366-4812.

FURNITURE

When you go shopping, take a list of what you need and a floor plan drawing; staff at the showroom will help you temporarily furnish your new pad.
- **Cort Furniture Rental**, 8925 Lyndale Avenue South, Bloomington, 952-884-5622

- **Home Furniture Rental**, 318 East Lake Street, Minneapolis, 651-646-4000
- **Quality Furniture Rental**, 916 Rice Street, St. Paul, 651-487-2191; 9125 Lyndale Avenue South, Bloomington, 952-884-4741

TELEVISION, VCR, STEREO

Most of the furniture rental places offer TVs, VCRs, and stereos as well, but you may want to lease from an electronics specialist:

- **C and D Sales and Rental**, I-35W at New Brighton Boulevard, Minneapolis, 612-788-9268
- **Robert Paul TV**, 1789 North Lexington Avenue, Roseville, 651-489-8025

COMPUTERS

- **ASAP Computer Rental Company**, 612-888-2114, 612-882-9962, 888-886-2727, supplies computers for Minneapolis and St. Paul conventions and seminars.
- **Kinko's Copy Centers**, numerous locations throughout the Twin Cities: 8300 City Centre Drive, Woodbury, 651-578-9000; 80 IDS Center, Minneapolis, 612-343-8000. Kinko's has PCs and Macs available for in-store use.
- **University of Minnesota**, 612-624-2713, www.ebc.umn.edu—you can rent an entire computer lab from the University of Minnesota.

DOMESTIC SERVICES

HOUSE CLEANING

In addition to taking care of routine chores on a regular basis, most cleaning services also offer a one-time cleaning service, including a once-over after moving day (or after your house-warming party). This list is just to get you started, and recommendation should not be implied. Before you employ any cleaner or cleaning service, be sure to check references, and hire only those services that are insured. Check the Yellow Pages for additional services or ask your friends or co-workers for recommendations.

- **Cottage Care**, 612-944-8020
- **Housecare Extraordinaire**, 612-724-2664
- **My Maid**, 651-228-0755
- **Maids of Minnesota**, 612-378-0180

PEST CONTROL

Apart from mosquitoes, Minnesota pests tend to run to squirrels and bats that move into your attic, and raccoons and wood ducks that fall down your chimney. With that in mind, your first line of defense should be to make sure that all your chimneys and air vents are properly screened. Carpenter ants can also be a problem, so trim shrubbery back away from your foundation. Should you develop a problem that requires a professional solution, here are some local services.

- **Critter Control**, 952-475-0115
- **Diversified Mosquito Spraying**, 952-934-7064
- **Metropolitan Mosquito Control**, 651-645-9149
- **Orkin**, 612-559-2728
- **Plunkett's Pest Control**, 763-475-2100
- **Terminix**, 612-938-8363 or www.terminix.com
- **Wildlife Management Services**, 612-926-9988

MAIL SERVICE

Minneapolis' main post office is located downtown at 100 South First Street; hours of operation: Monday-Friday, 7 a.m. to 11 p.m., Saturday, 9 a.m. to 1 p.m. St. Paul's is at 180 East Kellogg Boulevard; hours are Monday-Friday, 6 a.m. to 6 p.m., Saturday, 8 a.m. to 1 p.m. You can't call them, or any other post office, directly anymore. The central number is 800-ASK-USPS (800-275-8777). Use this number for consumer complaints, postal rates, services and zip codes. You can also access this information on the Web at www.usps.com. For mail that needs to go out immediately, the Eagan post office, at 3145 Lexington Avenue South (located where I-494 and 35E converge), is open 24 hours a day.

Those needing to claim already sent mail (say wedding invitations that went out the day before the wedding was called off) can go to the local post office and fill out form 1509. Be sure to ask questions about the retrieval process, as incurred expenses will be charged to the applicant.

JUNK MAIL

To curtail the onslaught of mail newcomers are sure to receive after relocating, try these strategies: a written request, including name and address, asking to be purged from the Direct Marketing Association's list (Direct Marketing Association Mail Preference Service, P.O. Box 9008, Farmingdale,

NY 11735) will help, though some catalogue companies will need to be contacted directly with a purge request. Another option is to call the "Opt-out" line at 888-567-8688, requesting that the main credit bureaus not release your name and address to interested marketing companies.

MAIL RECEIVING SERVICES

If you're in-between addresses but still need a place to get your mail, there are dozens of businesses where you can rent a mailbox, or check with your local post office.

- **Mailboxes Etc.**, 40 locations metro-wide, 612-822-0022
- **Postal Service Plus, Inc.**, 3208 West Lake Street, Minneapolis, 612-922-4414
- **One Step Mail Shoppe**, 2200 West 66th Street, Richfield, 612-861-4826

SHIPPING SERVICES

- **Airborne Express (AirEx)**, 800-247-2676, www.airborne.com
- **DHL Worldwide Express**, 800-225-5345, www.dhl.com
- **Federal Express**, 800-238-5355, www.fedex.com
- **Roadway Package Systems (RPS)**, 800-762-3725, www.roadway.com
- **United Parcel Service (UPS)**, 800-742-5877, www.ups.com
- **US Postal Service Express Mail**, 800-222-1811, www.usps.com

CONSUMER PROTECTION—RIP-OFF RECOURSE

The best defense against fraud and consumer victimization is to avoid it. So read all contracts down to the smallest print, save all receipts and canceled checks, get the names of telephone sales and service people with whom you deal, check with the attorney general's office or the Better Business Bureau for complaints. But when you've been stung and negotiations fail, there still is something you can do.

The internet inclined should visit www.consumer.findlaw.com, where there is a wealth of information, including a Consumer Handbook with listings of consumer agencies and organizations. You can even file a complaint here with the Better Business Bureau or the National Consumer Complaint Center, or try:

- **Minnesota Attorney General's Office Consumer Division**, 651-296-3353, toll free 800-657-3787, TTY 651-297-7206, TTY toll free 800-366-4812

- **Better Business Bureau of Minnesota**, 2706 Gannon Road, St. Paul, 651-699-1111, www.minnesota.bbb.org
- **Federal Consumer Product Safety Hotline**, 800-638-2772
- **Housing Discrimination**, 800-669-9777
- **Minnesota Public Interest Research Group** (**MPIRG**), 2512 Delaware Street SE, Minneapolis, 612- 627-4035

Some people choose to take their complaints to conciliation court where suit can be filed for relief up to $7,500. You do not need a lawyer, and most people represent themselves. First obtain a complaint form from the conciliation court clerk: Hennepin County, 612-348-2713; Ramsey County, 651-266-8197; Washington County, 651-430-6264. Fill out the form with absolute accuracy, file the complaint with the clerk and pay the required fee. You and the person you are suing will receive a complaint/summons with a date to appear in court. Before heading to court, however, inform your adversary of your intentions, politely but firmly. You may force a settlement, thereby saving yourself the trouble of following through. Be aware that even if you win in court, you'll be on your own to collect your award.

If you feel you have been a victim of discrimination. The Minnesota Department of Human Rights is the state agency charged with protecting people from discrimination. Write them at 190 East 5th Street, St. Paul, MN 55101 or call 651-296-5663, 800-657-3704, TDD 651-296-1283.

IDENTITY FRAUD

While the overall crime rate in the US is on the decline, one crime that is on the increase is identity fraud. It can take years for the victims of such fraud to clear their names, so the best defense is to avoid becoming a victim. Don't have your Social Security number printed on your checks. Shred undesired pre-approved credit offers. Don't carry credit cards, social security cards, birth certificates or passports, except when you need them. Cancel all unused credit card accounts. Always take credit card and ATM receipts away with you and never toss them in a public trash container. Keep a list of all your credit cards, including information on customer service and fraud department telephone numbers. And never give out credit card information over the phone unless you initiated the call. If you have been a victim of identity fraud, call the **National Consumers' League**, 800-876-7060 or the **Privacy Rights Clearinghouse**, 800-773-7748. Other resources for victims of identity theft are the three major credit reporting bureaus: **Equifax**, 800-525-6285; **Trans Union**, 800-680-7289; and **Experian (TRW)** 800-301-7195.

GAY, LESBIAN, BISEXUAL, TRANSGENDER LIFE

Minnesota has some of the strongest civil rights protection laws in the country for Gays, Lesbians, Bisexual and Transgender (GLBT). It is the only state that includes transgender people under the umbrella of protection, and it is also the only state where you cannot be fired for being gay. Minneapolis has a well-established GLBT community with many organizations, businesses and publications that address their concerns and interests—too many to detail here. We mention the following as starting points.

- **OutFront Minnesota**, is a service center, clearing house and information line. It offers support services as well as a monthly newsletter, telephone directory that includes legal and legislative advocates, churches, bars, bookstores, hangouts, doctors and more. For visitors to the Twin Cities, it can make hotel reservations and supply an itinerary for a three-day visit. The OutFront Minnesota info line, 612-822-0127 ext. 0 or 800-800-0350 ext. 0, provides over two hours of recorded information about gay life in Minnesota. OutFront Minnesota is located at 310 38th Street East, Minneapolis; e-mail: outfront@outfront.org.
- **District 202 Community Center**, 1601 Nicollet Avenue South, Minneapolis, is a drug-free, alcohol-free, "safe space" for young people, many of whom are from minority communities, 612-871-5559.
- **Minneapolis Public Schools: Out 4 Good**, 612-668-0180
- **PFLAG (Parents & Friends of Lesbians & Gays)** sponsors monthly programs and discussions. Call 612-825-1660, or check www.pflag.org.
- **St. Paul Public Schools: Out for Equity**, 651-603-4942 provides support to students, staff and families.

NEWSPAPERS AND NEWSLETTERS

- *focusPoint*: weekly local and national news, arts, calendar; free at bookstores, coffee shops, restaurants, bars; Also available by subscription, 612-288-9008; e-mail: fPReader@aol.com.
- *Lavender* magazine: a biweekly publication covering culture, arts, news, comics, bar scene. Free at bookstores, coffee shops, restaurants and bars, also available by subscription, 612-871-2237; e-mail: info@lavendermagazine.com; www.lavendermagazine.com.

- ***Rainbow Families Newsletter***: quarterly, free to members of Rainbow Families. Membership is $18 per year. Contact Rainbow Families, 310 East 38th Street, Suite 204, Minneapolis, MN 55409, 612-370-6651; rainbows@visi.com.
- ***UP*** magazine: biweekly culture, fashion, great map of GLBT hangouts in every issue. Geared toward twenty-somethings. Free at bookstores, coffee shops, restaurants, bars. Also available by subscription, 651-822-8355; e-mail: info@upmagazine.com; www.upmagazine.com.

Gay USA: Where the Babes Go by Lori Hobkirk, also published by First Books, offers an extensive profile of lesbian life in Minneapolis.

ENTERTAINMENT

- **Twin Cities Gay Men's Chorus** performs six times a year at the Ted Mann Concert Hall at the University of Minnesota. For tickets call 612-339-SONG, or purchase tickets online; www.tcgmc.org.
- **Gay 90s Theatre Cafe and Bar**, 408 Hennepin Avenue, Minneapolis, has been voted the Twin Cities' best gay bar. Call 612-333-7755.

HOUSING

If you're looking for like minded GLBT neighbors, try the following neighborhoods: Lowry Hill, Uptown, Longfellow, East Isles, and downtown in the Near North Side in the Itasca Building and along First Avenue North. Gays are gentrifying the Near Northeast around Hennepin and Central, south of Broadway and north of Hennepin Avenue; and along University Avenue. In the suburbs GLBT residents are likely to be found in Golden Valley in North Tyrol Hills. Golden Valley is one of the most heterogeneous of the suburbs, with large African-American and GLBT communities.

MOVING TO A NEW PLACE MEANS RUNNING LOTS OF ERRANDS— from buying new curtains that fit to replacing mops and brooms that didn't make it into the moving truck. The Twin Cities present you with many shopping choices, from major national department stores to boutiques, from antique shops to flea markets, from major discount chains to malls of discount specialty shops. If you're looking for something trendy, start in Uptown; if sophisticated is your style, try 50th and France; and if it's toilet bowl brushes, school supplies and a good price on a small appliance, beat feet to Target. If your passion is fashion, there are choices from Ragstock's vintage jeans to designer boutiques—and there is no sales tax on clothing!

Partly because of the long, severe winters and partly because of the massive urban sprawl and resultant car culture, indoor malls dominate retail shopping here, with Southdale Mall in Edina said to be the first indoor retail center built in the United States. There are dozens more now and the list below will help guide you.

MALLS

Planes full of shoppers fly in from all over the world to spend their money at the **Mall of America**, Highways 77 & I-494 in Bloomington, 952-883-8800, www.mallofamerica.com. This is the largest fully enclosed shopping and entertainment complex in the United States, and is the most visited attraction in the US. Its anchor stores are **Bloomingdale's**, **Macys**, **Nordstrom** and **Sears**, but you can find over 500 other stores here with everything imaginable. For those not interested in shopping, there are sharks in Underwater World, Legoland, Golf Mountain, a race car simulator, and an indoor roller coaster at Camp Snoopy, among other attractions.

Most of the following malls have a mix of practical and pricey shopping, except for the Galleria and Gaviidae Common, which consist mainly of specialty stores and boutiques:

- **Apache Plaza**, 38 NE Avenue & Silver Lake Road, St. Anthony, 612-788-1666
- **Brookdale**, Brookdale, Brooklyn Center, 763-566-6672
- **Burnsville Center**, County Road 42, Burnsville, 952-435-8181
- **Calhoun Square**, Hennepin Avenue & Lake Street, Minneapolis, 612-824-1240
- **Eden Prairie Center**, Highway 212 and I-494, Eden Prairie, 952-941-7650
- **Galleria**, 3510 Galleria, Edina, 952-925-9534
- **Gaviidae Common**, 6th Street & Nicollet Mall, Minneapolis, 612-372-1222, children like the jumping fountain in front of Nieman Marcus and you'll appreciate the valet parking available at the 5th and 6th street entrances.
- **Har-Mar Mall**, 2100 North Snelling Avenue, Roseville, 651-631-0340
- **Maplewood Mall**, I-694 & White Bear Avenue, St. Paul, 651-770-5020
- **Ridgedale**, 12401 Wayzata Boulevard, Minnetonka, 952-541-4864
- **Rosedale**, Hwy. 36 & Fairview Avenue, Roseville, 651-633-0872, www.rosedalecenter.com
- **Southdale**, 6601 France Avenue South, Edina, 952-925-7885, www.southdale.com

SHOPPING DISTRICTS

In no way are malls the whole story. Many shopping districts thrive with a variety of useful and one-of-a-kind stores. Besides unique shopping possibilities, they also offer many opportunities to get a bite to eat or a cup of cappuccino.

- **Uptown**, Hennepin Avenue at Lake Street, Minneapolis, is as urban and edgy as Minnesota gets. Here business suited conservatives shop side-by-side with orange haired multiply pierced twenty-somethings. Besides the numerous cafes, bars and art galleries, close to a hundred trendy clothing, housewares, furniture, and home decorating stores are located here. For those interested in acquiring the work of local artists, the Minneapolis College of Art and Design operates a gallery in Calhoun Square, the three-story SoHo inspired mall that anchors the Hennepin-Lake corner. Lake Street, east of Hennepin, tends toward discount and warehouse stores, including Cheapo, 1300 West lake, 612-827-0646, a great used record/CD store (check the White Pages for other locations). North of Lake on Hennepin there are a number of antique and specialty shops. Uptown is the site of summer festivities including Aquatennial events at Lake Calhoun in July and the massive Uptown Art Fair in August. There is food here for all tastes and budgets, from Figlio's bistro to Bruegger's Bagels.

- **Grand Avenue**, St. Paul, is a thriving street made up of shops selling stylish clothing, travel books, running shoes, housewares, antiques, art and unique accessories. Grand runs east and west one block south of Summit Avenue, from Crocus Hill to the St. Paul Seminary. Toward the east end of the street, Victoria Crossing at Victoria Street is a chic crossroads with trendy boutiques and popular restaurants and bars. Cafe Latte has a line out the door anytime of the day or night, but it moves fast—and its light cuisine of healthy salads and soups will alleviate your guilt for choosing a slice of their turtle cake, 651-224-5687. You'll recognize the Red Balloon Bookstore down the street by its tree-trunk sculpture of "The Three Bears" in the front yard, 651-224-8320. Further west Ruminator Books (formerly the Hungry Mind Bookstore) at 1648 Grand Avenue, 651-699-0587, is what a bookstore ought to be: stacks to the ceiling and intellectual exchanges ongoing in every narrow aisle. During Grand Old Days in June, the whole street becomes one long block party.
- **Nicollet Mall**, Minneapolis, the city's famous downtown pedestrian mall is home to sophisticated national and local housewares and home furnishings stores and department stores such as Saks Fifth Avenue, Ann Taylor, Dayton Hudson, Nieman-Marcus and Williams-Sonoma. Getting around from store to store in winter is made easier by the second-story skyway system. Gaviidae Common offers valet parking service at its 5th and 6th Street entrances. Orchestra Hall anchors the west end of Nicollet Mall, and the Minneapolis Library anchors the east. In between, there is an on-the-mall farmers' market in the summer and the Holidazzle Parade between Thanksgiving and Christmas.
- **Dinkytown**, 10th Avenue to 17th Avenue SE, west of U of M campus, Minneapolis, offers a variety of affordable student-oriented shops and bars.
- **Linden Hills**, 43rd Street and Upton Avenue South, Minneapolis, is the location of several first-rate, locally-owned shops, with two especially good stores for children: Wild Rumpus children's book store, 2720 43rd Sreet, 612-920-5005, and Creative Kidstuff which inspires

with its toys, music, arts and crafts, 4313 Upton, 612-927-0653. Sebastian Joe's ice cream, 4321 Upton, is another treat for the whole family. Turtle Bread Company, 3415 West 44th Street, 612-924-6013, is worth a special trip.

- **50th and France Avenue**, Edina, www.50thandfrance.com, is as close as Edina comes to having a downtown. This hub has a hundred classy boutiques, trendy accessories, a drapery/slipcover workroom, Lund's grocery and Wuollet's Bakery, 612-922-4341. Shopping begins at 44th and France, where Durr, Ltd., 952-925-9146, sells unique French/English country furniture and accessories. Across the street is the famed Oriental rug dealer, Karagheusian, 952-920-5008. On 50th, Marathon Sports is where to go to get fitted for athletic shoes, 612-920-2606, and Tejas restaurant, 952-926-0800, is the place to run to— for gourmet Southwestern fare. The crossroad and surrounding streets are transformed into an exotic bazaar in June during the Edina Art Fair.
- **Midway**, University Avenue at Snelling Avenue, St. Paul, provides the necessities to the people of the western side of St. Paul, with grocery stores, banks, warehouse and discount department stores, second-hand furniture and clothing retailers.
- **South Robert Street**, West St. Paul, transcends nationality with ethnic groceries, well-known national department stores, discount stores, housewares, and electronics.
- **Stillwater** (See **Quick Getaways** chapter.)
- **Wayzata**, on Lake Minnetonka west of Minneapolis out I-394, offers preppy, upscale shopping, with half a dozen small malls and waterfront specialty clothing stores, boutiques, gifts and half a dozen restaurants. The Gold Mine, 332 Broadway Avenue South, 952-473-7719, specializes in antique china, silver, and glass on consignment from Minnetonka's finest families. The sign on the Wayzata Home Center at 1250 Wayzata Boulevard says it all: "London, Paris, Wayzata." These antique shops have something for everyone, but excel in opulent bedroom suites. American Vacuum, in the lower level, sells and services better brands of vacuum cleaners, 952-473-6861. Across the street, The Sports Hut, 473-8843, in Colonial Square is an authority on skiing, biking and most other sports. When exploring Wayzata in warm weather months, park your car and walk or use the trolley to get around.
- **White Bear Lake** features one-of-a kind shops clustered in a friendly downtown with a turn-of-the-century resort quality. This is a good place to visit if you're into quilting, needlepoint, knitting or other crafts. White Bear is also home to the Outdoor Cooking Store, 2225 4th Street, 651-653-6166, which has everything to do with grilling.

OUTLET MALLS

Some shoppers travel hundreds of miles by car and charter bus in search of huge discounts at outlet malls—whether they really offer the expected savings, though, is open to debate. There are several outlet malls and factory outlet stores near the Twin Cities, among them:

- **Baby Plus Teens**, 5740 Wayzata Boulevard, Golden Valley, 763-544-5422, an outlet for childrens' furniture and accessories.
- **Horizon Outlet Center**, 50 miles south of Minneapolis on Interstate Highway 35, Exit 48, between Owatonna and Faribault, 507-455-4111, 42 stores sell Nike, Liz Claiborne, Mikasa as well as Norwegian sweaters at Devold, women's sportswear at Koret, and bedding at The Company Store.
- **Prime Outlets**, East of St. Paul at I-94 and County Road 19, Exit 251, Woodbury, 651-735-9060, www.primeoutlets.com; Eddie Bauer and Spiegel are the anchors, but there are 45 other stores: London Fog, Hush Puppies, West Point Stevens for linens, Welcome Home for gifts and home accessories, and Kasper ASL for women's career clothing. Register at the web site for coupons.
- **Room and Board**, 4680 Olson Memorial Highway, Minneapolis, 612-529-6089, sells contemporary furniture, open Saturdays and Sundays.
- **Tanger Outlet Center**, I-35 North, Exit 147, North Branch, 800-409-3631, is home to a Black and Decker tool outlet, Carter's Children's Wear, Big Dog and Pfaltzgraff. Coupons are available at the Carter's store and mall office.

DEPARTMENT STORES

If you have trouble living without Bloomingdale's or Nordstrom or some other top of the line department store, you can breathe easier, most of the national one-stop shopping giants are here, ready to make your life in the Twin Cities as livable as it was anywhere else. But don't forget to try out the hometown favorite, Dayton's (it's the same company that owns the popular discount store, Target).

- **Bloomingdale's**, Mall of America, Bloomington, 952-883-2500
- **Dayton's**, 700 Nicollet Mall, Minneapolis, 612-375-2200 (check the White Pages for other locations).
- **Herberger's**, Apache Plaza, St. Anthony, 612-789-2422 (check the White Pages for other locations).
- **JC Penney**, Brookdale, Brooklyn Center, 763-566-2100 (check the White Pages for other locations).

- **Macys**, Mall of America, Bloomington, 952-888-3333
- **Neiman-Marcus**, 505 Nicollet Mall, Minneapolis, 612-339-2600
- **Nordstrom**, Mall of America, Bloomington, 952-883-2121; this chain has built its reputation on excellent service, and this store is no exception. Check out the clearance items at Nordstrom's Rack, 952-854-3131 on the third floor.
- **Saks Fifth Avenue**, 655 Nicollet Mall, Minneapolis, 612-333-7200
- **Sears, Roebuck & Co.**, Mall of America, Bloomington, 952-853-0500; 425 Rice Street, St. Paul, 651-291-4330 (check the White Pages for other locations).

DISCOUNT STORES

- **Bank's**, 615 1st Avenue Northeast, 612-379-2803, has a changing inventory of furniture and clothing. Call 612-379-4321 for weekly sales updates.
- **Lands' End Inlet**, Lyndale and I-494, Richfield, 612-861-4100 (check the White Pages for other locations) stocks closeout merchandise from the Lands' End catalogue.
- **Loehmann's**, 5141 West 98th Street, Bloomington, 952-835-2510, is great for fancy dresses and gifts.
- **Nordic Ware Factory Outlet Store**, Highways 7 and 100, St. Louis Park, 952-924-9672, sells cooking equipment.
- **Sam's Club**, 3745 Louisiana Avenue South, St. Louis Park, 952-924-9450 (check the White Pages for other locations) offers a wide variety of merchandise to members.
- **Sportsman's Guide**, 411 Farwell Avenue in South St. Paul, 651-552-5248; a liquidation showroom and retail outlet store, it offers name brand shoes like Timberland and apparel.
- **Target**, 1300 University Avenue West, St. Paul, 651-642-1146 (check the White Pages for other locations).
- **TJ Maxx**, IDS Center, Nicollet Mall, Minneapolis, 612-321-9107 (check the White Pages for other locations).
- **Tuesday Morning**, 6405 City West Parkway, Eden Prairie, 952-943-2267 (check the White Pages for other locations).

APPLIANCES & ELECTRONICS

- **Audio King**, 7435 France Avenue South, Centennial Lakes Plaza, Edina, 952-830-0100 (check the White Pages for other locations).

- **Audiophile HiFi Sound Electronics**, 1226 Harmon Place, Minneapolis, 612-339-6351
- **Best Buy**, 1647 West County Road B2, Roseville, 651-636-6456 (check the White Pages for other locations).
- **Circuit City**, 1750 West Highway 36, Roseville, 651-636-2505; Southdale Mall, Edina, 952-832-5200.
- **Fireplace Center**, 12460 Wayzata Boulevard, Minnetonka, 952-454-3797, installs and sells fireplace inserts, stoves, Holland grills, and fireplace equipment.
- **Guyer's**, 13405 15th Avenue North, Plymouth, 612-553-1445 (check the White Pages for other locations). Check prices here first for major appliances, cabinets, carpets, and fireplaces.
- **Van's Coating Systems**, 612-331-9442, will come to your house and refinish your appliances so you don't have to buy new ones.
- **Radio Shack**, Ridgedale Center, Minnetonka, 952-546-1112; 312 City Center, 612-333-3954; 894 Arcade Street, 651-771-0773 (check the White Pages for other locations).

COMPUTERS/SOFTWARE

Try the Yellow Pages for computer listings not included here, including specialized dealers who also provide training. The larger electronics vendors, such as **Circuit City**, **Radio Shack** and **Best Buy**, have become competitive in computer and software products. Then there are the mail-order catalogs, such as **MacWarehouse**, 800-255-6227, from which you can shop without leaving that warm spot on your couch. If you're on a tight budget or don't need the very latest technology, try one of the used computer vendors.
- **CompUSA**, 4220 West 78th Street, Bloomington, 952-820-8090; 11500 Wayzata Boulevard, Minnetonka, 612-512-0087; 2480 Fairview Avenue, Roseville, 651-635-0770; 8320 Tamarack Village, Woodbury, 651-578-0078
- **Computer Renaissance, Inc.**, 1305 West Lake Street, Minneapolis, 612-825-3007; 2335 Fairview Avenue, Roseville, 651-638-9808
- **Used Computer Bank**, 2500 Highway 88, St. Anthony, 612-789-6910.
- **Dan Patch Computer**, 3802 West Highway 13, Burnsville, 952—894-1683, deals only in Macintosh computers and accessories.
- **Midwest Mac**, Robbinsdale, call for directions—they're complicated, 763-537-5000.

ART

Artists who live and work in Northeast Minneapolis and Lowertown in St. Paul periodically open their studios for public sales. Keep an eye on the paper, or check out the Art-A-Whirl web site, www.art-a-whirl.org. There are numerous galleries, especially in Uptown or the Minneapolis warehouse district. And, don't forget the art schools. The Minneapolis College of Art and Design runs a gallery in Calhoun Square and also holds a students' art sale every December, 612-874-3654. The Minnetonka Center for the Arts, 2240 North Shore Drive, Orono, 612-473-7361, has frequent shows and sales. The Art Collective, 1620 Central Avenue, NE, Minneapolis, 612-788-8613, is an excellent resource for handcrafted furniture, pottery, glass, lighting, drawings, paintings, soap, jewelry, and many other types of artwork.

ART SUPPLIES

- **Art Scraps**, 1459 St. Clair Avenue, St. Paul, 651-698-2787
- **Creative Kidstuff**, Valley Creek Plaza, Woodbury, 651-735-4060 (Check the White Pages for other locations.)
- **Wet Paint**, 1684 Grand Avenue, St. Paul, 651-698-6431, carries thousands of different papers, so it's a favorite with calligraphers.

BOOKSTORES

The Twin Cities are home to many excellent new and used bookstores. They include chains such as **Barnes & Noble**, **Borders**, **B. Dalton** and **Walden Books**, all of which have multiple locations. Independent booksellers, who survive by virtue of their customer service and erudition, are harder to find, so a few of them are listed below:

- **Bookcase of Wayzata**, 607 East Lake Street, 952-473-8341; connected to Caribou Coffee
- **Books for Travel**, 857 Grand Avenue, St. Paul, 888-668-8006, premier selection of travel related books and accessories.
- **Excelsior Bay Books**, 36 Water Street, Excelsior, 952-401-0932 is a real neighborhood bookstore known for its children's books and fiction.
- **Magers & Quinn**, 3038 Hennepin Avenue South, Minneapolis, 612-822-4611; for the friendly atmosphere, scholarly staff and a sense that there are treasures to be found here, this bookstore is a favorite among the Twin Cities' many excellent used book stores.
- **Micawber's Books**, 2238 Carter Avenue, St. Paul, 651-646-5506

- **Once Upon A Crime**, 604 West 26th Street, Minneapolis, 612-870-3785, for the mystery lover.
- **The Red Balloon**, 891 Grand Avenue, St. Paul, 651-224-8320, is a fantastic children's bookstore that stages many fun family events throughout the year.
- **Ruminator Books** (previously Hungry Mind Books), 1648 Grand Avenue, St. Paul, 651-699-0587, 800-760-9532, is located next door to Macalester College. The atmosphere here is academic, the book inventory huge, and the book readings hosted by famous authors. You'll feel smarter just by walking through the door.
- **Uncle Edgar's Mystery Bookstore**, 2864 Chicago Avenue, Minneapolis, 612-824-9984
- **Wild Rumpus**, 2720 West 43rd Street, Minneapolis, 612-920-5005, is a Linden Hills children's bookstore with a kid-sized door and pet animals. The ambiance alone is certain to turn children into bookworms.

CHILDREN

- **Capers**, 205 Water Street, Excelsior, 952-474-1715; carries cards, stickers, shirts, picture frames, and trendy accessories
- **Creative Kidstuff**, 12977 Ridgedale Drive, Minnetonka, 952-540-0022, offers innovative toys and crafts to stimulate the imaginations of parents and kids alike. (Check the White Pages for other locations.)
- **Gymboree**, 12535 Wayzata Boulevard, Minnetonka, 952-591-9598; children work out singing, dancing and playing interactive videos while parents' shopping nets plenty of imaginative merchandise. (Check the White Pages for other locations.)
- **The Glasses Menagerie**, 3142 Hennepin Avenue (Uptown), Minneapolis, 612-822-7021, www.Kidseyes.com
- **Zany Brainy** children's playshops, 2487 North Fairview Avenue, Roseville, 651-635-0067, and Brandon Square, 3533 West 70th Street, Edina, 952-920-0410, offers crafts, story-time, costumed storybook characters, and myriad other learning activities to capture the magic of childhood.

FURNITURE

- **Chanhassen Furniture Galleries**, 521 West 78th Street, Chanhassen, 952-934-5801, is an excellent resource for stylish pieces.
- **Dayton's**, 700 On the Mall, Minneapolis, 612-375-2200; Southdale,

Edina, 952-896-2160; Rosedale, 651-639-2040; warehouse store, 411 Cedar Street, St. Paul, 651-292-5222, offers medium to higher quality furniture, accessories and carpeting of all styles; check out the bargains at the warehouse store.

- **Gabberts**, 3501 Galleria, Edina, 952-927-0725; everything from mattresses to carpeting to tables to a complete range of furniture and celebrity decorators, all located in one showroom in the Twin Cities' premier home furnishings store. Gabbert's is pricey; check their Odds 'n Ends room for bargains.
- **Elements**, 2941 Hennepin Avenue, Minneapolis, 612-824-5300; 1655 West County Road B2, Roseville, 651-633-3515; 2940 West 66th Street, Richfield, 612-866-0631; specializes in clean-lined design and reasonable prices.
- **International Market Square**, 275 Market Street, Minneapolis, 612-338-6250, is the local to-the-trade designers' showroom. Go there with a designer or catch the once-a-year sample sale in September.
- **Room and Board**, 2875 Snelling Avenue North, Roseville, 651-639-0591 (check the White Pages for other locations). Look here for less expensive contemporary and children's furniture.
- **Rosenthal Furniture**, 22 North 5th Street, Minneapolis, 612-332-4363, is a warehouse-type showroom which also special-orders from hundreds of manufacturers.
- **Seasonal Concepts**, Har Mar Mall, St. Paul, 651-636-5900 (check the White Pages for other locations), stocks seasonal merchandise including an excellent selection of high-quality outdoor furniture and great fake Christmas trees.
- **Unpainted Place, Inc.**, 1601 Hennepin Avenue, Minneapolis, 612-339-1500, is an excellent source for unpainted pine and oak furniture.

BEDS, BEDDING & BATH

Department stores can handle all your bedding needs, from the beds themselves to shams and comforters; but if you don't want to spend a bundle, check out **Tuesday Morning** (see **Discount Stores** above), which always has some designer linens on sale at closeout prices.

- **Comforest Adjustable Beds**, 5019 University Avenue NE, Columbia Heights, 763-572-8361
- **The Company Store**, 800-285-3696 or www.thecompanystore.com; this catalog company sells many products including cotton sheets and down-filled bedding.

- **Deep Sleep Inc.**, West Broadway and Bass Lake Road, Crystal, 763-533-2400
- **Duxiana/The Dux Bed**, 7507 France Avenue South, Edina, 952-835-7682
- **F & B Linen Shoppe**, 844 Grand Avenue, St. Paul, 651-602-0844, specializes in high thread count ready-made or custom bedding, tablecloths and napkins. Look here for unusual sizes or new pieces to mix with Grandma's vintage sets.
- **Futon Gallery**, 2601 Hennepin Avenue, Minneapolis, 612-377-9440; 799 Grand Avenue, St. Paul, 651-227-2644 (check the White Pages for other locations).
- **Linens 'N Things**, 1585 South Plymouth Road, Minnetonka, 952-541-9704 (check the White Pages for other locations).
- **Mattress Giant**, 1845 East Co. Road D, Maplewood, 651-770-1800
- **Restwell Mattress Company**, 3540 Belt Line Boulevard, St. Louis Park, 952-920-3348
- **Slumberland Furniture**, 7801 Xerxes Avenue South, Bloomington, 952-888-6204 (check the White Pages for other locations). Clearance operations are at: 1925 Suburban Avenue, St. Paul, 651-738-6230; 4140 Excelsior Boulevard, St. Louis Park, 952-925-9035

CARPETS & RUGS

- **Carpet King**, 773 Cleveland Avenue South, St. Paul, 651-690-5448 (check the White Pages for other locations).
- **Cyrus Carpets**, Galleria, Edina, 952-922-6000, deals in fine Oriental rugs.
- **Dayton's** (see **Department Stores** above).
- **Gabberts**, 3501 Galleria, Edina, 952-927-0725
- **Karagheusian**, 44th and France Avenue, Edina, 952-920-5008

LAMPS & LIGHTING

- **Cartier Lighting**, 151 Cheshire Lane, Plymouth, 763-476-9555
- **Citilights**, 1619 Hennepin Avenue, Minneapolis, 612-333-3168
- **Creative Lighting**, I-94 at Snelling Avenue, St. Paul, 651-647-0111
- **Lamp Depot**, Brighton Village Center, I-694 at Silver Lake Road, New Brighton 763-332-6626 (check the White Pages for other locations).
- **Michael's Lamp Studio**, 3101 West 50th Street, Minneapolis, 651-926-9147

HARDWARE STORES

In the Twin Cities you can find the national chains, as well as a number of locally owned, neighborhood hardware stores. Check in your Yellow Pages under "Hardware Stores" for those nearest you. For specialty decorative hardware, however, the last three listed here are excellent resources.

- **Ace Hardware**, 1344 Coon Rapids Boulevard Northwest, Coon Rapids, 7632-755-1762; 4401 Winnetka Avenue North, New Hope, 763-537-1634; 10809 University Avenue Northeast, Blaine, 763-754-0364; 1804 Nicollet Avenue, Minneapolis, 612-870-0511; 3805 Nicollet Avenue, Minneapolis, 612-822-3121 (check the White Pages for other locations).
- **Coast to Coast**, 4140 West Broadway Avenue, Robbinsdale, 763-533-2758; 10530 France Avenue South, Bloomington, 952-884-2209; 4020 Bloomington Avenue, Minneapolis, 612-822-4155 (check White Pages for other locations).
- **Mills Fleet Farm**, 8400 Lakeland Avenue North, Brooklyn Park, 763-424-9668 (check the White Pages for other locations).
- **Home Depot**, 6701 Boone Avenue North, Brooklyn Park, 763-533-1200; 400 West 79th Street, Bloomington, 612-881-7020; 1520 New Brighton Boulevard, Minneapolis, 612-782-9594; 1705 Annapolis Lane North, Plymouth, 763-509-9590; 5800 Cedar Lake Road South, St. Louis Park, 952-512-0109 (check the White Pages for other locations).
- **Menards**, 6800 Wayzata Boulevard, Golden Valley, 763-541-9300; 7701 Nicollet Avenue, Richfield, 612-798-0508; 7800 Lakeland Avenue North, Brooklyn Park, 763-424-8575 (check the White Pages for other locations).
- **Art and Architecture**, 404 Washington Avenue North, Minneapolis, 612-904-1776
- **The Brass Handle**, Galleria, Edina, 952-927-7777
- **Nob Hill**, 7317 Cahill Road, Suite 209, Edina, 952-646-5408

GARDEN CENTERS/NURSERIES

One of the biggest problems for any gardener is choosing the right plants for his/her hardiness zone. The Twin Cities are in hardiness zone 3b, which means that our average minimum temperature is in the minus 25-35 degrees Fahrenheit, range. But summer temps often climb into the 90s or even over 100; making the climate inhospitable to many popular garden plants. Good advice: start cultivating a fondness for hostas and daylillies—they are two plants that actually thrive here.

For gardeners, there is one good thing about our long winter, it provides a respite for aching bodies and also offers an interval in which to plan for the next season. So if the thought of morning sun slanting across pink hollyhocks makes your heart sing, here are some nurseries just for you:

- **Ambergate Gardens**, 8730 County Road 43, Chaska, 952-443-2248, is owned by a horticulturist who was at the Minnesota Landscape Arboretum for a number of years. His nursery sells vigorous, cold-hardy perennials, with emphasis on the out of the ordinary. Call for directions or a catalogue.
- **Bachman's**, 10050 6th Avenue North, Plymouth, 763-541-1188 (check the White Pages for other locations), is the all-purpose garden center for the Twin Cities.
- **Bergman's**, Highway 36 and County Road 15, Stillwater, 651-439-4294
- **Green Value Nursery**, 3801 Edgerton, Vadnais Heights, 651-483-1176
- **Landscape Alternatives**, 1705 Saint Albans Street North, Roseville, 651-488-3142, sells native wildflowers, ornamental grasses and perennials.
- **Nature's Harvest**, 320 East Wayzata Boulevard, Wayzata, 952-473-4687
- **Prairie Restorations**, Princeton, Minnesota, 763-389-9377, designs low maintenance natural gardens and also sells native grasses and wildflowers and prairie kits.
- **Linder's Greenhouse & Garden**, 270 Larpenteur Avenue West, St. Paul, 651-488-1927, is another all-inclusive garden center.
- **Rice Creek Gardens Nursery**, 11506 Highway 65 Northeast, Blaine, 763-754-8090, is a great place to visit, both to buy plants and to see new ideas for using perennials in the landscape.
- **Savory's Gardens**, 5300 Whiting Avenue, Edina 952-941-8755; founded by a former president of the Hosta Society, this nursery offers its own hosta introductions in addition to other shade-tolerant plants.
- **University of Minnesota Landscape Arboretum**, 3675 Arboretum Drive, Chanhassen, 952-443-2460, holds a plant sale every May, usually around Mother's Day.

HOUSEWARES

- **Crate & Barrel**, 915 Nicollet Mall, Minneapolis, 612-338-4000; Southdale Center, Edina, 952-920-2300

- **Homeplace**, Circuit City Plaza, Edina, off I-494, 952-832-0059 (check the White Pages for other locations).
- **Pottery Barn**, Mall of America, Bloomington, 952-858-9030; Galleria, Edina, 952-925-1610; www.potterybarn.com
- **Pier One**, 1433 West Lake Street, Minneapolis, 612-825-5367; 733 Grand Avenue, St. Paul, 651-228-1737 (check the White Pages for more locations).
- **Lechters Housewares**, Rosedale Shopping Center, 651-636-7725; Ridgedale, 952-546-1202
- **Williams-Sonoma**, Mall of America, Bloomington, 952-858-8530; Galleria, Edina, 952-925-0039; IDS Center, Minneapolis, 612-376-7666

SPORTING GOODS

Contrary to what some newcomers might believe, outdoor recreation is a year-round phenomenon in these parts. Many Minnesotans look forward to the winter months for the chance to go skiing, skating, snowboarding, or curling. In October, die-hard cross-country skiers can be seen polling along the parkways on skates, training for the first snow. And in the glorious days of summer with its longer northern days, there's lots of time for biking, swimming, fishing, in-line skating, camping, sailing, volleyball—whatever your heart desires. For those in need of gear, we offer the following list of places to start shopping. If you're counting your pennies, remember to shop the season-end sales, and if you're not sure whether you want to buy an expensive item, inquire about testing or renting—or investigate the second-hand sporting goods stores.

- **Alternative Bike and Board Shop**, 2408 Hennepin Avenue South, Minneapolis, 612-374-3635, advertises overnight repairs.
- **Cabelas**, 3900 Cabela Drive, Owatonna, Minnesota, off I-35 south of the cities, 507-451-4545, is the definitive sports equipment shopping experience.
- **Erik's Bike Shop**, Minnetonka Boulevard at Texas Avenue, St. Louis Park, 952-920-1790 (check White Pages for other locations), encourages you to test-ride before you buy.
- **The Golf Connection**, 500 Lake Street, Excelsior, 952-474-9073; golfers come from far away to get custom-made, reasonably priced golf clubs here; hours vary so call first.
- **The House**, located at the junction of 35E and 694 at 300 South Owasso Boulevard, St. Paul, 651-482-9995, has a great selection and great prices on windsurfing equipment and lessons, and snowboards

and more. They also have catalogue sales.

- **Hoigard's**, 3550 South Highway 100, St. Louis Park, 952-929-1351, can outfit you for almost any sport with equipment and clothing. This is also a good place to look for a winter coat and patio furniture. Don't miss its giant tent sales.
- **Midwest Mountaineering**, 309 Cedar Avenue South, Minneapolis, 612-339-3433, near the U of M, sells outdoor equipment, clothing and holds a spectacular fall sale.
- **Now Bikes and Fitness**, 1298 County Road 42, Burnsville, 952-435-6832 (see White Pages for other locations), stocks the top brands and offers a trade-in program for children's bikes.
- **Play It Again Sports**, 3505 Hennepin Avenue South, Minneapolis, 612-824-1231; 1669 Grand Avenue, St. Paul, 651-698-3773 (see the White Pages for other locations), markets used equipment that's still in good shape.
- **REI (Recreational Equipment, Inc.)**, 750 West 98th Street, Bloomington, 952-884-4315; 1995 West County Road B2, Roseville, 651-635-0211, has bikes, skis, canoes and camping gear, and a monster climbing wall.
- **2nd Wind**, 6819 Wayzata Boulevard, St. Louis Park, 952-544-2540, sells new and used better-grade exercise equipment.
- **Sports Hut**, Colonial Square Shopping Center, Wayzata, 952-473-8843, sells and services skis, bikes and other sports equipment and carries name brand sports clothing.
- **Twin City Tennis Supply**, 4747 Chicago Avenue South, Minneapolis, 612-823-9285, www.tctennis.com; this is where the champions shop.

WINTERWEAR

In the introduction, we warned you about the winter months and the need for warm clothes. No kidding, even with global warming, winters here are no joke. If you arrived without the right winter gear, the following are a few places where you can get the coats and boots you'll need to stay warm and happy from Thanksgiving to Easter. Don't forget the department stores.

- **Burlington Coat Factory** 3700 South Highway 100, St. Louis Park, 952-929-6850
- **Hoigard's** (see **Sports Equipment** above).
- **L.L. Bean** catalogue, 800-341-4341, www.llbean.com—L.L. Bean not only guarantees its merchandise, it also rates it. Buy a 50-below

coat and you'll be dancing comfortably on the ice in February.
- **United Stores**, 449 Snelling Avenue North, St. Paul, 651-646-3544 (check the White Pages for other locations).

SECOND HAND SHOPPING

ANTIQUE SHOPS AND FLEA MARKETS

The Twin Cities have many antique and junk shops which tend to be clustered together, such as 7th Street in St. Paul, or the cities of Excelsior, Wayzata, Stillwater, and Buffalo. In Minneapolis, venerable dealers are found in the warehouse district along 1st and 3rd Avenues North. The Decorative Arts Council of the Minneapolis Institute of Arts sponsors an annual fundraising Antiques Show and Sale at International Market Square every October. The weekend includes a preview party and lectures, and antiques from some of the nation's leading dealers.

There are also many interesting shops to be found off the beaten path. So hitch up the U-haul, and happy hunting! Here are some places to start:
- **Medina Flea Market**, Sunday mornings in the Medina Ballroom parking lot on Highway 55 west of Minneapolis.
- **Farmstead Flea Market**, New Richmond Heritage Center, 1100 Heritage Drive, New Richmond, Wisconsin, 715-246-3276, Saturdays, 7:30 a.m. to 2 p.m. and Sundays, 11 a.m. to 4 p.m.
- **Antiques Minnesota**, 1197 University Avenue, St. Paul, 651-646-0037, has about a hundred dealers under one roof selling everything from kitschy collectibles to nice antiques.
- **Architectural Antiques**, 801 Washington Avenue North, Minneapolis, 612-332-8344, and 316 North Main Street, Stillwater, 651-439-2133; every corner is filled with artifacts saved from the wrecking ball. They can lend an atmosphere of grace to new construction or contribute authenticity to a renovation.
- **Walden Woods**, 213 Washington Avenue North, Minneapolis, 612-338-2545, and Buffalo, west of Minneapolis off Highway 55, 763-682-5667
- **French Antiques**, 74 7th Street West, St. Paul, 651-293-0388, and 3016 Lyndale Avenue South, Minneapolis, 612-824-8181, carries a variety of furniture (new and antique) imported from France.
- **Rose Galleries**, 2717 Lincoln Drive, Roseville, 651-484-1415, www.rosegalleries.com, is an auction house where you can sometimes find very fine pieces.

- **Postal Service auctions of unclaimed and undeliverable goods** are held every eight weeks in St. Paul. This is one of only three locations in the country (the others are Atlanta and San Francisco) where these auctions are conducted. Auction information is posted in the post offices.

THRIFTS AND VINTAGE SHOPS

If you're renovating an old house, there are architectural artifact sources listed under **Antiques** above. But make your first stop **The Reuse Center**, 2216 East Lake Street, Minneapolis, 612-724-2608. You may find just the right door there, plus they'll even show you how to hang it in one of their many do-it-yourself classes. For those more interested in shopping than doing, Minnetonka and Edina are considered garage sale Heaven. Look in the papers on Wednesdays and map out your route to cover the Thursday-Saturday garage sales for deals on toys, camping equipment, sports equipment, and furniture. Estate sales are also held on weekends, and are often the better place to look for nice furnishings. If you're hunting for a funky outfit or gently-used designer clothing, it's fun to shop the vintage and consignment stores—and don't forget to check out the Goodwill. If you like to shop the internet, check www.bargains.org for great prices on specific models of electronics, watches, sporting goods and other items.

- **The Clothes Line**, 2901 Hennepin Avenue, Minneapolis, 612-822-3212, is operated by the Minneapolis Junior League and sells modern high-quality clothes. Look here for a gown for the Symphony Ball.
- **Lula's**, 1587 Selby Avenue, St. Paul, 651-644-4110 and 710 West 22nd Street, Minneapolis, 612-872-7090, sells vintage clothes from the 1960s and before.
- **Maternity Closet**, Hugo, 651-407-1818, by appointment, www.maternitycloset.com, rents special occassion and business maternity clothes on a month-to-month basis.
- **Maternity Style**, Eden Prairie, 952-934-5565, by appointment only, makes and rents maternity business and formal wear on a month-to-month basis.
- **Nu Look Consignment**, 4956 Penn Avenue South, Minneapolis, 612-925-0806, stocks women's, children's and maternity fashions.
- **Once Upon A Child,** 14200 Wayzata Boulevard, Minnetonka, 952-540-0477 (check the White Pages for other locations), advertises "kids' stuff with previous experience."
- **Paris Flea Market**, 5005 France Avenue South, Edina, 952-928-9923, carries vintage and costume jewelry.

- **PPL Shop**, 850 15th Avenue NE, Minneapolis, 612-789-3322; 370 Toronto Street, St. Paul, 651-224-7019; PPL stands for Project for Pride in Living, a nonprofit organization whose mission is to help low- and moderate-income people become self-sufficient. Donations of used office equipment come from companies such as General Mills and Honeywell. A cabinet manufacturer donates kitchen cabinets twice a year. Stolen and recovered merchandise, used computers and electronics, and new jewelry and home accessories are also sold here.
- **Ragstock Clothing**, 315 14th Avenue SE, Minneapolis, 612-331-6064; 1433 West Lake Street, Minneapolis, 612-823-6690; 1515 University Avenue West, St. Paul, 651-644-2733; Warehouse, 830 7th Street North, 612-333-8520; www.ragstock.com, has lots of denim, Hawaiian print shirts, bell-bottoms and is tops with teens and college kids.
- **Rose's Tea Room**, 429 2nd Street, Excelsior, 952-474-2661, sometimes has clothing and always has china, books, silver, music, linens, jewelry—and lunch!
- **Rodeo Drive Consignment Boutique**, 4110 Minnetonka Boulevard, St. Louis Park, 952-920-0188, specializes in designer clothes, sizes 2-28. Look for their summer and winter sales.
- **Tatters Clothing**, 2922 Lyndale Avenue South, Minneapolis, 612-823-5285, has men's and women's vintage clothes mostly from the 1940s through the 70s, as well as motorcycle jackets.

HARD-TO-FIND SERVICES

- **Anthony's Furniture Restoration**, 4553 Bryant Avenue South, Minneapolis, 612-824-1717, offers French polishing and cleaning for your fine antiques, as well as refinishing and repair.
- **Bob's Shoe Repair**, Wayzata Bay Center, Wayzata, 952-473-8248, stays open until 9 p.m.
- **Oexning Silversmiths**, 9 North 4th Street, Minneapolis, 612-332-6857, can restore your family heirlooms to their original beauty by re-plating, straightening and polishing anything silver, from flatware to tea services.
- **Van's Coating Systems**, 612-331-9442, will come to your house and apply a new finish to your appliances so you don't have to buy new ones.

FOOD

You can live without lamps, but you can't live without dinner. So soon after moving, you're going to have to go to the grocery store or a restaurant. Here are some suggestions:

GROCERY STORES

Cub and **Rainbow** are warehouse food stores. Their aisles are lined with formidable towers of boxes, cans, and produce. Both are 24-hour enterprises, enabling you to go on late-night shopping sprees. Both chains have bakeries and delis, as well as small health food sections. If you're stocking up on cleaning products and other staples, these are good places to go. Another warehouse chain is **Sam's Club**, (see above under **Discount Department Stores**) which has five stores; you will need to become a member if you want to shop here for anything other than liquor.

Lund's, **Byerly's**, **Kowalski's**, and **New Market** grocery stores generally offer such amenities as gourmet and imported foods, fresh flowers, specialty meats and seafood, and clerks who bag your groceries. Each of these enterprises has stores throughout the metro area; check the White Pages for the nearest one. **Jerry's** is also in this category but limits its stores to Edina and Eden Prairie. Byerly's conducts weeklong **Kids' Cooking Camps**, call 612-929-2492 for information.

FOOD CO-OPS

If your idea of quality is organically grown produce and health foods, you'll be able to find a limited selection in most supermarkets, but one of the Twin Cities' many grocery co-operatives may come closer to meeting your needs. Besides offering unsprayed produce and the gamut of "free" foods (wheat-free, free-range, etc.), co-ops sell many foods in bulk, allowing you to get the exact amount you need. Recently added to many of the health food stores are take-out delis offering good for you gourmet fare. Co-ops sell shares and distribute dividends to members; some allow you to volunteer at the store for a discount on groceries. Following are well-known grocery co-ops in the metro area:

- **Capital City Co-op**, 28 West 10th Street, St. Paul, 651-298-1340
- **Hampden Park Co-op**, 928 Raymond Avenue, St. Paul, 651-646-6686

- **Lakewinds Natural Foods**, 17523 Minnetonka Boulevard, Minnetonka, 952-473-0292, www.lakewinds.com
- **Linden Hills Co-op**, 2813 West 43rd Street, Minneapolis, 612-922-1159
- **Mississippi Market**, 1810 Randolph Street, St. Paul, 651-690-0507 or 622 Selby Avenue, St. Paul, 651-224-1300
- **North Country Co-op**, 1929 South 5th Street, Minneapolis, 612-338-3110
- **Seward Community Co-op**, 2111 East Franklin Avenue, Minneapolis, 612-338-2465
- **Valley Natural Foods**, 14015 Grand Avenue South, Burnsville, 952-892-6667
- **Valley Co-op**, 215 North William Street, Stillwater, 651-439-0366
- **Wedge Community Co-op**, 2105 Lyndale Avenue South, Minneapolis, 612-871-3993

In a class of their own are **Tao Foods** and **Whole Foods**. Tao Foods, at 2200 Hennepin Avenue in Minneapolis, 612-377-4630, is a small shop that combines food and medicine, offering homeopathic remedies, herbal tonics and a juice bar. Whole Foods, 30 Fairview Avenue South, St. Paul, 651-690-0197, is a national chain offering organic and health foods, as well as gourmet foods and a bakery. This is not a place to shop for bargains.

FARMERS' MARKETS

If you're shopping for the highest quality in fruits and vegetables, nothing beats buying directly from the growers. Seasonal garden produce is sold at scores of markets and vegetable stands throughout the metro area. Following are a few of the largest markets. If a drive to the country with a stop to pick fresh raspberries or apples sounds like a cure for your city blues, get the full listing of farm stands in Minnesota from this address: Minnesota Grown, Minnesota Department of Agriculture, 90 West Plato Boulevard, St. Paul, Minnesota 55107 or call 651-297-8695. A local farm cooperative offers another way to get your vegetables fresh as can be— straight from the farm. The Land Stewardship Project has produced a directory of farms which sell directly to consumers. You may also be able to participate in events at the farms including hayrides, festivals and chore weekends. For more information contact the **Land Stewardship Project**, 2200 4th Street, White Bear Lake, MN 651-653-0618.

- **Minneapolis Farmers' Market**, 612-333-1718, two locations: one block south of Highway 55 on Lyndale Avenue North, open daily, 6 a.m. to 2 p.m., April 24 to December 24; and Nicollet Mall, Thursdays, 6 a.m. to 6 p.m., May to November. Minnesota's largest open-air market offers fresh produce, fish, meats, bedding plants, fresh flowers, maple syrup, wreaths and trees before Christmas—go early!

- **St. Paul Farmers' Market**, has locations in St. Paul as well as many other sites: East St. Paul, West St. Paul, Burnsville, Woodbury, Cottage Grove, Roseville and Maplewood. Call the hotline at 651-227-6856 or visit www.stpaulfarmersmarket.com for locations and hours. The largest market is at Fifth and Wall Street, St. Paul: Saturdays, 6 a.m. to 1 p.m., April to November; Sundays, 8 a.m. to 1 p.m., May to October; Wednesdays, 2 to 5 p.m., July to September. Buy fresh produce, honey, eggs, fresh-cut flowers, plants, trout, buffalo meat, Hmong handiwork.
- **Afton Apple Orchards**, 651-436-8385, junction of South 90th Street and County Road 21, Afton; open daily, 8 a.m. to 6 p.m. (or until picked out), June and July; 10 a.m. to 6 p.m., August to October. Pick up or pick your own strawberries, raspberries, apples and pumpkins. Call ahead for harvest information. Also available are honey, preserves, maple syrup, cider, and hayrides in the fall.
- **Apple Jack Orchards**, 763-972-6673, Highway 55 West to Wright County Road 115 South, Delano, offers apples, berries, wagon rides to the fields and a hay mound for children to play in.
- **Berry Brook Farm**, 763-424-8700, 10311 Noble Avenue North, Brooklyn Park; road stand, open Tuesday-Saturday, 7:30 a.m. to 11 a.m., 5:30 p.m. to 8 p.m. (in season). Pick your own strawberries, blueberries, and raspberries.
- **Deardorff Orchards**, 952-442-1885, 2.6 miles west of Victoria and 1 mile north of Highway 5 on Parley Lake Road; open Tuesday-Sunday, 9 a.m. to 5 p.m., September and October, for pick-your-own or pre-picked apples, honey, pumpkins, hayrides and crafts.
- **Emma Krumbee's**, Belle Plain, 952-873-3006, has an orchard, bakery and a restaurant and is a favorite outing for families.
- **Pine Tree Apple Orchards**, 651-429-7202, 450 Apple Orchard Road, White Bear Lake, offers wagon rides to the strawberry field in season and cross country skiing in winter. Pick your own or buy apples, strawberries, pumpkins, and other produce or baked goods from their bakery. Call for hours and availability.
- **Sponsel's Minnesota Harvest Apple Orchard and Bakery**, 952-49-APPLE, 169 South two miles past Jordan, then left on 59 and follow the signs; open Monday-Saturday, July-April; closed Sundays.

This is entertainment shopping: accordion music, restaurant, pony rides, pick-your-own and pre-picked apples, other produce in season, and many gift items.

- **University of Minnesota Horticultural Research Center**, Highway 5, Zumbra Heights (between Chanhassen and Victoria), 952-474-9440; you'll find old favorites as well as experimental apples, cider, and other products; tours.

COMMUNITY GARDENS

For the ultimate in freshness, you need to grow your own. It doesn't take much space; a window box will do for many herbs, even with the long Minnesota winters.

Many neighborhoods have community gardens, particularly in Minneapolis. These are available for free or for a nominal rental fee to people who want to grow vegetables and flowers. Often created to improve the looks of vacant lots, urban gardens bring neighbors together during the warm months and serve as symbols of urban renewal. Many community gardens are found in neighborhoods which have lower property values: the Phillips neighborhood, for example, has more than twenty community gardens, while areas with more expensive real estate often have none. In St. Paul, Farm-in-the-City uses the grounds of Concordia College, community schools and parks to provide garden-based summer programs for children, with proceeds distributed to the hungry. Check with your own neighborhood organization for possibilities. Also call **Urban Lands**, 612-872-3291, or **Minnesota Green**, 651-643-3601. To take a look at this movement in a national context, visit the **American Community Gardening Association** Web site at www.communitygarden.org.

SEAFOOD

- **Coastal Seafood**, 2330 Minnehaha Avenue, Minneapolis, 612-724-7425; 74 Snelling Avenue, St. Paul, 651-698-4888

HOME DELIVERY

- **Bag Boy Express**, 2900 Bryant Avenue South, 612-749-8678 or www.bagboyexpress.com
- **Morris and Christie Market**, 3048 Hennepin Avenue, 612-825-2477
- **Simple Simon**, 612-537-2800

BAKERIES

- **Breadsmith**, 1111 East Wayzata Boulevard, Wayzata 952-475-0099; 1434 West Lake Street, Minneapolis, 612-825-8775; the Edina location, 3939 West 50th Street, 952-920-2778, is a kosher bakery.
- **French Meadow Bakery and Restaurant**, 2610 Lyndale Avenue, Minneapolis, 612-870-7855 or 612-870-4740
- **The Country Cake Cupboard**, 491 Willow Drive Long Lake, 952-476-0222
- **Turtle Bread Company**, 3415 44th Street, Minneapolis, 612-924-6013
- **Wuollet's**, East Lake Street, Wayzata, 952-473-8621 (check the White Pages for other locations).

ETHNIC MARKETS

Nothing satisfies the eyes, the ears, and the taste buds like a visit to an ethnic market. In Minneapolis, take a walk down Nicollet Avenue between 24th and 29th streets and you will hear and smell the world. This bustling market community has Asian, Greek, Mexican, and Middle-Eastern groceries—and restaurants, as well. In the same spirit, the Mercado at 1515 East Lake Street, with many small shops under one roof, and Concord Street in West St. Paul, are centers for the Hispanic community. University Avenue east of Lexington and the Rice Street in St. Paul serve that purpose for members of several Asian communities. Other ethnic markets are scattered throughout the Twin Cities. Even though many of the local supermarkets and co-ops offer a selection of foods for ethnic cooking, try some of these below for a more authentic experience—and, remember, in no way is this a complete list:

AFRICAN
- **Merkato African Groceries**, 605 Cedar Avenue South, Minneapolis, 612-673-0308

GREEK, MIDDLE EASTERN
- **Bill's Imported Foods**, 721 West Lake Street, Minneapolis, 612-827-2891
- **Holy Land Bakery & Deli**, 2513 Central Avenue NE, Minneapolis, 612-781-2627
- **Sinbad Mideastern Grocery**, Bakery and Deli, 2528 Nicollet Avenue, Minneapolis, 612-871-6505

ITALIAN

- **Broder's Cucina Italiana**, 2308 West 50th Street, Minneapolis, 612-925-3113
- **Buon Giorno Italian Market**, 335 University Avenue East, St. Paul, 651-224-1816
- **Cossetta's**, 211 West 7th Street, St. Paul, 651-222-3476

LATINO/MEXICAN

- **El Burrito Mercado**, 175 Concord Street, St. Paul, 651-227-2192, www.elburritomercado.com
- **Las Americas**, 340 East Lake Street, Minneapolis, 612-827-3377

ASIAN

- **Asia Import Food & Video**, 1840 Central Avenue NE, Minneapolis, 612-788-4571
- **Phil Oriental Foods**, 789 University Avenue West, St. Paul, 651-292-1325
- **Shuang Hur Oriental Market**, 2710 Nicollet Avenue, Minneapolis, 612-872-8606

SCANDINAVIAN/RUSSIAN/EASTERN EUROPEAN

- **European Delicacies**, 11044 Cedar Lake Road, Minnetonka, 952-541-5494
- **Ingebretsen's**, 1601 East Lake Street, Minneapolis 55407, 612-729-9333, 800-279-9333 (for A catalogue), www.ingebretsens.com
- **Kramarczuk Sausage Co.**, 215 Hennepin Avenue East, Minneapolis, 612-379-3018

SPICES

- **Penzeys, Ltd.**, 674 Grand Avenue, St. Paul 651-224-8448, www.penzeys.com

DRINKING WATER

Minneapolis and St. Paul supply municipal water to their residents and some suburbs from surface sources, principally the Mississippi River. Others drink groundwater from municipal or private wells. Increasingly, people here have become concerned about the quality and taste of their water. In particular, well water is often undrinkable because of its bad taste from dissolved minerals, and recently there have been a number of problems with iron bacteria growing in wells. As a result, sales of bottled drinking water (which may or may not, depending on the supplier, be any better than your own water) have soared. Grocery stores sell bottled water, and there are a number of drinking water delivery services that rent coolers as well. Artesian water is available at a local brewery in St. Paul. An increasingly popular option is a water purifier for your tap water. Check the White Pages for suppliers. Drinking water services include:

- **Prairie Water**, 2125 Broadway NE, Minneapolis, 612-379-4141
- **Culligan**, 7165 Boone Avenue North, Brooklyn Park, 763-535-4545 or 1001 Marie Avenue South, St. Paul, 651-451-2241
- **Glenwood Inglewood Co.**, 225 Thomas Avenue North, Minneapolis, 612-374-2253
- **Great Glacier, Inc.**, Princeton, 763-333-6944
- **Minnesota Brewing Co.** (April to November), 882 West 7th Street, St. Paul, 651-228-9173; bring your own container, there is a small charge per gallon.

RESTAURANTS

The Twin Cities have restaurants for every taste. Many of them are clustered in Minneapolis' warehouse district and around Uptown; they also line Selby, University and Grand Avenues in St. Paul. Some of the best restaurants are totally smoke free. A free directory of smoke-free restaurants is available from the Association for Nonsmokers-Minnesota (ANSR), 2395 University Avenue West, Suite 310, Saint Paul, MN 55114-1512, 651-646-3005. The restaurants below have become **local institutions**:

- **Adele's Frozen Custard and Old Fashioned Ice Cream**, 800 Excelsior Boulevard, Excelsior, offers the best ice cream, period. Sandwiches and yogurt, too. Take a book when you go, you may wait in line a long time, but it's worth it. Call for hours and the flavor of the day, 952-470-0035.
- **Cafe Latté**, 850 Grand Avenue, St. Paul, 651-292-1665; don't be deterred by the long lines, this cafeteria always has a place for you to sit. Recognized every year for having the "best desserts," the rest of the food is first-rate, too. Great place for any occasion including those after-the-theater dates you don't want to end. Parking can be a problem; smoke-free.
- **Cam Ranh Bay**, 8244 Commonwealth Drive, next to Shinder's, Eden Prairie, 952-943-1127; so small you'd think only the locals

would know about it, but people come from all over the metro area to eat here. Order the Cam Rahn Bay shrimp. Order everything; smoke-free.

- **Figlio's**, 3001 Hennepin Avenue, Uptown, Minneapolis, 612-822-1688; the rosemary potatoes, ravioli and death by chocolate are sublime!

- **Goodfellow's**, 40 South 7th Street, Minneapolis, 612-332-4800; a Hall of Fame restaurant, this is everyone's favorite for classy dining— especially if someone else is paying. Call at 9 a.m. on June 1st (no kidding!) to make a reservation to eat in the kitchen sometime during the next year.

- **Hennepin Technical College**, 9200 Flying Cloud Drive, Eden Prairie, 952-550-3136; is where the new chefs train. Call for scheduled lunches and dinners. Reservations required. Closed in the summer.

- **Kozlak's Royal Oak Restaurant**, 4785 Hodgson Road, Shoreview, 651-484-8484; no fern-bar here, but excellent meat, and a salad so good you'll want to order a second one for dessert.

- **Ristorante Luci,** 470 Cleveland Avenue South, St. Paul, 651-699-8258; this tiny restaurant serves superb hand-cut pastas and rare wines that are good bargains when the house pours. Reservations required; smoke-free.

- **Mud Pie Vegetarian Restaurant**, 2549 South Lyndale, Minneapolis, 612-872-9435; looks like nothing, but over and over again, vegetarians name this as their favorite restaurant; smoke-free.

- **No Wake Cafe**, 100 Yacht Club Road, St. Paul, 651-292-1411, is on a boat moored on Harriet Island across from downtown St. Paul. The banana cream pie will really float your boat. Make reservations-and reserve a piece of pie at the same time; smoke-free inside.

- **Taste of the Nation**, www.taste.org, is an April benefit to end hunger where you can sample the food.

WELCOME TO THE STATE WHERE THE HEALTH MAINTENANCE Organization (HMO) was invented. Even the venerable Mayo Clinic and University of Minnesota participate in HMOs and managed care. In fact, nearly 50% of Minnesotans are enrolled in HMOs, and most of the rest are involved in other managed care plans.

On paper, the state health care situation looks good. Compared to other states, Minnesota has a high number of community clinics, a high rate of immunizations, a low infant mortality rate, and life expectancy here is long enough that by the year 2020, one-fourth of the population of Minnesota will be 60 years old or older. That's the good news. The bad news is that along with the rest of the country, Minnesotans and their doctors feel a lot of frustration with health plans and managed care. Originally conceived as a way to hold down costs through preventive care measures, some feel that managed care actually prevents doctors from delivering the level of care their patients deserve.

Frustration aside, some medical coverage is better than none. To avoid coverage pitfalls, be sure to read through your policy before a medical emergency. Start with the "Coverage" section to determine which illnesses or conditions appear to be covered. Next, read the "Exclusions" section and find out what treatments or medical costs are not covered. Finally, read the rest of the policy to determine whether any conditions apply such as obtaining pre-authorization from the health plan before you can seek treatment, deductibles, co-payments, or limitations with respect to the health care providers you may use.

For more Information, the Minnesota Attorney General's Office has published a handbook entitled, "Managing Managed Health Care." This booklet will help you navigate today's managed health care system. To request a free copy, contact the Attorney General's Office at: 1400 NCL Tower, 445 Minnesota Street, St. Paul, MN 55101; or call 651-296-3353 or 800-657-3787, TTY 651-297-7206 or 800-657-3787.

Most insurance companies have a wide range of products that include HMOs and managed care and it is important to understand what you are purchasing. Before making a decision about your health plan, consult each plan's web page or call their customer service representatives:

- **Allina Health System/Medical Health Plans**, 5601 Smetana Drive, Minnetonka, MN 55343, 612-992-2000, www.allina.com and www.medica.com, serves residents of Minnesota, western Wisconsin, eastern North Dakota and eastern South Dakota. Twin Cities facilities include Abbott Northwestern, Mercy, Unity, and United hospitals, Phillips Eye Institute and Sister Kenny physical rehabilitation institute.
- **Blue Cross and Blue Shield/Blue Plus of Minnesota**, 3535 Blue Cross Road, Eagan, 55122, 651-456-8000, www.bluecrossmn.com, markets a range of health products including indemnity insurance, comprehensive managed care, and Delta Dental insurance. It also administers benefits packages for large self-funded health plans.
- **HealthPartners**, Member Services, P.O. Box 1309, Minneapolis, MN 55440-1309, 612-883-5000, www.healthpartners.com, operates a network of primary care clinics in the Twin Cities that are staffed by HealthPartners Medical Group physicians. It also contracts with several thousand physicians throughout Minnesota, Wisconsin, North Dakota and South Dakota. HealthPartners owns Regions Hospital, and has affiliations with North Memorial, St. John's, Fairview Ridges, Fairview-University, Children's and Mercy.
- **Mayo Health Plan**, 21 1st Street NW, Rochester, MN 55902, 507-287-3329, www.mayo.edu; offers a full range of health services through a network of community based providers, primarily in southern Minnesota; check out your health concerns on their Web page.
- **Metropolitan Health Plan**, Member Services, 822 South 3rd Street, Suite 140, Minneapolis, MN 55415, 612-347-6308, serves people on medical and general assistance only.
- **PreferredOne**, 200 South 6th Street, Suite 300, Minneapolis, MN 55402, 612-623-8282, www.preferredone.com, provides healthcare services to members, employers, insurance companies and third party administrators throughout the Upper Midwest.
- **UCare Minnesota**, 2550 University Avenue West, Suite 201-S, St. Paul, MN 55114, 651-647-2632, 800-203-7225 or www.ucare.org, administers Prepaid Medical Assistance Program (PMAP) for Minnesota residents who receive medical assistance and general assistance medical care: MinnesotaCare is a statewide program for those

Minnesotans who don't have access to health insurance; Minnesota Senior Health Options (MSHO) is for those 65 and older who are eligible for both Medicare and Medicaid; and UCare for Seniors, is a health program that provides affordable coverage to Medicare beneficiaries.

HEALTH CARE ASSISTANCE PROGRAMS

The state insurance plan is called MinnesotaCare. It is a subsidized health care program for people who live in Minnesota and do not have access to health insurance. Applicants must be below a certain income, ranging from about $14,000 for a single adult and $19,000 for a couple, to almost $30,000 for a single parent with one child to about $60,000 for a family with six children. MinnesotaCare's information number is 651-297-3862.

CLINICS—U OF M

If you're strapped for cash while in transition, or would like to receive cutting-edge care, the **University of Minnesota School of Dentistry's Dental Clinics** provide general and special dental care in Moos Health Sciences Tower, 515 Delaware Street SE, Minneapolis, on the East Bank Campus. The U's programs include dental (D.D.S.) and dental hygiene (D.H.) post-graduate training in endodontics ("root canals"), oral and maxillofacial surgery, orthodontics, pediatric dentistry, periodontics, and prosthodontics. They also run TMJ/Facial Pain and Cleft Palate and Craniofacial Anomalies Clinics. Fees vary based on the type of program in which you receive care, and are lowest in the pre-doctoral and dental hygiene programs where services cost 35% to 50% less than they would in the general community. Treatment at this level takes longer, however, because each step must be checked by a supervising faculty member. To become a patient in the Pre-doctoral D.D.S. clinical program, call 612-624-8400 to schedule an initial appointment or 612-625-2495 for additional information. Treatment in the Family Dentistry Clinic takes less time than in the pre-doctoral program but fees are somewhat higher, though still 20% to 35% less than in the general community. Call 612-625-5441 for an appointment. The Faculty Practice Clinic is a state of the art facility where consultative and second-opinion services are provided by faculty specialists who are engaged in dental education and research. Call 612-626-3233 for an appointment. Even those who are not already patients, but have a dental emergency during regular clinic hours, can call the Family Dentistry Clinic for help, 612-625-4908.

COMMUNITY CLINICS

These nonprofit clinics may be the most affordable for routine visits such as physicals or minor health problems:

- **Cedar-Riverside People's Center**, 2000 South 5th Street Minneapolis, 612-332-4973
- **Central Avenue Clinic**, 2610 Central Avenue NE, Minneapolis, 612-781-6816
- **Family Medical Center**, 5 West Lake Street, Minneapolis, 612-827-9800
- **Fremont Clinic**, 3300 Fremont Avenue North, Minneapolis, 612-588-9411
- **Hennepin Care North**, 6601 Shingle Creek Parkway, Brooklyn Center, 763-569-3737
- **Hennepin County Medical Center**, 701 Park Avenue Minneapolis, 612-347-2121
- **Pilot City Health Center**, 1313 Penn Avenue North, Minneapolis, 612-302-4600
- **Planned Parenthood of Minnesota**: 6900 78th Avenue North, Brooklyn Park, 763-560-3050; 2530 Horizon Drive, Burnsville, 952-890-0940; 1965 Ford Parkway, St. Paul, 651-698-2406; St. Paul Clinic, 1700 Rice Street, 651-489-1328
- **Red Door**, 525 Portland Avenue South, Minneapolis, 612-348-6363, provides confidential treatment for sexually transmitted diseases.
- **St. Paul Public Health Center**, 555 Cedar Street, St. Paul, 651-292-7727
- **Sheridan Women's and Children's Clinic**, 342 13th Avenue NE, Minneapolis, 612-362-4111
- **Southside Community Clinic**, 4243 4th Avenue South, Minneapolis, 612-822-3186
- **West Side Health Center**, 153 Concord Street, St. Paul, 651-222-1816
- **Women & Children's Health Center**, 810 1st Street South, #220, Hopkins, 952-569-2660

SERVICES FOR PEOPLE WITH DISABILITIES

The slogan for a disabled advocacy program on a community radio station, KFAI, is "Disabled and Proud—Not an Oxymoron!" This slogan could also describe the supportive environment for the disabled in the Twin

Cities. Here the physically challenged will find visibility (a reporter for one of the local TV stations works from a wheelchair), organization, communication, and reliable mobility. Of course, the reviews are mixed.

In accordance with the 1990 Americans and Disabilities Act, public buildings are required to be handicapped-accessible. Every parking lot has handicapped spaces, and non-disabled people who park in them face fines of up to $200. Most city sidewalks have curb cuts, and in the downtowns, with ramp parking and skyways, it is possible to go for miles without stepping outside. The Guthrie and other theaters and concert halls set aside special sections for people in wheelchairs, and many facilities have hearing augmentation devices or signed performances. By state law, Minnesota schools are required to offer special needs students a full range of services. Call the Department of Education at 651-582-8689 for more information. The library systems offer services for the hearing and vision impaired such as books on tape and high-magnification lenses. Call 952-541-8530 for At Home services of Hennepin County libraries; Minneapolis, 612-630-6000; Ramsey County, 651-486-2200; St. Paul, 651-266-7000; and Washington County, 651-731-8487. There is an active community of animal lovers who train service dogs in three programs: Paws for People, Cambridge, 763-689-4129; Helping Paws of Minnesota, Hopkins, 952-988-9359; Hearing and Service Dogs of Minnesota, Minneapolis, 612-729-5986. Application fees range from $20 to $50; there is no further charge.

The area offers a multitude of sports and outdoor recreation opportunities for the physically challenged. The **Power Hockey** league allows anyone in a power wheelchair to participate. If you want to sign up, call the **US Electric Wheelchair Hockey Association**, 612-535-4736 or www.usewha.org. If it's camping or canoeing you like to do, **Wilderness Inquiry** creates outdoor adventures for people of all ages, abilities, and backgrounds. They plan trips by canoe, sea kayak, dog sled, horseback, and backpack to over 30 destinations including the Apostle Islands in Lake Superior and the Boundary Waters. For information or to reserve a spot, call 612-379-3858, 800-728-0719 or go online, www.wildernessinquiry.org/trip. For those who love horses, Minnesota has a **We Can Ride** chapter, offering therapeutic horseback riding and cart driving for children and adults at four locations: Hennepin County Home School in Eden Prairie, Carver-Scott Educational Cooperative in Waconia; Shriner's Ranch in Independence and Pine Meadow Farm in Delano. Call 612-934-0057 to sign up or volunteer.

On the downside, Twin Cities' public transportation for the disabled is sorely lacking, and winter weather provides great challenges for wheelchairs, canes and crutches. Winter plowing, un-shoveled walks and the process of freezing and thawing may make it impossible to get around for days or weeks at a time. And, though the downtown has an extensive sky-way system, most downtown parking ramps will not accommodate large vans. Whatever your disability, the **Minnesota State Council on Disability**, Voice/TTY, 651-296-6785, www.disability.state.mn.us, is the number to call when you are looking for any kind of help.

GETTING AROUND

DISABLED CERTIFICATES AND CAR LICENSE PLATES

To apply for a disability certificate or disabled car license plates call 651-297-3377. You may apply after a physician or chiropractor certifies that you meet the state requirements for a disabled person. If your disability is permanent and you are the owner/primary driver of a vehicle, you may apply for disabled plates at the time of vehicle registration. There is a $5 fee for disabled certificates, but no additional cost for car license plates.

BUS TRANSPORTATION

All buses designated with a wheel chair symbol on the front and curbsides of the bus are lift-equipped. By 2003 all buses should have lifts. In 2000, the following routes were lift-equipped: Minneapolis routes 4, 5, 6, 7, 10, 14, 16, 17, 18, 19, 21, 22, 28, 80 and 94B; St. Paul routes 4, 14, 16, 21, 22, 50, 54 and 94B. All Metro Transit drivers are trained to recognize "bus identifier cards" used by vision or hearing impaired to display the bus route number they are waiting for. These cards are color-coded by disability so the driver can offer proper assistance. Call Metro Transit Customer Relations, 612-373-3333, www.metrocouncil.org/transit/access for these cards.

Metro Mobility certification takes three weeks, but once certified, participants receive door-through-door public transportation. Reservations should be made in advance. Door-through-door service means that drivers will help riders through the first set of doors at both their pick-up points and their destinations. This is a shared-ride system structured to transport multiple passengers to multiple destinations. It works well to get disabled people to and from work. To apply, you must complete an Americans with Disabilities Act (ADA) application. Call Customer Services at 651-602-1111, TTY 651-221-9886, for an application form. ADA-certified customers also are entitled to use regular route transit for $.50. The off-peak fare for Metro

Mobility is $2.00 per one way trip; the peak hour fare is $2.50 per one way trip. The fare may be paid in cash or with Fare Tickets, sold in books of ten. Call Metro Mobility Customer Services at 651- 602-1111, TTY 651-221-9886, between 8 a.m. and 4:30 p.m., Monday through Friday or e-mail, mmscmail@metc.state.mn.us.

WHEELCHAIRS AND SCOOTERS

If you need to rent or purchase a scooter or motorized wheelchair, these are some places to start looking:
* **Jackson Medical**, 651-645-6221
* **Gopher Medical Supply**, 612-623-7706
* **Health East/Medical Home**, 612-881-2635
* **Macalester-Plymouth United Church**, 1658 Lincoln Avenue, St. Paul, 651-698-8871

COMMUNICATIONS

DEAF AND HARD OF HEARING

If you are deaf or hard of hearing, the consultants at the **Metro Regional Service Center for Deaf and Hard of Hearing People**, Voice 651-297-1316, TTY 651-297-1313, can assist you.

    Telephone Relay Service, known as TDD or TTY, is the communication system for the hearing and speech impaired. It is available 24 hours a day, 365 days a year throughout the Twin Cities for those properly equipped. The Regional Service Center for Deaf and Hard of Hearing People (listed above) will help you obtain the necessary keyboard, amplifiers and message lights. Financial assistance is available for those in need. For **Minnesota Relay Service** call 800-627-3529; Consumer Relations Voice/TTY, 800-657-3775. The Minnesota Department of Public Service offers updates on Minnesota Relay, check www.dpsv. state.mn.us or call 651-296-5120 for more information. **Federal Relay Service (FRS)**, for the hard of hearing and speech disabled can be accessed online at www.gsa.gov/frs, or call 800-877-8339. **The National Association of the Deaf** can be accessed online, www.nad.org or call 301-587-1788, TTY 301-587-1789. **Metropolitan Council Assistance** for the hearing impaired is available at the following numbers: Transit Information, 612-341-0140; Customer Service, 612-349-7439; Human Resources, 612-349-7565.

BLIND AND VISUALLY IMPAIRED

Minnesota has a special homestead tax credit for the blind and visually impaired. Call the state's Services for the Blind (see below) for information.

Minnesota provides many adaptive services to the blind. Make your first call to the **Minnesota Department of Economic Security, Services for the Blind**, Voice 651-642-0500, TTY/TDD 651-642-0506, or toll free Voice/TDD 800-652-9000. It serves the blind and visually impaired, offering job and independent living rehabilitation classes and services, including group classes for the blind elderly. Its communications center provides Radio Talking Books and voice-edition newspapers. It also has a store that sells adaptive aids at cost. Transportation is provided to group classes.

Vision Loss Resources Inc. provides services to people who are out of school. Their West Metro facility houses a rehab and community center, 1936 Lyndale Avenue South, Minneapolis, Voice/TTY 612-871-2222. Their East Metro facility is located at 216 South Wabasha, St. Paul, Voice/TTY 651-224-7662. This organization provides services for visually impaired seniors and those with chronic illnesses including diabetes education. E-mail, internet access, and computer training for blind people also are available here.

BLIND Inc. (Blindness Learning In New Dimensions) is a non-profit training facility where people learn to live independently, use Braille, cook, clean, and sew. It also teaches industrial arts and job readiness skills. Call 612-872-0100. Additional resources to consider:

- **Minnesota Library for the Blind**, 800-722-0550
- **Minnesota Chapter of National Federation of the Blind**, 612-872-0100
- **American Council of the Blind of Minnesota**, Wally Waranka, President, 651-698-5059

HOUSING

People with disabilities are among those qualified to receive subsidized housing or to live in public housing, where residents pay no more than 30% of their adjusted gross income for rent.

City Housing and Redevelopment Authorities (HRA) take applications for Section 8 subsidized housing. For information, call the St. Paul HRA, 651-298-5459, or Minneapolis HRA, 612-342-1400. Applications for subsidized units are received by the the managers of the buildings you're interested in. It's a good idea to have your name added to the waiting list at all of the buildings in which you'd like to live.

Public housing is available through the local Public Housing Authority (PHA). To apply, contact the individual county or city you prefer and complete and return the application, even if there are no vacancies. Then have your name added to the waiting list at all of the buildings in which you'd like to live. Public Housing Authorities include: Columbia Heights, 612-782-2854; South St. Paul, 651-451-1838; St. Louis Park, 952-924-2500; Minneapolis, 612-342-1413; Forest Lake, 651-464-4406; Hopkins, 612-939-1329; St. Paul, 651-298-5158; Mound, 952-472-5078; Plymouth, 952-509-5410.

Other agencies which give special needs assistance include: **Accessible Space**, a non-profit corporation that provides disability-adaptive housing, including group homes, for adults with mobility impairments, brain injuries and physical disabilities, 651-645-7271 or 800-466-7722; **Lutheran Social Services**, whose services include Share a Home, a program designed to enable seniors, single-parent families and disabled people to stay in their homes by matching them with people who are looking for affordable housing, 612-879-5354; and the **National Handicapped Housing Institute (NHHI)** which rents apartments to the handicapped and disabled, 651-639-9799.

There is a critical shortage of affordable housing in the Twin Cities, so it may take a long time to locate an acceptable apartment. Start your search early. The Metropolitan Center for Independent Living has a list of subsidized buildings (see Independent Living section below). Some buildings may also offer units to people with disabilities who do not need wheelchair accessibility.

Minnesota law requires that a disabled person and his/her family must be given priority with respect to handicapped-equipped rental housing. This means that if a family without a disabled member is living in handicapped-equipped housing, they can be asked to move to another unit in the same rental complex to make way for a family that does include a disabled person. For help finding barrier-free housing or housing assistance programs for the disabled, call the National Handicapped Housing Institute (651-639-9799).

For information about accessible hotels and motels in the Twin Cities area check **Temporary Lodgings**.

INDEPENDENT LIVING

The **Metropolitan Center for Independent Living (MCIL)** is one of eight such centers in Minnesota. It offers up-to-date information about community resources related to people with disabilities, including housing and benefits referral. This organization is an amazing resource. It lists job openings, provides e-mail links to Minnesota's US Senators and Representatives, accessible conference space, a computer lab for consumer use, advocacy, subsidized personal assistance, and classes for people with disabilities to acquire the skills they need for independent living. The Senior Companion program provides necessary support to seniors wanting to stay in their own homes. The Ramp Project assists those needing ramps. The Transition Program assists students and young adults with disabilities, ages 14 through 24, to make a successful transition from high school to post-secondary education, to employment and adult independent living. Call Voice 651-646-8342, TTY 651-603-2001, or visit www.macil.org/mcil.

ADDITIONAL RESOURCES

Following is a variety of resources, both governmental and non-profit, that may be of use to those with special needs:

- **Minnesota State Council on Disability**, 651-296-6785, www.disability.state.mn.us. With this number, you can meet any challenge. Call here first, for any need.
- **ADA Minnesota**, Voice 651-603-2015, TTY 651-603-2001, is the Minnesota resource for information about the Americans with Disabilities Act.
- **ARC Minnesota**, www.mtn.org/arcminn, provides advocacy with the legislature and state agencies, referrals for services and educational materials. Call the nearest office: Hennepin County, 952-920-0855; Anoka/Ramsey County, 651-523-0876; Minnesota Office, 3225 Lyndale Avenue South, Minneapolis, 651-523-0823.
- **Closing the Gap**, www.closingthegap.com, provides a technology forum for "special people."
- **Courage Center**, 3915 Golden Valley Road, Golden Valley, is Minnesota's most famous rehabilitation center. It is a non-profit organization that provides rehabilitation and independent living services for people who have physical disabilities and neurological impairments. It also operates Camp Courage in Maple Plain. For service and program information, call 763-520-0520, TDD 763-520-0245, www.freenet.msp.mn.us/ip/health/courage_center.
- **"Disabled and Proud"** airs on Tuesday nights at 7:30 on KFAI, 90.3 FM in Minneapolis and 106.7 FM in St. Paul.

- **Epilepsy Foundation**, 800-779-0777
- **First Call for Help** is a comprehensive information referral service. Call 612-335-5000 for Minneapolis and west suburban resources; 651-224-1133 for St. Paul and east suburban resources; and 800-543-7709 for referrals outside these areas.
- **Johns Hopkins Health Information** homepage www.intelihealth.com includes a drug search, men's and women's health information and an easily searched disease and conditions index.
- **Minnesota Department of Health**, www.health.state.mn.us, is a detailed Web site where you can order birth or death certificates. It offers information to health professionals as well as the general public.

O NE OF THE MOST DIFFICULT PROSPECTS PARENTS FACE WHEN moving to a new area is finding good child care and schools. While the process is not an easy one, with a little time and effort it is possible to find what you're looking for, be it in-home care, an after-school program or on-site day care.

DAY CARE

Probably the best way to find a good day-care provider is by referral from someone you know and trust. That notwithstanding, there are four area agencies that should be able to assist you with you search. **Minnesota Child Care Resource and Referral Network**, 651-665-0150, is a state-wide information service. Call with your zip code and they will transfer your call to the agency that provides child care referrals in your area. For those in the Twin Cities metro area, you will likely be connected with either **Resources for Childcaring**, 651-641-6601 or the **Greater Minneapolis Day Care Association** (**GMDCA**), 612-341-1177, www. radiochildcare.org/GMDCA. Both agencies provide a variety of services including training for child care providers, funds to help parents pay for child care, information about employing in-home workers, referral service for licensed child care, and listings of nanny services. For child care referrals in South Minneapolis, the University Area, or downtown, call the **Early Childhood Resource Center**, 612-721-0265. The **Adult and Children's Alliance's (ACA)** members are licensed home-based care givers. There is no charge for referrals. Call 651-481-9320 or 800-433-8108.

For University of Minnesota-affiliated families, the **University of Minnesota Child Care Center** operates year-round in a new facility on the East Bank, 612-627-4014. The waiting period can be more than one year, but the center can provide a list of other centers in the area. Child care is also offered at both Como and Commonwealth student housing cooperatives, 612-331-8340. You do not have to be a resident at the cooperatives to enroll your child.

The **Downtown Childcare Center**, 244 10th Street East, St. Paul, is a non-profit organization providing child care for children six weeks to 12 years of age. In 2000 rates ranged from $193 per week for infants to $143 per week for school-age children. It is licensed to care for over 100 children year-round. Business hours are 6:30 a.m. to 6:00 p.m. Monday-Friday, excluding legal holidays and two in-service days per year. For information call 651-222-7140, or log on to www.downtownchildcare.org.

When searching for the best place for your child, be sure to visit prospective day care providers—preferably unannounced. In general, look for safety, cleanliness and caring attitudes on the part of the day care providers. Check that the kitchen, toys and furniture are clean and safe. Ask for the telephone numbers of other parents who use the service and talk to them. It's a good idea to request a daily schedule—look for both active and quiet time, and age appropriate activities. In this part of the country, four to five months of the year are spent indoors, so you should ask about active time in the winter.

Keep in mind that being licensed does not necessarily guarantee service of the quality you may be seeking. If you think a licensed provider might be acceptable, be sure to call your county's day care licensing bureau and ask them to run a background check—they can go back up to ten years: Hennepin County (Minneapolis), 612-348-3883; Ramsey County (St. Paul), 651-266-3779; Washington County, 651-430-6488.

If you're only looking for part-time child care, or if the day care service of your choice has a waiting list, call ADA (above) for a licensed referral. For drop-in child care while you go shopping or to a movie, **Clubkid** is popular. It accepts children age 18 months to ten years at four locations: Burnsville, 952-435-6263; Edina, 952-831-1055; Minnetonka, 952-545-1979; and Roseville, 651-631-1492. In 1999 rates were $4.95 per hour for one child, $5.70 for a toddler, and there is a family discount. While reservations are not necessary, call first to be sure they have room on a particular day.

Minnesota Parent magazine is published monthly and is an excellent resource for child care information and activities for families. Free copies are available at public libraries, grocery stores and restaurants around town, or contact the publishers directly at 612-375-1203 to have one mailed to you.

ONLINE RESOURCES—DAY CARE

Care Guide, www.careguide.com, offers assistance to those needing child or elder-care. This free service offers pertinent care-related news articles and advice. Another internet site, funded by the US Maternal and Child Health Bureau, is the National Resource Center for Health and Safety in Child Care. Here you'll find a section on health and safety tips, state child care licensure regulations, a list of national health and safety performance standards, etc. Check www.nrc.uchsc.edu for more information or call 800-598-KIDS. Other child care resources include the National Child Care Information Center's internet site, www.nccic.org, which provides links to other child care sites on the web, or call Child Care Aware at 800-424-2246 for assistance; they provide free referrals to child care agencies in your community.

NANNY SERVICES

If it's a nanny you prefer, in the Twin Cities you can expect to pay $400-$475 per week for a live-in nanny, depending on the nanny's experience, education and whether housekeeping is expected. The GMDCA, 612-341-1177, www.radiochild care.org, and Ramsey County Resources for Childcaring, 651-641-6601, provide referrals to nanny agencies. Look in the Yellow Pages under "Nanny Services" for a complete list of area businesses. Local licensed and bonded nanny agencies include:
- **LovingCare**, 651-450-6692, www.citilink.com/~lcare
- **Above and Beyond Nannies**, 612-894-0200, 888-933-0200
- **Umbrella Child Care Services**, 612-536-7772

Online, try the **Minnesota Nanny Center**, 651-698-9373, www.mnnanny.com. This is not an agency, but an information clearinghouse that can help with the difficult task of finding and employing a nanny. At the site is a nanny registry made up of experienced nannies seeking positions in Minnesota, tips for hiring a nanny and a variety of other resources that will answer your questions regarding background checks, taxes, training, video surveillance and more.

Be sure to check all references given to you by applicants. Do-it-yourselfers can check for an applicant's record of arrests and criminal convictions in Minnesota by calling the **Bureau of Criminal Apprehension**, 651-642-0670; the cost is $8. (Convictions for driving while intoxicated may not always be reported to the state.) If you prefer a professional background check, **Verified Credentials**, 952-985-7200, 800-473-4934, www.verifiedcredentials.com is a Minnesota firm that specializes in pre-employment screening. A check of criminal history, credit history, driving record and employment history costs an average of $200. **California Trustline**, an agency of the state of California, conducts fingerprint searches through the FBI for high misdemeanors and felonies in all states. This service is available to prospective child care employers who live in any state, but searches do require three or four months to complete. Call 800-822-8490 or check www.trustline.org.

If you are contracting directly with your nanny for his or her services (rather than through an agency), there are certain taxes that will have to be paid, such as social security, Medicare, federal and state unemployment and income taxes. These obligations apply to both full- and part-time, in-home workers who are paid more than $1100 annually. You will also need to carry workers compensation, which you may be able to purchase through either your homeowner's or automobile insurance provider. For assistance call the Minnesota Department of Labor and Industry, 651-296-2432. For more information about Minnesota taxes, consider ordering *Hiring An In-Home Childcare Giver, Your Tax Responsibilities As An Employer*, produced by Resources for Childcaring, and available from Redleaf Press, 800-423-8309, for a small fee. Also check the Nanitax Web site, www.4nannytaxes.com, 800-NANITAX.

AU PAIRS

The US Information Agency oversees and approves the organizations which offer this service where young adults between the ages of 18 and 26 provide a year of in-home child care and light housekeeping in exchange for airfare, room and board, and a small stipend per week. The program offers a valuable cultural exchange between the host family and the (usually European) au pair, as well as a flexible child care schedule for parents. The downside is that the program only lasts one year and the au pairs don't have the life or work experience of a career nanny. The agencies that bring over the au pairs run background checks before making placements. **European Au Pair**, 952-476-4236, www.euraupair.com, is located in Wayzata. Their au pairs come primarily from western Europe—Germany, France, Scandinavia—though some come from South Africa and Japan, and contract to work up to 45 hours a week for a stipend which, in 2000, was $139.05.

Red Wing's **Southeast Technical College**, 651-385-6300, offers a professional nanny degree-granting program. They do not run a place-ment agency, but contact the school and any interested graduates will call you back. Any of the following national agencies can connect you with a local coordinator who will match your family with an au pair:

- **EF Au Pair**, 800-333-6056
- **Interexchange, Au Pair USA**, 800-479-0907 or 800-287-2477
- **Au Pair International**, 800-654-2051
- **Au Pair in America**, 800-928-7247

SCHOOLS

There is probably nothing that can affect your family's happiness in a new place as much as your child's comfort at school. Minnesota offers school-ing options galore: public or private; ten-months or year-round; charter schools, magnet schools, or open enrollment. Enrichments offered at some schools include Early Childhood Family Education, college credit, and extended-day child care.

As public and private, urban and suburban schools compete more aggressively with each other for students, new choices are becoming avail-able every year. Minneapolis and St. Paul, for example, have opened a half-dozen downtown schools, including Downtown Open, Saturn, and Interdistrict, to serve the families of commuters who work in the urban core; the Catholic Archdiocese is thinking of doing the same. Other choices include language-immersion; special needs schools; and the public, residen-tial arts high school, Perpich Center for Arts Education, in Golden Valley. Several year-round schools are up and running in the metro area including: Minneapolis' School of Extended Learning, St. Paul's Four Seasons A Plus School, and Tri-district Elementary, an integration magnet school serving St. Paul, Roseville and North St. Paul/Maplewood/Oakdale. Most of these schools are in session for 45 days, with an "intersession" break for 15 days and then close for the traditional, but shorter, winter and summer breaks.

If the school in your district doesn't work out, the State of Minnesota offers the open enrollment option, which allows students to attend public schools outside the districts in which they live. Parents may obtain informa-tion and application forms from any school district office, but to transfer, you will need the approval of both the district you want to leave and the dis-trict into which you wish to transfer. For more information, call the **Enrollment Options Hotline**, 651-582-8701.

To better become better acquainted with the different districts call for a copy of *Schoolhouse Magazine*, 651-227-1519, $6.95 per single copy.

Updated annually, this publication contains general information provided by the public school districts and private and charter schools. Another resource you may want to try is **SchoolMatch**, a firm that maintains a database on public and private schools, including student-teacher ratios, test scores and per-pupil spending; call 800-992-5323. They'll fax you independent reports about requested schools. The cost for a basic "snapshot" of a school district's national ranking is $19; $49 will get you a more comprehensive "report card" and for $97.50, School Match's "full search service" will give you a statistical analysis of up to ten school systems. School Match's services are less expensive if initiated through the internet, www.schoolmatch.com.

Even if your oldest child is not yet in school, call your school district's administration office, to assure your child's inclusion in the district's database, to insure your being notified about early childhood screening and kindergarten registration. It will also connect you with the district's Early Childhood Family Education (ECFE) services.

All school districts provide ECFE programs for children, birth to kindergarten. These programs include parent education and support, and child learning experiences. Fees vary from school to school, with reduced fees or no fees available upon request. Transportation is sometimes provided. Classes are led by licensed educators and programs vary from choices for discipline, family fun-fests, playgroups, Saturday mornings with dads, to field trips. To find out about ECFE services call your local school district (see numbers below) or contact First Call for Help, 800-KIDS-709, and they will give you the number of the ECFE program nearest you.

School districts also provide free Early Childhood Screening for children ages three and four. This includes a check for vision, hearing, developmental and growth status, and an immunization review. Nurses who work in these programs will answer questions you have about your child's development or childhood diseases, and are often knowledgeable about a variety of community and health resources. Call your local school district office to receive a brochure or to schedule an appointment.

CHOOSING A SCHOOL

Most of the literature tells you to compare costs per pupil, graduation rates and test scores. While these objective measures may support your choice, there really is only one way to choose a school: visit, visit, visit and talk, talk, talk.

When visiting a school, your gut reactions will probably tell you everything you need to know. Ask yourself these questions: am I comfortable here? Are elementary-age students moving around naturally, but staying on task? What are the halls like in junior-high and high schools when classes change? Are students engaged in discussions or projects? Is student work displayed? Ask elementary teachers about reading and math groups and if children move up as they build skills. Find out if there are any special programs offered to assist new students with their transition to their new school. Check for after-school or enrichment activities that your child will enjoy. Ask if parents are encouraged to volunteer in the classroom. Finally, look at the facility and equipment. Are adults a presence in all parts of the building and grounds? Are the computer labs up to date with enough computers? Are instructional materials plentiful and new? Do textbooks cover things you think are important? Do you see opportunities for your child to do things he/she likes to do-art, music, science, etc.? If all passes muster then the next step is registering.

SCHOOL REGISTRATION

Register in person at the school your child will attend. If you intend to register during the summer months, call the school first to make sure the staff member you need to see will be available. If you are registering a kindergarten student, you will be asked to bring proof of birthday—children need to be five by September 1st in order to enter kindergarten. You don't need to bring anything to register students who are in first grade or higher, but you will be asked to sign a form allowing the district to request records from your child's previous school. Take medical records with you, if possible, because you will have to provide proof of vaccinations at the beginning of the school year.

EDUCATIONAL STANDARDS

The Minnesota State Board of Education has developed Profile of Learning standards that represent what students need to know and be able to do in order to be successful in life. Students, statewide, must complete 24 standards to graduate from high school. There are Basic Standards and High Standards. The Basic Standards are rudimentary skills tests at different grade levels in reading, mathematics and writing. Such testing is considered a "safety net," ensuring that no students graduate without learning these fundamental skills needed to live and work in society. The High Standards are oriented toward excellence. For more information, access the state's Web site at www.children.state.mn.us or call the Minnesota Department of Children, Families and Learning Grad Standards Hotline, 651-582-8693 or 800-657-3927.

In addition to the High Standards program, public and private school students can earn free college credits by participating in the Post-Secondary Enrollment Option Program, which allows high school juniors and seniors to take courses at Minnesota colleges, universities, technical schools and degree-granting trade schools. For information, check with the counselors at your high school or call 651-582-8701.

PRIVATE SCHOOLS

The metropolitan area is home to many excellent private and parochial schools. Blake and Breck are the schools most people think of first, followed quickly by Benilde-St. Margaret's, Akiva Jewish Academy and St. Paul Academy. Often, private schools are better able to meet children's special needs than the public schools. Be aware, however, that private junior high and high schools draw from a wide area, so your child will have friends from all over, which can present a challenge when scheduling events for younger teenagers. And it can be heart-stopping when your newly-licensed teenaged driver is dating somebody who lives 40 miles across town.

PUBLIC SCHOOLS

BLOOMINGTON #271
1998-99 K-12 Enrollment: 10,991
District Office: 952-885-8450, www.bloomington.k12.mn.us
Cities Served: Bloomington

Bloomington has two high schools serving grades 9-12 (Jefferson in West Bloomington and Kennedy in East Bloomington), two middle schools for grades 7 and 8; one intermediate school—grades 5 and 6, one community school for grades K-6, and nine elementary schools—grades K-4. The district also offers Kids' Safari school-age child care. This district serves an increasingly diverse population.

EDEN PRAIRIE #272
1998-99 K-12 Enrollment: 10,318
District Office: 952-975-7000, www.edenprairie.k12.mn.us
Cities Served: Eden Prairie

Eden Prairie schools serve most of Eden Prairie, but some areas along the northern edge of the community are in the Minnetonka and Hopkins school districts. It has one high school—grades 9-12, one middle school—grades 7 and 8, one intermediate school—grades 5 and 6, four elementary schools—grades 1-4, each serving a quadrant of the city; and a Central Kindergarten Center which is attended by almost all kindergarten students. The ninth-grade year is called the Freshman Academy, and serves as a transitional step to ease students into the high school. Like the community, the school district is growing rapidly; its enrollment has more than doubled in the last 10 years. It has been named one of the nation's "Top Ten Districts Overall" with over 90% of its graduates go on to college. This district's facilities are excellent and parent volunteers welcome. The district recently opened the Prairie Dome sports facility and a performing arts center. The center has six regulation-size basketball courts, 12 volleyball courts and a walking track. The district is considering offering an all-day kindergarten. The YMCA's in-school child care programs provide entertaining morning and afternoon play environments for children grades 1-6.

EDINA #273
1998-99 K-12 Enrollment: 6,760
District Office: 952-928-2500, www.edina.k12.mn.us
Cities Served: Edina

In Minnesota, Edina's schools are the standard by which all other schools are judged. Consistently, it has been rated among the top school districts in the nation. Facilities include: one high school—grades 10-12; two middle schools—grades 6-9; and six elementaries—grades K-5. There are several elementary options: traditional "neighborhood" programs; continuous progress, multi-age programs offering multilevel groupings and the same teacher for more than one year; and French Immersion. Edina is an affluent area and students from this district score well on all the standardized tests. Over 90% of seniors go to college and nearly 90% graduate from college within five years. Over half of Edina's graduates qualify for advanced placement or credit at the college level. The district has graduated a number of National Merit finalists and commended scholars. Kids in this district are participants—in sports, choir, orchestra, newspaper, literary magazine, band. Parents are involved, too, with over half of them volunteering in the schools. The district also partners with many businesses for mentorships, classroom resources and financial support. (When house hunting, be aware that some neighborhoods have Edina addresses, but the children attend Richfield or Hopkins schools.)

FOREST LAKE #831
1998-99 K-12 Enrollment: Approximately 8,000
District Office: 651-982-8100, www.forestlake.k12.mn.us
Cities Served: Forest Lake, Marine on St. Croix, Wyoming, Columbus, Linwood, Lino Lakes, Scandia, Bethel, Ham Lake, Hugo, Stacy

Forest Lake has seven neighborhood elementary schools, two junior highs—grades 7-9, a senior high and an Area Learning Center for at-risk students. Some of the elementary schools make use of team-teaching, and Columbus houses a K-6 Montessori program. Grades 5-8 participate in two one-day special events: the Young Authors Conference which gives talented young writers the opportunity to hear and work with successful authors, artists and illustrators; and the Creativity Conference which brings together well known writers, cartoonists, mimes, inventors, musicians and students from across the metro area. The district also runs a summer Technology Camp. District teams have won state and world Odyssey of the Mind championships.

HOPKINS #270
1998-99 K-12 Enrollment: 8,100
District Office: 952-988-4000, www.hopkins.k12.mn.us
Cities Served: Hopkins, Minnetonka, Golden Valley, Eden Prairie, Edina, Plymouth, St. Louis Park

This district is loved by parents for its ability to nurture and meet the individual needs of its students. In fact, it was named in the "What Parents Want" national award program by SchoolMatch and the high school was chosen one of the best in the nation by *Redbook Magazine*. It has seven elementary schools, two junior highs—grades 7-9, one senior high, and four community centers. Buildings are located in Hopkins, Minnetonka and Golden Valley. The District is also a partner in a multi-disciplinary community arts facility, the Hopkins Center for the Arts, 1111 Main Street, Hopkins, 952-979-1111. Its strong academic program has produced many National Merit finalists, Commended Scholars, and, to date, seven Presidential Scholars. In grades K-4, all classroom teachers also have resource teachers. All students in grades 4-6 take Spanish; junior high students may choose among Spanish, French or German. The high school also offers Japanese, Russian and Chinese. This district has one of the most extensive music programs in Minnesota. Each elementary school has an extended-day schedule, and the district's Parent-to-Parent Program is a model for K-12 parent support. Student turnover is high here, with about 20% moving in or out of the district each year.

MAHTOMEDI #832
1998-99 K-12 Enrollment: Approximately 3,000
District Office: 651-407-2000
Cities Served: Dellwood, Mahtomedi, Pine Springs, Willernie, Grant, Hugo, Lake Elmo Oakdale and White Bear Lake

Mahtomedi has two elementary schools (K-2 and 3-5), a middle school—grades 6-8, a high school and a District Education Center which houses a preschool for the disabled, Early Childhood Family Education and child care programs. The language arts curriculum is literature-based and multi-disciplinary. Science classes emphasize experimentation. Middle school classes are team-taught. Specialty courses are provided through interactive television. At least 75% of students are involved in extracurricular activities. Mahtomedi does not participate in open enrollment. While this area is growing, the schools are still small and have an intimate atmosphere and involved teachers and parents.

MINNEAPOLIS #1
1998-99 K-12 Enrollment: Approximately 50,000
District Office: 612-668-0000, www.mpls.k12.mn.us
City Served: Minneapolis

Minneapolis has 50 elementary schools, 16 K-8, one K-9, eight middle schools and seven high schools. Don't discount this school district! Yes, the test scores are low, but remember that the district serves a high percentage of students for whom English is a second language or who require special education. But the Minneapolis School District has produced National Merit finalists and Rhodes Scholars. Families who can afford private schools often opt to send their children here, for both the cultural opportunity and for the academic program. The magnet schools, in particular, are well regarded by parents. Due to its myriad program offerings, beginning even in kindergarten, the district has opened several Welcome Centers around the city to answer your questions, explain the district's options and handle registrations:

East/Northeast, 612-668-0150, North, 612-627-7080, South, 612-668-5070, and Southwest, 612-627-7090.

MINNETONKA #276
1998-99 K-12 Enrollment: Approximately 7,500
District Office: 952-906-2500, www.minnetonka.k12.mn.us
Cities Served: Minnetonka, Chanhassen, Deephaven, Eden Prairie, Excelsior, Greenwood, Shorewood, Tonka Bay, Victoria and Woodland

Minnetonka has six elementary schools—grades K-5; two middle schools— grades 6-8, one high school and a community education center which houses the district's Early Childhood Family Education program. The elementary schools are focal points of community life. The high school has an in-school coffee shop open after school, early evenings and some special weekends. While the district has a long-standing reputation for being an excellent school district, it also has an equally long-standing reputation for being extremely cliquish. Children who thrive in this highly homogeneous district tend to be high achievers and involved in athletics. Ninety-five percent of the district's graduates attend college.

MOUNDS VIEW #621
1998-99 K-12 Enrollment: Approximately 12,000
District Office: 651-639-6212, www.district.moundsview.k12.mn.us
Cities Served: Mounds View, New Brighton, Shoreview, North Oaks,Vadnais Heights, Arden Hills, Roseville

Mounds View has eight elementary schools, three middle schools—grade 6-8, two senior high schools and three alternative senior highs. This district offers adaptive physical education, physical and occupational therapy and many other special services. Mounds View has almost no children for whom English is a second language. Mounds View High School was close to the top ranking schools in the state on the 1999 10th-grade writing test. Eighty-four percent of its graduates continue to college.

NORTH ST. PAUL-MAPLEWOOD-OAKDALE #622
1998-99 K-12 Enrollment: 11,402
District Office: 651-748-7622 www.isd622.k12.mn.us
Cities Served: Lake Elmo, Landfall, Maplewood, North St. Paul, Oakdale, Pine Springs, Woodbury

This district has an early childhood education center, ten elementary schools, three middle schools—grades 6-8, and two high schools, Tartan in Oakdale and North Senior High in North St. Paul. The district is also a partner in Valley Crossing Community School and the Community Cultures/Environmental Science School, both of which have year-round options. This district is unusual in that many teachers at the high schools actually graduated from the district, giving the schools a small-town feeling and strong sense of tradition.

OSSEO/MAPLE GROVE #279
1998-99 K-12 Enrollment: 21,417
District Office: 763-391-7000, www.osseo.k12.mn.us
Cities Served: Brooklyn park, Maple Grove, Plymouth, Brooklyn Center, Osseo, Corcoran, Hassan and Dayton

The Osseo School District serves an extensive and rapidly developing area of the northwestern suburbs of Minneapolis. It has 20 elementary schools—grades K-6, located in Maple Grove, Brooklyn Park, Brooklyn Center and Osseo, four junior highs—grades 7-9, in Brooklyn Park, Maple Grove and Osseo, and three senior highs in Maple Grove, Osseo and Brooklyn Park. The schools offer a variety of options including all-day kindergarten and multi-age classrooms. Electives are available to junior high students. The senior highs offer French, German, Spanish and additional languages through a cooperative arrangement with the local technical college. High school programs include studio courses in art, early graduation and mentorships.

PERPICH CENTER FOR ARTS EDUCATION
1998-99 Enrollment: 306
Office: 952-591-4700, 800-657-3515, or www.mcae.k12.mn.us
Cities Served: Statewide

This is a residential, tuition-free, public high school for artistically talented 11th and 12th grade students from Minnesota. Located in Golden Valley, it offers innovative coursework in the arts as well as an intensive academic program. Students are selected for admission based on demonstrated ability in the arts and/or potential for growth in an art area. All students who apply to the Arts High School must participate in an arts review session that includes an interview, spontaneous art activity, an arts oriented assignment, and presentation of one or more examples of the applicant's work.

RICHFIELD #280
1998-99 K-12 Enrollment: 4,447
District Office: 612-798-6000, www.richfield.k12.mn.us
Cities Served: Richfield, Edina

This district has two (K-2) elementaries, one 3-5 elementary, one middle school—grades 6-8, one intermediate school—grades 3-5, and one high school—grades 9-12. Writing is emphasized here and incorporated across the curriculum. The Reading Recovery program provides one-on-one tutorials for at risk first graders. Multiple-choice tests have been banished and replaced by essay tests. Nevertheless, only 82% of Richfield's students passed the 10th-grade writing test. However, this is a district where more than 30% of the students move in or out of the district in any given year. The academic program utilizes Richfield's Wood Lake Nature Center and offers six foreign languages.

ST. ANTHONY-NEW BRIGHTON #282
1998-99 K-12 Enrollment: Approximately 1,450
District Office: 612-706-1000, www.stanthony.k12.mn.us
Cities Served: New Brighton, St. Anthony Village

Located in the middle, between Minneapolis and St. Paul, this district has one elementary school—grades K-5, a middle school—grades 6-8, and a high school. The highly-regarded academic program utilizes the area's urban cultural resources such as nearby art and science museums. Their traditional classroom program is augmented with enriched programs in language arts, math, and science. Options include multi-age grouping and multi-year looping. St. Anthony-New Brighton middle school has been named a National School of Excellence and National Blue Ribbon School. Here, parent-teacher conferences have been replaced by student-led parent-advisor conferences. The high school and middle school have recently been renovated and the district's technology has been updated. St. Anthony is one of the districts that is collaborating in the K-8 Downtown School. Together with Edina, St. Anthony-New Brighton led the metro area in scores on the 1999 10th-grade writing test.

ST. LOUIS PARK #283
1998-99 K-12 Enrollment: Approximately 4,300
District Office: 952-928-6000
Cities Served: St. Louis Park

St. Louis Park has five elementary schools (two K-3, two 3-6, and one Spanish immersion school), a junior high—grades 7-8, and one senior high. Many of the schools have been named National Schools of Excellence. Elementary schools offer multi-age and self-contained (traditional) classrooms. The cultural diversity of the city is mirrored in the diversity of the language program: Spanish immersion, French, German, Hebrew and Japanese are also offered. About 75% of St. Louis Park's graduates go to college. Thirteen percent of the district's students are in special education programs.

ST. PAUL #625
1998-99 K-12 Enrollment: Approximately 45,000
District Office: 651-632-3701, www.stpaul.k12.mn.us
Cities Served: St. Paul

St. Paul has 51 elementary schools, five middle schools—grades 6-8, four junior highs—grades 7-8, seven high schools, a K-12 open school, a special education school and several alternative learning centers. Non-traditional schools include Creative Arts School, the Adult Diploma Program, Downtown Kindergarten, Saturn/Riverfront Academy, Boys Totem Town and Guadalupe Project. St. Paul sits with Minneapolis near the bottom of most rankings of school excellence. Yet it too has produced many National Merit finalists and semi-finalists. Also like Minneapolis, this district serves a tremendously diverse population, many of whom have limited English language skills. To meet the incredible variety of needs, the school district has developed a large range of choices including: traditional neighborhood schools, magnets, Montessori programs, year-round schools, language immersion programs, and extended day school-age child care. Languages offered: Spanish, French, Chinese, German, Ojibwe, Latin, Russian, Swahili, Vietnamese and American Sign Language.

SOUTH WASHINGTON COUNTY #833
1998-99 K-12 Enrollment: Approximately 14, 600
District Office: 651-458-6300, www.sowashco.k12.mn.us
Cities Served: Cottage Grove, Newport, St. Paul Park, Grey Cloud, Afton, Denmark, Woodbury

South Washington has 11 elementary schools, four junior highs—grades 7-9, two senior highs—grades 10-12, and a 7-12 alternative. Students may also apply to attend Valley Crossing Community School, grades K-6, which is a cooperative venture of the three school districts that serve Woodbury. South Washington County school district is a parent's dream with respect to co-curricular activities. At the elementary level, Rainbow Kids Klub provides before- and after-school child care in each elementary building for all students, including children with special needs. Elementary Intramurals, an after-school sports program for students in grades 3-6, is available at all 11 elementary schools. There are also after school, evening and weekend enrichment classes which include golf, babysitting, sign language, dance, sports card trading, and Sensational Science Saturday. Junior high sports include boys' and girls' basketball, track, golf and downhill skiing, boys' football and wrestling and girls' volleyball and cheerleading. The high school program includes Junior Air Force ROTC. Both high schools have gone to a four-period day. Ninety-two percent of Woodbury High's students passed the 1999 10th-grade writing test. About 78% of the district's graduates attend college. South Washington does not participate in open enrollment.

STILLWATER #834
1998-99 K-12 Enrollment: Approximately 9,000
District Office: 651-351-8340, www.stillwater.k12.mn.us
Cities Served: Afton, Bayport, Lake Elmo, Lakeland Shores, Lake St. Croix Beach, Marine on St. Croix, Oak Park Heights, St. Mary's Point, Stillwater, Withrow, Woodbury

Stillwater has nine elementary schools, two junior highs—grades 7-9; one senior high and an Alternative Learning Program. District students also attend Valley Crossing, a three-district cooperative elementary school in Woodbury. This is a big district, covering 146 square miles, and it has some big schools; the newest elementary houses 800 students and the high school has 2600. Stillwater Area High School is located in Oak Park Heights. Each class has its own office, with an assistant principal and office staff that move with the classes. Adjacent to the high school is the 52-acre Environmental Learning Center (ELC). High school sports include gymnastics, synchronized swimming and boys' and girls' hockey, however, football "rules." The St. Croix Valley Alternative Learning Program serves district residents, age 16 to 20, who are behind in high school credits or academic achievement, parents to young children, chemically dependent, abused or homeless. Several of the district's schools have been named National Schools of Excellence, and its fine arts program, especially music, is one of the most highly regarded in the state. Stllwater does not participate in open enrollment.

WAYZATA #284
1998-99 K-12 Enrollment: Approximately 8,500
District Office: 952-745-5000, www.wayzata.k12.mn.us
Cities Served: Corcoran, Maple Grove, Medicine Lake, Medina, Minnetonka, Orono, Plymouth and Wayzata

Wayzata has seven elementary schools—grades K-5, three middle schools— grades 6-8, and a high school, built in 1997. Only one middle school lies within the city limits of Wayzata—the rest are in neighboring Plymouth. Virtually all students are bused, with an average bus ride of 15 minutes. All of the schools are accredited and about 80% of the graduates continue on to college. All of the secondary schools have been named National Schools of Excellence and the fine-arts department is ranked among the nation's top 25. It has an environmental learning center, nine computer labs at the high school and offers advanced placement courses as well as special education. A wide range of activities are offered, including sports, middle school yearbook, language-travel programs, and community volunteering. Nearly 25% of the students move in or out of the district in any given year.

WESTONKA #277
1998-99 K-12 Enrollment: Approximately 2,500
District Office: 952-491-8000, www.westonka.k12.mn.us
Cities Served: Independence, Lyndale, Minnetrista, Mound, Navarre, Orono, Shorewood, Spring Park

The Westonka district has two primary schools—grades K-4, a middle school—grades 5-7, a high school preparatory program—grades 8-9, and one high school. The middle school program includes twice-weekly asset-building activities; foreign languages are offered as after-school enrichment. Westonka advertises small classes and access to technology. Ninety percent of the district's 10th-grade students passed the 1999 statewide writing test. Three-fourths of the district's graduates attend college.

WHITE BEAR LAKE #624
1998-99 K-12 Enrollment: Approximately 9,700
District Office: 651-773-6000, www.whitebear.k12.mn.us
Cities Served: Birchwood, Gem Lake, Hugo, Little Canada, North Oaks, Vadnais Heights, White Bear Lake, White Bear Township

White Bear Lake has nine elementary schools—grades K-5, two middle schools—grades 6-8, one senior high with grades 9 and 10 on its North Campus and grades 11 and 12 on its South Campus, and an Alternative Learning Center. The elementary program emphasizes basic skills and writing, but offers alternatives like multi-age grouping and extended days. Lakeaires Elementary broadcasts a daily, student-run morning news show, and has several choirs. Within the past few years, Central Middle School has undergone major renovation, and added a new wing. French, German and Spanish are offered in grade 8. The high school curriculum includes College in the Schools, a program in conjunction with the University of Minnesota which offers advanced courses. A recent $1 million gift from a former student will be used to endow scholarships and improve teaching. Approximately three-fourths of the district's graduates go on to college.

ONLINE RESOURCES—SCHOOLS

Elementary through high school students can find help with their homework from volunteer teachers online at the Star Tribune's Homework Help, www.startribune.com/education/homework.

L IVING IN THE TWIN CITIES YOU'RE NEVER FAR AWAY FROM A COLLEGE and its accompanying academic atmosphere—you're reminded every time you go into a coffee shop where half the people are studying. It seems everyone is enrolled in some course—from bartenders and waitresses to corporate exceutives and retirees, not to mention 18 to 24 year olds.

Minnesota's oldest college is Hamline, founded in 1854. The land grant University of Minnesota followed soon after. Today the Twin Cities metropolitan area is home to over a dozen colleges and universities, and an equal number of technical schools. Five of the colleges, Hamline, Macalester, Augsburg, St. Thomas and St. Catherine's, have joined together to form the Associated Colleges of the Twin Cities (ACTC). Students at these schools may sign up for courses at any of the ACTC campuses and parents whose children are enrolled in some of these schools may audit courses there for free.

The **Interstate Tuition Reciprocity Program**, which allows students to attend an out-of-state public institution in Wisconsin, Iowa, and North and South Dakota for the same tuition they would pay at a comparable Minnesota public institution, is an option for students wanting to go to an out-of-state school. Students can also get discounted tuition at certain institutions in Michigan, Missouri, Kansas and Nebraska.

The **Minnesota Higher Education Services Office (MHESO)**, www.mheso.state.mn.us, includes information on tuition discounts, tax and savings incentives, and financial aid. For a rated list of colleges and universities, try **CollegeNet**, www.collegenet.com, or *US News'* **Colleges and Careers Center** at www.usnews.com/usnews/edu. To receive brochures from the college of your choice try either www.embark.com or contact the school directly. If you're interested in a public Minnesota college, visit the **Minnesota State Colleges and Universities' (MnSCU)** web page, www.mnscu.edu. It has links to campus profiles, a searchable program index, and transfer and financial information, or call 888-667-2848, 651-296-8012. The **Minnesota Private Colleges'** homepage, www.mn-colleges.org, has links to Minnesota's 16 private colleges as well as financial and admissions information.

Whether you're just beginning your college search or looking for continuing education opportunities, the colleges and universities in the metropolitan area are a good place to start. Also keep in mind that concerts, plays, lecture series and many other cultural opportunities abound at these institutions of higher learning for both students and non-students alike.

TWIN CITIES UNIVERSITIES AND COLLEGES

- **Augsburg College**, 731 21st Avenue South, Minneapolis 55454, 612-330-1000, 800-788-5678, www.augsburg.edu; set on the Mississippi West Bank, Augsburg is a private, four-year liberal arts college of the Evangelical Lutheran Church in America. Known for its ability to work with special needs students, it also offers a program called Weekend College, where adult students can earn a college degree, complete a second major, pursue a personal interest, or develop a job-related skill. Degrees offered: Bachelor of Arts, Bachelor of Music, Bachelor of Science, Master of Arts in Leadership, Master of Social Work, Teaching Licensure. Pre-Professional Programs: dentistry, engineering, law, medicine, ministry, pharmacy, veterinary science. The college also offers credit and non-credit courses through its continuing education program. Enrollment: about 1,500.

- **Bethel College**, 3900 Bethel Drive, Arden Hills 55112; 651-638-6400, 800-255-8706, www.bethel.edu, is a four-year, liberal arts Baptist college located in a wooded, lakeside setting about 15 minutes from downtown St. Paul and Minneapolis. The college is highly regarded for its music and education programs. Degrees offered: Associate of Arts, Bachelor of Arts, Bachelor of Music, Bachelor of Music Education, Bachelor of Science. Teaching Licensure programs: elementary and secondary levels. Pre-Professional programs: engineering, law, medicine, physical therapy. Enrollment: about 2,000.

- **College of St. Catherine**, 2004 Randolph Avenue, St. Paul, 55105; 651-690-6000, 800-945-4599, www.stkate.edu; this Catholic college for women does admit men to its masters programs and its two-year campus in Minneapolis. Degrees offered: Bachelor of Arts, Bachelor of

Science. Licensure programs: early childhood, pre-kindergarten, kindergarten, elementary and secondary education. Pre-professional programs: dentistry, engineering, forestry and environmental studies, law, medical technology, medicine, optometry, pharmacy, physical therapy, veterinary medicine. Certificate programs: accounting, business administration, pastoral ministry, pastoral music ministry, piano pedagogy, with numerous masters programs available. Their weekend college program offers women the opportunity to earn a college degree in four years by attending classes every other weekend, from early September through June. Enrollment: about 1,700.

- **Concordia University-St. Paul**, 275 North Syndicate Street, St. Paul, 55104; 651-641-8230, 800-333-4705, www.csp.edu; a private college with a Lutheran heritage which offers a liberal arts education. Degrees offered: Associate in Arts, Bachelor of Arts, Master of Arts in Education. Teaching Licensure programs: elementary and secondary education. Pre-professional programs: dentistry, law, medicine, seminary, veterinary science. Enrollment: about 1,000.

- **Dunwoody Institute**, 818 Dunwoody Boulevard, Minneapolis 55403-1192; 612-374-5800, 800-292-4625, www.dunwoody.tec. mn.us; famous for its National Baking Center devoted to traditional baking (which they sell to the public), Dunwoody has been training men and women for technical careers since 1914. It is one of the top technical schools in the US in automotive, electronics, tool and die manufacturing and many other technical fields.

- **Hamline University**, 1536 Hewitt Avenue, St. Paul, 55104; 651-523-2207, 800-753-9753, www.hamline.edu; this nationally recognized coeducational Methodist college of liberal arts and sciences is composed of an undergraduate College of Liberal Arts, School of Law and Graduate School. Incoming freshmen are placed in mentoring groups of four to six students. Hamline guarantees that if a student begins college work at Hamline and the university fails to make it possible to graduate in four years, the fifth year's tuition is free. Ninety-seven percent of Hamline's full-time faculty hold a doctorate or the highest degree in their field. Degrees offered: Bachelor of Arts, Master of Arts in Education, Master of Arts in Liberal Studies, Master of Arts in Public Administration, Doctorate in Public Administration, Master of Fine Arts in Writing, Master of Arts in Non-Profit Management, Master of Arts in Management with Conflict Resolution Emphasis, Juris Doctor, with many pre-professional programs available. Hamline offers a growing number of courses and programs of continuing and community education and graduate-level courses with specialization in the Humanities. Enrollment: undergraduate, 1,800; graduate, 1,400.

- **Hennepin Technical Colleges**, 9200 Flying Cloud Drive, Eden Prairie, MN 55347, 952-550-3112, 800-345-4655, www.mnscu.edu, has two campuses devoted to educating people for careers that do not require a baccalaureate degree for entry. Its largest programs are computer careers; machine trades; media, print, communications; and nursing. The cooking course operates a restaurant that is open to the public on a reservation basis. Degrees offered: Associate in Applied Science, certificates, and diplomas. The college partners with many Twin Cities industries and businesses for job-placement. Enrollment: over 13,000.

- **Macalester College**, 1600 Grand Avenue, St. Paul, 55105; 651-696-6357, 800-231-7974, www.macalester.edu, is a coeducational, undergraduate residential liberal arts college with a strong tradition of high academic standards and a reputation for producing dedicated social activists. Its handsome campus is located among the shops and cafés on Grand Avenue. Affiliated with the Presbyterian Church (USA), the college is non-sectarian in its instruction. Ninety-three percent of its full-time faculty have a doctorate or the highest degree in their field. Students of exceptionally high achievement are invited to undertake a special project of independent research or creative work in their senior year. Students may take one course per term at the Minneapolis College of Art and Design. Degree offered: Bachelor of Arts. Licensure programs: pre-kindergarten, kindergarten, elementary and secondary teaching. Pre-professional programs: architecture, engineering, law and medical fields. Enrollment: about 2,500.

- **Metropolitan State University**, 730 Hennepin Avenue, Minneapolis, 612-341-7250; 700 7th Street East, St. Paul, 651-772-7777, www.mnscu.edu, is a state-funded commuter school which offers day, evening and weekend classes to more than 8,000 students pursuing vocationally-oriented bachelor's degrees. Unique programs include individualized bachelor's degrees, law enforcement, applied mathematics and biology. Degrees offered: Bachelor of Arts, Bachelor of Science, Bachelor of Social Work, Master of Management and Administration, Master of Business Administration, Master of Science in Nursing. Enrollment: over 8,000.

- **Minneapolis College of Art and Design**, 2501 Stevens Avenue

South, Minneapolis, 55404, 612-874-3760, 800-874-6223, www.mcad.edu, is over one hundred years old. This private four-year college is adjacent to the Minneapolis Institute of Art, just south of downtown. The curriculum is structured with studio emphasis and a liberal arts core. Degrees offered: Bachelor of Fine Arts, Bachelor of Science, Master of Fine Arts. Sophomores, juniors and seniors may earn some of the liberal arts credits needed for graduation by taking classes at Macalester College in St. Paul. Opportunities for independent study on or off-campus; study abroad in Florence, Italy, and Canada; and study at other art schools. Enrollment: approximately 550.

- **Minneapolis Community and Technical College (MCTC)**, 1501 Hennepin Avenue, Minneapolis 55403; 612-341-7000, www.mnscu.edu, is a non-residential two-year community college located near downtown by Loring Park. MCTC offers associate degrees in dozens of liberal arts and technical areas. This is the most ethnically diverse campus in the state and has a large English-as-a-Second- Language (ESL) program and state-of-the-art technical equipment. The college also operates the Center for Criminal Justice and Law Enforcement, a Transportation/Aviation Training Center and the College for Working Adults. Degrees offered: Associate in Arts, Associate in Sciences, Associate in Applied Science, also diplomas and certificates. Enrollment: 10,500.

- **Normandale Community College**, 9700 France Avenue South, Bloomington 55431, 952-832-6000, www.mnscu.edu, is a non-residential two year community college offering associate degrees. The engineering and health sciences departments, in particular, are highly regarded by graduates who started there and continued to higher degrees in other institutions. Two-thirds of Normandale's graduates go on to four-year colleges. Degrees offered: Associate in Arts, Associate in Science, Associate in Applied Science. Enrollment: over 11,000.

- **University of Minnesota**, Washington Avenue at East River Road, Minneapolis 55455; Como Avenue at Cleveland Avenue, St. Paul, 612-625-5000, www.umn.edu; "The U," with its four campuses, consistently ranks among the top 20 public universities in the country. It is highly regarded as a major research institution, particularly with respect to agriculture, business, medicine and public service. The heart-lung machine, cardiac pacemaker, flight recorder (black box) for aircraft and the retractable seat belt for cars were all invented here. It is also the world's leading kidney transplant center. The Twin

Cities campus spans the Mississippi River with facilities in Minneapolis and St. Paul that are connected by the campus shuttle service. It is made up of 20 colleges and offers 161 bachelor's degrees, 218 master's degrees, 114 doctoral degrees, and 5 professional degrees. A Big 10 school, its Golden Gophers teams compete in Division 1 college athletics. The dynamic University community is a diverse mix of ethnic backgrounds, interests, and cultures. Students come from all 50 states and more than 100 foreign countries. Enrollment on the Twin Cities campus is more than 40,000.

- **University of St. Thomas**, 2115 Summit Avenue, St. Paul, 55105; 651-962-6150, 800-328-6819, www.stthomas.edu, is the largest private school in Minnesota. A coeducational Catholic liberal arts university, it emphasizes values-centered, career-oriented education. Degrees offered: Bachelor of Arts in 58 major fields; Bachelor of Science in manufacturing engineering, international business, and actuarial science; Master's degrees in 25 fields, and pre-professional programs also available. New College, the evening and weekend division, offers Bachelor of Arts degrees in 12 majors; a Bachelor of Science in manufacturing engineering and certificate programs in business and computer science. Enrollment: approximately 10,000.

- **William Mitchell College of Law**, 875 Summit Avenue, St. Paul, 55105; 651-227-9171; founded in 1900, this 1,100-student private law school set among the mansions of Summit Avenue boasts two Chief Justices among its alumni—Warren E. Burger, graduated in 1931 and served on the US Supreme Court from 1969 to 1986, and Douglas K. Amdahl, graduated in 1951 and served as Chief Justice on the Minnesota Supreme Court from 1980 to 1988.

NEARBY COLLEGES

- **Carleton College**, 100 South College Street, Northfield, Minnesota 55057; 507-646-4190, 800-995-CARL, www.carleton.edu, is regarded as one of the country's best small liberal arts colleges. This coeducational, residential, four-year college attracts students from nearly every state and many foreign countries. Ninety-five percent of its faculty have a doctorate or highest degree in their field. Carleton and St. Olaf students may take courses on either campus. Degree offered: Bachelor of Arts. Offers a Secondary Education Certificate Program. Pre-professional programs: architecture, business and management, chemistry, dentistry, engineering, hospital administration or health systems, journalism and publishing, law, library science, medicine, ministry, nursing, social work and veterinary science. Enrollment: 1,720.

- **Gustavus Adolphus College**, 800 West College Avenue, Saint Peter, Minnesota 56082; 507-933-7676, 800-GUSTAVUS, www.gac.edu; this private, residential, liberal arts college is located in a small town about an hour and a half from the Twin Cities. Degree offered: Bachelor of Arts. Teaching majors in elementary and secondary subjects. Pre-professional programs also available. Enrollment: about 2,500.

- **St. Olaf College**, 1520 St. Olaf Avenue, Northfield, 55057; 507-646-3025, 800-800-3025, www.stolaf.edu, is a four-year, coeducational, residential, Lutheran liberal arts college with a beautiful campus. It is recognized nationally for its strong music, mathematics, and study abroad programs. The St. Olaf College Christmas Festival is the hottest holiday ticket in Minnesosta. Check it out online, at www.stolaf.edu/publications/christmas. St. Olaf and Carleton students take courses on either campus. Continuing education programs are specially designed for parents, alumni, congregations of the Evangelical Lutheran Church in America, businesses, professional groups and local residents. Degrees offered: Bachelor of Arts, Bachelor of Arts in Nursing, Bachelor of Music, Bachelor of Arts–Paracollege. Pre-professional programs also available. Enrollment: about 3,000.

MINNESOTA'S CLIMATE MAY BE COLD, BUT LOCAL CULTURE IS on fire—and it isn't all polka bands and Whoppee John Wilfart. The Walker Art Center is internationally famous for its contemporary exhibits. The Guthrie Theater is considered one of the finest classic repertory companies in the country. The St. Paul Chamber Orchestra is held in high regard by classical music aficionados everywhere. And popular music acts from Bob Dylan to Soul Asylum to Prince originated in the thriving club scene here. Did we mention the hundreds of small galleries, ballet troupes and avant-garde theater stages? By some measures, the arts activity is hotter here than it is in New York. And while Minnesotans don't dance in the aisles, every performance ends in a standing ovation.

TICKETS

Ticket prices are lower than New York's, but you can still drop a bundle on a good seat. The best prices come with series tickets, but if you take training as an usher you can often enjoy performances for free. Many venues have their own box offices, and many organizations sell tickets online. Or try Ticketmaster, 612-989-5151, www.ticketmaster.com; their ticket centers are located at Dayton's, Mervyn's California, and Rainbow Foods stores. Pick up discount TREATSEATS at the ticket centers and you'll save on performances, museums and many events. Season ticket holders often turn in tickets they can't use, so sometimes a last minute call to the box office will net you wonderful seats.

MUSIC—SYMPHONIC, CHORAL, OPERA, CHAMBER

The level of artistry in the Twin Cities is extraordinary. For classical music, start with the Minnesota Orchestra and St. Paul Chamber Orchestra, or take your pick from the following:

- **American Composers' Forum**, 332 Minnesota Street, #E145, St. Paul, 651-228-1407; concert series and other forums for emerging composers are the forte of this unique organization. Check them on the web at www.composersforum.org.

- **The Bach Society of Minnesota**, 313 Landmark Center, 75 West Fifth Street, St. Paul, 651-225-8101; choral performance of the works of Johann Sebastian Bach and other baroque contrapuntal composition in three to five subscription concerts a year and many educational programs and special events.

- **Chamber Music Society of Minnesota**, 33 South Sixth Street, Minneapolis, 612-339-2264; musicians from the Minnesota Orchestra, The Saint Paul Chamber Orchestra and the faculties of the Universities of Minnesota and Wisconsin present several concerts annually, usually on Sunday afternoons at the 3M Auditorium of the Minnesota History Center, 345 Kellogg Avenue, St. Paul.

- **Dale Warland Singers**, 119 North Fourth Street, # 510, Minneapolis, 612-339-9707; one of the world's finest a-cappella choral ensembles. Online at www.dalewarlandsingers.org.

- **Encore Winds Percussion**, 375 Oakwood Drive, Shoreview, 651-483-4912; this fine band performs six concerts per season, usually at Bethel College.

- **Minnesota Boychoir**, 651-292-3219; this concert choir made up of 48 boys ages 8-14 from all over the Twin Cities, performs at churches, the Minnesota Orchestra and the Guthrie Theater—when they're not away on tour, www.boychoir.org.

- **Minnesota Chorale**, 528 Hennepin Avenue, #211, Minneapolis, 612-333-4866; this 150-voice chorus performs regularly with the Minnesota Orchestra and the St. Paul Chamber Orchestra.

- **Minnesota Opera**, 620 North 1st Street, Minneapolis, 612-333-6669; this professional opera company has achieved an international reputation for originating opera productions. The company offers four main-stage productions each season at the Ordway Music Theatre, as well as an acclaimed educational touring production.

- **Minnesota Orchestra**, Orchestra Hall, 1111 Nicollet Mall, Minneapolis, 612-371-5656, www.mnorch.org; music Director Eiji Oue is attracting some of America's most in-demand musicians to perform with one of America's great symphony orchestras in evening and coffee concerts, weekend pops series and at the Viennese Sommerfest at Orchestra Hall in Minneaplois and St. Paul's Ordway Theater.

- **Minnesota Sinfonia**, 1820 Stevens Avenue South, Suite E, Minneapolis, 612-871-1701; this chamber orchestra produces adventurous and educational family-oriented performances which are free to the public and held in centrally located, easily accessible locations.

- **Minnesota Youth Symphonies**, 790 Cleveland Avenue South, Suite 203, St. Paul, 651-699-5811, provides pre-professional orchestral training for children, elementary through college levels. Three major concerts are presented each season at Orchestra Hall, Minneapolis; and O'Shaughnessy Auditorium, St. Paul.

- **National Lutheran Choir**, P.O. Box 6450, Minneapolis, 612-722-2301; professional musicians perform sacred choral works from early chant to large works with orchestras.

- **Nautilus Music-Theater**, 308 Prince Street, #250, St. Paul, 651-298-9913, creates new operas and other forms of music theater.

- **North Star Opera**, 1863 Eleanor Avenue, St. Paul, 651-690-6700; musical theater, operetta and opera are presented in English. Musicians are drawn from the Minnesota Orchestra and St. Paul Chamber Orchestra, with costumes and staging from the Guthrie Theater and Children's Theater.

- **Philomusica**, 2748 Salem Avenue South, St. Louis Park, 952-922-5365; this chamber music orchestra performs a half-dozen concerts a year at Theatre de la Jeune Lune and other locations throughout the Twin Cities.

- **Plymouth Music Series**, 1900 Nicollet Avenue, Minneapolis, 612-624-2345; this innovative series reinvents Bach, presents the oratorios of Handel, hosts world-famous orchestral and choral performers and assists emerging composers. Performances are given at the Plymouth Congregational Church, Basilica of St. Mary and Orchestra Hall in Minneapolis and other venues around the Twin Cities. Their schedule always includes a holiday gala. They mail notes on each program to ticket-holders a week in advance. Call 612-547-1475 for concert previews or visit their Web site at www.plymouthmusic.org.

- **The Saint Paul Chamber Orchestra**, Hamm Building, Suite 500, 408 St. Peter Street, St. Paul, 651-291-1144; this internationally-famous 32-player ensemble is the only full-time chamber orchestra in the US. It performs at numerous churches and synagogues around town, but most often at the Ordway Music Theatre in St. Paul. For a newcomer's kit that includes a voucher for two tickets for the price of one, call 651-291-1144.

- **The Schubert Club**, 302 Landmark Center, 75 West Fifth St., Saint Paul, 651-292-3268; established in 1882, this non-profit arts organization presents eight concert series annually, operates the Museum of Musical Instruments, sponsors an annual scholarship competition for music students, provides after-school music lessons at the Martin Luther King Center in Saint Paul and the Sabathani Center in Minneapolis, presents master classes, commissions new musical works and produces recordings and books.

COMMUNITY MUSIC

The Twin Cities' community choral societies, bands, orchestras and musical theaters range from ensembles of professionals to volunteer organizations whose purpose is to give people who love music a chance to participate. If you're interested in playing, this list of organizations will give you a place to get started. If you're only interested in listening, these groups are a treat! For a comprehensive listing of community bands and links to bands that have web pages, visit www.visi.com/~diazwalby/band.

- **Allegro Symphonia**, 952-707-8144; this orchestra rehearses and performs at Wayzata Community Church, Wayzata Boulevard at Ferndale Avenue, Wayzata. Its repertoire includes symphonic classics and the works of new Minnesota composers.

- **The Apollo Male Chorus**, Eisenhower Community Center, Highway 7, Hopkins, 952-933-6322; one of the oldest male choruses in the country, the Apollo Chorus has sung continuously since 1895. Most performances are at the Ted Mann Theater at the University of Minnesota. It performs major winter and spring concerts as well as special concerts in churches and at corporations and community events. Tickets range $14 to $18.

- **The Bel Canto Voices**, 1917 Logan Avenue South, Minneapolis, 612-377-5928, www.belcantovoices.org; concert choirs for girls grades two through twelve perform in venues as diverse as their music.

- **Bells of the Lake**, 511 Groveland, Minneapolis, 612-871-5303;

this hand-bell choir tours internationally, but also plays about 15 concerts a year in the Twin Cities in churches, at conventions, parties and weddings.

- **Dakota Valley Civic Orchestral Association**, Alimagnet Parkway, Box 4, Burnsville, MN 55337, 952-894-1924, www.spacestar.net/dvcoa, consists of three orchestras and a chorus. They perform about 20 concerts each year, primarily in Dakota County. Tickets cost from $3-$7.

- **Eagan Summer Theatre**, 651-683-6964, presents one production each summer at the Eagan High School Auditorium. Performances sell out fast, so they run a waiting list for tickets.

- **Eden Prairie Community Band**, Eden Prairie City Hall, 952-949-8453; home base for this band is Starring Lake in Eden Prairie; they also perform at Edinborough Indoor Park, and the Lake Harriet Bandshell.

- **Gilbert and Sullivan Very Light Opera Company**, P.O. Box 580172, Minneapolis, MN 55458-0172, 612-925-9159, presents the works of those eminent Victorians Gilbert and Sullivan, fully staged and with an orchestra of more than twenty. These productions are usually presented in the spring and frequently sell out in advance.

- **Grand Symphonic Winds**, P.O. Box 75675, St. Paul, MN 55175, 651-690-9842; this civic wind ensemble performs music of many periods and styles. They present about six concerts per season at churches and the Minnesota History Center and 3M Auditorium, 345 Kellogg Boulevard West in St. Paul. Visit their Web site at www.sky-point.com/~kjb/gsw.

- **Greater Twin Cities Youth Symphonies**, 430 Oak Grove Street Suite 205, Minneapolis, 612-870-7611; eight full youth orchestras perform about 15 concerts a year at Orchestra Hall and Benson Great Hall at Bethel College. Tickets are $10 for adults, $6 for seniors and students.

- **Kenwood Chamber Orchestra**, St. Olaf Catholic Church, 215 South 8th Street, Minneapolis, 612-949-9045; founded in the Lake of the Isles area, this 40-member group of serious amateur musicians rehearses at St. Olaf's Church downtown and is open to members from anywhere. They perform five or six programs a year at churches, the St. Paul Rheinfest, Walker Art Center, Lake Harriet Bandshell and occasional nursing homes. Concerts are usually free.

- **Linden Hills Orchestra**, 5017 Kingsdale Drive, Minneapolis, 952-893-9149; this adult amateur orchestra performs several concerts a year at churches, Southwest High School and the Lake Harriet Bandshell in Minneapolis. There is no charge for admission.

- **Medalist Concert Band**, 10305 Berkshire Road, Bloomington, 55437, 952-820-4634; this 70-member adult concert band has a 30-year history of performances throughout the midwest and abroad and has been described by the National Band Association as "one of the foremost community bands in the nation." It presents over 20 concerts each year throughout the area.

- **Metropolitan Boys Choir**, P.O. Box 19348, Minneapolis, 612-827-6501, is an organization of 400 young men, ages five to 18, from the Minneapolis-St. Paul area. The choirs perform at Orchestra Hall and a variety of national and international venues.

- **The Metropolitan Symphony Orchestra**, P.O. Box 581213, Minneapolis, MN 55458, 612-288-9581; in order to share live symphony music with communities that might otherwise not have an opportunity to hear it, the MSO performs free-of-charge in different sectors of the Twin Cities.

- **Minneapolis Pops Orchestra**, 1611 West 32nd Street, Minneapolis, 612-825-2922; free concerts by professional musicians who play together only in July at Lake Harriet in the Bandshell in a concert tradition that started over 100 years ago.

- **Minneapolis Vocal Consort**, 1400 Searle Street, St. Paul, 651-778-9628; their repertoire draws from centuries of choral music, including new works by local composers.

- **Mississippi Valley Orchestra**, 5309 28th Avenue South, Minneapolis, 55417, 612-722-7867; this semi-professional group is one of the premier orchestras in the area. Their music is challenging and varied, they also perform the Nutcrcacker Ballet at O'Shaughnessy Auditorium every winter with the Ballet Minnesota. Also check for them at the First Lutheran Church at Columbia Heights and Augustana Lutheran Church in West St. Paul.

- **Music Association of Minnetonka**, Eisenhower Community Center, 1001 Highway 7, Hopkins, 612-935-4615, provides choral and orchestral opportunities for musicians of all ages. Its ten ensembles present 70 public performances each year at convenient locations throughout the western suburbs, Minneapolis and St. Paul.

- **Music in the Park Series—St. Anthony Park**, 1333 Chelmsford

Street, St. Paul, 651-645-5699, produces seven chamber music concerts in the St. Anthony Park United Church of Christ and three sets of family concerts at the St. Anthony Park Public Library each year. Tickets range from $13 to $8 for chamber concerts; family concert tickets range from $4 advanced purchase for kids to $6 at the door. This is one of the best music series in the Twin Cities.

- **North Suburban Concert Band**, 4171 88th Lane NE, Blaine, 763-784-8997; this organization includes three groups, the orchestra, Big Band Jazz Ensemble, and German Band. They perform at Twin Cities' parks and also with local high school bands.

- **Shoreview Northern Lights Variety Band**, 5864 Oxford Street, Shoreview, 55126, 651-483-4283, www.snlvb.com, draws its musicians from all over the Twin Cities and performs at community events and the Como Park Pavilion. Holiday and spring concerts are presented in Benson Great Hall at Bethel College in Arden Hills.

- **St. Anthony Civic Orchestra**, 3301 Silver Lake Road NE, St. Anthony, 612-788-3516; started as a project for the Bicentennial, this adult group performs and rehearses at St. Anthony Community Center. They perform about ten concerts a year including classical concerts in the fall and spring, a holiday gala and summer pops.

- **St. Louis Park Band**, 2109 Robin Circle, 952-933-7175; this full concert band, made up of hobby musicians, plays at local parks including Oak Hill Park at 34th and Rhode Island Avenue in St. Louis Park and Edinborough Indoor Park in Edina. Every second year, they perform a concert at Orchestra Hall in Minneapolis with 5th-and 6th-graders from the St. Louis Park school district. They also give to The Gift of Music, a program which repairs used musical instruments and distributes them to children who are unable to afford them.

- **South St. Paul Male Chorus**, South St. Paul Senior High School, South St. Paul, 651 455-8843; this 40-voice chorus sings a variety of concerts and joins with the 3M Male Chorus and Lockheed-Martin Chorus in a Fall Musical Traditions Concert each November. It also presents a community concert at Christmas. Visit their Web site at www.tc.umn.edu.

- **Star of the North Concert Band**, 942 Northland Court, Stillwater; the extensive repertoire of this band includes symphonic band arrangements, marches, classical works, Dixieland, big band, musical theatre, original compositions, and instrumentals with vocal solos. They perform locally at Como Park, Town Square, and Landmark Center in St. Paul; Lake Harriet in Minneapolis; Edinborough Park and Centennial Lakes in Edina; Ojibway Park in Woodbury; the Maplewood Community Center; and Pioneer Park in Stillwater. Their international tours include Australia, New Zealand, Wales and England.

- **Twin Cities Gay Men's Chorus**, 528 Hennepin Avenue, Suite 701, Minneapolis, 612-339-SONG, performs six times a year at the Ted Mann Concert Hall at the University of Minnesota. Tickets can also be purchased on-line at www.tcgmc.org.

MUSIC–CONTEMPORARY

The Twin Cities have a long, rich history of great popular music. From Bob Dylan, who started out playing the coffeehouses of Cedar-Riverside, to Prince rocking the house at First Avenue, to garage-rock bands such as the Jayhawks and country-blues stars like Little Johnny Lang, the Twin Cities have been and continue to be a place to catch great gigs and perhaps experience music history in the making. The following venues are best-known for the category under which they're listed, although many of them book a variety of acts. Keep in mind that clubs that book popular music are often "here today, gone tomorrow;" our advice is to call first.

RHYTHM & BLUES

- **Blues Alley**, 15 North Glenwood Avenue, Minneapolis, 612-333-1327
- **Blues Saloon**, 601 Western Avenue, St. Paul, 651-228-9959
- **Bunker's**, 761 Washington Avenue North, Minneapolis, 612-338-8188
- **Cabooze**, 917 Cedar Avenue South, Minneapolis, 612-338-6425, www.mtnorg/TCJS
- **Five Corners Saloon**, 501 Cedar Avenue South, Minneapolis, 612-338-6424
- **Lyon's Pub on Sixth**, 16 South 6th Street Minneapolis, 612-333-6612
- **Nikki's Cafe and Bar**, 107 3rd Avenue North, Minneapolis, 612-340-9098
- **Schuller's Tavern**, 7345 Country Club Drive, Golden Valley, 763-545-9972
- **Viking Bar**, 1829 Riverside Avenue, Minneapolis, 612-332-4259
- **Whiskey Junction**, 901 Cedar Avenue, Minneapolis, 612-338-9550

COUNTRY, BLUEGRASS

- **Buckboard Saloon**, 464 South Concorde, South St. Paul, 651-455-9995
- **Dulono's**, 607 West Lake Street Minneapolis, 612-827-1726
- **Homestead Pickin' Parlor**, 6625 Penn Avenue South, Richfield, 612-861-3308

FOLK

- **Bryant-Lake Bowl**, 810 West Lake Street, Minneapolis, 612-825-3737
- **Cedar Cultural Centre**, 416 Cedar Avenue South, Minneapolis, 612-338-2674
- **Chang O'Hara's Bistro**, 498 Selby Avenue, St. Paul, 651-290-2338.
- **Fine Line Music Cafe**, 318 First Avenue North, Minneapolis, 612-338-8100
- **Ginkgo Coffeehouse**, 721 North Snelling Avenue, St. Paul, 651-645-2647
- **Loring Cafe**, 1624 Harmon Place, Minneapolis, 612-332-1617
- **Minneapolis Cafe**, 2730 West Lake Street, Minneapolis, 612-920-1401

IRISH & CELTIC

- **Half Time Rec Bar**, 1013 Front Street, St. Paul, 651-488-8245
- **Kieran's Irish Pub**, 330 2nd Avenue South, Minneapolis, 612-339-4499
- **O'Donovan's**, 700 1st Avenue North, Minneapolis, 612-317-8896

JAZZ

- **Hot Nights, Cool Jazz**, 50th & France, Edina, free, summers only, 5:30-7:30 p.m. in front of the TCF Bank, 3924 West 5th Street, 952-922-1524.
- **Free Summer Concerts**, St. Anthony Main, 7:30 to 10:30 p.m., Fridays, Saturdays and 4 to 7 p.m., Sundays, in the public courtyard between Anthony's Wharf and Tugg's River Salon.
- **Cafe Luxx**, 1101 LaSalle Avenue, Minneapolis, 612-332-6800
- **D'Amico Cucina**, 100 North 6th Street, Minneapolis, 612-338-2401
- **Dakota Bar and Grill**, Bandana Square, St. Paul, 651-642-1442

POLKA, LOUNGE MUSIC

- **Ivories**, 605 Waterford Park Tower, Plymouth, 763-591-6188
- **Mayslack's**, 1428 4th Street NE, Minneapolis, 612-789-9862
- **Nye's Polonaise Room**, 112 Hennepin Avenue East, Minneapolis, 612-379-2021

ROCK—ALTERNATIVE

- **First Avenue**, 701 1st Avenue North, Minneapolis, 612-332-1775
- **7th Street Entry**, 701 1st Avenue North, Minneapolis, 612-332-1775
- **Four Hundred Bar**, Cedar at Riverside Avenue, Minneapolis, 612-332-2903
- **O'Gara's Garage**, 164 North Snelling Avenue, St. Paul, 651-644-3333
- **Saloon**, 830 Hennepin Avenue, Minneapolis, 612-332-0835
- **Whole Music Club**, Coffman Union, U of M, 300 Washington Avenue SE, Minneapolis, 612-624-8638

ROCK—METAL, CLASSIC

- **Cat Ballou's**, 12 North Main Street, Stillwater, 651-439-4567
- **Hexagon Bar**, 2600 27th Avenue South, Minneapolis, 612-722-3454
- **Neon's**, 1955 English Street, Maplewood, 651-774-8787
- **Ryan's**, 4th & Sibley Street, St. Paul, 651-298-1917

NIGHTCLUBS AND DISCOS

- **Gator's**, Mall of America, Bloomington, 952-858-8888
- **Gay 90s**, 408 Hennepin Avenue, Minneapolis, 612-333-7755
- **Ground Zero**, 15 NE 4th Street Minneapolis, 612-378-5115
- **Quest Club**, 110 5th Street North, Minneapolis, 612-338-3383
- **Terminal Bar**, 409 East Hennepin Avenue, Minneapolis, 612-623-4545

CONCERT HALLS, ARENAS

- **Benson Great Hall**, Bethel College, 3900 Bethel Drive, Arden Hills, 651-638-6333
- **Fitzgerald Theatre**, 10 East Exchange Street, St. Paul, 651-290-1221
- **Guthrie Theater**, 725 Vineland Place, Minneapolis, 612-377-2224

- **Landmark Center**, 75 West 5th Street, St. Paul, 651-292-3225; Ma Barker and John Dillinger were tried in the courtroom in this castle-like edifice which today serves as a cultural center.
- **Hubert H. Humphrey Metrodome**, 900 South 5th Street Minneapolis, 612-335-3370
- **Northrop Auditorium**, 84 Church Street SE, Minneapolis, 612-624-2345
- **Orchestra Hall**, 1111 Nicollet Mall, Minneapolis, 612-371-5656 or 800-292-4141
- **Orpheum Theater**, 910 Hennepin Avenue South, Minneapolis, 612-339-7007
- **Ordway Music Theater**, 345 Washington Street, St. Paul, 651-224-4222
- **O'Shaughnessy Auditorium**, 2004 Randolph Avenue, St. Paul, 651-690-6701
- **RiverCentre/Roy Wilkins Auditorium**, 175 Kellogg Boulevard, St. Paul, 651-265-4800
- **Target Center**, 6001st Avenue North, Minneapolis, 612-673-1300]
- **University Theatre**, Rarig Center, 330 South 21st Avenue, Minneapolis, 612-625-4001

MUSIC LESSONS

Besides lessons, the following places offer classes and open jam sessions.
- **Homestead Pickin' Parlor**, 6625 Penn Avenue South, Richfield, 612-861-3308, offers classes and individual lessons in all folk instruments.
- **MacPhail Center for the Arts**, 1128 LaSalle Street Minneapolis, 612-321-0100; music, theater and dance lessons for children and adults.
- **Minneapolis Drum and Dance Center**, 3013 Lyndale Avenue South, Minneapolis, 612-827-0771; classes in drumming and ethnic dance.
- **Rymer School of Music**, 2256 Lexington Avenue North, St. Paul, 651-488-6100; private lessons for children and adults in all orchestra instruments, as well as voice and acting.
- **West Bank School of Music**, 1813 South 6th Street Minneapolis, 612-333-6651; classes and individual lessons in a variety of musical instruments.

DANCE–PERFORMANCE GROUPS

O'Shaughnessy Auditorium in St. Paul is the venue for many Twin Cities dance performances. Some of the following groups are cross-listed below as organizations that also offer dance lessons:

- **Ballet Arts Minnesota**, 528 Hennepin Avenue, Minneapolis, 612-340-1071
- **Ballet of the Dolls**, 1620 Harmon Place, Minneapolis, 612-333-2792
- **Ethnic Dance Theater**, 2337 Central Avenue NE, Minneapolis, 612-782-3970
- **Minnesota Dance Theater**, 528 Hennepin Avenue, Minneapolis, 612-338-0627
- **Zenon Dance Company**, 528 Hennepin Avenue, Minneapolis, 612-338-1101

DANCE LESSONS

- **Arthur Murray School of Dance**, 10 South 5th Street Minneapolis, 612-333-3131; 5041 France Avenue South, Edina, 952-920-1900
- **Ballet Arts Minnesota**, 528 Hennepin Avenue, Minneapolis, 612-340-1071
- **Ballet of the Dolls**, 1620 Harmon Place, Minneapolis, 612-333-2792
- **Classical Ballet Academy of Minnesota**, 249 East 4th Street, St. Paul, 651-290-0513
- **Nancy Hauser Dance School**, 1940 Hennepin Avenue, Minneapolis, 612-871-9077, free sample classes for children and adults.
- **Tapestry Folk Dance Center**, 310 East 38th Street Minneapolis, 612-722-2914
- **Zenon Dance Company**, 528 Hennepin Avenue, Minneapolis, 612-338-1101

THEATERS

The Twin Cities have something for everyone—from Broadway musicals to avant-garde experiments, and is second only to New York in the number of theater seats per capita. Some shows—like "The Lion King" and "Romeo and Juliet, the Musical" are coming here before opening on Broadway.

- **Brave New Workshop**, 3001 Hennepin Avenue South, Calhoun Square, 612-332-6620, is the nation's oldest ongoing satiric theatre.

- **Chanhassen Dinner Theatres**, 501 West 78th Street Chanhassen, 952-934-1525, offers lavish stagings of well-known plays in a dinner theater.
- **Children's Theatre Company**, 2400 3rd Avenue South, Minneapolis, 612-874-0400, is a nationally known company that interprets classical children's plays. A must for people of all ages.
- **Great American History Theatre**, 30 East 10th Street St. Paul, 651-292-4323, stages productions relevant to American history, particularly in the Midwest.
- **Guthrie Theater**, 725 Vineland Place, Minneapolis, 612-377-2224; a Twin Cities landmark, this repertory theater stages innovative interpretations of classic and modern dramas.
- **Hennepin Center for the Arts**, 528 Hennepin Avenue, Minneapolis, 612-332-4478
- **Hey City Stage**, 824 Hennepin Avenue, Minneapolis, 612-673-0404, www.heycity.com, presents "Tony n' Tina's Wedding," participatory theatre where members of the audience are the wedding guests. If you go, it's fun to take a gift—something tacky that is beautifully wrapped will get you a lot of attention from the cast.
- **Illusion Theater**, 528 Hennepin Avenue, Minneapolis, 612-339-4944. A non-profit professional group that writes and produces new plays, with a focus on overcoming interpersonal violence.
- **In the Heart of the Beast Puppet and Mask Theater**, 1500 East Lake Street Minneapolis, 612-721-2535, stages spectacular mask-and-oversized-puppet performances, often with a political theme.
- **Jungle Theater**, 711 West Lake Street Minneapolis, 612-822-7063, is a 100-seat capacity theater that produces intense interpretations of both well-known and obscure plays.
- **Lakeshore Players**, 5820 Stewart Avenue, White Bear Lake, 651-429-5674
- **Loring Playhouse**, 1633 South Hennepin Avenue, Minneapolis, 612-332-1617, is a professional performance company that has staged new plays and dance performances with an experimental bent.
- **Mixed Blood Theatre Company**, 1500 South 4th Street, Minneapolis, 612-338-6131; innovative productions, often with multicultural and racial themes.
- **Music Box Theatre**, 14th and Nicollet, Minneapolis, 612-673-0404
- **Mystery Cafe**, is not a place, it is an interactive murder mystery theater company operating in several different locations throughout the Twin Cities. To participate, and have a chance to win prizes for the

most creative solution, check 612-566-CLUE or www.themys-terycafe.com.

- **Nautilus Music Theatre**, 308 Prince Street, St. Paul, 651-298-9913
- **Old Log Theater**, 5175 Meadville Street, Excelsior, 952-474-5951, www.oldlog.com, is the oldest continuously operating dinner theater. It stages comedies and British farces.
- **Ordway Music Theatre**, 345 Washington Street, St. Paul, 651-224-4222, is a lavish space that hosts nationally touring musicals, dance troupes and concerts.
- **Orpheum and State Theatres**, 910 and 805 Hennepin Avenue, Minneapolis, 612-339-7007; after a city-funded rehab, these two grand theaters provide an opulent setting for touring musicals and concerts.
- **Park Square Theatre**, St. Peter Street at Kellogg Boulevard, St. Paul, 651-291-7005; interpretations of popular plays.
- **Patrick's Cabaret**, 506 East 24th Street, Minneapolis, 612-724-6273; performance art, experimental theater.
- **Penumbra Theatre Company**, 270 Kent Street, St. Paul, 651-224-3180; an acclaimed professional theater company, staging established and new plays with African-American themes.
- **Plymouth Playhouse**, I-494 and Highway 55, 763-383-1073, is home of the long-running musical, "How to Talk Minnesotan."
- **Red Eye Collaboration**, 15 West 14th Street Minneapolis, 612-870-0309; alternative theater and dance, performance art, films.
- **Southern Theater**, 1420 Washington Avenue South, Minneapolis, 612-340-1725; alternative productions, dance and performance art.
- **Stages Theatre Company**, 1111 Main Street, Hopkins, 952-979-1111, www.stagestheatre.org.
- **Theatre de la Jeune Lune**, 105 North 1st Street, Minneapolis, 612-333-6200. Founded by French and American actors, this group stages ambitious performances in a rehabbed warehouse district building.
- **Theatre in the Round**, 245 Cedar Avenue, Minneapolis, 612-333-3010, www.theatreintheround.org, is a community theater that stages the classics as well as new plays.

MOVIE THEATERS

The Uptown, Lagoon, and Parkway all show new releases that are not bound for the mega-multi-plex at the mall. The U Film Society shows a combination of new movies and revivals, and hosts the Rivertown Film Festival, a yearly smorgasbord of hundreds of international films. The Oak

Street runs a revival series. The Walker Art Center and Minneapolis Institute of Arts host film screenings in conjunction with other programs. For more commercial fare, check the newspapers and the Yellow Pages for the theater of your choice. Movie listings are available online at www.startribune.com/movieguide; for *Star Tribune* reviews of recent films, call 612-673-9050.

- **American Swedish Institute**, 2600 Park Avenue, Minneapolis, 612-871-4907
- **Cinema Cafes**: Burnsville, Valley Ridge Center, 952-894-8810; New Hope, Midland Center, 763-546-2336; Woodbury, Valley Creek Mall, 651-714-5500; eat and watch a fairly recent movie—$2.50, $1.25 matinees and Tuesday evenings.
- **Hopkins Cinema 6**, 1118 Main Street, Hopkins, 612-931-7992, $2 a seat; half-price on Tuesdays.
- **Imation IMAX Theatre**, Minnesota Zoo, 952-431-4629
- **Lagoon Theater**, 1320 Lagoon Avenue South, Minneapolis, 612-825-6006
- **Minneapolis Institute of Arts**, 2400 3rd Avenue South, Minneapolis, 612-870-3131
- **Movies in the Parks**: Hyland Lake Park, Bloomington, and Baker Park Reserve, Medina, 612-559-9000
- **Oak Street Cinema**, 309 Oak Street Minneapolis, 612-331-3134
- **Omnitheater-Science Museum**, 651-221-9444
- **Parkway**, 48th Street and Chicago Avenue, Minneapolis, 612-822-3030
- **Red Eye Collaboration**, 15 West 14th Street Minneapolis, 612-870-0309, presents films by local filmmakers.
- **Riverview**, 3800 42nd Avenue South, Minneapolis, 612-729-7369, $2 tickets
- **Springbrook 4**, 141 North 85th Avenue, Coon Rapids, 763-780-3706, all shows $1
- **U Film Society**, Bell Auditorium, University of Minnesota, 17th Avenue SE and University Avenue, Minneapolis, 612-627-4430
- **Uptown Theater**, 2906 Hennepin Avenue, Minneapolis, 612-825-6006
- **Vali-hi Drive-in**, I-94 at Manning, 651-436-7464
- **Walker Art Center**, 725 Vineland Place, Minneapolis, 612-375-7622

COMEDY

Some clubs feature comics on certain nights only. Call for schedules.

- **Acme Comedy Company**, 708 North 1st Street Minneapolis, 612-338-6393

- **Bryant-Lake Bowl Show Lounge**, 810 West Lake Street Minneapolis, 612-825-8949
- **The Brave New Workshop**, 3001 Hennepin Avenue South, Calhoun Square, 612-332-6620
- **Knuckleheads Comedy Club**, Mall of America, Bloomington, 952-854-5233
- **Stevie Ray's Improv Troupe**, 4608 Columbus Avenue South, Minneapolis, 952-825-1832

CULTURE FOR KIDS

- **Children's Theatre Company**, 3rd Avenue South, Minneapolis, 612-874-0400, is the Twin Cities' premier children's theatre.
- **Circus Pizza** serves up food and fun at several Twin Cities locations. Call the party hotline, 612-754-1263, or individual stores listed in the White Pages.
- **Como Zoo**, Midway Parkway and Kaufman Drive, St. Paul, 651-487-8200; Como Zoo was established at the turn of the century on Harriet Island (on the river!) before floods forced it to relocate. It's a traditional zoo, featuring a menagerie of exotic animals. Buildings open daily, April-September, 10 a.m. to 6 p.m.; October–March, 10 a.m. to 4 p.m.
- **Film Board Hotline**, 612-333-0436, www.mnfilm.org, list auditions, workshops, talent searches.
- **General Cinemas** at Mall of America, Centennial Lakes, Shelard Park, and Har Mar Mall show kids' movies at 10 am and noon on Wednesdays during the summer. $2 includes movie, popcorn and drink.
- **Kit and Kaboodle Music and Comedy for Kids of All Ages**; a former preschool teacher and professional comedian team up for about 200 shows a year at The Mall of America, The St. Paul Civic Center, parks, school assemblies and birthday parties. Call 651-653-7738 or visit www.kitandkaboodle.com for games and their performance schedule.
- **Lake Harriet Fine Arts Camp**, 2428 Aldrich Avenue South, Minneapolis, 612-374-9508, is an integrated arts experience that includes music, dance, sculpture and storytelling.
- **MacPhail Center for the Arts**, 1128 LaSalle Street Minneapolis, 612-321-0100; music, theater and dance lessons for children and adults.
- **Minnetonka Center for the Arts**, 2240 North Shore Drive, Wayzata, 952-473-7361, offers numerous classes for kids (and adults).
- **Minnesota Children's Museum**, 10 West 7th Street, St. Paul, 651-225-6000; buttons, gizmos, interactive make-believe, a theater and

hands-on exhibits that change frequently, make every trip an adventure. Admission is $5.95; over 59 and ages 1 to 2, $3.95, call for hours.

- **Minnesota Orchestra's** series of award-winning NotesAlive!® videos bring children's stories to life with live-performance symphonic music and animation. Videos include Dr. Seuss' "My Many Colored Days," and "The Untold Story and On the Day You Were Born." The Orchestra also presents KinderKonzerts to school groups and special family concerts for the general public. Videos are available through the orchestra, 612-371-5656.
- **Minnesota Zoo**, 1300 Zoo Boulevard, Apple Valley, 952-432-9000; one of the largest zoos in the country, it houses animals brought from climate zones around the world similar to Minnesota's. As a result, it's open year 'round. It features Discovery Bay marine exhibit and hosts outdoor concerts in the summer. Visit "Walk on the Wild Side" light display evenings, from Thanksgiving through December, or sleep over with the dolphins. Call 952-431-9320 for information and available dates. Admission is $8; $5 over 65; $3 children 3 to 12. Open daily 9 a.m. to 6 p.m., Memorial Day to Labor Day and 9 a.m. to 4 p.m., Labor Day to Memorial Day.
- **The Splatter Sisters**, 651-488-8490, performs upbeat children's songs for dancing and creative movement and old favorites for listening and singing, as well as their hit songs from Radio AAHS. Catch them at parks, libraries, hospitals, the Mall of America, RiverFest and the Minnesota State Fair. Their schedule is posted on their web site, www.splattersisters.com.
- **Stages Theatre**, 1111 Main Street, Hopkins, 952-979-1111; each production is a collaboration between adult and youth actors.
- **Stepping Stone Theatre for Youth Development**, Landmark Center, 75 West 5th Street, St. Paul, 651-225-9265, offers numerous classes and performing arts camps.
- **The Teddy Bear Band** performs free-of-charge throughout the Twin Cities. Watch the local papers for announcements of their appearances.

MUSEUMS–ART

If you want to experience the art scene up close, attend gallery openings and Saturday night "gallery crawls"—a night of openings in Minneapolis' and St. Paul's warehouse districts. Call a gallery and they'll tell you where and when these fun evenings take place. The Arts and Museums Pass provides admission to ten of the Twin Cities' top museums as well as discounts in the museums' shops. Passes can be purchased at the Explore Minnesota store at the Mall of America or from the Greater Minneapolis Convention and Visitors Association, 888-767-6757, 621-661-4700.

- **Minneapolis Institute of Arts**, 2400 South 3rd Avenue, Minneapolis, 612-870-3131; the permanent collection spans over 5,000 years from the Doryphoros of ancient Rome to a Tibetan sand mandala. Traveling exhibitions from the world's great museums are also hosted every year. Admission is free except for special exhibition galleries. Open 10 a.m. to 5 p.m., Tuesday, Wednesday and Saturday; 10 a.m. to 9 p.m. Thursday; noon to 5 p.m. Sunday; closed Mondays. For exhibition and class information, check out the Institute's web site at www.artsmia.org.

- **Minnesota Museum of American Art**, Landmark Center, 5th and Market Streets, St. Paul, 651-292-4355; a museum focusing on the diverse history of American artists, it offers many adult and children's classes. Donations. Open Tuesday-Saturday 11 a.m. to 4 p.m.; Thursday 4 to 7:30 p.m.; Sunday 1 to 5 p.m.; closed Mondays and holidays. Visit www.mtn.org/mmaa.

- **Walker Art Center**, 725 Vineland Place, Minneapolis, 612-375-7577, events information line, 612-375-7622; a Twin Cities landmark, in more ways than one: the permanent collection of twentieth-century art is world-famous; and the outdoor sculpture garden's Spoonbridge and Cherry fountain has become the Twin Cities' symbol. The Walker also sponsors classes, off-site performance art shows and summer movies in nearby Loring Park. Admission is $4 for adults and $3 for young adults and seniors; children under 12 free. Admission is free to the sculpture garden. Hours are Tuesday-Sunday 10 a.m. to 5 p.m.; open Thursday until 8 p.m.; closed Mondays; Thursdays and the first Saturday of each month are free. The museum's resources are accessible online at www.walkerart.org.

- **Frederick R. Weisman Art Museum**, 333 East River Road, University of Minnesota, Minneapolis, 612-625-9494; the Frank Gehry-designed stainless steel and brick building reflects the colors of the sunset and the adjacent Mississippi gorge. Best known for its collection of American art from the first decades of the twentieth century, the museum owns works by Georgia O'Keeffe and Arthur Dove. Free admission, open Tuesday-Friday 10 a.m. to 5 p.m.; Thursday, 5 to 8 p.m.; Saturday, Sunday 11 a.m. to 5 p.m.; closed Mondays and University holidays.

MUSEUMS—OTHER

- **American Swedish Institute**, 2600 Park Avenue, Minneapolis, 612-871-4907; a massive turn-of-the-century stone house shows a permanent collection of Swedish artifacts and hosts traveling exhibits. Admission $4. Seniors and 6-12, $3; free the first Wednesday of the month. Open Tuesday-Sunday, noon to 4 p.m.; Wednesday 4 to 8p.m.; Sunday 1 to 5 p.m.; closed Mondays.
- **Bell Museum of Natural History**, 17th Avenue SE and University Avenue, University of Minnesota, Minneapolis, 612-624-7083; exhibits, classes and other activities for adults and children with a focus on natural history. Admission $3; $2 seniors and age 3-16; free Thursdays. Open Tuesday-Friday 9 a.m. to 5 p.m.; Saturday 10 a.m. to 5 p.m.; Sunday noon to 5 p.m. Closed Mondays. Fun for kids—a slumber party at the Bell. Bring your sleeping bags, explore the museum by flashlight, and fall asleep to a spooky animal bedtime story.
- **Historic Fort Snelling State Park**, Highway 5 at Highway 55, Minneapolis, 612-726-1171; the first permanent structure built here by European settlers, the fort overlooks the confluence of the Mississippi and Minnesota Rivers. Costumed guides present demonstrations, give tours, and talk to you like it's still 1827. Admission $4 for two-day state park permit. Open daily, 8 a.m. to 10 p.m.
- **Minneapolis Planetarium**, Minneapolis Public Library, 300 Nicollet Mall, Minneapolis, 612-630-6150; the Planetarium re-creates the night sky each day, and gives a series of special lectures and presentations. Admission $4; $2.50 under 13. Call for show times. Special shows at Christmas.
- **Minnesota History Center**, 345 West Kellogg Boulevard, St. Paul, 651-296-6126; the Center's archive holds correspondence and records of historical figures, photographs, and maps of properties, among other material. A genealogy research center, three exhibit galleries and an excellent cafe are also to be found here. The History Center administers several historic buildings in the city, such as the James J. Hill mansion. Donations. Open Tuesday-Saturday 10 a.m. to 5 p.m.; Sunday noon to 5 p.m.; closed state holidays.
- **Science Museum of Minnesota and Omnitheater**, 120 West Kellogg, St. Paul, 651-221-9444, www.smm.org; brand new for the millennium, the Science Museum is a multi-level extravaganza of hands-on exhibits, creative demonstrations, 3D multimedia laser-theater, and 180-degree screen Omnitheater that shows science-related

films. Admission to either the museum or the Omnitheater is $7 for adults; $5 for ages 3-12 and seniors. A super admission pass allowing entrance to everything is $12.50 for adults, $9.50 for children and seniors. Open Tuesdays and Wednesday, 9:30 a.m. to 5 p.m.; Thursday-Saturday, 9:30 a.m. to 9 p.m.; Sunday 10 a.m. to 7 p.m.; mid-December through Labor Day, Monday 9:30 a.m. to 5 p.m. Make reservations for Omnitheater shows. Parking is conveniently located at a ramp next door.

B OB HOPE ONCE SAID, "IF YOU WATCH A GAME, IT'S FUN. IF YOU play it, it's recreation. If you work at it, it's golf." You'll have plenty of occasion for all three here, and many more besides. To the hale and hearty, this climate is not an impediment, but an opportunity to try out a whole new list of games. Ice boating, anyone?

Many sporting events take place at the **Hubert H. Humphrey Metrodome**, 900 South 5th Street, Minneapolis, 612-335-3370, www. stadia.com/metrodome. A calendar of Twin Cities sporting events is posted online at www.twincitiessports.com, or pick up a free copy of *Twin Cities Sports* at your local grocery or sporting goods store. Tickets for many games and events can be purchased through **Ticketmaster**, 612-989-5151, www.ticketmaster.com.

PROFESSIONAL SPORTS

Sports fans in Minnesota teeter between ecstasy and frustration. They remember with pride the performances of hometown heroes like Kirby Puckett when the Twins won the World Series in 1987 and 1991. But, fame is fleeting and recent lackluster seasons as well as the Twins' constant threats to move have caused baseball fans to exchange their "Homer Hankies" for pigs' snouts and head over to St. Paul for Saints games and cheaper beer. Basketball is one sport where the picture is getting brighter. The NBA's Timberwolves are packing in the crowds and Minnesota is home to the WNBA's Minnesota Lynx. Football take heart, Purple Pride is strong here after the Vikings almost made it to the 1999 Super Bowl. The big football rivalry is with Green Bay, whose fans wear "cheese heads." In comparison, the Minnesota fans' Viking horns and milkmaid braids don't look bad.

BASEBALL

The American League's **Minnesota Twins** play 80 or so games a year in the Hubert H. Humphrey Metrodome in Minneapolis. For tickets, call 612-33-TWINS. For game statistics, schedules and player information visit the Twins' Web site at www.majorleaguebaseball.com/u/baseball.

The **St. Paul Saints** play in the Northern League (A). Dozens of home games are played at the tiny Municipal Stadium in St. Paul's Midway. Off-diamond sideshows include grandstand massages, haircuts, a pig mascot that carries out the ball, lots of giveaways and affordable food and drink. Call 651-644-6659 for ticket information or you can buy tickets online at www.home.digitalcity.com/twincities/saints. Tickets are priced $3-$7.

BASKETBALL

The WNBA's **Minnesota Lynx** arrived in the Twin Cities in 1999, and play at the Target Center in Minneapolis. Tickets are available at the Target Center Box Office or Ticketmaster (see above). For team updates visit www.home.digitalcity.com/twincities/sports.

The NBA's **Minnesota Timberwolves** also play at the Target Center. For game tickets, call Ticketmaster (see above). For Timberwolves statistics check www.nba.com/timberwolves.

FOOTBALL

The **Minnesota Vikings** are perennial contenders in the National Football League. They play eight home season games at the Humphrey Metrodome, as well as pre-season games. The NFL schedule comes out in May. In July, when single-game tickets go on sale, die-hards camp out in front of the Vikings ticket office at the Metrodome to be first in line. For season tickets, call 612-33-VIKES. For team information access www.nfl.com/vikings.

HOCKEY

Professional NHL hockey is back with the **Minnesota Wild** at their new state-of-the-art arena in downtown St. Paul! Check www.wild.com for details or call 651-222-WILD.

SOCCER

The fast action and grace of soccer can be enjoyed by watching the **Minnesota Thunder** at the National Sports Center in the northern suburb of Blaine. Call 651-785-3668 for tickets or check out www.home.digitalcity.com/twincities/sports.

COLLEGE SPORTS

College sports generate a lot of enthusiasm. For an inexpensive and fun night out with the family, call the college nearest you for season and schedule information (see the **Higher Education** chapter for telephone numbers). The biggest college draw here is, of course, the University of Minnesota, which plays in the Big Ten Conference. Call 612-GOPHERS for schedules and tickets to any U of M event.

- **Baseball**—the University of Minnesota Golden Gophers men's baseball team plays at Siebert Field. The women's softball team plays at Bierman Field.
- **Basketball**—has quite a following here, especially the women's team. University of Minnesota's Golden Gopher men play at Williams Arena, and the women play at the Sports Pavilion.
- **Football**—University of Minnesota Big Ten Conference rivalries are heated, and the games uproarious. Home games are held at the Metrodome, so you don't have to worry about hypothermia. The football Gophers can be checked out at www.home.digitalcity.com/twincities/sports.
- **Hockey**—the popular U of M Golden Gophers have been a power in their conference. They play at Mariucci Arena.

The U of M conducts several "sports schools" for young athletes during the summer that teach tennis, golf, diving, sailing and more. Children can also enroll in "Gopher Adventures" day camps. For information call the U of M Youth and Community Programs, 612-625-2242 or look online at www.recsports.umn.edu/youth.

PARTICIPANT TEAM AND INDIVIDUAL SPORTS

BICYCLING

The Twin Cities are blessed with an abundance of bicycle routes (on-street bike lanes), paved off-road trails, and parkways. You can make your first 100-mile "century" ride without ever leaving the Twin Cities' trail system or riding twice over the same stretch. Bike commuting has tripled since 1970, and it's not unusual to see bikers wheeling to and from work dressed in suits, with important papers stowed in backpacks—even in the winter! Minneapolis accommodates bike commuters as much as possible. Several off-street bike routes are either built or under construction, many of them are located on abandoned railroad beds. The city is also collaborating with other metro-area municipalities to link existing trails and lanes in a wide web going from the western suburbs all the way to Stillwater. Pick up a Minneapolis Parks and Recreation trail map at the Park office in the Grain Exchange building at 4th Street and 4th Avenue South. An excellent map published by the University of Minnesota Extension Service, "Bicycle Guide and Commuter Map" is available at area bike shops or from the Commuter Connection, located on the Pillsbury Center skyway level. *Fred's Best Guide to Twin Cities Bicycling* contains maps and information covering 700 miles of routes sells for $15.95 at bike shops and bookstores. Online, check www.startribune.com/biking, for local biking news and events. In and around the Twin Cities, try these popular and scenic routes:

- Trails are on both sides of the **Mississippi River**: from downtown to the south city limits, into St. Paul and continuing south to the Crosby Farm Nature Area, and on the west side of the river through the downtown riverfront to Plymouth Avenue North.
- Around the **Minneapolis chain of lakes** (Harriet, Calhoun, Lake of the Isles, Cedar) on any one or all of the four circular loops. Pedestrian paths and bike trails are separate.
- **Theodore Wirth Park**
- **West River Parkway to Minnehaha Park**
- **Southwest Regional LRT Trail** from Hopkins west to Victoria or Hopkins southwest to Chanhassen—call 612-559-9000 for more information.
- **Como Park** in St. Paul
- **Summit Avenue**, from the Mississippi River to the St. Paul Cathedral, there is a separate bike lane for about five miles.
- **The Gateway Trail** begins just south of Wheelock Parkway and east of I-35E in St. Paul, and extends 18 miles to Pine Point Park in Stillwater.

Wheelchair accessible, this trail connects with parks, swimming areas, and biking, hiking, cross-country skiing, and horseback riding trails. **Out of town** try:

- **Cannon Valley Trail** near Red Wing. Bike or skate alongside the Cannon River on one of Minnesota's most popular rails-to-trails pathways. In May the wetlands are filled with bright yellow marsh marigolds. In the summer, you might see bluebirds.
- **Gandy Dancer Trail** is a paved surface from St. Croix Falls to Danbury in Wisconsin. It's shady and there are many parks along the route, 800-222-7655.
- **Root River Trail** from Fountain to Houston in southeastern Minnesota is a 40-mile paved trail that features great views of the limestone bluffs of the Red River Valley. There are inns and antique shops along the way and a trail shuttle runs seasonally, 800-428-2030.

For more maps to more routes (there are many more) call the following numbers:

- **Minneapolis Department of Public Works**, 612-673-2352
- **Minneapolis Parks and Recreation Board**, 612-661-4800, www.byways.org/grandrounds
- **St. Paul Division of Parks and Recreation**, 651-266-6400, www.stpaul.gov
- **Hennepin County Parks**, 612-559-9000 or www.hennepinparks.org
- **Ramsey County Parks**, 651-748-2500 or www.co.ramsey.mn.us/parks
- **Washington County Park Division**, 651-430-8368
- **Minnesota Department of Natural Resources**, 651-296-6157, 888-646-6267, www.dnr.state.mn.us, click on "Trails" for information about the 11 state trails the DNR manages.
- **Minnesota Office of Tourism**, 651-296-5029, 800-657-3700, www.exploreminnesota.com, offers an excellent guide called *Biking Minnesota which* lists trails and mountain-biking locations as well as lodging and trail pass requirements.
- The **Alternative Bike Shop**, 2408 Hennepin Avenue South, Minneapolis, 612-374-3635, rents tandem bicycles.

BOATING

It's not called the Land of Ten Thousand Lakes for nothing. There are hundreds of lakes within the metro area alone, and most of them are host to boats of some kind. Many of these lakes are connected by rivers, marshes and estuaries, all of which offer splendid paddling and fishing. If you've got a craft, you'll need a license and some suggestions on where to put in. A boat license is good for two years, and the cost depends on the type of boat. For a license application, call the Department of Natural Resources, 651-296-6157, www.dnr.state.mn.us.

Lake Minnetonka, the St. Croix River, and the Mighty Mississippi are the most popular boating waters. They all have many public launch sites. Prior Lake, south of the Twin Cities, is loved by water-skiers for its calm waters.

If you're looking for a loaner, call one of the following boat rental services. Most of the popular lakes Up North offer plenty of rentals on location.

- **Como Lakeside**, 1360 North Lexington Parkway, St. Paul, 651-488-4927, offers canoes and paddleboats.
- **Minneapolis Parks**: the park system rents canoes and paddleboats at many of the metro area lakes. Call 612-661-4800 for rental information on Minneapolis lakes.
- **Midwest Mountaineering**, 309 Cedar Avenue South, Minneapolis, 612-339-3433, offers canoes, kayaks.
- **Minnetonka Boat Rentals**, Mound, 952-472-1220, rents pontoons and fishing boats.
- **Midwest Boat Club, Inc.** advertises "boating without owning," 952-473-0965.

Be advised that operating a motorboat while under the influence of alcohol, a controlled substance or illegal substance is unlawful in Minnesota. Penalties include fines, jail sentences, loss of motorboat operating privileges, and may result in loss of motor vehicle operating privileges also. For additional canoeing possibilities see the Boundary Waters National Canoe Area in the **Quick Getaways** chapter.

BOWLING

You betcha! Bowling is making a comeback. It's a sport of concentration, but it's also a casual night out. The Bryant Lake bowl even offers a wine and espresso bar and a performance space!

- **Bryant Lake Bowl**, 810 West Lake Street, Minneapolis, 612-825-3737
- **Elsie's Bowling Center**, 729 NE Marshall Street, 612-378-9701, has black light bowling at 9 o'clock every night.
- **Maplewood Bowl**, 1955 English Street, Maplewood, 651-774-8787
- **Midway Pro Bowl**, 1556 University Avenue, St. Paul, 651-646-1396
- **West Side Lanes**, 1625 South Robert Street, West St. Paul, 651-451-6222

BRIDGE

The **Bridge Center of the Twin Cities**, 6020 Nicollet Avenue, 612-861-4487, teaches lessons and sponsors duplicate tournaments.

CASINOS

Indian gaming is one of Minnesota's biggest industries, and most casinos remain open all night. You have to be 18 to gamble, though most establishments have some kind of facility for children, such as an arcade. For more information on casinos in Minnesota check www.midwestcasinoguide.com/minnesota.

- **Black Bear Casino**, 601 Highway 210, Carlton, 888-771-0777
- **Grand Casino**, Mille Lacs, 800-626-LUCK
- **Grand Casino**, Hinckley, 800-GRAND-21
- **Grand Portage Lodge and Casino**, Box 307, Grand Portage, 800-543-1384
- **Jackpot Junction**, Morton, 800-538-8379
- **Little Six**, 2354 Northwesr Sioux Trail, Prior Lake 952-445-8982
- **Mystic Lake Casino**, Prior Lake, 800-262-7799
- **Treasure Island Casino**, Highway. 61 and 316, Red Wing, 800-222-7077

CHESS

- **Castle Chess Club**, 1381 Marshall Avenue, St. Paul, 651-459-2371, dwvoje@msn.com, meets Monday, Wednesday and Thursday nights and Saturday mornings and afternoons. There is a monthly membership or fee per tournament.
- **North Suburban Chess Club** meets 6 p.m. Wednesdays at the Har Mar Mall Barnes and Noble Bookstore, Roseville; free.
- **West Suburban Chess Club** meets at 6:30 p.m., Mondays, at Borders Books, 1501 South Plymouth Road, Minnetonka, 952-937-0444; free.
- **South Suburban Chess Club**, 952-890-2644, holds monthly tournaments at Thunderbird Hotel, Bloomington
  The Minnesota State Chess Association web site is www.rocsegg.com/mnchess. Tournament information is available on the Chess Information Line at 612-890-3708.

CURLING

If you've always wanted to bowl outdoors in the winter, the closest you'll come to fulfilling your dream is this old-fashioned game that uses "curling stones" and is played on polished ice. Contact the **St. Paul Curling Club**, 470 Selby Avenue, St. Paul, 651-224-7408.

DANCE

Dancing is in again! Twin Cities dance clubs offer lessons, host dances, participate in competitions and perform at festivals and fairs. For Square Dance lessons in the Minneapolis-St. Paul area, call the Square Dance Hotline, 612-557-5113. Your call will be returned, referring you to lessons in your area. For regular ballroom dancing, check the Yellow Pages under "Dance Instruction." Local dance clubs include:

- **Dakota Grand Squares**, South St. Paul; square dance lessons are given at the Heritage Middle School, 181 West Butler Avenue in West St. Paul. Call 651-454-2942 or visit www.spacestar.com/users/acj/wss. All square dancers and round dancers are welcome.
- **The Westonka Whirlers** square dance at Grandview Middle School in Mound, 1/2 mile north of Co. Rd. 15 on Co. Rd. 110. Call 952-550-9770 or visit www.home.att.net/~westonka_whirlers for information and their demonstration schedule.

DOGS

Community services and recreation departments often offer doggie-obedience classes. Before registering, try to talk to someone who has gone through the course. Ask how handlers and their canines are treated as well as how many dogs there are in a class. For beginners through experts, for those who want to compete, or who want to participate in activities like flyball, agility or tracking, the training clubs listed below will help you train your dog:

- **Animal Inn**, 845 North Meadow Lane, Golden Valley, 763-529-6585; 1252 Town Centre Drive, Eagan, 651-454-3458; Highway 5, 1 mile east of 694, Lake Elmo, 651-777-2317
- **Bloomington Obedience Training Club**, 8127 Pleasant Avenue South, 952-888-4998
- **Training Camp Inc.**, Heavenwood Farm, Stillwater, 612-922-1114; herding classes
- **Twin Cities Obedience Training Club**, 2101 NE Broadway Street, Minneapolis, 612-379-1332

For those who are looking for a purebred dog, area dog shows are good places to check out the different breeds and connect with breeders. Watch for notice of these shows in the newspaper:

- **Land O'Lakes Kennel Club**, January, River Centre, 143 West 4th Street, St. Paul
- **Lake Minnetonka Kennel Club**, June at the Waconia Fairgrounds
- **Minneapolis Kennel Club**, November, Minneapolis Convention Center
- **St. Croix Valley Kennel Club**, August at the Washington County Fairgrounds

It's hard to find a place to exercise your dog off-leash, but there is one area at Battle Creek Regional Park in Maplewood. Call the Ramsey County Parks for rules and other information, 651-748-2500 or visit www.co.ramsey.mn.us/parks. The Hennepin County parks' **off-leash exercise areas** can be found at Crow-Hassan Park Reserve, Rogers; Elm Creek Park Reserve, northwest of Osseo; and Lake Sarah, near Rockford. To buy the $25 special use permit call 612-559-9000.

FISHING

You are now in fishing country and the fishing license is just about as prevalent as the Minnesota drivers' license. Really! Everything stops for the fishing season opener in the spring. The Department of Natural Resources (DNR) stocks lakes in the metro area as well as those Up North. Don't forget ice fishing, either. For information about a fishing license, call the DNR at 651-296-6157, check www.dnr.state.mn.us, or purchase one at a bait shop or sporting goods store. Regulations are Byzantine in their complexity. The DNR publishes a free brochure on catch rules as well as information about the best lakes. Noted metro-area lakes are often surrounded by homes, but crowded with walleye and bass. Hang your hook in Lake Minnetonka, Lake Elmo, Lake Waconia or Forest Lake and you might come home with a record-winner. For those who want to travel, Lake Mille Lacs has northerns as well as exciting walleye action around its shallow rocks, and Leech Lake is home to big walleye and muskie. Lake of the Woods bills itself as the "Walleye Capital of the World." Call 800-382-FISH or visit www.lakeofthewoodsmn.com for resort information. Plastic-coated maps that show the good fishing spots on each lake are sold at bait and sporting goods stores. For a list of maps and ordering information, send a stamped, self-addressed envelope to: Lakemaps, 3965 Minnehaha Avenue South, Minneapolis, MN 55406.

GOLF

Having just moved, you may not be quite ready to join a country club, but don't worry, many public courses here are as good as the clubs. The **Minnesota Golf Association** can give you lots of information, 612-927-4643 or www.mn.golf.org. New to the Twin Cities is the Tournament Players Club (TPC) of the Twin Cities, a private course off 35W in Blaine/Circle Pines. Owned and built by the Professional Golfers Association, the TPC, which opened in the spring of 2000, is used once a year for the Coldwell Banker Burnet Classic Tournament, and will be available to members the other 51 weeks of the year. For information call 763-795-8508. For reviews of approximately 35 golf courses, visit www.mnsportspage.com. To reserve tee times at most courses, call **Teemaster** at 612-525-7800 or make your reservations online at www.teemaster.com. Here are some public courses Twin Cities golfers say rank with the best:

- **Baker National**, 2935 Parkview Drive, Medina, 763-473-0800, owned by Hennepin County Parks; holes: 18, par: 72, yardage: red 5395, white 6271, blue 6752; description: scenic, water, lots of pines.
- **Braemer Golf Course**, 6364 John Harris Drive, Edina, 952-826-6799; holes: 27/9/9, par; 36-35-36/29/27, yardage: red 5730, white 6386, blue 6739; description: national tournaments played here; rolling, good for sledding in winter.
- **Bunker Hills**, Highway 242 & Foley Boulevard, Coon Rapids, 763-755-4141; holes: 27/9, par: 36-36-36/32, yardage: north/east red 5618, white 6428 blue 6799; description: a lot of sand and huge greens.
- **Chaska Town Course**, 3000 Town Course Drive, Chaska 952-443-3748; holes: 18, par: 72, yardage: red 4853, white 6038, green 6382, black 6817; description: bentgrass throughout, rolling hills, water on eight holes, beautiful prairie land with flowers all over course.
- **Edinburgh USA**, 8700 Edinbrook Crossing, Brooklyn Park 763-493-8098; holes: 18, par: 72, yardage: red 5255, yellow 5799, white 6335, blue 6701; description: bentgrass fairways, silica sand-traps, rolling countryside; 40,000 square foot green; designed by Robert Trent Jones II.
- **Lakeview**, 405 North Arm Drive, Orono, 952-472-3459; holes: 18, par: 70, yardage: red 4894, white 5236, blue 5468; description: no sand; harsh undulating greens, rolling hills.
- **Meadowbrook**, 201 Meadowbrook Road, Hopkins, 952-929-2077; holes: 18, par: 72, yardage: red 4811, gold 5593, white 6156, blue 6457; description: 11 holes with water, 12 ponds, back nine hilly.
- **Keller Golf Club**, 2166 Maplewood Drive, St. Paul, 651-484-3011;

holes: 18, par: 72, yardage: red 5373, white 6041, blue 6566; description: rolling, tree-lined, old-style course.

- **Prestwick**, 9555 Wedgewood Drive, Woodbury, 651-731-4779; holes: 18, par: 72, yardage: red 5252, gold 5694, white 6354, blue 6732; description: rolling tree-lined fairways, good-sized greens.
- **Rush Creek**, 7801 Troy Lane, Maple Grove, 763-494-8844; holes: 18, par: 72, yardage: green 5317, silver 6223, blue 6640, gold 7020; description: 12 holes with water, mature trees, marshland, rolling.
- **Stonebrooke**, 2693 County Road 79 South, Shakopee 952-496-3171; holes: 18, par: 71, yardage: red 5033, white 6069, blue 6611; description: many elevation changes, trees and prairie, water on 13 holes, sand-traps.
- **The Wilds**, 3151 Wilds Ridge Prior Lake 952-445-4455; holes: 18, par: 72, yardage: orange 5095, green 6276, purple 6538, Weiskopf 7025; description: rolling, mature oaks, designed by Tom Weiskopf.

HIKING

The amount of green you see on the Minnesota State map speaks for itself—a good part of the northern third of the state is either state or national forest. There are dozens of state parks nearby and four national parks within a day's drive. For information on some interesting hikes call one of the hiking clubs. For additional hiking opportunities see the **Quick Getaways** and **Lakes and Parkways** chapters. Many hiking trails are also available for cross-country skiing.

- **Afton State Park**, Hastings, 651-436-5391; hike the rolling bluffs along the St. Croix River.
- **Carver Park Reserve**, west of Chanhassen off Highway 5, 952-559-9000, has 12.2 miles of turf hiking trails and another 8.5 miles of paved trails.
- **Fort Snelling State Park**, Highways 5 & 55, St. Paul, 612-725-2390, is a historic site with trails that connect to the metro parkways.
- **Hyland Lake Park Reserve**, Highway 28, Bloomington, 952-941-4362, offers pleasant meadow trails.
- **North Hennepin Trail Corridor**, 763-424-5511; paved trails connecting two park reserves, Coon Rapids dam and the Elm Creek Park Reserve. Hiking clubs include:
- **Minneapolis Hiking Club**, 612-661-4800
- **St. Paul Hiking Club**, 651-644-7502
- **Thursday Night Hikes**, 651-454-0340

HORSEBACK RIDING

Hennepin County used to have the most horses per capita of any county in the US. Now, if you want to keep horses, you really need to move farther out. Washington County toward Stillwater, and Medina/Maple Plain/Delano, and Lakeville still have room, and zoning friendly to horses. Baker Park in Medina, 763-476-4666, has just over nine miles of trails to ride, and Lake Elmo Park has an equestrian center with about 20 miles of trails. Call Hennepin Parks, 612-559-9000 or check www.hennepinparks.org for information about other horse trails in the Hennepin Park system. The **Minnesota Trail Riders Association** can also help you find places and horses to ride, 320-963-3087, www.kkreate.com/mtra. Canterbury Park in Shakopee runs thoroughbred and quarterhorse races during the summer months, 952-445-7223.

For boarding, lessons, training, showing and sales try:

- **Alpine Farms**, 2182 Homestead Trail, Long Lake, 763-473-1361
- **Centre Pointe**, 5756 Ehler Avenue South, Delano, 763-972-6397
- **Twin City Polo Club**, 6755 Turner Road, Maple Plain, 763-479-4307
- **Volz Stables**, 11755 Partridge Road, Stillwater, 651-430-1763
- **Woodbear Stables**, 9630 Eden Prairie Road, Eden Prairie, 952-934-4176
  For livery stables:
- **Brass Ring Stables**, 9105 Norris Lake Road, Elk River, 763-441-7987; trail rides
- **Bunker Park Stables**, Coon Rapids, 763-757-9445
  Horse shows and events:
- **Animal Humane Society Hunter and Jumper Show**, June, at Alpine Farms (see above).
- **Polo Classic**, August, West End Farm, Maple Plain; benefit for the Children's Home Society of Minnesota. Call 651-646-7847, ext. 118.
- **Tanbark Cavalcade of Roses**, for Saddlebreds, held at the Minnesota State Fairgrounds Coliseum, St. Paul, in June; benefit for We Can Ride. Call 952-492-6673 for information or visit www.state-fair.gen.mn.us.

ICE SKATING/HOCKEY/BROOMBALL

If you enjoy gliding across a smooth lake surface under the stars, you've come to the right neck of the woods. Nearly every lake in the Twin Cities `a rink and warming house in the winter, and they're lighted at night. If you're not a skater (yet), just watching a slow circle of skaters can be meditative. Hockey and broomball leagues play and practice on separate rinks. For locations and information about the numerous rinks in the state, visit Where's the Rink, www.geocities.com/~miama. For beginning ice-skating instruction, the park boards are good resources: **Minneapolis Parks and Recreation Board**, 612-661-4800; **St. Paul Division of Parks and Recreation**, 651-266-6400. The following ice arenas are inside and most of them are open nearly year 'round. Many of them participate in the United States Figure Skating Association's "Learn How to Skate" program, and offer open skating:

- **Aldrich Arena**, 18850 White Bear Avenue, Maplewood, 651-748-2511 or 651-777-5317
- **Augsburg College Arena**, 2323 Riverside Avenue, Minneapolis, 612-330-1251
- **Bloomington Ice Garden**, 3606 West 98th Street, Bloomington, 952-948-8842
- **Braemer Arena**, 7501 Highway 169, Edina, 952-941-1322
- **Breck School Ice Arena**, 5800 Wayzata Boulevard, Minneapolis, 763-545-1614
- **Burnsville Ice Center**, 251 Civic Center Parkway, Burnsville, 952-895-4651
- **Chaska Ice Arena**, 1661 Park Ridge Drive, 952-448-5446
- **Cottage Grove**, 8020 80th Street South, Cottage Grove, 651-458-2846
- **Eden Prairie Ice Arena**, 16700 Valley View Road, Eden Prairie, 952-949-8470
- **Highland Arena**, 800 Snelling Avenue South, St. Paul, 651-695-3766
- **Maple Grove Community Center**, 12591 Weaver Lake Road, Maple Grove, 763-494-6500
- **Minnetonka Ice Arena**, 3401 Williston Road, Minnetonka, 952-939-8310
- **Plymouth Ice Arena**, 3650 Plymouth Boulevard, Plymouth, 952-509-5250
- **Parade Ice Garden**, 600 Kenwood Parkway, Minneapolis, 612-370-4846
- **Richfield Ice Arena**, 636 East 66th Street, Richfield, 612-861-9351
- **Schwan's Super Rink**, 1850 105th Avenue NE, Blaine, 763-785-3687
- **White Bear Lake Sports Center**, 1328 Highway 96, WhiteBear Lake, 651-429-8571

Boys and men have been playing ice hockey forever in Minnesota. In fact the United States Hockey Hall of Fame is located in Eveleth. But girls' ice hockey has just recently taken off as a high school sport. To learn more, visit www.lifetimehockey.com. Then there's broomball, which is like hockey, but played with a broom instead of a stick. Check it out or, if you're brave, go ahead and join one of the many co-ed, post-college teams. For information about either sport, check with your park and recreation department or your local school district's Community Services. To sign up for broomball, you might also ask at your favorite bar, or call **Lord Fletcher's** in Spring Park on Lake Minnetonka, where many of the broomball leagues play, 952-471-8513.

IN-LINE SKATING

It is fitting that here in the home of Rollerblade®, one of the most popular warm-weather activities is to strap on in-line skates and cruise the marvelous greenbelt path system. Heavily used lake routes, such as along Lake Calhoun and Lake of the Isles, have separate paths for people on and off wheels, so in-line skaters can mix it up with bikers. The Summit Avenue bike lane and Mississippi River parkways are popular in-line routes as well. In the winter, the hallways of the Metrodome are regularly opened to in-line skaters. It's spacious, and it's the home of the Vikings; what more could you ask for? Or try the **Roller Garden**, 5622 West Lake Street, St. Louis Park, 952-929-5518; lessons are available. The session cost includes roller skate rental, but in-line skates are $3 extra.

PLAYGROUNDS

Here are two playgrounds guaranteed to wear out the kids, and are fun for parents, too:
- **Chutes and Ladders**, Hyland Park Reserve, Bloomington, has climbing options and slides suitable for almost any skill level, 952-941-4362.
- **Lake Minnetonka Regional Park**, Minnetrista, 612-559-9000 or 952-474-4822

RACQUET SPORTS

The courts listed here are either public courts or private institutions that offer daily rates for non-members. Keep in mind that many health clubs contain racquetball and indoor tennis courts; see listings below under **Health Clubs**. All of the following are indoor courts except for the Nakoda Club, which is worth mentioning because of its high quality clay courts (usable from April through October). Other outdoor courts can be found at parks and schoolyards throughout town. Don't overlook the school district community services catalogues as sources for lessons, leagues and partners.

- **Daytona Club**, 14740 North Lawndale Lane, Dayton, 763-427-6110
- **Minikahda Club**, 3520 Xenith Avenue South, Minneapolis, 612-924-1663
- **Nicollet Tennis Center**, 4005 Nicollet Avenue, Minneapolis, 612-825-6844

ROCK CLIMBING

The granite bluffs of the Upper Midwest offer some worthy challenges to climbers. The best rock climbs nearby are the quartzite bluffs at Devil's Lake State Park near Baraboo, Wisconsin, about a four-hour drive southeast. It's a beautiful hiking area, too. Climbers also like the sheer basalt walls on the banks of the St. Croix River at Interstate State Park in Taylors Falls. To practice on indoor walls, visit the following places:

- **Footprints Adventure**, 9208 James Avenue South, Bloomington, 952-884-7996; lessons available.
- **Midwest Mountaineering**, 309 Cedar Avenue South, Minneapolis, 612-339-3433
- **REI Recreational Equipment**, 750 West 79th Street, Bloomington, 952-884-4315
- **Vertical Endeavors**, 844 Arcade State, St. Paul, 651-776-1430

RUNNING/WALKING

Even in the glacial cold of January you see hardy Minnesotans jogging along the streets and parkways. The parkway system around the lakes is popular with runners, as is the system of paths on both sides of the Mississippi, from Fort Snelling to the U of M. For route suggestions, race information and running mates, call the following numbers. Also listed is an annual event that (briefly) transforms distance running here into a spectator sport, the Twin Cities Marathon. For more local clubs visit www.twincitiessports.com.

- **All-American Trail Running Association**, www.trailrunner.com gives the run down on trails and clubs all over the country
- **American Lung Association Running Club**, 612-476-8720
- **Minneapolis/St. Paul Skywalkers Club**, 651-268-1494, coordinates walking year round.

- **Minnesota Distance Running Association**, 952-927-0983; Race Hotline: 952-925-4749
- **Northwest Athletic Clubs Club Run**, 612-673-1282
- **Team Run N Fun**, 651-290-2747; informal running group, meets twice a month
- **Twin Cities Marathon**: this 26-mile road race winds around the city lakes of Minneapolis and along the Mississippi River to the finish line at the state capitol. Held in crisp October, it is billed as one of the most beautiful marathons in America and attracts thousands of runners and cheering spectators who line every foot of the way. Call 612-673-0778. If you want to run in this race, enter early and train hard—the entries fill fast, and just so you know, there's a punishing uphill late in the race.

SAILING/WINDSURFING/ICE BOATING

Minnesota waters are known to boaters across the country. Lake Minnetonka and White Bear Lake in the Twin Cities suburbs and Lake Calhoun in the shadows of Minneapolis' skyscrapers are home to nationally competitive yacht clubs and experienced sailing schools. Lake Superior is one of the finest sailing grounds in the world. Online, tack over to www.ussailing.com for answers to all your questions including programs for sailors with special needs. Locally, contact:

- **Blue Waters Sailing School**, 2337 Medicine Lake Drive West, Plymouth, 612-559-5649, BluWtrSS2@aol.com.
- **The Calhoun Yacht Club and Sailing School** races an x-boat fleet, Cs, M16s, Optimists, and Lasers on Lake Calhoun in Minneapolis and has camps and classes for kids 6-16. Call the sailing school at 612-912-2994 or pick up a brochure at Lake Calhoun. For club information call 612-944- 2213, www.lakecalhoun.org.
- **Minneapolis Parks and Recreation Board**, 612-661-4875, offers beginner-level evening lessons for adults at Lake Calhoun.
- **Minnetonka Power Squadron**, 612-253-2628, www.sb.usps.org/minn, provides public boating safety instruction.
- **Minnetonka Yacht Club and Sailing School**, 19800 Minnetonka Boulevard, Deephaven, 952-474-4457 or 952-404-1645, www.mtka-yc.com, races several classes of shows as well as Yinglings and J-22s. Its web page will link you to a number of other sailing sites including *Northern Breezes* magazine, the free local sailing news mag., 763-542-9707.

- **Sailboats, Inc.**, Lake City, MN, and Bayfield and Barker's Island, WI, 800-826-7010 or www.sailboats-inc.com offers instruction and charters on Lake Pepin and Lake Superior.
- **St. Paul Sail and Power Squadron**, 2014 Mesabi Avenue, Mound, 612-472-9300
- **Upper Minnetonka Yacht Club**, 4165 Soreline Drive, Spring Park, 952-479-6325
- **Wayzata Yacht Club and Sailing School**, 1100 East County Road 16, Wayzata, 952-473-0352, www.wyc.org, races keelboats and joins with the Minnetonka Yacht Club to conduct a sailing school for children and adults.
- **Women in the Wind**, P.O. Box 754, Long Lake, MN 55356, 952-476-6821

Ice boating and windsurfing are not as organized as sailing, but there are some races and there are plenty of guys out there experimenting with their "sleds," particularly on Lake Minnetonka, Lake Calhoun and Lake Waconia. Those interested should contact the Upper Minnetonka Yacht Club (see above) or the Lake Minnetonka Yacht Club (see above). For windsurfing, these places can outfit you with equipment and arrange for lessons:

- **Bavarian Surf**, 5 West 15th Street, Minneapolis, 612-728-9833
- **The House**, located at the junction of 35E and I-694 at 300 South Owasso Boulevard, St. Paul, 651-482-9995
- **Scuba Center Windsurfing**, 5015 Penn Avenue South, Minneapolis, 612-925-4818

SCUBA DIVING

Diving is a year 'round sport in Minnesota—no kidding. They just cut holes in the three-foot-thick ice. Good dives are found at Square Lake County Park in Washington County and in Lake Superior. There is also diving in the Crosby-Ironton mines "Up North." The following places can get you certified and equipped, but also check with your school district's Community Services.

- **Scuba Dive and Travel**, 4741 Chicago Avenue South, Minneapolis, 612-823-7210
- **Scuba Daddy's Dive Shop**, 14844 Granada Avenue, Apple Valley, 952-432-7070

SKIING—CROSS-COUNTRY

Once it snows, cross-country ski tracks seem to magically appear on all the lakes, parks and golf courses. You can follow them or, if you want to get out into the woods and forge your own twin tracks, try just about any of the State Parks listed in the **Lakes and Parkways** chapter. The Great Minnesota Ski pass, available from the Department of Natural Resources, 651-296-6157, will allow you to ski on nearly 200 trails in the state. An annual pass for an adult, 16 years or older, is $10 plus a $1 issuing fee. The DNR also sells $3 daily and $25 three-year passes. Many county parks also groom trails for skiing. Try Baker Park Reserve, 763-476-4666, its amenities include an unobstructed sliding hill and a cozy chalet. County ski licenses cost $5 plus a park pass. Maps of groomed ski trails throughout the state, as well as information about lodging, are available from the Minnesota Office of Tourism, 800-657-3700, 651-296-5029, www.exploreminnesota.com.

For an invigorating winter getaway, rent a cabin on the North Shore (the arrowhead-shaped part of the state north of Duluth), and tour the area's granite bluffs and woods by cross-country skis. For a package of North Shore tourist information, call 218-722-4011. For a more isolated experience, the Boundary Waters Canoe Area is open to cross-country skiers in the winter; call 218-365-7681. For statewide snow conditions call the DNR's snow hotline at 651-296-6157, www.dnr.state.mn.us. The Minnesota Department of Tourism, 800-657-3700 also reports statewide snow conditions.

Neighboring Wisconsin is host to the famous American Birkebeiner cross-country ski race. Starting at Hayward, Wisconsin, about a three hours' drive from the Twin Cities, this 51-kilometer race is held every February. The "Birkie," as it's affectionately known, is open to world class competitors and well-conditioned amateurs. Call 800-872-2753 or 715-634-5025 for information; pick up entry forms at local ski shops; enter online at www.birkie.org; or write the American Birkebeiner Foundation, P.O. Box 911 Hayward, WI 54843.

The park districts offer free cross-country ski lessons. Call the following numbers for more information:

- **Minneapolis Parks and Recreation Board**, 612-661-4800
- **St. Paul Division of Parks and Recreation**, 651-266-6400
  For rentals, sales, and advice, try the following (among others):
- **Aarcee Rentals**, 2910 Lyndale Avenue South, Minneapolis, 612-827-5746

- **Joe's Ski Shop**, 935 North Dale Street, St. Paul, 651-488-5511
- **Midwest Mountaineering**, 309 Cedar Avenue South, Minneapolis, 612-339-3433
- **North Country Inc.**, 8980 East Hudson Boulevard, St. Paul, 651-739-3500

SKIING—DOWNHILL

While Minnesota is not mountainous, it is hilly, and its short runs have turned out some of the top ski racers in the country—Cindy Nelson grew up at Lutsen and Kristina Koznick learned to race at Buck Hill. For the rest of us, the nearby slopes offer a fun day out, with most time spent skiing instead of riding lifts. Snowboarding and snow skating are allowed at most areas. For information about clubs, go to the Ski and Sports Show at the Minneapolis Convention Center in October. Most of the following ski areas have rentals available at the lodge. Snow information can be had at the DNR's snow hotline, 651-296-6157, www.dnr.state.mn.us, or call the Minnesota Department of Tourism, 800-657-3700.

- **Afton Alps**, 6600 Peller Avenue South, Afton, 651-436-5245, www.aftonalps.com; large area with many runs.
- **Buck Hill**, 15400 Buck Hill Road, Burnsville, 952-435-7174, www.skibuck.com; convenient, small area, sells half-day tickets and has an excellent racing program; crowded.
- **Hyland Hills Ski Area and School**, 8800 Chalet Road, Bloomington, 952-835-4604; good place to learn, excellent racing program through Mt. Gilboa Racing, snowboarding, toddler's ski school.
- **Indianhead Mountain**, Wakefield, Michigan, 800-3INDIAN; gets a lot of snow.
- **Lutsen Mountain Ski Area**, Lutsen, 800-642-6036 or 218-663-7281; the closest Minnesota comes to mountain skiing, beautiful views of Lake Superior.
- **Spirit Mountain**, Duluth, 800-642-6377, www.spiritmyn.com; municipal ski area, with views of Lake Superior.
- **Welch Village**, North of Redwing off Highway 61 on County Road 7, 1-651-258-4567 or 651-222-7079; even people accustomed to Colorado enjoy skiing here.
- **Wild Mountain Ski Area**, Taylors Falls, 651-257-3550 or 800-447-4958; fun area with many special events, popular with boarders.
  For certified ski and snowboard instruction or race coaching contact:

- **Afton Ski Racing**, 651-436-7652
- **Blizzard Ski and Snowboard School**, 952-945-9192
- **Buck Hill**, 952-435-7174 or www.skibuck.com
- **Mt. Gilboa Alpine Racing Inc.**, 952-930-9422, www.teamgilboa.com
- **SkiAway**, Sports Hut, Colonial Square, Wayzata, 952-546-3622, offers lessons for women taught by women.
- **SkiJammers**, 1175 East Wayzata Boulevard, Wayzata, 952-473-1288, offers instruction for school aged children.

SOCCER

Soccer is rapidly becoming Minnesota's most popular youth sport, and it's an exciting spectator sport as well. The 50 fields at the172-acre National Sports Complex/Blaine Soccer Complex in Blaine are home to the professional Minnesota Thunder and also the site of the USA Cup, the premier youth soccer tournament in the country. For information about soccer programs in your community check your community services or contact the **Minnesota Youth Soccer Association**, 11577 Encore Circle, Minnetonka, MN 55343, 952-933-2384, www.minnyouthsoccer.org.

SNOWMOBILING

In winter, this is the state "sport" for Minnesotans who love their motorized vehicles. A Snowmobile Vacation Guide is published in the December issue of *Snowgoer* magazine, 601 Lakeshore Parkway, Minnetonka, 952-476-2200. Also call the DNR, 651-296-6157, www.dnr.mn.us, for locations of trails, or pick up bags of information at the Ski and Winter Sports Show at the Convention Center in the fall. For snowmobile rentals contact **Bay Rentals Inc.**, Minnetonka, 952-474-0366.

SWIMMING BEACHES

Beaches in the metro area are guarded from early June to mid-August. None are open to dogs. If you sign your children up for beach swimming lessons, be advised that June is often stormy and the beaches are sometimes closed during the hottest days of summer because of parasites in the water that cause swimmers' itch. Lake Ann just west of Chanhassen off Highway 5 and Lake Independence in Baker Park west of Wayzata, 763-476-4666, are very popular swimming beaches and picnic facilities. The latest addition to the Twin Cites' inventory of swimming beaches is Lake Minnetonka Regional

Park, which has a nearly two-acre swimming pond with chlorinated lake water and a handicapped-accessible ramp that extends into the pool, 952-474-4822. Another chlorinated, sandy-bottomed swimming pond can be found at Lake Elmo Park Reserve. Minneapolis' most popular beach is on Lake Nokomis, although the beaches on Cedar, Calhoun and Harriet are also heavily used. St. Paul, while it does not have as many beaches as Minneapolis, does operate a beach on spring-fed Lake Phalen. In the western suburbs, Shady Oak Lake on Shady Oak Road in Hopkins is so heavily used it may be difficult to find a parking spot. For more information, call Minneapolis Parks, 612-661-4800; Hennepin County Parks (for beaches outside the city) 612-559-9000, www.hennepinparks.org; Ramsey County Parks, 651-748-2500, www.co.ramsey.mn.us/parks; St. Paul Parks, 651-266-6400, www.stpaul.gov.

MINNEAPOLIS BEACHES
- **Cedar Lake**, South Shore on Cedar Lake Parkway; First Street at Cedar Lake Parkway
- **Lake Calhoun**, North Shore at Lake Street; 32nd Street at Calhoun Parkway; Thomas Avenue at Calhoun Parkway
- **Lake Harriet**, North Shore at Lake Harriet Parkway; Minnehaha Parkway at Lake Harriet Parkway
- **Lake Hiawatha**, 45th Street at 28th Avenue South
- **Lake Nokomis**, 50th Street at Nokomis Parkway; West Shore at 50th Street
- **Wirth Lake**, Glenwood Avenue at Wirth Parkway

ST. PAUL BEACHES
- **Lake Como**, Como Boulevard at Horton Avenue
- **Lake Phalen**, Phalen Park on Wheelock Parkway

HENNEPIN COUNTY PUBLIC BEACHES
- **Baker Park Reserve**, County Roads19 and 24, Maple Plain
- **Bryant Lake Regional Park**, 6400 Rowland Road, Eden Prairie
- **Cleary Lake Regional Park**, 18106 Texas Avenue South, Prior Lake
- **Elm Creek Park Preserve**, 13080 Territorial Road, Maple Grove
- **Fish Lake Regional Park**, 14900 Bass Lake Road, Maple Grove
- **French Lake Regional Park**, 12615 County Road 9, Plymouth
- **Lake Minnetonka Regional Park**, Minnetrista
- **Lake Rebecca Park Preserve**, 9831 County Road 50, Rockford

RAMSEY COUNTY PUBLIC BEACHES
- **Bald Eagle Lake**, 5800 Hugo Road, White Bear Township
- **Gervais Lake**, 2520 Edgerton Street, Little Canada
- **Lake Johanna**, 3500 Lake Johanna Boulevard, Arden Hills
- **Long Lake**, 1500 Old Highway 8, New Brighton
- **White Bear Lake**, 5050 Lake Avenue, White Bear Lake

MUNICIPAL SWIMMING POOLS

Minneapolis' outdoor swimming pools are open from June to late August; in St. Paul, they're open June to September. For additional information on municipal pools, call the same numbers listed (above) for beaches. Once it gets cold, check your school district community services book, the YMCA and listings in the "Health Clubs" section of the Yellow Pages.
- **Chaska Pool** (open to Chaska residents), Chaska Community Center, 1661 Park Ridge Drive, 952-448-5633
- **Como Pool**, Como Avenue at Lexington Parkway North, St. Paul, 651-489-2811
- **North Commons**, 1701 Golden Valley Road North, Minneapolis, 612-370-4945
- **Oxford Pool**, Lexington Parkway at Iglehart Avenue, St. Paul, 651-647-9925
- **Richfield Pool and Water Slide**, 630 East 66th Street, 952-861-9355
- **Rosacker Pool**, 1500 Johnson Street NE, Minneapolis, 612-370-4937
- **St. Louis Park Pool**, 5005 West 36th Street, 952-924-2545; good for all ages
- **Valley View Pool**, 201 East 90th Street, Bloomington, 952-881-0900
- **Webber Pool**, 4300 Webber Parkway North, Minneapolis, 612-370-4915

HEALTH CLUBS, YMCA, YWCA, & GYMS

If you work for a larger company, ask human resources about company discounts that are offered by fitness centers. Or, try these:
- **Arena Health Club**, 600 1st Avenue North, Minneapolis, 612-673-1200
- **Bally Total Fitness**, for the nearest location, call 800-695-8111
- **Calhoun Beach Club Inc.**, 2925 Dean Parkway, Minneapolis, 612-927-9951

- **Flagship Athletic Club**, 755 Prairie Center Drive, Eden Prairie, 952-941-2000
- **Lilydale Club**, 945 Sibley Memorial Highway, Lilydale, 651-457-4954
- **Lonna Mosow's**, 7500 Flying Cloud Drive and 6409 City West Parkway, Eden Prairie, 952-941-9448
- **Northwest Racquet, Swim & Health Clubs**, 5525 Cedar Lake Road, St. Louis Park, for many other locations, call 952-525-CLUB.
- **Regency Athletic Club and Spa**, 1300 Nicollet Avenue, Minneapolis, 612-343-3131
- **The Gym**. Bloomington, 952-884-9144; Elk River, 763-441-4232; Fridley, 763-571-9555; Plymouth, 763-553-0171
- **The Marsh**, 15000 Minnetonka Boulevard, Minnetonka, 952-935-2202; this peaceful, affirming exercise facility has a yoga tower and two pools along with the normal equipment rooms and aerobics classes. Physical therapy is available here as well. The restaurant serves gourmet food and is open for lunch and dinner.
- **The University Club**, 420 Summit Avenue, St. Paul, 651-222-1751
- **YMCA**; a monthly membership may cost much less than for a private club. Volunteering at the Y can get you a discount. Call for locations of numerous branches. The downtown Y provides summertime fun day care for K-8th Graders. Locations: downtown Minneapolis, Ninth and Hennepin, 612-371-8750; downtown St. Paul, 476 North Robert Street, 651-292-4100
- **YWCA**; Minneapolis (downtown Branch), 1130 Nicollet Mall, 612-332-0501; Uptown Branch, 2808 Hennepin Avenue South, 612-874-7131; St. Paul, 198 North Western Avenue, 651-222-3741—Fitness Center, 651-225-9922

JUST FOR KIDS

- **Gymboree**, 5011 Ewing Avenue South, Edina, 952-404-1519 or 800-520-PLAY, www.gymboree.com; infants to 4 years.
- **My Gym Children's Fitness Center**, 956 Prairie Center Drive, Eden Prairie, 952-906-0028, www.my-gym.com, serves ages three months to nine years, and is available for birthday parties.

PARKS AND RECREATION

For more about services offered within your parks district, see **Parks and Recreation** in the **Useful Phone Numbers and Web Sites** chapter.

PPROXIMATELY TEN THOUSAND YEARS AGO, WHEN THE MOST recent ice age ended, the receding glaciers left behind a landscape filled with lakes, marshes, bogs and fens. When European settlers arrived they found this wet land difficult to develop, so thousands of acres were preserved, quite accidentally. Today, many of these wetlands are parks where everyone congregates for recreation and relaxation. Amazingly though, the wetlands almost didn't become parks.

By the 1880s, Twin Cities' lakes had become popular locations for resorts and houses, and while state officials coveted the prime waterfront areas as regional parks their plan was not well received. City leaders didn't want to give up direct control over any area in their domain, and citizens were afraid it was a speculation scheme by conspiratorial insiders. Park proponents prevailed, though, by citing the success of New York's Central Park. Soon, Theodore Wirth, in the persistent manner of New York City's Robert Moses, was tearing down houses on the east shore of Lake Calhoun and marshaling the park system into what it is today. Wirth Park is named after him. His idea was to link the lakes and green spaces together into a coherent system of paths or parkways. Although they don't quite make a complete circle, this 50-mile circuit of Minneapolis' green space is today affectionately known as the Grand Round. Here's how to traverse the **Grand Round**:

Begin at **Minnehaha Park**, a 171-acre regional sports and nature area surrounding Minnehaha Falls where Minnehaha Creek empties into the Mississippi River. On summer afternoons and weekends, the park is packed with family reunions and company picnics. There are well-marked paths for hiking and nature viewing. Of particularly dramatic prospects are the frozen falls in mid-winter, seen from the ski trails below. And in the early spring when ice melt from Lake Minnetonka pours thousands of gallons a minute thundering over the rocks, this spectacular display makes it easy to understand Henry Wadsworth Longfellow's inspiration as he wrote his "Song of Hiawatha." In the summer, many people make a day canoeing trip, putting in at Gray's Bay at the east end of Lake Minnetonka, and taking out at Minehaha Park, *before* the falls.

Continuing a tour of the Grand Round, pick up Minnehaha Parkway from the northern end of Minnehaha Park and head west. In about a mile, you'll reach **Lake Nokomis** (picnic grounds, swimming, playing fields). Hiawatha Golf Course and **Lake Hiawatha** are just across the road to the north. You can do a loop of about three miles around Lake Nokomis or continue west on the Parkway past charming houses and interesting gardens. Approximately five miles farther, you'll come upon **Lake Harriet**. This park offers sailing, summer concerts in the band shell, secluded picnic spots, swimming at "Beard's Plaisance," and a rock garden with dwarf conifers, flowering trees and perennials, and a rose garden adjacent to Lakewood Cemetery.

A full circle around Lake Harriet is about three miles, but it's only a short jog from the north end over to Lake Calhoun. The **Lake Calhoun** Parkway is thick with runners, bikers and skaters most of the year. The trip around the lake is, again, about three miles. This park is host to volleyball games, picnics, paddle-boaters, sailors, canoers, and summertime sunbathers. Lunch at an Uptown cafe is just a short walk from the lake's eastern shore.

About two miles east of Lake Calhoun and a couple of blocks south of Lake Street is a park not directly connected to the parkway system, but no less used and appreciated, **Powderhorn Park**. This park got its name from the lake's original crescent "powderhorn" shape, a shape lost when it was dug out at the turn of the century to drain away wetlands along its shores (wetlands preservation was not yet a concept). A welcome break from its urban surroundings, Powderhorn Park offers sledding hills, cross-country skiing, and community events including the annual Powderhorn Festival of the Arts in August, a weekend juried art show plus music, entertainers, children's activities and ethnic food.

Back at Lake Calhoun the parkway continues its path around the Minneapolis Chain of Lakes. One route from the northern tip of Calhoun loops around **Lake of the Isles** and its elegant mansions. Again, the circuit is nearly three miles around, not counting extra steps to dodge goose-droppings. At the northern end of the lake you'll notice **Kenwood Park**, a patch of wooded hills with outdoor tennis courts. Detour here to Sebastian Joe's Ice Cream on Franklin, just a few blocks east. From the west shore of the lake, take Benton Boulevard to Dean Parkway and connect with Cedar Lake Parkway, which follows the west side of Cedar Lake for a mile before heading northward to Wirth Park.

Wirth Park offers a mix of woods, prairie, picnic areas and beaches, with marked nature trails that wind through the woods and paved paths for running and biking. Families enjoy exploring the woods after dark at the monthly "Full Moon Walks" in the Eloise Butler Wildflower Garden, 612-370-4903, open April to November.

From Wirth Park, the Parkway heads straight north and becomes Xerxes/Victory Memorial Drive. The west side of the street is in Robbinsdale and the east side is in Minneapolis. This ballfield-wide grass boulevard lined with 1940s and '50s vintage houses cuts due east above 44th Street and continues through far-north Minneapolis until it runs into **Webber Park** on the bank of the Mississippi. From here, scenic West River Parkway will take you all the way to Minnehaha Falls Park past many little parks and the Grain Belt brewery, or you can cross the river on the 42nd Avenue bridge. But then you'll have another choice to make: drive parallel to the river on Marshall Avenue down to St. Anthony Main, or take St. Anthony Boulevard east for three more miles across Northeast Minneapolis, passing through Columbia Park to Stinson Boulevard. That's where the parkways end, unfortunately. From here, if you're biking, it's street riding to complete the magnificent circle of the Grand Round. During the winter, in addition to the roadway surfaces, a single paved trail is kept clear throughout the system for shared use by pedestrians and cyclists.

Another place to tour the parkways is along the narrow corridor that the Mississippi River carves through Minneapolis and St. Paul. This 72-mile route is one of the most diverse and complex ecosystems on earth. Shallow and narrow at its upper end, by the time the Mississippi reaches its confluence with the Minnesota River at Fort Snelling, it has become a wide and powerful feature of the largest inland navigation system on earth. At this point, it "becomes what the Mississippi *is*," a symbol of our nation, a critical migration and transportation corridor at the heart of America's history, and one of the planet's most identifiable features when observed from outer space.

Within the fifty-four thousand-acre riverfront, dozens of state and local parks provide outstanding recreation opportunities. For those who feel the river is best experienced by watercraft, be sure to plan ahead and obtain navigational charts, particularly if you are boating on the section of the river that is part of the inland waterway system. Not only are there locks, dams and shoals to navigate, but you will also be sharing the channels with trains of towed commercial barges that cannot maneuver out of your way. If that thought is enough to make you take back your captain's hat, try the Padelford tour boats, 651-227-1100 or 800-543-3908. Their daily sightseeing cruises, running Memorial Day to Labor Day, also include lunch or dinner.

The parkways along either bank are lovely for walking and bird watching. The **St. Anthony Falls Heritage Trail** is a self-guided tour along the Mississippi River on West River Parkway, from the Stone Arch Bridge (built for trains 150 years ago and now the exclusive domain of pedestrians and bicyclists) to Hennepin Avenue, crossing the Hennepin Avenue Bridge onto Nicollet Island, jogging over to Merriam Street and crossing the river on the Merriam Street Bridge. From there, the trail proceeds along SE Main Street to the Stone Arch Bridge and crosses the river once again to complete the loop. Interpretive markers and kiosks along the way describe the history of Minneapolis' birthplace. If your mood is romantic, stroll here on a moonlit evening and enjoy the skyline reflected in the black river.

For longer tours, you can follow West River Parkway and eventually reach Minnehaha Park on the city's far south side, or follow East River Parkway/East Mississippi River Boulevard south, going through the University of Minnesota campus, to **Hidden Falls Park**, a picnic area with a marina on the riverbank. A little farther along the parkway is Fort Snelling State Park, the place where the Minnesota and Mississippi Rivers meet and the site of a stone fort built on the bluff in the 1820s. The parkway ends at **Crosby Farm Nature Area**, off Gannon Road at Shepard Road, St. Paul. This secluded preserve of Mississippi River estuaries and marshes, on the edge of Fort Snelling State Park, features a boardwalk through the marsh and is one of the few places in the metro area where nesting warblers can be found.

The entrance to Fort Snelling State Park is off Post Road, south of State Highway 5. A day-use park with no camping allowed, the waterfront boasts a swimming beach, handicapped accessible fishing pier, and boat access.

Not directly connected to these paths, but well worth visiting, is the vast acreage of the **Minnesota River National Wildlife Refuge**, which stretches 34 miles along the Minnesota River from Fort Snelling State Park to Jordan. An interpretive center is located south of I-494 via the 34th Street exit.

St. Paul's lakes and parks also deserve a tour. Besides the traditional-style zoo and conservatory, **Como Park**, south of Larpenteur, offers visitors a Japanese garden, public swimming pool, golf course, and paved paths for walking and biking. In the summer you can rent canoes, paddleboats and bikes to use here. In winter, ski rentals are available. The Victorian-era Como Conservatory has an amazing collection of palm trees and orchids, a grotto and goldfish pond—a lovely escape on a minus 30° day. East on Wheelock Parkway from Como Park will take you to **Phalen Park**, a complex made up of a lake that is a source of water for the city, a swimming beach, a substantial expanse of rolling hills and wooded bluffs, an excellent golf course, amphitheater, picnic grounds and a paved running path. In the summer visitors may rent sailboats on Lake Phalen, and when the snows arrive the park offers cross-country ski lessons. Pick up the **Munger Trail** at Lake Phalen to bike through Maplewood.

Like Minneapolis, St. Paul has extensive riverfront parks. **Pig's Eye Lake Park**, located three miles downstream from downtown St. Paul, is actually a 500-acre backwater of the Mississippi that serves as a valuable refuge for migrating birds such as great blue herons, egrets, and cormorants. At the north end of Indian Mounds Park, just off of Mounds Boulevard, is an overlook on top of the bluffs. From here, you can gaze down on Minnesota's first city, and upon the transportation network that gives it life—the river, the railroad, the freeways, and the St. Paul Airport—all laid out before you like a map. South on Highway 61 to Lower Afton Road is the entrance to **Battle Creek Regional Park**. This park is promoted as an active recreation area and is recommended for "creative play." Your dog can run off leash here, if you have a permit. Internet surfers can check www.co.ramsey.mn.us/parks for rules and a map to the off-leash area at Lower Afton Road and McKnight Road. You can also try your skill at the Winthrop Street mountain-biking course. In winter, this park is open to cross-country skiers.

That's a quick tour of some of the better-known city parks and lakes. Certainly Theodore Wirth's original multi-use vision has turned out to be a most enjoyable reality. Check the **Sports and Recreation** chapter of this book, under **Boating, Dogs, Hiking, Swimming** and **Skiing** for phone numbers of numerous beaches and suggestions for park use. The **Metropolitan Council** web site, www.metrocouncil.org/parks, has maps you can search by area and activity. The **Minneapolis Parks and Recreation Board**, 612-661-4800, can provide information on rentals and lessons for swimming, canoeing, sailing, paddleboats, diving, golf, tennis, windsurfing at city parks. The **Hennepin Parks District** can provide particulars on their programs, 612-559-9000, www.hennepinparks.org. For information on beaches, trails and rentals in **St. Paul** call 651-266-6400 or check www.stpaul.gov. For **Ramsey County Parks**, try 651-748-2500, www.co.ramsey.mn.us/parks. In Washington County call 651-430-8368, www.co.washington.mn.us.

REGIONAL LAKES

- **Christmas Lake**, east of Excelsior and south of Highway 7, is spring-fed and famous for its fishing and water-skiing. The easiest public access is off the Highway 7 service road, just east of Christmas Lake Road.
- **Lake Minnetonka,** west of Minneapolis between highways 12 and 7, is the largest body of water in the Twin Cities area. With over 120 miles of shoreline, it is accessible at numerous public boat ramps; the closest to Minneapolis is at Gray's Bay off Highway 101. Popular for fishing both summer and winter, this lake is full of bass, crappies, sunfish, northerns, and walleyes, and several national bass fishing contests are held here each year. Water skiers gravitate to St. Alban's Bay and the quieter waters at the west end of the lake. On the north side of Big Island, between Excelsior and Wayzata, and Lord Fletcher's at Spring Park, are the places where motor boaters go to see and be seen. Families will enjoy Lake Minnetonka Regional Park, west of Excelsior, which features a swimming pond, boat ramp, and extraordinary playground.
- **Lake Waconia**, west of Minneapolis off Highway 5 in Waconia, is popular for fishing, windsurfing and sailing.
- **White Bear Lake**, east of Highway 61 at White Bear, is a shallow lake with a sandy bottom. It is a favorite for swimming, sailing, windsurfing, ice boating, and fishing for carp, bluegills and bullheads.

Fishing seasons for walleye, muskellunge, and large and small-mouth bass are generally mid-May to mid-February. Fishing for lake trout runs mid-May through September. For more information on fishing seasons see **Fishing** in the **Sports and Recreation** chapter and check the DNR's web site, www.dnr.state.mn.us.

STATE PARKS

There are four state parks in the metro area: Afton, Fort Snelling (see above), Minnesota Valley Trail, and William O'Brian. For complete listings and descriptions of the state parks, call the **Department of Natural Resources Parks and Recreation Division's** hotline, 651-296-6157. The annual state park pass is a bargain. There is an additional charge for camping. Camping reservations may be made 3 to 90 days in advance if you pay by credit card. Call 612-922-9000 or 800-246-CAMP or reserve online at www.dnr.state.mn.us.

- **Afton State Park**, Washington County Road 21, Hastings, MN 55033, 651-436-5391; located twenty miles southeast of the Twin Cities is a roller-coaster terrain of grassy ridges and deep wooded ravines overlooking the St. Croix River. This area has enthralled visitors from the earliest explorers to today's downhill skiers. It offers primitive campsites and is not handicapped accessible. With 20 miles of hiking/cross-country skiing and five miles of horseback riding trails, this park features narrow ravines that drop 300 feet to the river from native prairie uplands.
- **William O'Brien State Park**, Minnesota Highway 95, Marine-on-St.Croix, 651-433-0500; located 35 miles northeast of the Twin Cities and two miles north of the town of Marine-on-St. Croix, this rolling expanse of maple-basswood-oak forest, lakes, marshes, and meadows offers 11 miles of hiking and cross-country ski trails that loop through the uplands and along the river. Rent a canoe for the short paddle out to Greenberg Island, a refuge for mink, beaver, deer, fox, warblers and ovenbirds. The heron rookery is at the south end of the park on the river. Bald eagles feed, but do not nest, in the park. Snow-shoeing is popular here in the winter. Seven camp sites, the fishing pier and two miles of trails are all handicapped-accessible.
- **Minnesota Valley State Recreation Area**, Railpark Boulevard, Jordan, 952-492-6400; located 40 miles south of the Twin Cities, the park office is near the junction of Highway 282 and US Highway 169. This thirty-five mile multi-use (including horse and snowmobile) trail on the south bank of the Minnesota River passes through wetlands, floodplain forests, and oak savannas. Autumn color peaks in October, but so do the hunters. Be very careful if you use this trail during hunting season. Campsites, including some suitable for groups, are available.

FORESTS

- **Riley Creek Woods Conservation Area**, Pioneer Trail and Dell Road, is a 43-acre remnant of the Big Woods forest that once spanned the middle of the state, from St. Cloud to Mankato. It is severely pressured by surrounding development.
- **Wolsfeld Woods**, Highway 6 at Brown Road, Long Lake, is 185 acres of old growth forest so tall that sunlight pierces the trees like arrows. This is a mystical place where you can feel the deepness of time. If you're a birdwatcher, look for wood thrushes and scarlet tanagers near the lake.

ADDITIONAL RESOURCES—TOURS

For comprehensive recreation information for the entire state, call the **Minnesota Office of Tourism**, 121 Seventh Place East, St. Paul 55101, 651-296-5029, 800-657-3700, www.exploreminnesota.com. Order park maps from the **Minnesota Department of Natural Resources**, 651-296-6157, www.dnr.state.mn.us. To reserve a campsite at one of the many state parks, call the **DNR's reservation line** at 800-246-2267. If skiing is on the menu, call the **Snow Hotline** at 651-296-6157 during business hours, or check their web site (see above). For a free **Wisconsin vacation guide** call 800-432-TRIP or check www.travelwisconsin.com. The **North Dakota Tourism Department's** number is 800-435-5663. For **Travel Michigan** dial 888-784-7328. The **National Park Service** is online at www.nps.gov/noco. For other recreational opportunities, see **Quick Getaways**, or try these:

- **Afton Cruise Lines**, Afton, 651-436-8883
- **Alexis Bailly Vineyard**, Hastings, 651-437-1413
- **Anson Northrup Riverboats**, Minneapolis, 651-227-1100
- **Down in History Tours**, St. Paul, 651-292-1220, 651-224-1191
- **Gray Line Sightseeing Tours**, Minneapolis, 612-469-5020, 800-530-9686
- **Governor's Residence Tour**, St. Paul, 651-297-8177
- **Heartland Tours Twin Cities**, St. Paul, 651-777-7170
- **Landmark Center**, St. Paul, 651-292-3225
- **Metro Connections Sightseeing Tours**, Minneapolis, 612-333-TOUR, 800-747-TOUR
- **Minnehaha Steamboat**, Excelsior, 952-474-2115, 952-474-4801
- **Minnesota State Capitol**, St. Paul, 651-297-3521, 651-296-2881
- **Minnesota Zephyr Dinner Train**, Stillwater, 651-430-3000, 800-992-6100
- **Padelford Packet Boat Company**, St. Paul, 651-227-1100, 800-543-3908.
- **Queen of Excelsior excursion boats**, Excelsior, 952-474-2502
- **River City Trolley**, Minneapolis, 612-204-0000
- **Saint Paul Gangster Tours**, St. Paul, 651-292-1220, 651-224-1191
- **Summit Brewing Company Tours**, St. Paul, 651-265-7800
- **Taylors Falls Scenic Boat Tours**, Taylors Falls, 651-257-3550, 800-447-4958
- **UnderWater World**, Mall of America, Bloomington, 952-883-0202

- **University of Minnesota Landscape Arboretum**, Chanhassen, 952-443-2460
- **Valley Tours, Inc.**, Stillwater, 651-439-6110
- **Wayzata Towne Trolley**, Wayzata, 952-473-9595

Finally, a cautionary note to hikers and nature lovers, the woods and fields of Minnesota and Wisconsin are not 100% safe during deer hunting season. Generally, bow season begins in mid-September and firearm season begins in early November. If you feel the need to take a late fall walk in the woods, be sure to wear hunters "blaze" orange. And if you are taking Fido with you, put an orange vest on him as well. For more information on hunting seasons and regulations check www.dnr.state.mn.us.

VOLUNTEERING FOR AN ORGANIZATION IS A SATISFYING WAY TO make a difference in your new community while at the same time meeting people who share similar interests. There is a great tradition of organized volunteerism in Minnesota. At the turn of the century, women here fought for prison reform, bought and rehabbed buildings, established parent-teacher associations, and of course, helped gain the right to vote. These days, Twin Cities' service organizations are known for their work in everything from refugee assistance to addiction recovery. Area schools, hospitals and museums are always in need of volunteers.

VOLUNTEER PLACEMENT SERVICES

The following organizations coordinate many volunteer activities in the Twin Cities. Call them and they will help you find a place in need of your special talents:

- **Community Volunteer Service of the St. Croix Valley Area (CVS)**, 200 Orleans Street West, Stillwater, 651-439-7437, www.presenter.com/~cvs, serves Washington and St. Croix counties.
- **United Way Volunteer Center**, Minneapolis, 404 South 8th Street, Minneapolis, 612-340-7621, www.msp.org; hours are 8:30 a.m. to 4:30 p.m., Monday-Friday. They maintain a database of organizations that need volunteers.
- **The Volunteer Center**, St. Paul Area, 166 East 4th Street, St. Paul, 651-644-2044, www.thevolunteercenter.org
- **Volunteers of America**, Minnesota Office, 5905 Golden Valley Road, Golden Valley, 612-546-3242, www.voa.org
- ***The Twin Cities Volunteer's Handbook*** by the Earthworks Group and Metro Volunteer Centers is a comprehensive guide to community service. Free, call 612-904-1234.

AREA CAUSES

The following are some of the Twin Cities service organizations that need volunteers:

AIDS

- **AIDS Emergency Fund**, P.O. Box 582943, Minneapolis, 612-331-7733
- **AIDS Project Minnesota**, 1400 South Park Avenue, Minneapolis, 612-341-2060
- **The Aliveness Project**, 730 East 38th Street, Minneapolis, 612-822-7946
- **Red Door Clinic**, 525 Portland Avenue, Minneapolis, 612-348-6363
- **Youth & AIDS Projects**, 428 Oak Grove Street, Minneapolis, 612-627-6820

ALCOHOL AND DRUG DEPENDENCY

- **American Indian Services**, 735 East Franklin Avenue, Minneapolis, 612-871-2175, offers culturally specific transitional treatment
- **Arrigoni House**, Inc., 508 University Avenue SE, Minneapolis, 612-331-6582
- **Eden Programs**, 1025 Portland Avenue, Minneapolis, 612-338-0723
- **African-American Family Services**, 2616 Nicollet Avenue, Minneapolis, 612-871-7878
- **Park Avenue Center**, 2525 Park Avenue, Minneapolis, 612-871-7443

ANIMALS

- **Animal Humane Society**, 845 North Meadowbrook Lane, Golden Valley, 612-522 4325; 14-18 youth program and adult program
- **Humane Society of Ramsey County**, 651-645-7387, needs volunteers to walk dogs and clean cages.
- **We Can Ride**, 612-934-0057, offers therapeutic horseback riding and cart driving for children and adults at four locations: Hennepin County Home School in Eden Prairie, Carver Scott Educational Cooperative in Waconia; Shriner's Ranch in Independence and Pine Meadow Farm in Delano.

BUSINESS

- **SCORE Business Counseling**: 5217 Wayzata Boulevard; St. Louis Park 55416, 612-591-0539; 350 St. Peter Street, St. Paul 55102, 651-223-5010, is an organization of business people who have a wide range of expertise.

CHILDREN/YOUTH

- **Boys and Girls Club of Minneapolis**, 2323 11th Avenue South, 612-872-3640
- **Boy Scouts of America Viking Council, Inc.**, 5300 Glenwood Avenue, Golden Valley, 612-545-4550
- **Big Brothers & Big Sisters**: St. Paul, 166 E. 4th Street, 651-224-7651; Minneapolis: 2915 Wayzata Boulevard South, 612-374-3939
- **The Bridge for Runaway Youth**, 2200 Emerson Avenue South, Minneapolis, 612-377-8800
- **Children's Defense Fund**, 550 Rice St. #205, St. Paul, 651-227-6121
- **Children's Home Society of Minnesota**, 2230 Como Avenue, St. Paul, 651-646-6393
- **Family and Children's Service**, 414 South 8th Street, Minneapolis, 612-339-9101
- **Girl Scout Council of Greater Minneapolis**, 5601 Brooklyn Boulevard, Brooklyn Center, 763-535-4602
- **Inner City Youth League**, 905 Selby Avenue, St. Paul, 651-221-9827
- **Pillsbury House**, 3501 Chicago Avenue South, Minneapolis, 612-824-0708
- **Project Offstreets**, 212 2nd Avenue North, Minneapolis, 612-252-1200
- **Sabathani Community Center**, 310 East 38th Street, Minneapolis, 612-827-5981

CULTURAL ORGANIZATIONS

- **American Indian Business Development Corporation**, 1433 East Franklin Avenue, Minneapolis, 612-870-7555, offers job creation and business help.
- **American Indian Center**, 1530 East Franklin Avenue, Minneapolis, 612-879-1700

- **Center for Asians and Pacific Islanders**, 3702 East Lake Street #101, Minneapolis, 612-721-0122, offers employment training, emergency services.
- **Centro Cultural Chicano**, 2025 Nicollet Avenue South, Minneapolis, 612-874-1412
- **Hmong-American Partnership**, 1525 Glenwood Avenue, Minneapolis, 612-377-6482
- **Jewish Community Center of Greater Minneapolis**, 4330 South Cedar Lake Road, St. Louis Park, 612-377-8330
- **Urban League**: Minneapolis: 407 East 38th Street, 612-823-5818; St. Paul: 4001 Selby Avenue, 651-224-5771

DISABILITY ASSISTANCE

- **Accessible Space**, 2550 University Avenue West, St. Paul, 651-645-7271
- **Alliance for the Mentally Ill**, 970 Raymond Avenue, St. Paul, 651-645-2948
- **ARC**, Twin Cities, 651-523-0823
- **Courage Center**, 3915 Golden Valley Road, Golden Valley, 763-588-0811
- **People Incorporated**, 317 York Avenue, St. Paul, 651-774-0011
- **Sister Kenny Institute**, 800 East 28th Street, Minneapolis, 612-863-4400

ENVIRONMENT

- **Clean Water Action**, 326 Hennepin Avenue East, Minneapolis, 612-623-3666
- **Land Stewardship Project**, 2200 4th Street, White Bear Lake, 651-653-0618
- **Minnesota Center for Environmental Advocacy**, 26 East Exchange Street, St. Paul, 651-223-5969
- **Nature Conservancy**, 1313 5th Street SE, Minneapolis, 612-331-0750
- **Sierra Club**, North Star Chapter, 1313 5th Street SE, Minneapolis, 612-379-3853

GAY, LESBIAN, BISEXUAL, TRANSGENDER

- ***focus Point Newspaper***, 612-288-9000; call for a G/L business and organization directory.

- **Gay & Lesbian Community Action Council**, 310 East 38th Street, Minneapolis, 612-822-0127
- **Pride Institute**, 14400 Martin Drive, Eden Prairie, 612-934-7554, offers chemical dependency counseling.

HEALTH AND HOSPITALS

Most hospitals welcome volunteers—give the nearest one a call. For specific health issues, try one of the following:
- **American Cancer Society**, 3316 West 66th Street, Edina, 952-925-2772
- **American Heart Association**, 4701 West 77th Street, Edina, 952-835-3300
- **American Lung Association**, 490 Concordia Avenue, St. Paul, 800-642-LUNG
- **Association for Nonsmokers—Minnesota**, 2395 University Avenue West, Suite 310, St. Paul, 651-646-3005
- **Minnesota NARAL (National Abortion and Reproductive Rights Action League**), 550 Rice Street, St. Paul, 651-602-7655, www.mtn.org/mnnaral
- **Planned Parenthood of Minnesota**: St. Paul: 1965 Ford Parkway, 651-698-2406, 1700 Rice Street, 651-489-1328; Minneapolis: 1200 Lagoon Avenue, 612-823-6300

HOMELESS SERVICES

- **Catholic Charities**, 404 South 8th Street, Minneapolis, 612-340-7500
- **People Serving People**, 917 5th Avenue South, Minneapolis, 612-333-1221
- **St. Stephen's Shelter**, 2211 Clinton Avenue, Minneapolis, 612-874-9292
- **Salvation Army**, 2300 Freeway Boulevard, Brooklyn Center, 763-566-2040; St. Paul, 651-771-0015

HUMAN SERVICES

- **American Red Cross**: Minneapolis: 612-871-7676; St. Paul: 651-291-6789
- **Amicus**, 100 North 6th Street #347B, Minneapolis, 612-348-8570, provides services for ex-inmates.

- **Citizens' Council**, Minneapolis, 612-340-5432, offers assistance to families of inmates, victims; mediation.
- **House of Charity Soup Kitchen**, 714 Park Avenue South, Minneapolis, 612-594-2009
- **Neighborhood Involvement Program**, 2431 Hennepin Avenue South, Minneapolis, 612-374-3125
- **Phyllis Wheatley Community Center**, 919 Fremont Avenue North, Minneapolis, 612-374-4342
- **Second Harvest Food Bank**, 651-484-5117
- **Sharing and Caring Hands**, 425 North 7th Street, Minneapolis, 612-338-4640

LEGAL AID

- **American Civil Liberties Union**, 1021 West Broadway, Minneapolis, 612-522-2423
- **Legal Aid Society**, 612-334-5970
- **Legal Rights Center**, 808 East Franklin Avenue, Minneapolis, 612-337-0030

LITERACY

- **English Learning Center for Immigrants and Refugee Families**, 2315 Chicago Avenue South, Minneapolis, 612-827-4709
- **Minnesota Literacy Council**, 475 North Cleveland Avenue #303, St. Paul, 651-645-2277

MEN'S SERVICES

- **The Fathers Resource Center**, 430 Oak Grove Street #105, Minneapolis, 612-560-8656

POLITICS–ELECTORAL

- **Democratic—Farmer-Labor Party** (Democrats), State Office, 651-293-1200
- **Independent Republican Party** (Republicans), State Office, 651-222-0022
- **League of Women Voters of Minnesota**, 550 Rice Street, St. Paul, 651-224-5445
- **Reform Party**, 612-939-6601

POLITICS—SOCIAL

- **Association of Community Organizations for Reform Now (ACORN)**, 757 Raymond Avenue, #200, St. Paul, 651-642-9639
- **Common Cause in Minnesota**, 1010 University Avenue West, St. Paul, 651-644-1844
- **Friends for a Nonviolent World**, 1929 South 5th Street, Minneapolis, 612-321-9787
- **Minnesota Public Interest Research Group (MPIRG)**, 2414 University Avenue SE, Minneapolis, 612-627-4035
- **Minnesota Women's Political Caucus**, 550 Rice Street, St. Paul, 651-228-0995

REFUGEE ASSISTANCE

- **American Refugee Committee**, 2344 Nicollet Avenue South, #350, Minneapolis, 612-872-7060, offers health services for foreign refugees.

SENIOR SERVICES

- **Area Agency on Aging**, 1600 University Avenue West, St. Paul, 651-641-8612
- **Gray Panthers of the Twin Cities**, 3255 Hennepin Avenue South, Minneapolis, 612-822-1011
- **Little Brothers Friends of the Elderly**, 612-721-6215
- **Senior Resources**, 612-331-4063

WOMEN'S SERVICES

- **Domestic Abuse Project**, 204 West Franklin Avenue, Minneapolis, 612-874-7063
- **Minnesota Women's Press**, 771 Raymond Avenue, St. Paul, 651-646-3968. Call for a directory of women's businesses and organizations.
- **Sexual Offense Services of Ramsey County**, 1619 Dayton Avenue, #201, St. Paul, 651-298-5898
- **Sexual Violence Center of Hennepin County**, 2100 Pillsbury Avenue South, Minneapolis, 612-871-5100
- **Women of Color Health Alternatives Network**, 1060 Central Avenue West, St. Paul, 651-646-3775

WHILE THE LARGEST ACTIVE LUTHERAN CONGREGATION IN THE US can be found in south Minneapolis at the Mount Olivet Lutheran Church (www.mtolivet.org) not everybody in Minnesota is Lutheran, and in fact, Lutherans may be outnumbered by Catholics—and those two religious traditions may well be outnumbered by everybody else!

Obviously there are too many active houses of worship in Minneapolis and St. Paul to list here but we offer the following as a place to start. For a complete listing look in the Yellow Pages under "Churches" and "Synagogues."

CHURCHES

AFRICAN METHODIST EPISCOPAL

- **St. James AME Church**, 3600 Snelling Avenue, St. Paul, 651-721-4566
- **St. Peters AME Church**, 401 East 41st Street, Minneapolis, 612-825-9750
- **St. James AME Church**, 624 Central Avenue West, St. Paul, 651-227-4151

ANGLICAN

- **Anglican Church of St. Dunstan**, 4241 Brookside Avenue South St. Louis Park, 952-920-9122
- **Anglican Church of St. Luke**, 170 Virginia Street, St. Paul, 651-290-2565

APOSTOLIC

- **Rehoboth Church of Jesus Christ**, 916 31st Avenue North, Minneapolis, 612-529-2234

ASSEMBLIES OF GOD

- **Bethel Assemblies of God**, Nicollet Avenue & 57th Street, Minneapolis, 612-866-3227
- **Bloomington Assemblies of God**, 8600 Bloomington Avenue South, Bloomington, 952-854-1100
- **Summit Avenue Assembly of God**, 854 Summit Avenue, St. Paul, 651-228-0811

BAPTIST

- **Bethany Baptist Church**, Skillman & Cleveland Avenue, St. Paul, 651-631-0211
- **Bethesda Baptist Church**, 1118 South 8th Street, Minneapolis, 612-332-5904
- **First Baptist Church**, 10th & Hennepin Avenue, Minneapolis, 612-332-3651
- **First Baptist of White Bear**, Hwy. 61 at Buffalo Street, White Bear Lake, 651-429-9227

CHRISTIAN SCIENCE

- **Excelsior First Church**, 106 Center Street, Excelsior, 952-474-6267
- **Second Church of Christ, Scientist**, 228 South 12th Street, Minneapolis, 612-332-3368
- **Third Church of Christ, Scientist**, 42nd Street & Xerxes Avenue South, Minneapolis, 612-926-3511

CHURCH OF CHRIST

- **Minneapolis Central Church of Christ**, 1922 4th Avenue North, Minneapolis, 612-374-5481
- **Summit Avenue Church of Christ**, 10 South Grotto, St. Paul, 651-222-0872

CHURCH OF JESUS CHRIST OF LATTER-DAY SAINTS

- **Latter-Day Saints Institute**, 1205 University Avenue SE, Minneapolis, 612-331-1154

CONGREGATIONAL

- **First Congregational Church of Minnesota**, 500 8th Avenue SE, Minneapolis, 612-331-3816
- **Colonial Church**, 6200 Colonial Way, Edina, 952-925-2711
- **Plymouth Congregational Church**, 1900 Nicollet Avenue, Minneapolis, 612-871-7400
- **Woodbury Community Church**, 2975 Pioneer Drive Woodbury, 651-739-1427
- **Wayzata Community Church**, Ferndale and Wayzata Boulevard, Wayzata, 952-473-8876

DISCIPLES OF CHRIST

- **Bloomington Christian Church**, I-35W & 90th Street West, Bloomington, 952-888-4933
- **First Christian Church**, 2201 First Avenue South Minneapolis, 612-870-1868
- **Park Christian Church**, 700 Summit Avenue, St. Paul Park, 651-459-1098

EASTERN ORTHODOX

- **Russian Orthodox Church**, 1201 Hathaway Lane NE, Fridley, 763-574-1001
- **St. George Greek Orthodox Church**, 1111 Summit Avenue, St. Paul, 651-222-6220
- **St. Mary's Orthodox Cathedral**, 1701 NE 5th Street, Minneapolis, 612-781-7667
- **Ukrainian Orthodox Church of St. George**, 316 4th Avenue SE, Minneapolis, 612-379-1647

EPISCOPAL

- **Cathedral Church of St. Mark**, 519 Oak Grove Street, Minneapolis, 612-870-7800, www.st-marks-cathedral.org
- **Christ Episcopal Church-Woodbury**, 7305 Afton Road, Woodbury, 651-735-8790
- **Episcopal Diocese of Minnesota**, 1730 Clifton Place, Minneapolis, 612-871-5311
- **La Mision El Santo Nino Jesus**, 1524 Summit Avenue, St. Paul, 651-698-3408
- **Messiah Episcopal Church**, 1631 Ford Parkway, St. Paul, 651-698-2590
- **St. Alban's**, 6716 Gleason Road, Edina, 952-941-3065
- **St. David**, 13000 St. David's Road, Minnetonka, 952-935-3336
- **St. Edward the Confessor**, 865 North Ferndale Road, Orono, 952-473-2262
- **St. Martin's By the Lake**, County Road 15 and Westwood Road, Minnetonka Beach, 612-471-8429
- **St. Paul's**, Franklin and Logan at Lake of the Isles, 612-377-1273
- **St. Paul's Church on the Hill**, 1524 Summit Avenue, St. Paul, 651-698-0371
- **Trinity Episcopal Church**, 322 2nd Street, Excelsior, 952-474-5263

EVANGELICAL

- **First Covenant Church**, 810 South 7th Street, Minneapolis, 612-332-8093
- **First Evangelical Free Church of Minneapolis**, 5150 Chicago Avenue South, Minneapolis, 612-827-4705

FRIENDS (QUAKERS)

- **Minneapolis Friends Meeting**, 4401 York Avenue South Minneapolis, 612-926-6159

INDEPENDENT/INTERDENOMINATIONAL

- **Church Upon the Rock**, 7901 NE Red Oak Drive Minneapolis, 612-786-9555
- **Evergreen Community Church**, 1300 West 106th Street, Bloomington, 952-887-1646

- **Japanese Fellowship Church**, 4217 Bloomington Avenue, Minneapolis, 612-722-8314
- **Living Waters Christian Church**, 1002 2nd Sreet NE, Hopkins, 952-938-4176
- **Spiritual Life Church**, 6500 Shingle Creek Parkway, Brooklyn Center, 763-560-7221

JEHOVAH'S WITNESSES

- **Lake Harriet Congregation**, (with Spanish), 3715 Chicago Avenue South, Minneapolis, 612-825-6312
- **Como Park Congregation**, 270 Wheelock Parkway, St. Paul, 651-489-8925
- **Riverview Congregation**, (with Spanish), 1545 Christensen Avenue, West St. Paul, 651-457-7139

LUTHERAN

- **Bethlehem Lutheran Church**, 4100 Lyndale Avenue South, 612-823-8281
- **Calvary Lutheran Church**, 7520 Golden Valley Road, Golden Valley, 952-545-5659
- **Central Lutheran Church**, 333 South 12th Street, Minneapolis, 612-870-4416
- **Como Park Lutheran Church**, 1376 West Hoyt Avenue, St. Paul, 651-646-7127
- **Evangelical Lutheran Church Association**, 612-870-3610
- **Gloria Dei Lutheran Church**, 700 Snelling Avenue South, St. Paul, 651-699-1378
- **Hmong Community Lutheran Church**, 301 Fuller Avenue, St. Paul, 651-293-1279
- **Holy Trinity Lutheran Church**, 2730 East 31st Street, Minneapolis, 612-729-8358
- **Latvian Evangelical Lutheran Church**, 3152 17th Avenue South, Minneapolis, 612-722-4622
- **Lutheran Campus Ministry of U of M**, 317 17th Avenue SE, Minneapolis, 612-331-3552
- **Mt. Olivet Lutheran Church**, 5025 Knox Avenue South, Minneapolis, 612-926-7651
- **St. John's Lutheran Church**, 49th & Nicollet, Minneapolis, 612-827-4406

- **Shepherd of the Hills Lutheran Church**, 500 Blake Road, Edina, 952-935-3457

MENNONITE

- **Faith Mennonite Church**, 2720 East 22nd Street, Minneapolis, 612-375-9483
- **St. Paul Mennonite Fellowship**, 576 South Robert Street, St. Paul, 651-291-0647

METHODIST

- **Hamline United Methodist Church**, 1514 Englewood Avenue, St. Paul, 651-645-0667
- **Hennepin Avenue United Methodist Church**, 511 Groveland at Lyndale Avenue, Minneapolis, 612-871-5303
- **Epworth United Methodist Church**, 3207 37 Avenue South, Minneapolis, 612-722-0232
- **Walker Community United Methodist Church**, 3104 16th Avenue South, Minneapolis, 612-722-6612
- **Wesley United Methodist Church**, Marquette Avenue & Grant Street, Minneapolis, 612-871-3585
- **Woodbury United Methodist Church**, 7465 Steepleview Road, Woodbury, 651-738-0305, www.concentric.net/~wumc

NON-DENOMINATIONAL

- **The Rock**, meets at Blake School, near the Walker Art Center, 511 Kenwood Parkway, Minneapolis, www.rockthechurch.com; a church by young people and for young people.
- **Cedarcrest Church**, 1630 East 90th Street, Bloomington, www.cedarcrestchurch.org

PRESBYTERIAN

- **Aldrich Avenue Presbyterian Church**, 3501 Aldrich Avenue South, Minneapolis, 612-825-2479
- **Bryn Mawr Presbyterian Church**, 420 South Cedar Lake Road, Minneapolis, 612-377-5222
- **Central Presbyterian Church**, 500 Cedar Street, St. Paul, 651-224-4728

- **Christ Presbyterian Church**, 6901 Normandale Road, Edina, 952-920-8515
- **Knox Presbyterian Church**, 48th and Lyndale South, Minneapolis, 612-822-2181
- **Macalester-Plymouth United Church**, 1658 Lincoln Avenue, St. Paul, 651-698-8871
- **Presbytery of the Twin Cities**, 122 West Franklin Avenue, Minneapolis, 612-871-7281
- **Randolph Heights Presbyterian Church**, 435 South Hamline Avenue, St. Paul, 651-698-3889
- **St. Luke**, 3121 Groveland School Road, Minnetonka, 952-473-7378, www.churchnet.org/churchnet/stlukepres
- **Trinity Church**, 2125 Tower Drive, Woodbury, 651-738-0045
- **Westminster Presbyterian Church**, Nicollet Mall & 12th Street, Minneapolis, 612-332-3421

ROMAN CATHOLIC

The web site for the Archdiocese of St. Paul and Minneapolis, www.arch.spm.org, provides information about St. Paul's majestic cathedral and offers links to other Catholic resources.

- **Archdiocese of St. Paul and Minneapolis**, 226 Summit Avenue, St. Paul, 651-291-4400
- **Basilica of St. Mary**, 88 North 17th Street, Minneapolis, 612-333-1381, www.mary.org
- **Cathedral of St. Paul**, 239 Selby Avenue, St. Paul, 651-228-1766
- **Immaculate Heart of Mary**, 13505 Excelsior Boulevard, Minnetonka, 952-935-1432
- **Liberal Catholic Church of St. Francis**, 3201 Pleasant Avenue, Minneapolis, 612-823-4276
- **Our Lady of Guadalupe**, 401 Concord Street St. Paul, 651-228-0506
- **Pax Christi**, 12100 Pioneer Trail, Eden Prairie, 952-941-3150, www.paxchristi.com
- **Presentation of the Blessed Virgin Mary**, Larpenteur Avenue at Kennard Street, St. Paul, 651-777-8116
- **St. Albert the Great Church**, 2836 33rd Avenue South, Minneapolis, 612-724-3643
- **St. Bartholomew**, Wayzata Boulevard and Broadway, Wayzata, 952-473-6601

- **St. Olaf Catholic Church**, 215 South 8th Street, Minneapolis, 612-332-7471
- **St. Patrick's**, Valley View and Gleason Road, Edina, 952-941-3164
- **St. Stephens Catholic Church**, 2211 Clinton Avenue South, Minneapolis, 612-874-0311
- **St. Therese**, 18323 Minnetonka Boulevard, Deephaven, 952-473-4422

UNITARIAN

- **First Unitarian Society of Minneapolis**, 900 Mt. Curve Avenue, Minneapolis, 612-377-6608
- **Unity Unitarian Church**, 732 Holly Avenue, St. Paul, 651-228-1456
- **White Bear Unitarian Universalist Church**, 328 Maple Street, Mahtomedi, 651-426-2369

UNITED CHURCH OF CHRIST

- **First Congregational Church of Minnesota**, 500 8th Avenue SE, Minneapolis, 612-331-3816
- **Mayflower Congregational Church**, 106 East Diamond Lake Road, Minneapolis, 612-824-0761
- **Macalester Plymouth United Church**, 1658 Lincoln Avenue, St. Paul, 651-698-8871
- **St. Anthony Park United Church of Christ**, 2129 Commonwealth Avenue, 651-646-7173
- **St. Paul's United Church of Christ**, 900 Summit Avenue, St. Paul, 651-224-5809

WESLEYAN

- **Waite Park Wesleyan Church**, 1510 33rd Avenue NE, Minneapolis, 612-781-7434
- **Oakdale Wesleyan Church**, 6477 North 10th Street, Oakdale, 651-739-2940

SYNAGOGUES

Jewish Minnesota, www.jewishminnesota.org, lists local synagogues and organizations, and has links to other Jewish-related sites as well as arts and culture. This site also has links for singles and newcomers. The **Temple**

of Aaron, www.uscj.org/central/stpaulaaron, is a conservative congregation whose web site is rich with descriptions of rituals and customs.

Two area centers that may be of interest are the **Jewish Community Center-Greater Minneapolis**, 4330 Cedar Lake Road, St. Louis Park, 952-377-8330 and the **Jewish Newcomers-Shalom**, Minneapolis, 5901 Cedar Lake Road, 952-593-2600.

JEWISH-CONSERVATIVE

- **Beth El Synagogue**, 5224 West 26th Street, St. Louis Park, 952-920-3512
- **Sharei Chesed Congregation**, 2734 Rhode Island Avenue South, St. Louis Park, 952-929-2595
- **Temple of Aaron Congregation**, 616 South Mississippi River Boulevard, St. Paul, 651-698-8874

JEWISH-ORTHODOX

- **Lubavitch House**, 15 Montcalm Court, St. Paul, 651-698-3858

JEWISH-REFORM

- **Mount Zion Temple**, 1300 Summit Avenue, St. Paul, 651-698-3881
- **Temple Israel**, 2324 Emerson Avenue South, Minneapolis, 612-377-8680

ISLAM

For the Islamic community, the University of Minnesota's Muslim Students Association is online at www.tc.umn.edu/nlhome/g031/muslimsa.

- **Islamic Center of Minnesota**, 1401 Gardena Avenue NE, Fridley, 763-571-5604

FAR EASTERN

The Minnesota Zen Center site, www.mnzenctr.com, has information on the practice of Buddhism and the Twin Cities Buddhist community. Or try www.freenet.msp.mn.us/people/angelus/buddhism.

The Shambhala tradition has attracted interest because of its music and art. Check www.shambhala-mn.org for more information.

For more information about Hinduism in the Twin Cities check www.hindumandir.org. This site is associated with the Hindu Society of Minnesota where many events take place.

BUDDHIST

- **Karma Kagyu Minneapolis**, 4301 Morningside Road, Edina, 952-926-5048
- **Minnesota Zen Meditation Center**, 3343 East Lake Calhoun Parkway, Minneapolis, 612-822-5313
- **Soka Gakkai International USA**, 1381 Eustis Street, St. Paul, 651-645-3133

HINDU

- **Geeta Ashram Church**, 10537 Noble Avenue North, Brooklyn Park, 763-493-4229
- **Hindu Mandir**, 1835 NE Polk Avenue, Minneapolis, 612-788-1751

OTHERS

NEW AGE

- **Lake Harriet Community Church**, 4401 Upton Avenue South, Minneapolis, 612-922-4272
- **Meditation Center**, 631 University Avenue NE, Minneapolis, 612-379-2386
- **Minneapolis Satsang**, 2300 24th Avenue South Minneapolis, 612-721-4360

If you're an "eclectic practitioner," e.g., a Wiccan, Druid, tolerant Pantheist, etc., the **Orenda North Home Page**, www.geocities.com/Athens/Agora/5249, may be for you.

Finally, the **Minnesota Atheists Online**, www.mn.atheists.org, have a site that explains this oft-misunderstood belief system.

IF YOU WANT TO KNOW WHAT MINNESOTA IS LIKE IN THE WINTER, rent the movie, *Grumpy Old Men*. You'll see that Minnesotans don't just endure the winter, they enjoy it! Popular winter activities include ice fishing, skiing, skating, and even sailing! There's nothing quite like the clattering of an ice boat skipping across "stone water." With snow cover on the ground continuously for several months, it's no surprise that snowmobiles were invented right here in Minnesota. Originally developed as a serious way to get around in inclement weather, snowmobiles quickly became Minnesotans' preferred recreation vehicle, and there are now over 15,000 miles of snowmobile trails in the state. Free snowmobile trail maps and license information are available from the Minnesota Office of Tourism, 651-296-5029, 800-657-3700, or the Minnesota Department of Natural Resources License Bureau, 800-285-2000.

Winter, which really sets in here by November and lasts into April, is brought down by bitter cold weather systems that dip south from Canada. Be prepared for week-long periods of sub-zero (that's sub-zero, not sub-freezing) temperatures, and for the possibility of an April blizzard. Take winter seriously: if you don't stay active in the cold-weather months, cabin fever and shortness of daylight can result in malaise and even depression. Winters here can be a pleasure, and the following information should help to smooth your way.

APPAREL

Layering is the secret to staying comfortable here. You'll need a heavy coat (down-filled is usually warmest). Buy it here or from a catalogue company such as L.L.Bean, which rates its clothing for comfort at sub-zero temperatures. Bean's -50° Fahrenheit down hip-length or longer coats and parkas are popular here. For the proper clothing for more strenuous activities, consult the ski and sports stores. Snow boots will reduce your chances of suffering a major wipeout on the sidewalk, not to mention frozen toes. Adult Sorel boots are rated for very cold temperatures and are especially good for those who have to stand around outside. Sorel makes children's boots that are rated to -25°. Bugabootoos by Columbia have good traction and provide warmth to -25°. Because falling on ice causes many injuries, stores here sell metal-studded detachable soles that fit on the bottoms of your boots. L.L.Bean calls theirs "Stabil-icers." As for long underwear, there are numerous high-tech fabrics suitable for many different activity levels. Check with an outdoor sporting goods store for advice. For sleeping comfort, down comforters give immeasurable pleasure during frosty nights. Check the **Shopping for the Home** chapter for additional winter wear tips.

One final category: dressing up. Minnesota *couture* usually includes long sleeves and boots, and people carry their good shoes. So if you're throwing a winter housewarming, be sure to save room by the front door for the pile of boots.

By the way, your teenager will not dress sensibly, so give it up. Generations of Minnesota teens have proven that you *can* stand at a bus stop dressed in jeans and a short jacket wearing neither hat nor gloves, with temperatures at 20 below, and survive.

DRIVING

If you have four-wheel drive you may think winter driving will be a cinch, the truth is, four-wheel is better in snow, but no better on ice. Front wheel drive cars provide better control in icy conditions than rear-wheel drive, but none of it's any good if you're driving too fast, so slow down.

If the forecast includes bad road conditions, give yourself 15 to 30 extra minutes to get to your destination, including a few minutes to warm up your car. If the weatherman happens to mention "black ice," be especially careful. It is particularly prevalent at intersections and causes many accidents on bridges, freeway ramps and at exposed locations where the wind whips across the pavement. One such location, on I-494 between Minnetonka Boulevard and I-394, is particularly notorious. Your neighbors will be able to clue you in to similar locations near you. If you are taking the bus, you may want to catch an earlier run than you might otherwise; along with the rest of the traffic, buses move more slowly, and tend to fall behind schedule on slippery days.

Before winter really kicks in (sometime in October), take the following steps to winterize your vehicle. Change the radiator fluid and add anti-freeze. Some people switch to a lighter oil (more viscous at low tempera-tures) for winter. If you park outside overnight, 5W-30 oil will help your car start in the morning; if you park in a garage, 10W-30 is sufficient. Do consider buying snow tires and an engine block heater (the origin of the electrical cords you see hanging out of the grilles of some cars). These devices run a low electrical current through your engine to keep it warm overnight. They're particularly helpful if you don't have a garage, although you may find it impractical to run an extension cord out to your car. Finally, think about your battery. Be sure to clean the connections in the fall; and if it is four years old, replace the battery before winter. On those January mornings when it's -20° and you stick your key in the igni-tion, begging and swearing may not turn your engine over, but that new battery will.

Next, stash the following useful items somewhere inside your car:

- An ice scraper.
- A cell phone.
- A set of jumper cables, for yourself or for a coworker stranded in the parking lot.
- A bag of kitty litter (for traction) and a small snow shovel, to help dig your way out of a wipeout (car mats work for tire traction, too).
- A "stranded" emergency kit consisting of blankets, a bright-colored piece of cloth to use as a flag, Hot Hands heat packs, a candle in a cof-fee can (a makeshift heater), matches, a flashlight (with batteries that work), water and a couple of energy bars.

Once the Arctic weather has arrived, keep your gas tank from getting near empty—the water content of the fuel will actually freeze in the gas lines preventing any fuel from getting to the engine.

If you've never driven in snowy conditions before, a good place to practice is a parking lot. The trick to maintaining control when you start to "fishtail" (when the back wheels slide out to the left or right as you hit the brakes) is to steer, not too fast, into the direction that your back wheels are sliding. Try it, it works. Above all, drive as slowly as conditions demand.

As mentioned, you will have to leave a little extra time to drive any-where. Many drivers make an extra key for their car, so they can go out, start up their vehicle, lock it, and return to get ready while the inside of the car gets nice and warm. The police however, counsel against doing this, because of the easy (and warm!) target you leave for a car thief. On par-ticularly cold nights, start your car up for ten minutes or so before going to bed; it gives your engine and battery an extra charge for the morning. One safety tip: don't run your car while it's parked inside a garage—people here die every year that way.

For specific rules on winter parking, see Parking in the **Getting Settled** chapter.

Did we remember to tell you to drive slowly?

HOME INSULATION

Insulation is taken seriously in this climate. As of the year 1999, state building codes require a minimum of R-38 in ceilings with attics. To learn more about the state building code, check online at www.state.mn.us/ebranch/admin/buildingcodes/rules. The **Center for Energy and Environment** in Minneapolis, 612-335-5828, and the **St. Paul Neighborhood Energy Consortium**, 651-644-5436 are excellent resources for information about keeping your house cozy on those below-zero days. You can actually save a considerable amount of money on heating and cooling by making some relatively modest improvements to your home. Caulking or weather-stripping doors and windows can save as much as 10% on your annual energy bill. Storm doors and windows prevent drafts and can save as much as 15% in cold months. Insulating your attic floor or top floor ceiling reduces energy costs by about 5%, and insulating exterior walls can save on both heating and cooling by 20%. If there's a drafty window you'd like to fix without investing in a storm window, an ingenious product now available is clear sheet plastic for your window that contracts with heat. After sizing the sheet over the window, attach it to the frame using double-sided tape. Then, using a hair dryer, heat the plastic until it becomes taut. This should keep drafts out for the rest of the winter. In the spring, when the tulips start pushing out of the ground and you crave fresh air, the plastic detaches easily.

PETS

The two most important things you can do for your pet in the winter are to provide adequate shelter and plenty of water—animals cannot survive on the moisture in snow. You will also need to protect your pet's feet. Pet stores and catalogues sell dog booties, which protect tender paws from being cut or frozen while walking on the crusty snow. Look for booties that are tall enough to stay on. The New England Serum Company catalogue, 800-329-6372, sells waterproof tall booties with non-slip soles. Fido Fleece booties have a draw cord around the top which keeps out snow, www.fid-ofleece.com. You can also pick up booties from vendors at dog shows.

While acclimatized dogs can live outside in winter, many people appreciate the convenience of indoor-outdoor runs. It's an easy do-it-yourself project to install a dog door between the studs in a garage wall to create an out-of-the-elements place for your pet to sleep and be fed.

For those who dream of racing through the woods behind a team of huskies, you've come to the right state. Wintersong Woods Dog Sledding at Cotton, Minnesota, north of Duluth, offers trips that last from one hour to a full day. Contact them at 218-482-3296, www.angelfire.com/biz/wintersongwoods. Sled dog races are held during St. Paul's Winter Carnival and sometimes on Lake Minnetonka.

WEATHER-RELATED RESOURCES

For current weather conditions as well as a lot of weather-related links, WCCO Channel 4 News/WCCO Radio 830 posts extensive information on the web at www.weather.channel4000.com. If you want to check out the snow cover across the US, access www.rap.ucar.edu/weather. Lest you think the only interesting weather comes in winter, check out the Minnesota tornado page, www.tornadoproject.com. Minnesota's popular Weatherguide Calendars are sold for $14.95 in most book and grocery stores, or order one from the following address: Minnesota Weatherguide Calendars, Freshwater Foundation, Box 4, 2500 Shadywood Road, Navarre, MN 55331.

BY CAR

For better or worse, people in the Twin Cities get around by car. With increased growth and development, particularly in the outer suburbs, traffic congestion continues to intensify despite carpooling initiatives and road expansions. That's not to say that if you're coming from Atlanta, Seattle, LA or Denver that you won't find traffic here downright tolerable, but traffic on the main arteries does come to a grinding halt during rush hours. Be prepared.

The first thing to watch for on Twin Cities Interstate highways is the on-ramp metering. The on-ramp signal lights are meant to keep cars flowing smoothly onto the highway. They're bona fide traffic lights, so yes, you're supposed to stop until the light turns green. Another clever idea from the Department of Transportation: the accident alert sign. Most major arteries have hanging message signs on overpasses that give you early warning of upcoming traffic-stoppers. As you head for an exit, be aware of cars coming from the ever-present on-ramp placed just before an exit. This crossing traffic has confused many a new arrival. Then there are Minnesota's two road seasons—construction and pothole. Winter radio devotes a lot of airtime to favorite pothole, biggest pothole, and deepest pothole call-ins. For up-to-the-minute road and construction conditions, call the Minnesota Department of Transportation's (MNDOT) hotline at 800-542-0220 or check www.dot.state.mn.us.

As you get to know the area, you'll find alternatives to the big roads, but until then, here are some of the main arteries:

- The big north-south roadway is **I-35**. This highway splits in Burnsville into I-35W, which heads into Minneapolis, and I-35E, which goes through St. Paul. The two roads run through the northern suburbs before joining again in Lino Lakes. Interstate-35 ends in Duluth. As you near downtown Minneapolis from the south, keep right to stay headed north on I-35W or to get onto I-94 East, which leads to St. Paul. To the left, State Highway 65 ends quickly downtown. There is also an exit here for I-94 West. A congestion-relief tip: if you're heading for the Uptown area from I-35W, consider heading into downtown and taking a street south instead of getting onto I-94—or get in line and wait.

- Lesser north-south routes serving St. Paul are **State Highway 3** (South Robert Street), which connects southeastern suburbs to downtown St. Paul; **State Highway 61**, which winds along the Mississippi and cuts northwest into St. Paul (a beautiful drive near the river); and **State Highway 5**, which goes directly from the airport to West 7th Street.

- Lesser north-south routes on the Minneapolis side are **State Highway 77**, which is a link from Apple Valley to the Mall of America and the airport; **State Highway 100**, which runs from Bloomington through first-ring suburbs to Brooklyn Center; and **US 169**, which runs slightly to the west of Hwy. 100, from Eden Prairie to Maple Grove, and then becomes a state highway heading north. Also, **State Highway 280** joins I-94 to **State Highway 36**, an east-west route north of St. Paul to Stillwater.

- **Interstate-94** is the main east-west thoroughfare. It does not split in two the way I-35 does, but instead passes directly through downtown St. Paul, then cuts past downtown Minneapolis. I-94 then turns due north before heading out of town to the northwest. To continue westward, get onto I-394.

- Minor east-west arteries are **State Highway 62** (the Crosstown), which runs from Minnetonka to the airport, and **I-394** which heads west out of downtown Minneapolis; I-394 ends at US 12, east of Long Lake. **US 12** continues due west out of the metro area as a two-lane highway. The other east-west route is **State Highway 36**, which runs through suburbs north of St. Paul to Stillwater.

- The main encircling arteries are **I-694** to the north and **I-494** to the south and west. Minneapolis-St. Paul International Airport is off I-494/State Highway 5 in Bloomington; see below for best routes by which to approach it. The Mall of America is off I-494 in Bloomington.

CARPOOLING

After you've sat on I-494 and read an entire newspaper a few afternoons in a row, you might start to consider carpooling or vanpooling. Not only will you save time, you'll also save money, and the environment. The Metropolitan Council estimates that the annual cost of driving a roundtrip of just 17 miles a day to work is around $3,000. Plug your own numbers into the formula on the Met Council's web site, www.metrocouncil.org/commuter/cost.htm, and find out what commuting by yourself will cost you. To travel as part of a group, contact Metro Commuter Services which links people who want rides with others who work in the same area. Call them at 651-602-1602 or check out their web site at www.metrocommuterservices.org. If you're curious about how well commuting works for the people who do it, join the discussion online at www.startribune.com/gettingthere.

BY BIKE

Surprisingly large numbers of Twin Citians bike to work, and Minneapolis and St. Paul do their best to make their cities bicycle friendly. There are designated bike lanes throughout downtown Minneapolis; in St. Paul's downtown the bike trails come together at 5th Street, East 3rd Street and Kellogg Boulevard.

Think the climate is bicycle un-friendly? Think again. "There's no such thing as bad weather—just bad clothing," is the motto of dedicated bike commuters. Those making the year-round trek wear layers and cold-weather booties and mittens in the winter. Many others commute by bike only during the warm months, opting for buses or cars in the winter. One tip from dedicated two-wheelers: leave your business clothes at a health club or office and shower and dress there. And for those on the fence on this issue, consider the health benefits, and you may qualify for a discount on your auto insurance.

For those who want to bike *and* ride, there are bike racks on Minneapolis Route 6 buses all year round. Route 6 operates from Southdale to Rosedale via south Minneapolis, Uptown, downtown Minneapolis, U of M, and Dinkytown. Several locations along Route 6 have bike lockers, which offer safe, waterproof storage for a bike and equipment. Locker rental during biking season (April 1 through November 30) costs $40 plus a refundable $25 damage deposit.

For information about commuting by bike, call Metro Commuter Services, 651-602-1602. They will send you a packet of materials that includes maps, bike locker locations and prices, and can even pair you up with a "bike buddy."

GUARANTEED RIDE HOME

People who use alternative transportation don't have to worry about being stuck at work without a ride home when an emergency happens or you unexpectedly have to work late hours. Guaranteed Ride Home gives you two vouchers per year worth up to twenty dollars each to use for emergency taxis or buses. Contact them at 651-602-1602 or www.metro-commuterservices.org.

PUBLIC TRANSPORTATION

BY BUS

Unfortunately, the only mass transit currently available is the bus system, though Light Rail Transit is in the works (see below). The bus system, called MetroTransit, will transport you along many of the larger streets, into and between the two downtowns, and from the downtowns to suburban Park & Ride transit stations, and major shopping centers. If you live in outlying areas, you can park at a designated lot and take the bus into town. Bus stops are marked with the "T" logo.

The main number for Metro Transit is 612-373-3333, TTY 612-341-0140. Even if you live in the far-flung suburbs, call this number for information about your city's bus service. They will mail a transit system map to you and tell you about routes and schedules.

If you prefer, you can visit one of the following Metro Transit Stores to pick up a map, talk to someone in person, or buy a pass:

- **Minneapolis Transit Store**, 719 Marquette Avenue, open 7:30 a.m. to 5:30 p.m., weekdays.
- **St. Paul Skyway Store**, 101 East Fifth Sreet, Firstar Center, open 7:30 a.m. to 5 p.m., weekdays.
- **St. Paul Transit Store**, 1919 University Avenue, open 8:00 a.m. to 4:00 p.m., weekdays
- **Mall of America Transit Store**, 60 East Broadway (in the transit station), open 11:30 a.m. to 7 p.m. Tuesday-Saturday.

An adult non-rush hour base fare ($1.00) gets you one ride plus two transfers to complete a one-way trip. Express routes, which travel between the downtowns and to the suburbs, cost 50 cents extra. Rush hour fare costs an additional 50 cents. Seniors, children age 6-12, and those with disabilities ride for 50 cents. Children 5 and under ride free. You can pay as you go (the driver takes cash, but doesn't make change), buy 10-ride discount passes, or go all-out for a monthly unlimited pass. Ride in the Downtown Zone for 25 cents during non-rush hours and 50 cents during rush hours. SuperSavers let you ride the bus at discounted prices. For a SuperSaver order form, call 612-349-7681, or pull the form off Metro Transit's web site, www.metrocouncil.org/transit. You can also purchase SuperSavers at over 150 metro locations, including many Cub Foods and Rainbow stores, co-ops and drug stores.

People who are disabled must show some form of proof of disability. For information on disabled certification, call 612-349-7415, and see the **Health Care and Services for the Disabled** chapter.

If Metro routes aren't convenient for you, there are other options. Check the routes and schedules of the University of Minnesota Transit Service, 612-625-9000, which runs buses from many locations throughout the city to the University, though usually only on weekdays. Anyone can ride them, and they cost the same as a city bus. **Dial-A-Ride**, a shared curb-to-curb van and minibus service, is another option. Rides must be scheduled in advance, but they do accept standing orders. Your Dial-A-Ride driver can also give you a transfer ticket good for a bus ride. Fares are low, generally under $3. For more information about Dial-A-Ride, call MetroTransit at 612-373-3333 or check www.metrocouncil.org/transit under "Public Transit." To schedule a ride, call your area Dial-A-Ride:

- **Anoka County Traveler**, 763-323-5222
- **Hopkins Hop-A-Ride**, 952-935-8003
- **Maple Grove**, 763-493-2200
- **Northeast Suburbs**, 651-227-6378
- **Northeast and Lake Area Transit**, 651-644-8876
- **Plymouth Dial-A-Ride**, 763-559-5057
- **South (Washington) County Circulator**, 651-704-0799
- **South Shore Lake Minnetonka**, 952-474-7441
- **Southwest Metro Dial-A-Ride**, 952-974-3111
- **Westonka**, 952-474-7441
- **Woodbury**, 651-735-7433

There are also a few fun buses around. MetroTransit's Arts & Eats Express offers transportation to restaurants, museums and theaters located near the Convention Center and downtown hotels. Call 612-373-3333. The RiverCity Trolley offers narrated tours in turn-of-the-century reproduction trolley cars. The route runs from the Minneapolis Convention Center through downtown Minneapolis to the Mississippi Mile riverfront and back through the Warehouse District, May through October. Stations are at St. Anthony Main, Walker Art Center and Sculpture Garden, and the Convention Center. A trolley will also stop every twenty minutes at trolley signs along the route. The cost is $10 for all day; $8 for two hours; and $5 for seniors and children. Call 612-204-0000. St. Paul's Capital City Trolley operates between hotels, restaurants and entertainment; it costs 25 cents a ride, children are free. Call 651-223-5600 for trolley routes or check any St. Paul map. Wayzata has a free trolley that operates from May through October in downtown Wayzata and up to the Colonial Square shopping center on Wayzata Boulevard. Both the trolleys can be chartered for parties and to take you to special events like football games or the Symphony Ball.

LIGHT RAIL TRANSIT (LRT)

LRT finally received funding from the Minnesota legislature in 1999 and the line is expected to be operational between Fort Snelling Station and downtown Minneapolis in late 2003. The first segment to be completed will be the Hiawatha Corridor, along Hiawatha Avenue, which will connect downtown Minneapolis with the Minneapolis-St. Paul International Airport and Mall of America. Almost 12 miles long, this line will have stations at Nicollet Mall, Government Center, Humphrey Metrodome, Cedar/Riverside, East Franklin, East Lake Street, East 38th Street, East 46th Street/Minnehaha Park, the VA Medical Center, Ft. Snelling General Services Administration (GSA) Building Park & Ride, both airport terminals, 80th Street in Bloomington, and the Mall of America Park & Ride. Feeder bus service with timed transfers will connect with the LRT at the Metrodome, East Lake Street, 38th Street, 46th Street, GSA Building and Mall of America.

BY AIR

Minneapolis-St. Paul International Airport, 612-726-5555, www.mspairport.com, one of the busiest airports in the country, is located on State Highway 5 between Bloomington and St. Paul. It is the commercial aviation center for the entire region. Regional airports include Rochester, Duluth, Grand Rapids and Hibbing, all of which have some commercial service, frequently through Northwest/Mesaba Airline. The airport's Humphrey Terminal serves charter airlines and can be reached by going north from I-494 on 34th Avenue. The Humphrey Terminal is well-signed, as are its long-term and off-site parking lots. Unfortunately for consumers, a single airline, Northwest, dominates this market, so ticket prices are high and many Northwest connections must be made through Detroit. To reach the airport by car, use the following routes:

- From Minneapolis and points north, take I-35W south to State Highway 62 east to Highway 5 west or take Hiawatha Avenue all the way south from Minneapolis.
- From St. Paul and points northeast, take I-35E south, then State Highway 5 west.
- From western, southern and eastern suburbs, take I-494 to State Highway 5.

MAJOR AIRLINES

- **Northwest/KLM**, 800-225-2525, www.nwa.com; Northwest posts cybersavers, great deals on last minute travel, on its web site on Wednesdays at 12:01 a.m.
- **Sun Country**, 612-726-5559, www.suncountry.com
- **Iceland Air**, 800-223-5500
- **United**, 800-241-6522, www.ual.com
- **USAir**, 800-428-4322, www.usairways.com; US Airways' "e-savers" fares offer discounts for travel on the weekend, check for postings on the Wednesday prior.
- **Vangard**, 800-826-4827
- **Continental**, 800-642-1617 or www.coticket.com/coolweb

PARKING OPTIONS

The airport terminal always seems to be under construction, and parking is consistently at a premium. Check availability by calling the Parking Information Hotline, 612-826-7000. If possible, park off-site and take a shuttle to the terminal. Parking rates are cheapest off airport property. Terminal parking rates are:

- **Short-term** at the terminal: $1 for the first 1/2 hour; $1 for the second 1/2 hour; $1 each additional hour up to eight hours, then $2 per hour; maximum $34 in a 24-hour period.
- **Long-term**: $14 for 24 hours, $98 per week
- **Econo Lot** parking with free shuttle to the terminal: $2 first two hours, $1 each additional hour; $8 daily, summer; $10 daily, winter; $56 weekly, summer; $70 weekly, winter.
- Heated under-terminal **valet parking**: $8 first hour, $2 each additional hour; $20 daily, May-October; $25 daily, November-April.

AIRPORT BUS SERVICE

The airport bus stop is on the east side of the upper level roadway of the Main Terminal (Lindbergh). Metro Transit buses depart from the shelters on the Upper East roadway, across from doors 1 and 2. Inside Door 2 is a bus kiosk. The bus stop is connected to the main terminal by a skyway, or through the ground transportation center, using escalators or elevators. Ask for directions at the travelers-assistance booth, if necessary.

Daily Service is provided on the following routes: From the **Airport to Downtown Minneapolis**, Route 7 departs every 20 minutes; travel time is about 40 minutes. From the Airport to Downtown St. Paul, Route 54D departs every 30 minutes; travel time is about 25 minutes. From the Airport to the Mall of America, Route 7DEF departs every 20 minutes; travel time is about 12 minutes. Route 54M also provides daily service to the Mall of America, departing every 30 minutes; travel time is about 12 minutes.

From **Downtown Minneapolis to the Airport**, Route 7CDEF departs every 20 minutes; travel time is about 40 minutes. Catch this bus traveling east on 6th Street in Downtown Minneapolis. From **Downtown St. Paul to the Airport**, Route 54M departs every 30 minutes; travel time is about 30 minutes. Catch this bus traveling west on 6th Street in Downtown St. Paul. From the **Mall of America to the Airport**, Route 7, with a destination sign reading "Downtown," provides daily service to the Airport, departing every 20 minutes; travel time is about 12 minutes. Catch this bus at the Mall of America Transit Station, at Gate 2 on the lower level of the east side of the mall. Route 54D departs every 30 minutes; travel time is about 12 minutes. Also catch this bus at the Mall of America Transit Station.

From the **Southwest Suburbs to the Airport**: hourly SW Metro Transit/Express Shuttle Airport Park & Fly Service is provided daily, 6:30 a.m. to 8:30 p.m., from the Southwest Station in Eden Prairie. Twenty-four hour advance reservations are required for service to the airport. Call 952-827-7777. Parking at Southwest Station is free. Pick-up times are scheduled at 30 minutes past the hour with arrival at the airport at 10 minutes past the hour. Cost is $15 per person with advance purchase of tickets at Southwest Station. The cost is $17 when tickets are purchased from the driver. Tickets can be purchased at Southwest Station during regular business hours, 5:30 a.m. to 6:30 p.m. Catch the **return shuttle** at the airport's Ground Transportation Center, one level below baggage claim. Shuttles depart every 30 minutes daily, between 6:00 a.m. and 10:00 p.m., from the Scheduled Shuttle/Hotel Shuttle loading area. Tickets may be purchased at the Express Shuttle USA desk or directly from the driver.

You also have the option of hopping a hotel shuttle from one of the downtowns directly to the airport. It costs more than a bus but less than a taxi. Call a major hotel in either downtown—they all run shuttles. Of course, you can always call a taxi. And if you want to arrive in style, all the limousine services make runs to the airport. Check the "Limousine Service" listings in the Yellow Pages or call:

- **A Minnetonka Limousine Service**, 952-474-2244
- **A Knight Rider Limousine Service**, 651-489-9690

TAXIS

Unless you are in one of the two downtowns, at the airport, or perhaps in a few places such as Uptown and other commercial thoroughfares, you must telephone for a taxi rather than hailing one on the street. No problem, though, there are plenty here. Some only work in specific areas, so call the cab that covers your location.

METROPOLITAN AREA

- **Airport Taxi** (smoke free on request), 612-928-0000
- **Northwest Taxi and Limo**, 612-890-0980

MINNEAPOLIS

- **Blue & White Taxi**, 612-333-3333
- **Minneapolis Yellow Cab**, 612-824-4000

ST. PAUL

- **Citywide Cab**, 651-489-1111
- **St. Paul Yellow Cab**, 651-222-4433

SUBURBAN

- **Minnesota Taxi, Inc.**, 612-866-9999
- **Suburban**, 612-545-1234

AMTRAK

The Amtrak passenger station is centrally located in the Midway area of St. Paul. The Empire Builder stops in the Twin Cities on its route from Chicago (about 8 hours) to Seattle (48 hours plus).

Look for 'rail sale' entries at their web site, www.amtrak.com. Discounts are only available on the internet, and offer savings of up to 60% on long-distance coach train tickets.

- **Amtrak National Route Information**, 800-872-7245
- **Amtrak Twin Cities Passenger Station**, 730 Transfer Road, St. Paul, 651-644-1127

NATIONAL BUS SERVICE

The Greyhound Bus Lines national reservation number is 800-231-2222. Greyhound has terminals in the following Twin Cities locations:

- **Minneapolis**, 1100 Hawthorne, 612-371-3325
- **St. Paul**, 25 West 7th Street, 651-222-0509
- **Minneapolis-St. Paul International Airport**, 612-726-5118

There are also a number of **regional bus lines** you can use:

- **Jefferson Bus Lines**, 612-332-3224, serves the southern part of the state, including Albert Lea, Austin, LaCrosse, Northfield, Red Wing, Rochester and Winona, as well as many US cities further south.
- **Northfield Lines**, 612-339-3223, offers daily shuttles to Northfield.
- **Rochester Direct**, 612-725-0303, offers daily shuttles between International Airport and Rochester

CAR RENTAL

Most car rental agencies are based at the Minneapolis-St. Paul Airport:

- **Affordable Car Rental**, 6405 Cedar Avenue South, Richfield, 612-861-7545, 800-405-5444
- **Avis Rent A Car**, 800-831-2847
- **Budget Car And Truck Rental**, 612-727-2000
- **Dollar Rent A Car**, 800-800-4000, www.dollar.com
- **Hertz Rent A Car**, 612-726-1600
- **A MacFrugal Company**, 2401 East 79 Street, Bloomington, 952-854-8080
- **National Car Rental**, 800-227-7368, www.nationalcar.com

WHILE YOU SEARCH FOR A PERMANENT LIVING SITUATION, THE apartment search services listed in the **Finding A Place to Live** chapter can assist you with a short-term lease. Also, consider the following options, which vary in expense and accommodation. Rates quoted do not include state and city taxes.

HOTELS AND MOTELS

There are hundreds of hotels and motels in Minneapolis, ranging from the bare bones room-with-a-bed motel to luxurious hotel suites with breathtaking views of the city lakes and the Minneapolis skyline. Always remember to ask the hotel reservationist about discounts or weekend packages. Many lodgings have daily, unadvertised specials only offered if you inquire. Keep in mind that room rates vary by season and by convention (no discounts, usually, during large events). The following list of accommodations includes places that might otherwise be hard to find when you live out of town. For a more complete listing, check the online Yellow Pages under "Hotels and Motels," www.qwestdex.com, or call the major hotel chains listed in this chapter. Another good source for hotel and motel recommendations are *AAA Travel Guides*. Free to members, these listings are useful because AAA lists only those hotels that are up to their standards.

MINNEAPOLIS AREA

- **Baymont Inn**, Minneapolis Airport, 7815 Nicollet Avenue South, Bloomington; 6415 James Circle North, Brooklyn Center, 800-789-4103, www.baymontinns.com; rates range from $70 to $80.
- **Best Western American Inn**, 3924 Excelsior Boulevard, St. Louis

Park, 952-927-7731, 800-528-1234, $75 per night for one to two people; refrigerators available upon request.

- **Best Western University Inn**, 2600 University Avenue SE, Minneapolis, 612-379-2313, 800-528-1234; located five blocks from the University of Minnesota campus and Fairview University Hospitals. Some suites have kitchens. Free shuttle to campus and hospital. Rates from $79
- **Hawthorn Suites Hotel**, 3400 Edinborough Way, Edina, 952-893-9300, 800-527-1133; guests may use the ice skating rink, pool, track and playground in attached Edinborough Park. Accepts small pets. Two-room suites have kitchens. Serves breakfast and a light supper, Monday-Thursday. Rates vary with availability, expect to pay at least $145 for one person and $10 additional for each adult per night; lower rates for longer stays; corporate discounts available.
- **The Northland Inn**, 7025 Northland Drive, Brooklyn Park (off I-94/694), 612-536-8300, 800-441-6422, www.northlandinn.com; rates at this all-suite hotel range from $110 to $215.
- **Wyndham Garden**, 4460 West 78th Street Circle, Bloomington, 952-831-3131; this hotel has 13 two-room suites. Rates range from $89 to $159 per night for one person.

ST. PAUL AREA

- **Best Western Stillwater Inn**, 1750 West Frontage Road, Stillwater, 651-430-1300, 800-647-4039; the knotty pine decor will make you feel like you're in the north woods. Accepts pets. Rates from $74 for two people.
- **Day's Inn at RiverCentre**, 175 West 7th Street, 651-292-8929, 800-DAYS-INN; renovated in 1999; refrigerators available upon request. Rates range from $79 to $109 per night. Accepts pets. Weekly and monthly rates available.

HOSTELS

- **The City of Lakes International House**, 2400 Stevens Avenue South, Minneapolis, 612-871-3210, is located among the Victorian homes near the Minneapolis Institute of Arts. Convenient to downtown, it offers private rooms with a group kitchen for $36 per night for one or two people. Dormitories are available for $16 and $17 per night, depending upon whether you have a student ID card or not.

This hostel is only open to out-of-the-metropolitan-area and international visitors. Telephone is free for local calls; fax is available. Visit their web site at www.hostels.com/cityoflakes.

SHORT-TERM RENTALS AND EXTENDED-STAY HOTELS

For a comfortable transition, the following companies offer furnished rooms in convenient locations, such as downtown Minneapolis. Most apartments are equipped with linen, cooking utensils, etc.

- **Country Inns and Suites**, many locations, 800-456-4000 or www.countryinns.com
- **Embassy Suites**: Minneapolis Airport, 7901 34th Avenue South, Bloomington, 612-854-1000; Minneapolis Downtown, 425 South 7th Street, 612-333-3111; St. Paul, 175 East 10th Street, 651-224-5400
- **Executive Suites**, 431 South 7th Street, Minneapolis, 612-884-5266, 800-950-1191; studios and one-bed apartments, equipped kitchens, weekly and monthly rates
- **Midwest Guest Suites**, locations throughout the metro area, 651-735-8127; full suites, equipped kitchens, weekly and monthly rates
- **Oakwood Corporate Housing**, locations throughout the Twin Cities, 800-897-4610; equipped and furnished suites, monthly rates
- **Park Vista**, 387 East Arlington Avenue, St. Paul, 651-771-2084; one- and two-bedroom apartments, kitchen and linen packages. Offers month-to-month leases; located along Gateway biking and hiking trail.
- **The Residence Inn by Marriott**, 7780 Flying Cloud Drive, Eden Prairie, 612-829-0033, has one-and two-bedroom units with patios or balconies and fireplaces. Pets are accepted. Rates range from $109 to $195 per night.
- **Richfield Inn**, 7700 Bloomington Avenue South, Richfield, 612-869-3050, 800-245-3050; one- and two-bed apartments, short-term rates, equipped kitchens

BED & BREAKFAST INNS

If you really want to learn about your new hometown, try a bed & breakfast for your initial stay. Innkeepers always know their way around. The following rates are based on double occupancy for the most modest rooms available.

- **Chatsworth Bed & Breakfast**, 984 Ashland Avenue, Saint Paul, 651-227-4288, $75
- **Inn on the Farm**, 6150 Summit Drive, Brooklyn Center, in the Earle

Brown Heritage Center, 763-569-6330; this restored Victorian "Gentleman's estate" has ten rooms ranging in price from $110 to $140 a night.

- **Le Blanc House**, 302 University Avenue NE, Minneapolis, 612-379-2570 (Riverplace); rates range from $80-$110. Near U of M and only a short walk to downtown Minneapolis.
- **The Garden Gate Bed and Breakfast**, 925 Goodrich Avenue, St. Paul, 651-227-8430 (Victoria Crossing); this two-story Victorian duplex has four rooms. Rates from $55

LUXURY LODGINGS

- **Hyatt Whitney**, 150 Portland Avenue, Minneapolis, 612-339-9300; this converted flour mill overlooks the Mississippi at St. Anthony Falls. Rates range from $215 to $260.
- **Nicollet Island Inn**, 95 Merriam Street on Nicollet Island, Minneapolis, 612-331-1800; a restored factory located in a historic district on the Mississippi River. Rates range from $125 to $160.
- **The Saint Paul Hotel**, 350 Market Street, St. Paul, 651-292-9292; across the square from the Ordway and Landmark Center, this historic hotel has always been *the* place to stay in St. Paul. Rates range from $145 to $170.

HOTEL CHAINS

Hopefully, you'll be able to find an affordable and convenient place to stay from among the above options. For other ideas, and to get a packet of information on a wide variety of local accommodations, contact the Minnesota Office of Tourism at 651-296-5029, 800-657-3700. Or try the national chains in the Twin Cities:

- **Choice Hotels**: Sleep Inn, Comfort Inns, Quality, Clarion and Econo Lodge brands, 800-228-1222
- **Days Inn**, 800-432-9755
- **Hampton Inns**, 800-426-7866
- **Hilton Worldwide**, 800-916-2221
- **Holiday Inn**, 800-HOLIDAY
- **Hyatt**, 800-532-1496
- **LaQuinta Inns**, 800-221-4731
- **Red Roof Inns**, 877-222-7663

ACCESSIBLE ACCOMMODATIONS

The following national chains own hotels in the Twin Cities and have reputations for offering many services to the disabled: **Hilton Hotels**, 800-445-8667, TDD, 800-368-1133, **Hyatt Hotels**, 800-532-1496, **ITT Sheraton**, 800-325-3535, **Marriott Hotels**, 800-288-9290. However, accommodations may be relatively inconsistent from community to community, so be sure to call and talk over your specific needs with the reservations clerk. Be aware that federal law requires that if a hotel guarantees reservations for its regular rooms, it must also guarantee reservations for handicapped-accessible rooms. Another issue for people with disabilities is security: some experts advise that you ask the hotel to remove the handicap sign from your door if there is one.

You may have the best luck finding fully accessible accommodations outside the downtowns or in the newer hotels of Minneapolis, many of which are connected by skyways. A word of warning: if you travel in a large van, the downtown parking ramps will probably not be able to accommodate your vehicle, even though the hotels may be able to accommodate you. Some hotels with accessible accommodations are:

- **Crowne Plaza Northstar Hotel**, 618 South Second Avenue, Minneapolis, 612-338-2288, is on the skyway system. It has four handicapped accessible rooms, each with one king-sized bed; one bath with a roll-in shower, the rest with tubs with seats; TDD and strobe-light alarms are available; the elevators have Braille.
- **Hilton Minneapolis**, 1001 Marquette Avenue, 612-397-4875, has a number of fully accessible rooms, some with roll-in showers, and TDD. Located on the skyway system; can accommodate large vans in its parking ramp.
- **Holiday Inn/Bandana Square**, 1010 Bandana Square West, St. Paul, 651-647-1637, has five accessible rooms with king-size beds.
- **Holiday Inn Metrodome**, 1500 Washington Avenue South, 612-333-4646, is near the University of Minnesota campus and the HHH Metrodome. It has 12 accessible rooms, four with roll-in showers; some public areas have limited accessibility for those in wheelchairs.
- Minneapolis' **Hyatts** have some accessible rooms. At the Hyatt Whitney (see **Luxury Lodgings** above) two percent of its rooms and the public areas of the hotel are handicap accessible. It is located in downtown, but is not on the skyway system. The Hyatt Regency, 1300 Nicollet Mall, 612-370-1234, on the skyway system and has 18 fully-accessible rooms, half with roll-in showers and the rest with tubs and bars; TDD and strobe light alarms are available.

- **Minneapolis Marriott City Center**, 30 South 7th Street in the City Center shopping complex, 612-349-4000; connected to the skyway, this hotel's accessible rooms have two double beds, roll-in showers, railings, low fixtures, TDD and strobe light alarm. Make reservations at 800-288-9290.
- **Northland Inn and Executive Conference Center**, 7025 Northland Drive, Brooklyn Park, 763-536-8300 or www.northlandinn.com, is a suite hotel with fully accessible rooms.

WHEELCHAIRS AND SCOOTERS

If you need to rent a scooter or motorized wheelchair while you're here, these are some places to start looking:
- **Jackson Medical**, 651-645-6221
- **Gopher Medical Supply**, 612-623-7706
- **Health East/Medical Home**, 612-881-2635
- **Macalester-Plymouth United Church**, 1658 Lincoln Avenue, St. Paul, 651-698-8871

ONCE YOU'VE SETTLED IN, YOU'LL EVENTUALLY WANT TO GET away, if only for a weekend. Twin Citians tend to frequent the places described below. In addition to these, you may want to join the time-honored tradition of heading "**Up North**." It doesn't matter where you go—there are ten thousand lakes to choose from. One popular destination is **Lake Mille Lacs**, about two hours' drive north—except on Friday afternoons. Call 888-350-2692 or check www.millelacs.com for specifics. If you head that way, don't miss the giant Paul Bunyan in nearby **Brainerd**, it's a Minnesota thing. So is breaking the short trip to Duluth at Toby's Restaurant in **Hinckley**—everybody does it!

One word of general information: Minnesota law requires separation between smokers and non-smokers, except in bars, but restaurants' non-smoking sections are not always sufficient for people with allergies or lung or cardiovascular diseases. Some smoke-free restaurants are noted below, but you can obtain a free comprehensive guide to smoke-free restaurants throughout the state from The Association for Nonsmokers-Minnesota (ANSR), 2395 University Avenue West, Suite 310, Saint Paul, MN 55114-1512, 651-646-3005.

IN-TOWN GETAWAYS

You don't have to go far to get away from the rat race. Just head for **Lake Minnetonka**, west of Minneapolis or for the **St. Croix River Valley**, east of St. Paul. These are favorite destinations of day-trippers and also have romantic, restful inns and bed and breakfasts for those wanting to stay overnight.

Excelsior, on Lake Minnetonka, has a New England village feel with a waterfront common area and a variety of colorful houses. Take a walking tour of the historic buildings—sometimes a tour is led by local author Bob Williams, who uses Excelsior as the setting for his books.

A resort since the 1800s, Excelsior's ties to the lake are audible in the mellow whistles of the excursion boats that resound throughout the village. Two boats, the Queen of Excelsior and QE2 offer public brunch cruises on Sundays. For reservations call 952-474-2502 or access www.qecruise.com. The Minnehaha, a 1906 streetcar boat that has been raised and restored by community volunteers after being scuttled in Lake Minnetonka back in the 1920s, runs a scheduled route on weekends and holidays and will drop you off at the Wayzata dock so you can explore that village too.

The pace in Excelsior is casual: browsing in the shops on Water Street, swimming at the Common, cheering for the home team at a softball game by the lake. If you want to be more active, rent a jet ski from Bay Rentals, 952-474-0366, or a boat from Lake Minnetonka Boat Rentals, 952-472-1220. You can walk and bike the LRT trail from Hopkins through Excelsior to Victoria, or stroll through the gardens of the University of Minnesota Landscape Arboretum nearby. Lake Minnetonka Regional Park, 952-474-4822, several miles west in **Minnetrista**, has a swimming pond and boat launch, and recently completed a $500,000 children's playground that even adults will love.

Don't miss: Excelsior Bay Books, 36 Water Street, 952-401-0932, an independent bookstore well-known for its children's and fiction sections, and Leipold's Antiques and Gifts, 239 Water Street, 952-474-5880; Adele's Frozen Custard & Old Fashioned Ice Cream, on Excelsior Boulevard at the east end of town, is a good place to end your walking tour with a dish of the ultimate in ice cream. Be sure to catch a performance at the world-famous Old Log Theater, 5175 Meadville Street, 952-474-5951. The Old Log serves excellent dinners and is renowned for its British farces and for the famous actors who have starred in them.

The sense of community here is felt in many ways: shopkeepers who take time to get to know the tastes of their customers, people who say hello on the street, the turnout at the free concerts on the Common and Fourth of July fireworks, and the numbers who volunteer to work at Art on the Lake, the village's June arts and crafts fair.

If you decide to stay the night, there are two bed and breakfasts: The Christopher Inn, 202 Mill Street, 952-474-6816 and the James H. Clark House at 371 Water Street, 952-474-0196. Both are charming Victorians, centrally located.

For more information contact the Excelsior Chamber of Commerce, 440 Union Place 55331, 952-474-6461, www.excelsioronline.com.

Stillwater is a lively town with a history that pre-dates statehood. Despite the number of jails/prisons—there are four in the area including the Washington County jail at the government center and the maximum security Stillwater Correctional Facility up on the hill, Stillwater is a picturesque town nestled into the bluffs of the St. Croix River. Located just 20 miles east of downtown St. Paul, it was a thriving logging town into the late 1800s and is listed on the National Registry of Historic Places. Visitors enjoy the antiquing, canoeing and boating on the beautiful St. Croix, one of America's protected Wild and Scenic Waterways, or touring the river valley from a hot air balloon.

This is one town which did not tear down its past in order to build its present, so many of its elegant old mansions survive and have been turned into bed and breakfasts. Elephant Walk, 801 Pine Street West 55082, 651-430-0528, has beautiful gardens and is often recommended, as is Rivertown Inn Bed & Breakfast, 306 Olive Street West 55082, 651-430-2955. These are smoke-free. For other accommodations visit the Stillwater homepage, address below.

For dining the locals suggest The Dock Cafe, 425 Nelson Street East, 651-430-3770, a great place to sit and watch the river traffic and eat hamburgers. Joseph's Family Restaurant, 14608 60th Street North, 651-439-3336, is known for its pie, and Savories, 108 North Main Street, 651-430-0702, features homemade bread and bakery goods, varied cuisine, and is smoke-free.

Visit Stillwater during Lumberjack Days in July to watch professional and amateur loggers as they demonstrate log rolling, ax throwing and other lumberjack skills.

The Stillwater Chamber of Commerce, 324 South Main Street 55082, 651-439-4001, can give you more information, or access www.ci.stillwater.mn.us.

The St. Croix National Scenic Riverway from Stillwater upstream to Taylor's Falls is an unpolluted National Park. It is easy to navigate by canoe or powerboat and also attracts hikers, rock climbers, cross-country skiers, mountain bikers, and fishermen. There are three parks in this area: St. Croix Islands Scenic Reserve and William O'Brien State Park in Wisconsin; and Interstate Park at Taylor's Falls. For information, contact the Superintendent, St. Croix National Scenic Riverway, P.O. Box 708, St. Croix Falls, WI 54024, 715-483-3284. Information is available online from the National Park Service at www.nps.gov/sacn. The Minnesota Department of Natural Resources (DNR) number is 651-296-6157, www.dnr.state.mn.us.

DULUTH AND THE NORTH SHORE OF LAKE SUPERIOR

Duluth, about two hours' drive north of the Twin Cities up I-35, is an easy weekend destination. Here you can watch giant cargo ships from around the world enter Duluth's harbor under the Aerial Lift Bridge. There are a lot of other things to do here, in every season: downhill ski at city-owned Spirit Mountain; bike, hike or in-line skate the Munger Trail; stroll the boardwalk and visit the police horse stable at Canal Park; or hop on a tour boat to cruise the harbor, 218 722-6218 or www.visitduluth.com.

Walking the quiet residential streets of the historic East End is always a pleasure. The massive mansions and ornate Victorian houses here were built by wealthy turn-of-the century businessmen who could afford to bring master craftsmen over from Europe to build their regal homes. Glensheen at 3300 London Road is a Jacobean mansion on the lake where two infamous murders took place. It is open to the public June-October. Call 218-724-8863 for information, 888-454-4536 for tour reservations or visit www.d.umn.edu/glen.

For those who like to camp, the **Superior National Forest** or one of the several state forests along the North Shore are favorite destinations. For Superior National Forest information call 218-626-4300 or 877-444-6777 (reservations). For state forests, contact the DNR, 651-296-6157, www.dnr.state.mn.us.

If you're really adventurous, go kayaking in Lake Superior. Raven Moon Adventures leads guided tours and provides instruction, including women's kayaking workshops, 219-724-8914 or www.cpinternet.com/ravenmn. The University of Minnesota, Duluth offers sea kayaking/rock climbing tours, 218-726-6533, www.d.umn.edu/umd.outdoors.

If you're looking for a room with a lake view, try these three: Fitger's Inn, a renovated brewery at 600 East Superior Street 55802, 888-FITGERS or www.fitgers.com; The Mansion, 3600 London Road 55804, 218-724-0739, an especially elegant bed and breakfast right next door to Glensheen; or the interesting Mountain Villas on top of Spirit Mountain, 800-642-6377, www.spiritmt.com.

Popular events in and near Duluth are Grandma's Marathon from Two Harbors to Duluth in June and the North Shore In-line Marathon over the same route in September, Two Harbors Folk Festival in July, Bayfront Blues Festival in August, and the 400-mile John Beargrease sled dog race in February.

For help planning your trip contact the Duluth Convention and Visitors Bureau, 100 Lake Place Drive, Duluth, MN 55802, 800-4DULUTH, www.visitduluth.com.

If you have a little time, continue up the **North Shore** of **Lake Superior**, the largest freshwater lake on earth. Its mild appearance on a calm day belies the fact that these are some of the most dangerous waters anywhere in the world. Highway 61 along the shore is lined with markers memorializing the ships that have wrecked on Superior's iron-red rocks.

The views as you drive along the lake through Superior National Forest are stunning and minimalistic, often reduced to a rock against sky and water. Park and hike to Gooseberry Falls and Split Rock Lighthouse—the routes are well-marked from the highway.

A little farther up the coast, **Lutsen** is a famous resort area on the Lake Superior shore which offers downhill and cross-country skiing and snowmobiling in winter and hiking, sea kayaking, canoeing and fly fishing in summer. There are numerous motels and resorts here. Contact Lutsen Ski Area, 218-663-7281, the Village Inn and Resort at 800-642-6036, www.twin-cities.com/ski/lutsen or Lutsen-Tofte Tourism Association, 888-61-NORTH, www.mn.northshore.com.

Grand Marais, just up the road, is home to the Grand Marais Art Colony, www.boreal.org/arts/thecolony, which offers workshops for visual artists and writers throughout the summer. The galleries here are worth a stop. Contact Grand Marais Art Colony, Box 626, Grand Marais, MN 55604, 800-385-9585. For lodging and information call 888-922-2225 or check www.grandmaraismn.com.

Seventeen miles north of Grand Marais, the Gunflint Trail takes off into the **Boundary Waters Canoe Area Wilderness** (**BWCAW**). Extending 150 miles along the Canadian border, the BWCAW is a million-acre labyrinth of portage-linked lakes. Here you can canoe and camp just as primitively as the French-Canadian voyageur fur-traders did in the 1700s. Cross-country skiing, snowshoeing, dog sled trips, and wolf-calling are popular activities in the wilderness in winter. Whatever the season, you are in close contact with nature including bears and moose; be careful. Guides are available and permits are required for all visitors entering the BWCAW or neighboring **Quetico Provincial Park**, another million acres of wilderness on the Canadian side of the border. Motorized equipment is prohibited. Visit in the middle of the week or before Memorial Day or after Labor Day, and you will encounter fewer people. The main entry points to the BWCAW are through **Crane Lake, Ely, Tofte,** and **Grand Marais**, so that's where the outfitters are located. If you use an outfitter, as most people do, the outfitter will be able to arrange for your permit. For help finding outfitters, access www.exploreminnesota.com or contact the Grand Marais Chamber of Commerce, 800-622-4014, www.grandmaraismn.com; the Ely Chamber of Commerce, 800-777-7281, www.ely.org; or the Crane Lake Visitor and Tourism Bureau, 800-362-7405, www.cranelake.org. For Gunflint Trail lodgings and outfitters call 800-338-6932, www.gunflint-trail.com.

For information and to reserve an overnight permit to visit the BWCAW contact: BWCAW Reservation Office, P.O. BOX 462, Ballston, NY 12020, toll free 877-550-6777 or www.bwcaw.org. Information can also be obtained from the Superior National Forest at 218-626-4300, www.gis.umn.edu/snf. For permits for Quetico call 807-597-2735.

Seven miles south of the Canadian border, **Grand Portage National Monument** was once a large fur-trading post. Tour the reconstructed fort and hike or cross-country ski the 8.5-mile portage footpath to the awe-inspiring 200-foot high Pigeon River waterfall. For camping information contact the Superintendent, Grand Portage National Monument, P.O. Box 668, Grand Marais, MN 55604, 218-387-2788.

Grand Portage is the place to catch the ferry to **Isle Royale**, a wilderness park of rugged forests and unspoiled lakes located 22 miles out in Lake Superior. Home to wolves and moose, it is accessible only by boat or floatplane, April to October. Eighty percent of Isle Royale National Park is underwater and includes shallow warm-water ponds and fast streams as well as the cold, deep waters of Lake Superior. Sport fishing is popular here and trout, northern pike, walleye and perch are abundant, especially in spring and fall. Travel in the park is by foot or boat—no pets, no bikes. Campers, including boaters, need a permit (free at any ranger station) and should write for information before traveling to the park: Superintendent, Isle Royal National Park, 800 East Lakeshore Drive, Houghton, Michigan 49931, or call 906-482-0984. Reservations for Rock Harbor Lodge or housekeeping cabins may be made by calling the Lodge at 906-337-4993 or National Park Concessions, Inc., Mammoth Cave, Kentucky 42259, 502-773-2191. Floatplane service is available from Houghton, Michigan (see Superintendent above).

VOYAGEURS NATIONAL PARK

The quiet splash of the voyageurs' paddles dipping into sparkling water is long gone and has been replaced by crowds of house-boating wilderness-seekers and fishermen on the chain of 30 lakes that makes up Voyageurs National Park. There are primitive boat-in campsites scattered throughout the park, but public and private campsites, accessible by car, also are available. The Park Service maintains a number of trails for hiking and cross-country skiing. Snowmobiling and ice fishing are allowed on the frozen lakes in winter. Moose, bear, eagles, loons and wolves can be seen here. Three park visitor centers offer information, guidebooks, maps, navigational charts, naturalist-guided trips and campfire talks: Rainy Lake Visitor Center is open year round; Kabetogama Lake Visitor Center and Ash River Visitor Center are open seasonally. There are also narrated boat tours, which depart from Rainy Lake Visitor Center and visit an old lumber camp, gold and mica mines, and the nesting habitats of gulls and cormorants. Reservations are suggested: 218-286-5470.

You can enter Voyageurs Park from four points along US 53 between Duluth and International Falls: Crane Lake, Ash River, Kabetogama, and Rainy Lake. Year-round food, fuel, lodging and boat rentals are available outside the park at the four access points. There is also a park concession at Kettle Falls, which operates seasonally, providing food, lodging, boat rentals and a mechanized portage between Rainy and Namakan Lakes. Because this park spans the international border, you must report to customs before and after crossing the Canadian border. Contact Superintendent, Voyageurs National Park, 3131 US 53, International Falls, MN 56649-8904, 218-283-9821 or www.nps.gov. For lodging and boat rental around Rainy Lake call 1-800-FALLS-MN or www.intlfalls.org; Ash River is 800-950-2061; for Crane Lake, see BWCAW above.

MISSISSIPPI BLUFF COUNTRY

In sharp contrast to the rocky wildness of the North Shore drive, Highway 61, going south from the Twin Cities, is a pastoral route across rolling farmland and the tall wooded bluffs of the Mississippi River.

About an hour from the Twin Cities is **Red Wing,** a popular day or weekend destination. A big rock called Barn Bluff towers over downtown like a nose that is too big for its face. It's a hard climb, but worth it—the view of Red Wing, Lake Pepin and the surrounding river valley is breathtaking. People go to Red Wing for many reasons: the scenic drive, Antique Alley, factory outlets, proximity to Welch Village ski area and the Cannon Valley Trail, and the wonderful St. James Hotel, where they serve you coffee and hot chocolate in bed, 800-252-1875. If the St. James is full, there are many other delightful options, visit www.bbonline.com or www.red-wing.org or call the Convention Bureau, 800-498-3444, for more information on where to stay.

Lake Pepin at **Lake City** is another half-hour south. Lake Pepin is a natural wide spot in the Mississippi River where the sailing is wonderful, though it's shared with a lot of recreation and commercial traffic. The lush broad flood plain and majestic river bluffs of Lake Pepin's shoreline make it prime territory for bird watching. The large Lake City Marina, 651-345-4211, rents boats and has excellent shower and bathroom facilities as well as electric hook-ups, so you can sleep on board your boat if you choose.

A favorite fall color/apple-picking trip is to drive down the Minnesota side of the river on Highway 61, cross at Wabasha or Winona and come back up Wisconsin Route 35, eating at the famous, and smoke-free, Harbor View Cafe in **Pepin, Wisconsin**, 715-442-3893. Laura Ingalls Wilder's *Little House in the Big Woods* is replicated just north of the town. Contact the Pepin Visitor Information Center, 715-442-3011.

Along the way, visit **Frontenac**, on the Minnesota side, a village where little has changed since the 1880s. Frontenac State Park completely encircles the village and is a sanctuary for migratory warblers and bald and golden eagles. Hiking trails here overlook the valley and lead you to In-Yan-Teopa, a giant boulder that was sacred to the Dakota and Fox Indians. Look again for bald eagles at Read's Landing near Wabasha.

At **Winona**, you hit serious apple country. Winona County Road 1 is known as Apple Blossom Drive, but it is **LaCrescent**, which bills itself as the Apple Capital of Minnesota. Time your trip to catch the Apple Festival held here during the third week in September.

If you keep going far enough, **Trempealeau**, about three hours down on the Wisconsin side of the river, is a tiny town with the historic Trempealeau Hotel. Here you can rent bikes and canoes to explore nearby Perrot State Park and the Upper Mississippi National Wildlife Refuge. Spot herons, eagles, trains and river barges. Call 608-534-6898 for more information.

An alternative to the Minnesota/Wisconsin loop is to turn west at Winona, on US Route 14, and head for **Mantorville** where Greek revival buildings are listed on the National Register of Historic Places.

WISCONSIN

If you want to step outside of time, head for Bayfield and The Apostle Islands National Lakeshore. Cruise one of the great sailing grounds of the world. Fish one of the great fishing holes. Bike, hike and learn about nature from the rangers on the islands. Or just enjoy the ambience.

Start your vacation on the mainland in **Bayfield**, a gem of a town on the shore of Lake Superior that mixes art, antiques and Victorian brownstone mansions with hunting, fishing, camping and sailing. Take a sailboat cruise on the three-masted schooner, the Zeeto, or charter a boat yourself. Sailboats, Inc. at Bayfield and Superior, WI, operates a charter service/sailing school, 800-826-7010, www.sailboats-inc.com. Or try sea kayaking. Midwest Mountaineering and Raven Moon Adventures teach a three-day basic kayaking course which begins with a night on Lake Nokomis in Minneapolis and ends with an overnight in the Apostle Islands, 612-339-3433.

Bayfield is home to several active yacht clubs which conduct a full schedule of regattas. Try to catch the Blessing of the Fleet in June when fishing boats, sailboats, kayaks, rowboats, and even ferry boats decorated with flags weave their way through the Bayfield harbor in a colorful parade to welcome the summer season and receive an ecumenical blessing.

Bayfield is also a winter destination. The first weekend in February, you can Run on Water—a five-mile race to Madeline Island over the Madeline Island Ice Road. This weekend also features the Asaph Whittlesey Snowshoe Race.

Bayfield is known as a romantic destination, and its bed and breakfasts do their best to make it true. The most famous is the Old Rittenhouse Inn, 301 Rittenhouse Avenue, Bayfielde, WI 54814, 715-779-5111.

For further information, contact The Bayfield Chamber of Commerce, 42 South Broad Street, P.O. Box 138, Bayfield, WI 54814, 800-447-4094, or www.bayfield.org.

Then it's out to the islands. You can go back and forth easily on the ferry that travels from Bayfield Dock to Madeline Island every half-hour, 715-747-2051.

Sightseeing boats and island shuttles also depart from the Bayfield Dock. The Grand Tour sightseeing trip takes half a day and takes you past all 22 of the Apostle Islands. For campers, there is a shuttle to Stockton Island from the mainland. Stockton is the largest island and has the most extensive trail system, as well as civilized camping facilities and an awesome swimming beach. Devil's Island is famous for its sea caves.

Madeline Island is not part of the park, but is developed with summer and year-round residences, hotels and bed and breakfasts. Besides water sports, you can play golf and tennis at the Madeline Island Golf Club; explore the island on rented mopeds or bikes; or bird watch in the Madeline Island Wilderness Preserve.

Among the lodging choices on Madeline is Brittany Bed & Breakfast, Old Fort Road, P.O. Box 381, LaPointe, Wisconsin 54850, 715-747-5023, www.bbonline.com/wi/brittany. This peaceful waterfront complex was built in the style of an Adirondack camp, with a main house and several cottages. Its manicured croquet lawn begs for ladies in long white dresses and gentlemen in boaters. And after you peg out (finish the game in croquet talk), be sure to stop for a glass of wine in the formal garden's tea house.

The Madeline Island Chamber of Commerce can be reached at 888-475-3386. For information about the National Park write the Superintendent, Apostle Islands National Lakeshore, Route 1, Box 4, Bayfield, WI 54814, 715-779-3397 or contact the Sand Bay Information Center, 715-779-3397. For more information about sailing, contact US Sailing, 800 US Sail-1, www.ussailing.org. This web page will give you a lot of information including help for sailors with special needs.

Madison, the Wisconsin capital is four and a half-hours' drive southeast of St. Paul. Stop at Devil's Lake State Park on the way—it's a beautiful hiking area with quartzite cliffs, 608-356-8301. In Madison, enjoy University of Wisconsin events, or take in some live music or theater. American Players Theater, a Shakespearean repertory group, performs outdoors in Spring Green in the summer, 608-588-7401. Taliesen, Frank Lloyd Wright's architecture school, is also near Spring Green. The Greater Madison Convention and Visitors Bureau can give you more information, www.visitmadison.com or call 800-373-6376.

To contact the Wisconsin Department of Tourism call 800-372-2737 (neighboring states), 800-432-8747 (other states) or access www.tourism.state.wi.us. The Wisconsin Department of Natural Resources, 608-266-2105, is online at www.dnr.state.wi.us. You can reserve a state park campsite at www.maps1.reserveamerica.com.

NORTH COUNTRY NATIONAL SCENIC TRAIL

The nation's longest hiking trail, the North Country National Scenic Trail is a work in progress. Viewed on a map, it looks like the path of an ant, beginning at Crown Point State Historic Site on the Vermont-New York border and meandering over 4,000 miles through New York, Ohio, Pennsylvania, Michigan, Wisconsin, and Minnesota to Lake Sakakawea in North Dakota.

According to the National Park Service, the trail will captivate the mind "with a kaleidoscope of scenes of a developing America and the wild, undeveloped resources from which it grew. The hiker will experience the grandeur of the Adirondack Mountains, the tranquillity of the rural farm countryside, the splendor of placid lakes and sparkling steams among the forested hills, the boundlessness of the northern prairie, the merging of water and sky at the horizon of the Great Lakes, and the nostalgia of historic canals and abandoned logging and mining villages."

So far, though, there are a lot of gaps, and the trail is measured in segments. It comes into the Upper Midwest across **Michigan's Upper Peninsula**, passing through the **Pictured Rocks National Lakeshore** for 43 miles along the shore of Lake Superior, climbing from beach level to the tops of high sandstone cliffs. This is possibly the most awe-inspiring vista on the entire trail, although there are plenty of people who would vote for the spectacular **Black River Canyon** waterfalls a little farther west in **Porcupine Mountains Wilderness State Park.**

In Wisconsin, the longest segment of the trail is in the remote north-central wilderness of the **Chequamegon National Forest**. Because it is not very steep, this section of trail is not terribly difficult. Farther west the last segment in Wisconsin goes through **Brule River State Forest** near Solon Springs. The first two miles here are along a historic portage lined with commemorative stones which are inscribed with the names of early explorers and traders who passed through the area.

Water is the theme of the trail in **Minnesota** where there are several disconnected bits and pieces. In the east, a short segment in **Jay Cooke State Park** cuts through the rugged gorge of the **St. Louis River**. In the middle of the state, a beautiful 68-mile segment in the **Chippewa National Forest** traverses wetlands, lakes and streams and skirts **Leech Lake**—one of the largest lakes in the state. A short distance farther west, a segment is completed in **Itasca State Park**—the birthplace of the mighty Mississippi River. It is here that the trail begins to emerge from the northern forests and enters its final landscape, the grasslands of the Great Plains.

The vastness of the tall-grass prairie is evident when hiking two fairly long segments of certified trail in **North Dakota**: a 25-mile segment across the **Sheyenne National Grassland** and a 147-mile segment along the **New Rockford and McCluskey Canal** corridors and the **Lonetree Wildlife Management Area**. Cattle are allowed to graze the Sheyenne National Grassland; so Lonetree, which is being restored to natural prairie, is closer to what the pioneers saw. Ironically, the kaleidoscope of scenes ends in North Dakota at **Lake Sakakawea**, a man-made lake in the unspoiled land that once fascinated explorers Lewis and Clark.

Information, updates and brochures can be obtained from: North Country National Scenic Trail, 700 Rayovac Drive, Suite 100, Madison, Wisconsin 53711, 608-264-5610; or access the National Park Service homepage, www.nps.gov; the Great Outdoor Resources Page, www.gorp.com; North Country Trail Association, 49 Monroe Center NW, Suite 200B, Grand Rapids, Michigan 49503, 616-454-5506; E-mail at NCTAssoc@AOL.com, or homepage, www2.dmci.net.

CHICAGO

This just squeaks in as a "quick" getaway—it's an eight-hour drive, one way—but if you give yourself four days, you won't feel rushed. Or fly—there are often special fares between Minneapolis and Chicago. "The Windy City" needs no introduction, but as a reminder, you can visit the Art Institute, the Field Museum of Natural History, the Magnificent Mile of shopping on Michigan Avenue, eclectic shops and pubs on Clark Street, Old Town, blues and jazz festivals, and more. Yes, the Cubs still play at Wrigley Field. To get a packet of information, call the Chicago Office of Tourism at 312-744-2400.

ADDITIONAL RESOURCES

For general travel information and an excellent comprehensive travel guide for the entire state, call the Minnesota Office of Tourism, 121 Seventh Place East, St. Paul 55101, 651-296-5029, 800-657-3700 or www.exploreminnesota.com. For trip planning or park maps call the Minnesota Department of Natural Resources at 651-296-6157 or visit www.dnr.state.mn.us. To reserve a campsite at one of the many state parks, call the DNR's reservation line at 800-246-2267. In case your getaway involves skiing, call the Snow Hotline at 651-296-6157. For a free Wisconsin vacation guide call 800-432TRIP or www.travelwisconsin.com. The North Dakota Tourism Department's number is 800-435-5663. For Travel Michigan dial 888-784-7328. The National Park Service is online at www.nps.gov/noco. For help finding bed and breakfasts try B&Bs on the web, www.mnmo.com; The Bed and Breakfast Channel, www.bbchannel.com; or Bed and Breakfast online, www.bbonline.com. First-Fiddle, www.first-fiddle specializes in supplying information about lake resorts. For road condition and detour information call the Minnesota Department of Transportation (MNDOT), 800-542-0220.

MOSQUITOES EAT YOU IN SUMMER AND THE COLD FLASH-freezes you in winter, but if you're a Minnesotan, you'll be out and about anyway, dismissing such perceived life-threatening conditions as mild annoyances. All four seasons in the Twin Cities offer exciting annual celebrations, festivals, and shows. Here are just a few you may want to experience yourself.

JANUARY

- **St. Paul Winter Carnival**; this spectacular annual event includes parades, dog sled races, a treasure hunt, the selection of dance hall queen Klondike Kate, and fervent attempts by the Vulcans to warm up the winter. It runs into early February.
- **Land O'Lakes Kennel Club Dog Show**, RiverCenter, St. Paul, 651-224-9627; all breeds. This is the largest indoor show in the region.
- **Minneapolis Boat Show**, Minneapolis Convention Center, 612-827-5833

FEBRUARY

- **Chilly Open**; play golf on frozen Lake Minnetonka in Wayzata! There are three courses and lots of hot food and drink. For information, call 952-473-9595.
- **John Beargrease Dogsled Race**, Duluth, Minnesota.

MARCH

- **St. Patrick's Day Celebration,** March 17; St. Paul really knows how to celebrate its Irish heritage. Irish and non-Irish alike participate in the rowdiness—parade, bar-hopping and kilt-tilting—all over town.

- **Builders Association Spring Preview of Homes**, offers tours of newly built homes to acquaint you with builders, and the latest trends and developments. Call 651-697-1954 for a directory.
- **Maple Syruping** at the University of Minnesota Landscape Arboretum, 952-443-2460; Fort Snelling State Park, 952-725-2724; Wood Lake Nature Center, 612-861-9365
- **Minnesota State High School Hockey Tournaments**, 612-560-2262
- **Minnesota State High School Basketball Tournaments**, 612-560-2262

APRIL

- **Festival of Nations**, RiverCentre, 651-224-9627; Minnesota's largest multicultural extravaganza features ethnic cafes, folk dancing, and an international bazaar.
- **Annual Smelt Run** in rivers near Duluth.
- **Taste of the Nation Minnesota**, Minneapolis, www.taste.org, a benefit for hunger relief.

MAY

- **Minnesota Fishing Opener**, this *huge* event in the land of 10,000 lakes is the weekend we are all reminded that Minnesota has too many fishermen and too few roads heading "Up North."

JUNE

- **Edina Art Fair**, West 50th Street and France Avenue; outdoor art and craft bazaar featuring artists, food and entertainment.
- **Grand Old Day**, Grand Avenue, St. Paul; this three-mile-long family-friendly bash in the street includes a parade, food and drink, specials in Grand Avenue stores, arts and crafts, and great music on stages in every block. Contact 651-699-0029, www.GrandAve.com.
- **Juneteenth**, held in Theodore Wirth Park, Glenwood Avenue North, Minneapolis, is a family festival celebrating the abolition of slavery with food, music, athletic events and a film festival. Call 612-529-5553.
- **Midsommar Festival**, American Swedish Institute, 2600 Park Avenue South, Minneapolis, 612-871-4907; this traditional June 19th

Swedish summer solstice celebration welcomes summer with folk dancing and crafts.

- **Grandma's Marathon**, Duluth; the route parallels the shore of Lake Superior from Two Harbors to Duluth and draws competitors from all over the world. Pick up information at local sports stores.
- **Art On the Lake**, the Commons, Excelsior, is an outdoor art fair on the shore of Lake Minnetonka that includes entertainment, food and excursion boat rides.
- **Gay Lesbian Bisexual Transgender Pride Festival**, Loring Park, Grant and Willow streets, Minneapolis; includes music, dancing and drag queens. Call 612-996-9250.
- **Tanbark Cavalcade of Roses Horse Show**, the Coliseum, State Fairgrounds, St. Paul, is home to saddlebred horses strutting their stuff for four days. Free admission. Friday and Saturday stake nights are particularly exciting. For information call 612-448-5191.
- **Lake Minnetonka Kennel Club All-breed Dog Show**, Waconia Fairgrounds, is an outdoor show where approximately 2,000 dogs of all breeds from all over the country are exhibited.
- **Alpine Farms Hunter and Jumper Horse Show**; 2182 Homestead Trail, Medina, 763-473-1361; benefit for the Humane Society.
- **Dayton's Challenge Golf Tournament**; professionals and amateurs, men and women, play together with host, Tom Lehman, to raise money for the Children's Cancer Fund.

JULY

- **Taste of Minnesota** State Capitol grounds, St. Paul; the place to be for the Fourth of July weekend—three days of music, entertainment, delicious food from local restaurants and capital fireworks. For information check www.tasteofmn.org.
- **Hopkins Raspberry Festival** is a weeklong celebration of the time when Hopkins was an agricultural center. Events include a race, parade, fireworks and dancing.
- **Hamel Rodeo**; a professional rodeo and a lot of fun for families. Located at Highway 101 and County Road 10, Hamel, www.hamel-rodeo.org.
- **Rondo Days Festival and Parade**, Martin Luther King Recreation Center Park, St. Paul; host to the biggest African-American celebration in Minnesota. It includes a parade, arts and crafts, and a drill team competition.

- **Minneapolis Aquatennial**; celebrates water with ten days of events that appeal to all age groups and interests: Grande Day and torchlight parades, milk-carton boat race, water ski show, art fair, and plenty of fireworks. This is the biggest event of the summer. Contact 612-331-8371, www.aquatennial.org.
- **Basilica Block Party**, Basilica of St. Mary, Hennepin Avenue and 17th Street, Minneapolis; the church trades its choir for funky rock bands, two nights of music, food, drink and a raffle. Call 612-333-6023.
- **Minnesota Orchestra's Viennese Sommerfest**, Orchestra Hall, Nicollet Mall; the setting for nearly a month of concerts with famous guest soloists inside Orchestra Hall and free entertainment, food and dancing outside in the Peavey Plaza Marketplace. For $50 you can sit on stage with the orchestra. For concert tickets call 612-371-5656 or 800-292-4141 or order online at www.mnorch.org.
- **Rib Fest**, downtown Minneapolis, is a five-day contest among the nation's best BBQ rib joints for a $10,000 prize and you're the judge! Live music by major local and national bands. Call 612-673-0900 or check www.downtownmpls.com.
- **Lumberjack Days**, Stillwater's festival commemorates its lumber mill days with ax throwing, log-rolling, chainsaw carving, pole climbing, free concerts and a Bunyanesque fireworks display. Information can be accessed through Stillwater's home page, www.ci.stillwater.mn.us or call the Stillwater Chamber of Commerce, 651-439-4001.

AUGUST

- **Uptown Art Fair**, Hennepin and Lake in Minneapolis; a street fair crowded with artists' booths, food, and entertainment. This is one of the largest outdoor art fairs in the Midwest.
- **Minnesota Renaissance Festival** is a loose recreation of a renaissance town fair. Located off Highway 169, four miles south of Shakopee, it lasts seven weekends and Labor Day. Make merry with jousting tournaments, finger food, entertainers, and unique arts and crafts. Call 612-445-7361 for directions and ticket information.
- **Minnesota State Fair**, State Fairgrounds, Snelling Avenue, St. Paul, marks the end of summer with farm animals, art, fried cheese curds and Princess Kay of the Milky Way carved in butter—what more could you want? Runs through Labor Day. Check www.statefair.gen.mn.us or call 651-642-2200.

SEPTEMBER

- **North Shore In-Line Skating Marathon**, Two Harbors to Duluth.
- **Fall Festival** at the Minnesota Landscape Arboretum, Highway 5, Chanhassen, invites the public in for live music, children's activities and apple and plant sales. Call 952-443-2460 for date and directions.
- **Parade of Homes** is a tour of selected new homes in the Twin Cities, sponsored by the Builders Association of the Twin Cities, 651-697-1954.

OCTOBER

- **Twin Cities Marathon**; race starts in Minneapolis at the Metrodome, follows the parkways around the city lakes, along the Mississippi River, up Summit Avenue in St. Paul and ends at the state capitol. Pick up information at local sports stores.
- **MEA Week**, the Minnesota Education Association holds its annual convention, area schools schedule parent conferences.
- **Shadows and Spirits of the State Capitol**, Minnesota State Capitol, 651-296-2881
- **Spooky World**, Historic Murphy's Landing, Shakopee, 952-445-8555

NOVEMBER

- **A Christmas Carol** is an annual treat at the Guthrie Theater, 612-377-2224.
- **Dayton's Holiday Auditorium Show**, 8th Floor Dayton's, Nicollet Mall, 612-375-2200
- **Holidazzle Parade** down Nicollet Mall in Minneapolis, nightly, Thanksgiving through December.
- **Walk the Wild Side** at the Minnesota Zoo light display, Thanksgiving through December, 952-432-9000, 800-366-7811, www.mnzoo.com.

DECEMBER

- **Holiday Flower Show**, Como Park Conservatory, 651-487-8247
- **Holiday Traditions in the Period Rooms**, the Minneapolis Institute of Arts, 3rd Street, Minneapolis, 612-870-3131, is decorated for the holidays.

- **Handel's Messiah**, performed at several locations by the St. Paul Chamber Orchestra, 651-291-1144, and the Minnesota Orchestra, 612-371-5656
- **Nutcracker Fantasy**, performed by the Minnesota Dance Theatre at the Historic Orpheum Theatre, 612-989-5151.
- **A Capitol New Year,** Rice Park and other downtown St. Paul locations, rings in the New Year with ice skating, live music, and midnight fireworks.
- **Mississippi Mile-ennium**, Minneapolis' New Year's celebration, is sponsored by the Minneapolis Park and Recreation Board. It's filled with healthy ways to celebrate: snow shoeing, cross-country skiing, ice skating, and snow sculptures, with the "World's Largest Warming House" on Nicollet Island, and fireworks at 8 p.m. and midnight, 621-661-4817, www.mississippimile.com.

FROM SINCLAIR LEWIS AND F. SCOTT FITZGERALD TO CAROL BLY and Lavyrle Spencer, many fine writers hail from or have written about Minnesota. Is it the weather? Here are a few good reads with a Minnesota connection to get you started:

FICTION

- *Cry Vengeance, Dead Silence, Malice Intended* and *Savage Justice* by Ron Handberg are mystery thrillers.
- *The Dead Get By With Everything* and *The Heart Can Be Filled Anywhere On Earth: Minnesota, Minnesota* by Bill Holm
- *Dear James, Dean's List, Rookery Blues, North of Hope, Simon's Night, The Love Hunter,* and *Staggerford*; novels by Jon Hassler
- *Excelsior* by Bob Williams is a historical novel set on the Fourth of July in the 1800s when Excelsior was a popular resort.
- *In the Lake of the Woods* by Tim O'Brien; mystery
- *Killing Time in St. Cloud* by Judith Guest; a murder mystery
- *Main Street* by Sinclair Lewis is set in Sauk Center, which is on the way to Itasca from the Twin Cities.
- *Rules of Prey, Eyes of Prey, Shadow Prey, Night Prey, Certain Prey, Secret Prey, Mind Prey,* and *Sudden Prey* by John Sandford; mysteries set in the Twin Cities.
- *Red Earth, White Earth* by Will Weaver
- *A Superior Death* by Nevada Barr; a mystery about National Park Service employees that features Isle Royale
- *A Thin Town of the Heart* by Patricia Eilola is an autobiographical novel by a woman of Finnish ancestry.
- *The Windchill Factor* by Tom Gifford; a mystery set in Stillwater

REGIONAL HISTORY

- *All Hell Broke Loose* by William H. Hull, is the story of the November 11, 1940 Armistice Day storm—the worst blizzard that ever hit Minnesota.
- *Duluth* by Gore Vidal is about policewomen in Duluth.
- *Fitzgerald's Storm: The Wreck of the Edmund Fitzgerald* by Joseph MacInnis is the story of Lake Superior's most famous shipwreck.
- *Gunflint: Reflections on the Trail* and *Woman of the Boundary Waters* by Justine Kerfoot, are about an elderly woman who lived alone in the Boundary Waters area.
- *Me: a Memoir* by Brenda Ueland is the story of growing up in south Minneapolis.
- *Once There Were Green Fields: How Urban Sprawl is Undermining America's Economy and Social Fabric* by F.Kaid Benfield and others, published by the Natural Resources Defense Council, 212-727-2700, www.nrdc.org.
- *Root Beer Lady* by Bob Cary, is about Dorothy Molter, about a woman who lived alone in her cabin in the Boundary Waters until her death in 1986.
- *Secrets of the Congdon Mansion* by Joe Kimball, tells you everything they won't tell you on the tour of Glensheen.

ARCHITECTURE

- *Cape Cods and Ramblers: A Remodeling Planbook for Post-WWII Houses* will help you time-tune houses from the 1940s, '50s and '60s. Residents of Blaine, Brooklyn Park, Columbia Heights, Coon Rapids, Crystal, Fridley, Golden Valley, Hopkins, Mounds View, New Brighton, New Hope, Robbinsdale, Richfield, Roseville and St. Louis Park can purchase the book for $10 from their city halls. Those who live outside those communities can get a copy for $15 from the City of Brooklyn Park, 763-424-8000.
- *Longfellow Planbook:Remodeling Plans for Bungalows and Other Small Urban Homes* can be purchased from the Longfellow Community Council, 4151 Minnehaha Avenue South, Minneapolis 55406, 612-722-4529; $18.50, $10 for Longfellow residents.

CHILDREN

- *Betsy-Tacy books* by Maud Hart Lovelace; this whimsical series is about three friends, Betsy, Tacy, and Tib growing up in a turn-of-the-century Minnesota town based on Mankato. Read them to your children, then take the Betsy-Tacy walking tour.
- *The Gitter, The Googer and the Ghost* by Stephen Oliver; a children's book set in Red Wing.
- *Little House in the Big Woods* and *Little House on the Prairie* by Laura Ingalls Wilder are set in this region. The "Big Woods" was Pepin, Wisconsin, and "the Prairie" was Walnut Grove, Minnesota.

MINNESOTA IN PHOTOS

- *Chased by the Light: A 90-day Journey* by Jim Brandenburg.
- *Minnesota: A State of Beauty* by James LaVigne.
- *Minnesota on My Mind* is a collection of photos and quotations
- *Minnesota Wild* by Les Blacklock.

QUICK GETAWAYS

- *Biking with the Wind: Bicycling Day Trips in Minnesota and Wisconsin* by David Bixen
- *Boundary Waters: The Grace of the Wild* by Paul Gruchow is a mixture of natural history and stories about pioneers on Isle Royal and the Gunflint Trail.
- *Camper's Guide to Minnesota: Parks, Lakes, Forests, and Trails: Where to Go and How to Get There* by Mickey Little; a must have for anybody planning to explore Minnesota
- *Deep Water Passage: A Spiritual Journey of Mid-life* by Ann Linnea is the diary of a woman's solo kayaking trip around Lake Superior.
- *Natural Wonders of Minnesota: Parks, Preserves and Wild Places* by Martin Hintz.
- *Romancing Minnesota* by Kate Crowley and Michael Link is a complete guide to off-the-beaten-path Minnesota vacations.
- *Scenic Driving: Minnesota* by Phil Davies
- *Traveler's Guide to Wildlife in Minnesota*, Minnesota Division of Fish and Wildlife
- *Trial at Grand Marais* by Jean Andereck

- *Twin Cities Birding Map* by Little Transport Maps, P.O.Box 8123, Minneapolis, MN 55408, is available at bookstores; describes where to go, the habitat, and what birds are in the Twin Cities.

OTHER

- *Always on Sunday* by Eleanor Ostman, a cookbook
- *Blossoms and Blizzards* by Carol Bly; a collection of essays, poems, and stories.
- *Minnesota: Land of Lakes and Innovation* by Nood Wharton Reynolds is a book of corporate profiles.

WHILE THERE IS CLEARLY NO SUBSTITUTE FOR CONDUCTING newcomer business in person, a significant portion of preparatory, and getting acquainted work can be done by phone or online. Whether it is researching available apartment rentals, determining the closest library to your neighborhood or figuring out your daily commute, many of the details can be found even before you arrive.

What follows is a partial listing of phone numbers and web sites that cover a variety of services and attractions. In addition to the listings below there are many others embedded throughout this book. Check in your section of interest for additional numbers and sites.

ALCOHOL AND DRUG DEPENDENCY

- AA Alternative, 612-922-3392
- Al-Anon: Minneapolis, 612-920-3961; St. Paul, 651-771-2208
- Alcoholics Anonymous: Minneapolis, 612-922-0880; St. Paul, 651-227-5502
- Cocaine Anonymous, 612-323-3350
- Crisis Connection (24-hour), 612-379-6363
- Hennepin County Crisis Intervention, 612-347-3161
- Narcotics Anonymous, 612-639-3939
- *Phoenix Newspaper*, 800-983-9887, www.phoenixrecovery.com

ANIMALS

- Animal Bites, 911
- Animal Humane Society of Hennepin County, 612-522-4325

- Animal Inn Pet Cemetery, 651-777-0255
- Humane Society of Ramsey County, 651-645-7387
- Minneapolis Animal Control Shelter, 612-348-4250
- Minnesota Online Pet Resources, www.creatures.com/mn
- Minnesota Zoo Tigers, www.mnzoo.com
- NSP Bird Cam, www.nspco.com/nspbird.htm
- Pet Cemetery, Ramsey County Humane Society, 651-645-7387
- St. Paul Animal Control Center, 651-645-3953

ANIMAL EMERGENCY CLINICS

- Affiliated Emergency Veterinary Services: 763-754-9434 (Coon Rapids), 763-529-6560 (Golden Valley), 952-942-8272 (Eden Prairie)
- University of Minnesota Veterinary Hospitals 612-625-9711 (24 hour)

AUTOMOBILES

- AAA, 952-927-2600; 24-hour line, 952-927-2727
- Department of Public Safety—Motor Vehicle Division, 651-296-6911, www.dps.state.mn.us
- Minneapolis Impound Lot, 612-673-5777
- Minneapolis Parking Permits, 612-673-2411
- Twin Cities Automotive Web Site, www.carsoup.com

SERVICE CENTERS—VEHICLE REGISTRATION, DRIVER'S LICENSES
For a complete list of service centers, hours of operation, and addresses, check www.dps.state.mn.us/dvs.
- Bloomington Motor Vehicle License Bureau, 952-948-8719
- Minneapolis Driver and Vehicle Licenses, 612-348-8240
- Minnesota Driver's License Exam Station, Chaska, 952-448-3740
- Minnesota Driver's License Exam Station, Plymouth, 763-341-7149
- Richfield Motor Vehicle License Bureau, 612-861-9730
- Ridgedale Service Center, Minnetonka, 612-348-8241
- Southdale Service Center, Edina, 612-348-8241
- St. Paul/Midway Written Exam Station, 651-642-0808

BIRTH/DEATH CERTIFICATES

- Hennepin County Service Center (Minneapolis), 612-348-8241
- Ridgedale Service Center, Minnetonka, 612-348-8241
- Southdale Service Center, 612-348-8241

- St. Paul Health Center, 651-292-7730
- Minnesota Department of Health, 651-215-5800

CHILD ABUSE/PROTECTION

- Hennepin County Child Abuse/Neglect, 612-348-3552, 612-348-3552 (after hours)
- St. Paul Emergency Social Service (24 hour), 651-291-6795
- Dakota County (to report), 651-891-7400
- Ramsey County Child Protection, 651-266-4500
- Emergency Social Services (24 hours and holidays), 651-291-6795

CONSUMER AGENCIES

- Better Business Bureau of Minnesota, 651-699-1111, 800-646-6222, www.minnesota.bbb.org
- Federal Consumer Information Center, 800-688-9889, TTY, 800-326-2996, www.pueblo.gsa.gov
- Federal Communications Commission, 888-225-5322, www.fcc.gov
- Federal Trade Commission, 202-382-4357, www.ftc.gov
- Financial Consumer Information, www.moneytalks.org
- Insurance Federation of Minnesota, 612-222-3800, 800-642-6121
- Minnesota Attorney General, 651-296-3353, 800-657-3787, www.ag.state.mn.us
- Minnesota Department of Commerce, 651-296-2488
- Minnesota Extension Service, www.mes.umn.edu or www.extension.umn.edu.
- Minnesota Public Utilities Commission, 651-296-0406, 800-657-3782
- Minnesota State Attorney General-Consumer Information, www.ag.state.mn.us
- National Consumers' League, 800-876-7060, www.fraud.org
- Telecommunications and Research Action Center, www.trac.org
- United States Consumer Product Safety Line, 800-638-2772
- University of Minnesota Extension Service, 612-624-4771, www.extension.umn.edu

CRISIS LINES

- Abuse Hot Line, 800-799-SAFE
- Adult Protection, 612-348-8526, 651-266-4012
- Battered Women, 612-825-3333, 651-646-0994

- Bridge for Runaway Youth, 612-377-8800
- Bulimics/Anorexics Anonymous, 612-459-3097
- Child Protection, 612-348-3552, 651-266-4500
- Crisis Connection (24 hour crisis counseling), 612-379-6363
- Crisis Program (walk in), 651-221-8922
- Day One Project (find shelter in one phone call), 612-780-2330
- Emergency Social Service (24 hour), 651-291-6795
- Family Violence Network, 651-770-0777
- Minneapolis Crisis Intervention Center (24 hour), 612-347-3161
- Minneapolis/Hennepin Co. Crisis Nursery (24 hr), 612-824-8000
- Minnetonka Sojourner Battered Women's Shelter, 952-933-7422
- Missing Children Minnesota, 612-521-1188
- National Runaway Switchboard, 800-621-4000
- St. Paul Crisis Intervention Center, 651-221-8922
- Suicide Prevention, 612-347-2222

RAPE
- First Call for Help/West Metro, 612-335-5000
- First Call for Help/East Metro, 651-224-1133
- Minneapolis Rape/Sexual Assault Center (24 hour), 612-825-4357
- Minneapolis Sexual Violence Center (24 hour), 612-871-5111
- St. Paul Sexual Offense Services (24 hour), 651-298-5898

CULTURAL LIFE

- American Swedish Institute, www.americanswedishinst.org
- Bell Museum of Natural History, www.umn.edu/bellmuse
- Brave New Workshop, www.BraveNewWorkshop.com
- Bryant-Lake Bowl, www.bryantlakebowl.com
- Chanhassen Dinner Theatre, www.ChanhassenTheatres.com
- Frederick R.Weisman Art Museum, www.hudson.acad.umn.edu
- Hey City Theater, www.heycity.com
- Jungle Theater, www.jungletheater.com
- MacPhail Center for the Arts, www.macphail.org
- Minneapolis Institute of Arts, www.artsMIA.org
- Minnesota Museum of American Art, www.mtn.org/MMAA
- Minnesota Orchestra, www.mnorch.org
- Old Log Theater, www.oldlog.com
- Ordway Theater, www.ordway.org

- Saint John's Bible, www.saintjohnsbible.org, watch scribes as they create a handwritten, illuminated Bible for St. John's University, Collegeville, Minnesota
- Stages Children's Theater Company, www.stagestheatre.org
- Summer Music Camp for high school students, St. Olaf College, Northfield, MN, www.stolaf.edu
- Walker Art Center, www.walkerart.org

DISABLED, SERVICES FOR THE

- ARC Minnesota (disability rights), 651-523-0823
- Disabled Certificate/License Plates, 651-297-3377
- Epilepsy Foundation, 800-779-0777
- Federal Relay Service, 800-877-8339, www.gsa.gov
- Metro Council Assistance for Hearing Impaired, 612-341-0140
- Metropolitan Center for Independent Living, 651-646-8342, TTY 651-603-2001, www.macil.org
- Minneapolis Sign Language Coordinator, 612-673-3220
- Minnesota Disability Organizations and related sites PACER's listing, www.pacer.org
- Minnesota Library for the Blind, 800-722-0550
- Minnesota Relay Service, 800-627-3529 or 800-223-3131
- Minnesota State Council on Disability, 651-296-6785
- Minnesota State Services for the Blind, 651-642-0500, TTY 651-642-0506, 800-652-9000
- National Handicapped Housing Institute (NHHI), 651-639-9799
- National Association for the Deaf, 301-587-1788, TTY952-906-1198, www.nad.org
- Metro Regional Service Center for Deaf and Hard of Hearing People, 651-297-1316, TTY 651-297-1313

EDUCATION

- Minnesota School Districts, www.informns.k12.mn.us provides links to public school districts and private schools.

EMERGENCY

- Fire, Police, Medical, 911
- Poison Control, 612-825-4357

GAMBLING, Minnesota Compulsive Gambling Hotline, 800-437-3641

GOVERNMENT

MINNEAPOLIS
- Chamber of Commerce, 612-370-9132
- City Clerk, 612-673-2215
- City Council Members, www.tcfreenet.org
- City of Minneapolis Government Office, www.ci.minneapolis.mn.us, 612-673-3000
- Assessor, 612-673-2382
- City Hall (general information), 612-673-3000
- City Information Line (recording), 612-673-CITY
- Mayor's Office, 612-673-2100
- Minneapolis Community Development Agency, 612-673-5095
- Neighborhood Revitalization Program, 612-673-5140

ST. PAUL
- Chamber of Commerce, 651-223-5000
- City Clerk, 651-266-8989
- City Council Members, www.tcfreenet.org
- City of St. Paul Government Office, www.stpaul.gov, 651-266-8500
- City Hall (general information), 651-266-8500
- Mayor's Office, 651-266-8510
- Housing and Redevelopment Authority, 651-266-6700
- Residential Assessor, 651-266-2141

COUNTY
- Anoka County, www.co.anoka.mn.us
- Carver County, www.co.carver.mn.us
- Hennepin County, www.co.hennepin.mn.us, 612-348-3000
- Metropolitan Council, www.metrocouncil.org, 651-602-1000
- Ramsey County, www.co.ramsey.mn.us, 651-266-2000
- Scott County, www.co.scott.mn.us
- Washington County, www.co.washington.mn.us, 651-439-3220

STATE
- Attorney General, www.ag.state.mn.us, 651-296-3353
- Governors Office, 651-296-3391
- Information and Referral, 651-296-6013

- Secretary of State, www.sos.state.mn.us, 651-296-2805
- State of Minnesota, www.state.mn.us/minnesota, 651-296-6013
- State Operator, 651-296-6013

FEDERAL
- Social Security Administration, 800-772-1213, www.ssa.gov

HEALTH

- American Cancer Society-Minnesota, 800-227-2345
- American Red Cross, 651-291-6789
- Association for Nonsmokers-Minnesota (ANSR), 651-646-3005
- Centers for Disease Control and Prevention, 877-FYI-TRIP, www.cdc.gov
- Health Services Minneapolis, 612-673-2301
- Health Services St. Paul, 651-292-7711
- Hennepin County Community Health Dept., www.co.hennepin.mn.us
- Mayo Clinic Health Oasis, www.mayohealth.org, includes *The Virtual Cookbook*, and a first-aid section.
- Minnesota Council of Health Plans, www.mnhealthplans.org, provides Minnesota health care industry statistics and consumer information, addresses and links to the ten health care plans.
- Minnesota Department of Health, 612-676-5700, 800-657-3970, www.health.state.mn.us
- Minnesota Radon Project, www.physics.csbsju.edu/mnradon, includes maps of average radon concentrations in Minnesota
- Neighborhood Health Care Network, 651-489-CARE, medical and dental referrals
- Travel Health Resource Line, 612-676-5588
- Women's Cancer Resource Center, 612-729-0491
- Ramsey County Department of Public Health, 651-266-2400

HOSPITALS

- Burnsville Fairview Ridges, www.fairview.org
- Coon Rapids Mercy, www.mercy-unity.com and www.allina.com
- Edina Fairview Southdale, www.fairview.org
- Fridley Unity, www.mercy-unity.com and www.allina.com
- Maplewood HealthEast St. John's, www.healtheast.org
- Mayo Clinic, Rochester, www.mayo.edu
- Minneapolis Abbott Northwestern, www.abbottnorthwestern.com; www.allina.com

- Minneapolis Children's Health Center, www.childrenshc.org
- Minneapolis Fairview-University, www.fairview.org
- Minneapolis Hennepin County Medical Center, www.hcmc.org
- Minneapolis Veterans Affairs Medical Center, www.va.gov
- Minneapolis Phillips Eye Institute, www.allina.com
- Minneapolis Shriners' Hospital for Children, www.shrinershq.org
- Minneapolis Sister Kenny, www.abbottnorthwestern.com and www.allina.com
- Robbinsdale North Memorial, www.northmemorial.com
- St. Louis Park, Methodist, www.healthsystemminnesota.com
- St. Paul Children's, www.childrenshc.org
- St. Paul Gillete Children's, www.gillettechildrens.org
- St. Paul HealthEast Bethesda Lutheran Rehabilitation, www.health-east.org
- St. Paul HealthEast St. Joseph's, www.healtheast.org
- St. Paul Regions, www.healthpartners.com
- St. Paul United, www.unitedhospital.com; www.allina.com
- Shakopee St. Francis, www.allina.com
- Stillwater Lakeview, www.lakeview.org
- Waconia Ridgeview, www.ridgeviewmedical.org

HOUSING

MINNEAPOLIS
- Landlord and Tenant Information Network, 612-341-3504
- Minneapolis Assessor, 612-673-2387
- Minneapolis Housing Services, 612-673-3003
- Minneapolis Neighborhood Revitalization Program, 612-673-5140
- Minneapolis Rental Licensing information, 612-673-5856
- Minneapolis Department of Inspections: housing, 612-673-5858
- Minneapolis Tenant Advocacy, 612-673-3003
- Minneapolis Zoning Information, 612-673-5836

ST. PAUL
- St. Paul Department of Inspections: housing, 651-266-9016
- St. Paul Tenants' Union, 651-221-0501
- St. Paul Housing Information Office, 651-266-6000
- St. Paul Housing and Redevelopment Authority, 651-266-6700
- St. Paul Residential Assessor, 651-266-2141

STATE/FEDERAL

- Minnesota Building Codes, 651-296-4639
- Minnesota Department of Human Rights, 651-296-5663, TDD, 651-296-1283, 800-657-3704
- Minnesota Department of Public Service Energy Information Center, www.dpsv.state.mn.us
- Minnesota Multi-Housing Association, 612-858-8222
- Minnesota Tenant's Union, 612-871-7485
- US Department of Housing and Urban Development, 612-370-3000, www.hud.gov; Discrimination Hotline, 800-669-9777

LIBRARIES

- Hennepin County, 952-541-8530, www.hennepin.lib.mn.us
- Minneapolis, 612-630-6000, www.mpls.lib.mn.us
- Minnesota Historical Society, 651-296-2143
- Ramsey County, 651-486-2200, www.ramsey.lib.mn.us
- St. Paul, 651-266-7000, www.stpaul.lib.mn.us
- Washington County, 651-731-8487, www.washington.lib.mn.us,
- The State of Minnesota Web site, www.state.mn.us/libraries, provides links to regional and college libraries.
- Washington County, www.washington.lib.mn.us

MARRIAGE LICENSES

- Hennepin County Service Center (Minneapolis), 612-348-8241
- Ramsey County Vital Services Office (St. Paul), 651-66-8265
- Washington County (Stillwater), 651-439-3220

MINNESOTA ONLINE

City/neighborhood specific web sites can be found at the end of each neighborhood profile or check the **Surrounding Communities** section.
- Area Code 612 coverage: www.612.com/community
- Boulevards Minneapolis has links for hotels, restaurants, music and attractions, www.minneapolis.com.
- City sites: www.ci.minneapolis.mn.us, www.ci.stpaul.mn.us
- Explore Minnesota, www.exploreminnesota.com
- Family Fun Magazine, www.family.go.com
- The Mining Company, www.minneapolis.miningco.com, provides a guided tour of the Twin Cities.

- Minnesota Online, www.mnonline.org, is a comprehensive, categorized list of Minnesota web sites.
- Photo Tour, www.radparker.com/phototour
- Sidewalk.Com, www.twincities.sidewalk.com
- Twin Cities Freenet, www.tcfreenet.org or www.Minneapolis.about.com

MAPS
- Atlas of Minnesota, www.map.lib.umn.edu
- Books for Travel, 857 Grand Avenue, St. Paul, 888-668-8006, www.booksfortravel.com
- Color Landform Maps of Minnesota, www.fermi.jhuapl.edu/states/mn
- DNR Maps, www.dnr.state.mn.us/information_center/maps, includes lake depth maps, state park and trail maps

NEWSPAPERS AND MAGAZINES

- *Citybusiness*, www.amcity.com/twincities
- *Insight News*, www.insightnews.com
- *Lavender*, www.lavendermagazine.com
- *Minneapolis Star Tribune*, www.startribune.com
- *StarTribune Online*, www.startribune.com
- *St. Paul Pioneer Press*, www.pioneerplanet.com
- *City Pages*, www.citypages.com
- *Minneapolis St. Paul Magazine*, www.mspmag.com
- *Minnesota Monthly*, www.mnmo.com
- *Minnesota Parent*, www.parent.com
- *Minnesota Women's Press*, www.womenspress.com
- *Sun Newspapers*, www.mnsun.com
- *Twin Cities Parent*, www.tcparent.com
- *University of Minnesota Minnesota Daily*, www.daily.umn.edu
- *UP*, www.upmagazine.com

PARK AND RECREATION DEPARTMENTS

- City of Bloomington Parks and Recreation Facilities map, www.ci.bloomington.mn.us
- Hennepin County, www.hennepinparks.org, 612-559-9000
- Minneapolis, 612-661-4800, www.ci.minneapolis.mn.us
- Minnesota DNR, 651-296-6157, 888-646-6367, www.dnr.state.mn.us
- Minnesota State Park Reservations, 800-246-2267
- Ramsey County, www.co.ramsey.mn.us/parks, 651-748-2500

- St. Paul, www.stpaul.gov, 651-266-6400
- Washington County, www.co.washington.mn.us, 651-430-8368

POLICE

- Emergency, 911
- Minnesota State Bureau of Criminal Apprehension, 651-642-0670
- Safetynet, www.freenet.msp.mn.us/conf/safetynet is an online discussion about safety issues in Twin Cities neighborhoods

MINNEAPOLIS
- Community Crime Prevention (CCPSafe), 612-673-3015
- Crime Victim Crisis Center, 612-340-3552
- Downtown Command, 612-673-2655
- 2nd Precinct (Northeast), 612-673-5702
- 3rd Precinct (South and East of I-35), 612-673-5703
- 4th Precinct (North), 612-673-5704
- 5th Precinct (Southwest, West of I-35W), 612-673-5705
- Tele-Serv (to report non-emergency crimes), 612-348-9392

ST. PAUL
- Crime Prevention Coordinator, 651-292-3625
- Crime Statistic Map (STAT MAP), 651-292-3501
- General Information, 651-291-1111, www.st.paul.gov/police
- Central District, 651-292-3563
- Eastern District, 651-292-3565
- Western District (North), 651-292-3512
- Western District (South), 651-292-3549

RADIO/TV STATIONS

- KDWB 101.3 FM, www.kdwb.com
- KQRS 92 FM, www.92kqrs.com
- KS95 94.5 FM, www.ks95.com
- KSTP Radio AM 1500, www.am1500.com
- KSTP TV Channel 5, www.kstp.com
- KTCA PUBLIC TELEVISION, www.ktca.org
- KTCL 97.1 FM, www.cities97.com
- KNOW Minnesota Public Radio 91.1 FM, www.mpr.org
- WCCO Radio AM 830, www.wcco.com
- Radio archives, www.reelradio.com

- KMSP Channel 9, www.kmsp.com
- KFAI Community Radio, 90.3 FM Minneapolis, 106.7 FM St. Paul
- Radionet, www.radionet.com, listen to the radio over your computer

RELOCATION

- Apartments.com, www.apartments.com, includes short-term rentals and furniture rental
- Apartment Search.com, www.apartmentsearch.com, provides free help finding an apartment.
- www.erc.org, the Employee Relocation Council, a professional organization, offers members specialized reports on the relocation and moving industries
- www.firstbooks.com, relocation resources and information on moving to Atlanta, Boston, Chicago, Los Angeles, New York, Philadelphia, San Francisco and the Bay Area, Seattle, Washington, DC, as well as London, England
- www.homeadvisor.com, Microsoft's answer to home buying on the web; looks comprehensive and useful
- www.homefair.com, realty listings, moving tips, and more
- www.homestore.com, renting, buying, selling, and building; home improvement , and more
- www.moverquotes.com, comparison shop for mover quotes
- www.moving.com, a moving services site: packing tips, mover estimates, etc.
- www.moving-guide.com, movers and moving services
- www.moving.org, members of the American Moving and Storage Association
- www.rent.net, apartment rentals, movers, relocation advice and more
- www.springstreet.com, apartment rentals, moving tips, movers, and more
- www.usps.com, relocation information from the US Postal Service

ROAD CONDITION INFORMATION

- Metro Area, 651-405-6030
- Minnesota (MNDOT), 800-542-0220, www.dot.state.mn.us
- Snow Emergency Information Minneapolis, 612-348-SNOW, www.ci.minneapolis.mn.us
- Snow Emergency Information St. Paul, 651-266-PLOW, www.stpaul.gov
- Wisconsin, 800-762-3947

SANITATION—GARBAGE & RECYCLING

- Minneapolis Solid Waste and Recycling, 612-673-2917
- Ramsey County Neighborhood Energy and Recycling, 651-633-3279
- Minneapolis Solid Waste and Recycling, 612-673-2917
- St. Paul Neighborhood Energy Consortium, 651-644-7678

SENIORS

- AARPP (American Association of Retired Persons), 612-858-9040
- Hennepin County Services to Seniors, 612-348-4500
- Legal Aid, (assists people over 60 and low-income), 612-332-1441
- Metropolitan Senior Federation, 651-645-0261
- Senior Housing, Inc., 612-617-7842
- Senior Linkage Line, 800-333-2433

SOCIAL AGENCIES

- First Call for Help Minnesota provides a searchable database of over 10,000 service agencies and 45,000 social services in Minnesota.
- First Call for Help/West, 612-335-5000, www.firstcall-mn.org
- First Call for Help/East, 651-224-1133, www.firstcall-mn.org
- Ramsey County Homestead Department, 651-266-2100
- St. Paul Citizen Service Office, 651-266-8989

SPORTS & RECREATION

COLLEGE/PROFESSIONAL SPORTS
- Canterbury Park, www.canterburypark.com
- Golf Tee Times, www.teemaster.com
- Minnesota Lynx, www.wnba.com/lynx
- Minnesota Thunder, www.mnthunder.com
- Minnesota Timberwolves, 612-673-0900, www.nba.com/timber-wolves
- Minnesota Twins, 612-33-TWINS , www.wcco.com/sports/twins
- Minnesota Vikings, 612-333-8828, www.nfl.com/vikings
- Minnesota Wild-NHL, www.mnwild.com
- St. Paul Saints, 612-644-6659, www.spsaints.com
- University of Minnesota, (all teams), 612-624-8080, www.gopher-sports.com

PARTICIPANT SPORTS & ACTIVITIES
- Minnesosta Ski Areas, www.twin-cities.com/ski
- SkiJammers Ski School, www.wavefront.com/~skijammers
- StarTribune, www.startribune.com/sports
- Boundary Waters, www.canoecountry.com
- FishingNetwork, www.the-fishing-network.com
- Minnetonka Yacht Club, www.myc.com
- National Parks, www.us-national-parks.net, www.nps.gov
- Snowmobiling, www.sledcity.com
- State Trails, www.outdoorlink.com/amtrails

STREET MAINTENANCE

- Minneapolis (24 hour), 612-673-5720
- St. Paul (24 hour), 612-292-6600

TAXES

FEDERAL
- Internal Revenue Service, 800-829-4477, www.irs.ustreas.gov
- IRS Forms Distribution Center, 800-829-3676

PROPERTY
- Hennepin County, 612-348-3011, www.co.hennepin.mn.us
- Minneapolis, 612-348-3011, www.ci.minneapolis.mn.us
- Ramsey County, 651-266-2000, www.co.ramsey.mn.us
- St. Paul, 651-266-2000, www.stpaul.gov

STATE
- Income Tax and Forms, 651-296-3781, 800-652-9094
- Taxpayers Rights Advocate, 651-296-0992
- Refund Status, 651-296-4444
- Special Taxes, 651-297-1882

TELEPHONE

- AT&T, www.att.com
- MCI WorldCom, www.wcom.com
- Sprint, www.sprint.com
- Qwest, 800-244-1111, www.qswest.com
- Qwest Yellow Pages, www.qwestdex.com

TIME/TEMPERATURE/WEATHER, 612-331-2470

TRANSPORTATION

- Department of Public Safety Driver and Vehicle Services, www.dps. state.mn.us/dvs
- State Department of Transportation, 888-472-3389, www.dot.state.mn.us
- Road Restrictions for the State of Minnesota, 651-406-4701
- US Department of Transportation, 651-291-6150, www.dot.gov

AIRPORTS

- Minneapolis - St. Paul International Airport, 612-726-5555, www. mspairport.com; Parking Information Hotline, 612-826-7000
- Holman Field, St. Paul, 651-224-4306
- Northwest Airlines, www.nwa.com
- Sun Country Airlines, www.suncountry.com
- US Airways, www.usairways.com

COMMUTING

- Metro Commuter Services, 651-602-1602
- Guaranteed Ride Home, 651-602-1602
- www.startribune.com/gettingthere is an on-going discussion about commuting.

METRO TRANSIT

- Metro Mobility, 612-221-1931, TTY 612-221-9886
- Metro Commuter Services, 651-602-1602, www.metrotransit.org
- MetroTransit Bus Route & Schedule Information, 612-373-3333, TTY 612-341-0140, www.metrotransit.org
- MetroTransit 24-hour schedule information, 612-341-4BUS
- University of Minnesota Transit Service, 612-625-9000

NATIONAL TRAIN & BUS SERVICE

- Amtrak, 800-872-7245
- St. Paul/Minneapolis Midway Amtrak Station, 651-644-1127
- Greyhound Bus Lines, 800-231-2222

TAXIS

See **Transportation** chapter.

TOURISM

- Minnesota Office of Tourism, 651-296-5029, 800-657-3700, www.exploreminnesota.com
- Gunflint Trail, www.gunflint-trail.com
- North Shore, www.61north.com

US POSTAL SERVICE, 800-275-8777, www.usps.com

UTILITIES

- Electricity (NSP), 800-895-4999
- Gas (Minnegasco), 612-372-4727; gas leaks, 612-372-5050
- Gopher State One Call (buried cable locations), 651-454-0002
- Minnesota Public Utilities Commission, 651-296-0406, 800-657-3782

WEATHER

- Weather Line, 612-512-1111
- WCCO live camera view of downtown Minneapolis, www.weather.channel4000.com

WORSHIP

- Minnesota Council of Churches, www.mnchurches.org
- Jewish Minnesota, www.jewishminnesota.org
- Lutheran Brotherhood, www.luthbro.com

ZIP CODE INFORMATION, 800-275-8777, www.usps.com

INDEX

M

ELIZABETH CAPERTON-HALVORSON has lived in the Minneapolis area for 25 years. Raised in Virginia, her experience as a newcomer began with her marriage to a Minnesotan—and nearly ended when she realized she had worn her winter coat through the entire summer the first year she lived in the Twin Cities. She and her family soon discovered the exhileration of Minnesota skiing and the joy of sailing Lake Minnetonka by moonlight, and she now looks forward to the cycle of the seasons. She has worked as an elementary school teacher and newspaper reporter and is currently a writer and editor of corporate communications. Her family's hobbies revolve around art, bridge, gardening and sports.

MARIS STRAUTMANIS lived in Minneapolis and St. Paul for several years. A native of Wisconsin, Maris has worked as a journalist in Chicago, Austin, Minneapolis, and Portland, Oregon.

READER RESPONSE FORM

We would appreciate your comments regarding this second edition of the *Newcomer's Handbook®* for Minneapolis-St. Paul. If you've found any mistakes or omissions or if you would just like to express your opinion about the guide, please let us know. We will consider any suggestions for possible inclusion in our next edition, and if we use your comments, we'll send you a *free* copy of our next edition. Please send this response form to:

Reader Response Department
First Books
3000 Market Street N.E., Suite 527
Salem, OR 97301

Comments:

_____

_____

_____

_____

_____

_____

_____

_____

Name: _____

Address _____

_____

_____

Telephone (_____) _____

3000 Market Street N.E., Suite 527
Salem, OR 97301
503-588-2224
www.firstbooks.com

FIRST BOOKS

THE ORIGINAL, ALWAYS UPDATED, ABSOLUTELY INVALUABLE GUIDES FOR PEOPLE MOVING TO A CITY!

Find out about neigborhoods, apartment and house hunting, money matters, deposits/leases, getting settled, helpful services, shopping for the home, places of worship, cultural life, sports/recreation, vounteering, green space, schools and education, transportation, temporary lodgings and useful telephone numbers!

	# COPIES	**TOTAL**
Newcomer's Handbook® for Atlanta	_____ x $17.95	$_____
Newcomer's Handbook® for Boston	_____ x $14.95	$_____
Newcomer's Handbook® for Chicago	_____ x $14.95	$_____
Newcomer's Handbook® for London	_____ x $18.95	$_____
Newcomer's Handbook® for Los Angeles	_____ x $17.95	$_____
Newcomer's Handbook® for Minneapolis-St. Paul	_____ x $20.95	$_____
Newcomer's Handbook® for New York City	_____ x $18.95	$_____
Newcomer's Handbook® for Philadelphia	_____ x $16.95	$_____
Newcomer's Handbook® for San Francisco	_____ x $16.95	$_____
Newcomer's Handbook® for Seattle	_____ x $14.95	$_____
Newcomer's Handbook® for Washington D.C.	_____ x $16.95	$_____
	SUBTOTAL	$_____
POSTAGE & HANDLING (*$6.00 first book, $1.00 each add'l.*)		$_____
	TOTAL	$_____

SHIP TO:

Name _____

Title _____

Company _____

Address _____

City _____ State _____ Zip _____

Phone Number (_____) _____

Send this order form and a check or money order payable to:
First Books

First Books, Mail Order Department
3000 Market Street N.E., Suite 527, Salem, OR 97301

Allow 1-2 weeks for delivery

(435)

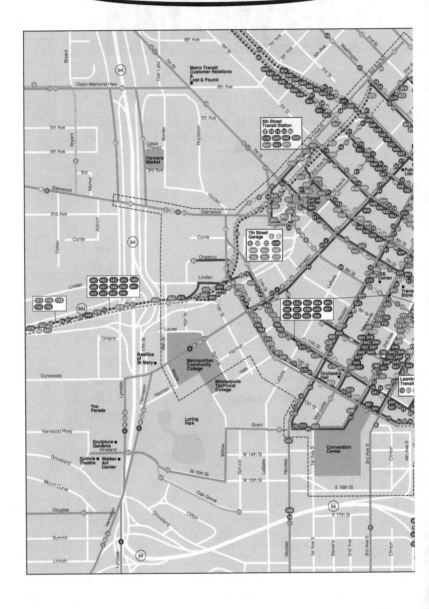

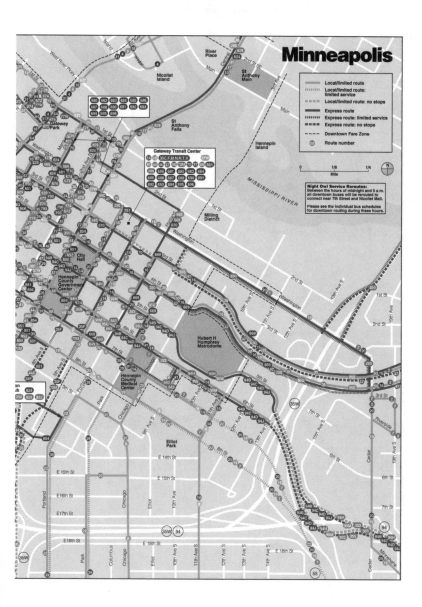

Minneapolis

Local/limited route
Local/limited route: limited service
Local/limited route: no stops
Express route
Express route: limited service
Express route: no stops
Downtown Fare Zone
Route number

Night Owl Service Reroutes:
Between the hours of midnight and 5 a.m. all downtown buses will be rerouted to connect near 7th Street and Nicollet Mall.

Please see the individual bus schedules for downtown routing during these hours.

0   1/8   1/4
Mile

N

Gateway Transit Center

River Place
St Anthony Main
Nicollet Island
St Anthony Falls
Hennepin Island
MISSISSIPPI RIVER
Milling District
Gateway Park
City Hall
Hennepin County Government Center
Hennepin County Medical Center
Hubert H Humphrey Metrodome
Elliot Park

West River Pkwy
Main
Washington
2nd St
Washington
2nd St
4th St
5th St
6th St
7th St
8th St
Portland
Park
Chicago
Elliot
10th Ave
11th Ave

E 14th St
E 15th St
E 15th St
E 16th St
E 17th St
E 18th St
E 18th St

Portland
Columbus
Chicago
Elliot
10th Ave
11th Ave S
12th Ave S
13th Ave S
14th Ave S

Cedar
19th Ave S
3rd St
2nd St
1st St
9th Ave S
Riverside
6th St
7th St
Minnehaha

35W
94
35W   94
55

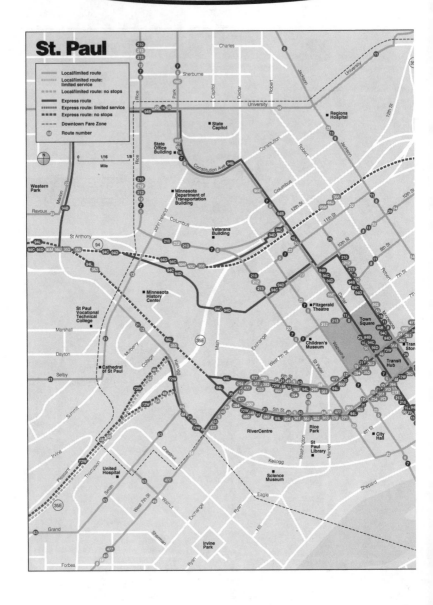

St. Paul

Legend:
- Local/limited route
- Local/limited route: limited service
- Local/limited route: no stops
- Express route
- Express route: limited service
- Express route: no stops
- Downtown Fare Zone
- (68) Route number

0   1/16   1/8
Mile

N